ON THE MEDITERRANEAN AND THE NILE

INDIANA SERIES IN SEPHARDI AND MIZRAHI STUDIES
Harvey E. Goldberg and Matthias Lehmann, *editors*

Aimée Israel-Pelletier

ON THE MEDITERRANEAN AND THE NILE

THE JEWS OF EGYPT

Indiana University Press

This book is a publication of

Indiana University Press
Office of Scholarly Publishing
Herman B Wells Library 350
1320 East 10th Street
Bloomington, Indiana 47405 USA

iupress.indiana.edu

© 2018 by Aimée Israel-Pelletier
All rights reserved

No part of this book may be reproduced or utilized in any form or by any means, electronic or mechanical, including photocopying and recording, or by any information storage and retrieval system, without permission in writing from the publisher.

The paper used in this publication meets the minimum requirements of the American National Standard for Information Sciences—Permanence of Paper for Printed Library Materials, ANSI Z39.48-1992.

Manufactured in the United States of America

Library of Congress Cataloging-in-Publication Data

Names: Israel-Pelletier, Aimée, author.
Title: On the Mediterranean and the Nile : the Jews of Egypt / Aimée Israel-Pelletier.
Description: Bloomington, Indiana : Indiana University Press, [2018] | Series: Indiana series in Sephardi and Mizrahi studies | Includes bibliographical references and index.
Identifiers: LCCN 2017046402 (print) | LCCN 2017047382 (ebook) | ISBN 9780253025784 (e-book) | ISBN 9780253025296 (cloth : alk. paper) | ISBN 9780253031921 (pbk. : alk. paper)
Subjects: LCSH: Jews—Egypt—Intellectual life. | Egyptian literature, Modern—Jewish authors—History and criticism. | Jews, Egyptian—Identity. | Egypt—In literature.
Classification: LCC DS135.E4 (ebook) | LCC DS135 .E4 I87 2018 (print) | DDC 305.892/4062—dc23
LC record available at https://lccn.loc.gov/2017046402

In memory of my grandmothers
  Emma Sasson Israel and Solange Dayan Cohen,
of my grandfathers
  Israel Ezra Israel and Solomon Cohen,
and in loving memory of my parents
  Saul Israel and Pauline Cohen Israel.

To the future and to the light of my eyes
  Luke Philippe Agopsowicz, my first grandchild,
my daughters Pauline Marietta Pelletier
  and Chloé Madeleine Pelletier,
and my nieces Rebecca Mintz,
  Leah Mintz, and Sarina Israel.

Contents

Acknowledgments — ix

Introduction — 1

1. Jacques Hassoun: Return to Egypt — 27
2. Jacqueline Shohet Kahanoff's Egypt: A View from the Nile — 68
3. Edmond Jabès: Egypt Recovered — 100
4. Paula Jacques, Resistance and Transmission: Transplanting Egypt on the Soil of France — 140
5. André Aciman and the Mediterranean: The Staging of Egypt as Elsewhere — 176

Epilogue — 202

Bibliography — 207
Index — 217

Acknowledgments

This book owes so much to the support and friendship of Norman A. Stillman. Both "Noam" and Dinah Assouline Stillman made Jewish Sephardic and Mizrahi Studies a second home for me. They cheered me on as I tried to bring Egypt into the fray from my place in French Studies. I thank them sincerely for making that crossing an amazing adventure that I expect has just begun.

The idea for this book would have been inconceivable were it not for Elie Patan. I owe him my unqualified gratitude for helping me recognize that the cultural heritage of the Jews of Egypt is rich and deep. I also thank him for introducing me to Ada Aharoni and Levana Zamir. They made it possible for me to participate in a small way in their efforts to make known the heritage of Egyptian Jewry. Their energy and dedication on behalf of this community cannot be overstated. Their work has been collaborative, appealing to broad interests, and restorative.

I want especially to thank Paula Jacques for welcoming me in Paris on many occasions. Her warmth and hospitality have touched me and our discussions of her work and her perspective on Egyptian Jewry have enriched my understanding of both. I also want to thank Pascale Hassoun, Jacques Hassoun's spouse, for sharing with me her insights on his work and his life, and for providing me with materials not easily available.

The library staff at the University of Texas at Arlington, Diane Shepelwich, Ava Nell Harris, Rachel H. Robbins, and Dean Rebecca Bichel, provided the institutional support I needed to undertake a project that had me examine works across various disciplines: History, Social Sciences, Literature, French, Jewish, and Arabic Studies. They have been there for me, supporting this effort. I am most grateful to them. I want to also thank Mark A. Cichock and the Charles T. McDowell Center for Critical Languages and Area Studies for needed assistance and collegial support. I want to also express my gratitude to Mary Edna Fraser for giving me permission to use her artwork *Nile Delta Desert Islands* for the cover of this book.

Writing this book took me at times to the happy places of my childhood in Cairo and Alexandria. But it also took me to some difficult ones. I want to thank

Carol Rogers for her guidance in getting me out of these places with speed, richer for having been there. I am lucky to have a sister who has been a friend all my life. Solange Israel-Mintz has been on the same journey with me inside and outside Egypt. I owe her so much for the laughter we shared and for shouldering some of the adversities our family has faced. I thank Paul S. Mintz for his constant devotion and warmth, and my brother Solomon Israel for his abiding love. I am indebted to others who, at different times in my life, have made an impact on my life. My parents, Saul and Pauline, have shown me what love really is and what courage looks like, in Egypt and long after we left. They are present in me and beside me every day; my beloved aunt Clemence Israel Saphir who has always been an inspiration to me from the time I was a "little pest" in Cairo to this day when we mull over the past we shared, a past she faces with frankness and generosity. I also want to recognize my aunt Germaine Stoliar Israel for her strength, her warm heart, and her teasing sense of humor. My love and sincere thanks to Arlette Romano Cohen and the late Edwin Cohen. They set the tone for how I would experience the "New World" for years by introducing me to its splendid variety. I want to express my love to those who grew up beside me outside Egypt, keeping memories alive, and providing vital continuity: Esther Rakib Captan and Nader Captan, Pierre (Moni) and Joseph Rakib, Jenny Rakib Brous, Ilana Israel Moas, Rena Israel Laniado, Miriam Israel Klechevsky, Israel Israel, Joe and Laurette Eliahou, Céline and Elie Eliahou, Chaoul Eliahou, Leon and Israel Bonan, and Allen, Nadine, and Leon Israel. Their love and friendship has mattered a great deal to me.

    I am fortunate to have supportive friends who kept me grounded during the writing of this book and who made our time spent together utterly sweet. My gratitude and love, as always, to Ruth V. Gross, the best of friends, and to the luminous Ellen Shapiro Pincus, to Lillian Mizrahi Gilbert, Klila and Brian Caplan, Judy Pelusi, Fran and Ben Weiger, Shirley and Elias Sassoon, Ken Licker, Danielle Snailer, and Richard Allen. I want to express my affection and appreciation to Cantor Sheri Allen and to Stuart Snow who have created around them a beautiful circle of caring, spirituality, and fun at Congregation Beth Shalom in Arlington, Texas. I thank them for inspiring me during Shabbat services to always remember the place of Egypt in Judaism and not to forget the legacy transmitted to our ancestors and to us.

    I would never have been able to complete this book without the support, patience, and unqualified love of Philippe André Pelletier, always my first and finest reader. My true love. I want to thank Philippe for overseeing many of the translations in this book, sometimes overhauling them, always bringing to them additional clarity and stylistic polish. I thank him dearly for that.

    Finally, I want to address directly my daughters Pauline and Chloé, the loves of my life whose brilliance and energy have kept me and continue to keep me on my toes. I thank you both for your love and the faith you place in me and in my work. I am, and always will be, your most ardent cheerleader. It is for you, and also for Rebecca, Leah, Sarina, and for Luke that I wrote this book. I wanted to shine a light on the legacy passed on to you by Saul and Pauline Israel, your grandparents and Luke's great-grandparents. My angle is narrow and my speak is academic. I apologize for that. But my hope is that this won't stop you from looking inside.

About the Cover Art

The cover art is *Nile Delta Desert Islands,* batik on silk by Mary Edna Fraser, 52 in. × 36 in.

The batik is based on an infrared aerial image of the Nile Delta where the fertile vegetation appears red. The shape of the delta suggests the lotus flower, an Ancient Egyptian symbol of rebirth. The greenish blue color at the mouth is caused by the flow of sediment from the Nile into the Mediterranean and visually highlights their intermingling. www.maryedna.com.

ON THE MEDITERRANEAN AND THE NILE

We Egyptian Jews, we were there with the Pharaohs, and with the Persians, the Babylonians, the Greeks, the Romans; and when the Arabs came, we were still there . . . and also with the Turks, the Ottomans. . . . We are natives, like the ibises, like the water buffalos, like the kites. Today, we are not there anymore. Not one of us is left. How can they live without us these Egyptians? And in my head, the divine Asmahane, Farid's sister, is singing: "Come to me, my love, come!"

    Tobie Nathan

Nous autres, Juifs d'Egypte, nous étions là avec les pharaons, puis avec les Perses, les Babyloniens, les Grecs, les Romains; et lorsque les Arabes sont arrivés, nous étions encore là . . . et aussi avec les Turcs, les Ottomans . . . Nous sommes des autochtones, comme les ibis, comme les bufflons, comme les milans. Aujourd'hui, nous n'y sommes plus. Il n'en reste plus un seul. Comment les Egyptiens peuvent-ils vivre sans nous? Et dans ma tête, la divine Asmahane, la soeur de Farid, continue de chanter: "Viens, ô mon aimé, viens!"

Introduction

> In exile with other writers in exile like me, I explore with them, see through their eyes, a cosmopolitan Mediterranean of the South that existed at one time, a Jewish and Muslim Mediterranean, now orphaned of Jews who inhabited it before Islam. The story each one of us tells is sometimes happy, sometimes cruel. The stories we tell recall a different time.
>
> Leïla Sebbar[1]

THANKS TO BOTH the Mediterranean Sea and the Nile River, Egypt has produced eminent cultures: Judaic, Pharaonic, Copt, Greco-Roman, Ottoman, European, and Arab. Together they have shaped Egyptian experience and identity. I appeal to the Mediterranean and the Nile to describe how Egyptian Jews thought and felt about Egypt and suggest that the great sea and the great river offer different nonbinary models for framing Jewish Egyptian identity. Along with the Egyptian people whose languages, gestures, voices, and gaits reflect the histories of migrations, invasions, travels, and exchanges traceable back millennia, the Mediterranean and the Nile are natural phenomena even before they take on mythic status. For Egyptian Jews, when all is said and done, the Mediterranean and the Nile provided a frame for imagining what they meant by home; these sites of memory confirmed their sense of belonging and heightened their attachment to Egypt. What they longed for in exile was the land, the sights, sounds, air, smells, tastes, and the feel of their Egyptian experience; they missed the voices, expressions, and manners of its people. I believe it matters that we keep sight of the material experience and engage with it when we examine how Egypt manifested itself in the imaginary of Egyptian Jews in the first half of the twentieth century and believe that it is in literature that we find one of the fullest expressions of this layered experience. This book makes the point that Jewish Egyptian identity and attachment to Egypt rely on an image that was best formulated in the 1920s by Egyptian territorial nationalists. Egyptian Jews identified themselves with an

Egypt that was both Mediterranean and Nilotic, an Egypt that was outward looking, hospitable, connected, and, at the same time, deeply rooted in the landscape and history that mark the country's uniqueness.²

Egyptian Jews are connected to Egypt by ties as ancient and enduring as Judaism itself, a history that is not lost on them. Rehearsing yearly the Passover story, all recognize they lived the part to the very end. This book examines different perspectives on what it was like for Egyptian Jews born and raised in Egypt in the middle of the twentieth century to feel that suddenly, much like Moses and his people had felt, they were foreigners in a "foreign land" (Exodus: 1:1–10:5). It draws a picture of how they lived, what they aspired to, how they perceived their collective identity, and responded to the changes taking place in Egypt in the first half of the twentieth century. To achieve these ends, I focus on the works of five writers, Jacques Hassoun, a psychoanalyst and activist (Alexandria; 1936–1999); Jacqueline Kahanoff, a public intellectual, essayist, and novelist (Cairo; 1917–1979); Edmond Jabès, a writer, poet laureate, and seminal thinker on the Jewish condition (Cairo; 1912–1991); Paula Jacques, a novelist, radio producer, and host (Cairo; b. 1949); and André Aciman, a novelist, essayist, and academic (Alexandria; b. 1951). I have also drawn on the works of ethnopsychiatrist Tobie Nathan and been informed by numerous others, such as the poet and artist Carole Naggar and the peace activists Ada Aharoni and Victor Teboul. Their works merit far greater attention than is provided here. The aim of this book is not to be comprehensive but to select exemplary works that address identity, attachment, and politics.

I approach these writers through the lens of literary and cultural studies to examine the imaginary of Egyptian Jews in the social and historical contexts that animate their particular issues of identity and belonging. The material I lean on comes from fiction, essays, and theoretical texts. The fundamental assumption of my approach is that the imaginary of individuals and communities, what Benedict Anderson has called imagined communities, invariably eclipses objective reality, judicial and political facts.³ The imaginary is an accumulation of conscious and unconscious materials (images, concepts, myths, and individual idiosyncrasies) that the mind holds on to and privileges. The imaginary acts on feelings, thoughts, and behavior; it shapes perceptions and forms the worldview of individuals and groups. Identity is not a legal or political category but a framework for the creative management of desires and affiliations. It is, finally, a construct that acts more powerfully on reality than any reasoned discourse.

This study has three overlapping objectives: 1) to make known the work of five commanding writers whose works are both issue oriented and rich in affect; among them only Edmond Jabès has rightfully enjoyed considered attention; 2) to draw out from their works an insider's picture of how Egyptian Jews lived in Egypt, and how once they were in exile they described that experience, conceived their identity, and made sense of their expulsion; 3) to show that, as I stated, Egyptian Jews shared with Egyptian territorial nationalists a collective image of Egypt and Egyptian identity, an image that became unsustainable with the establishment of pan-Arab nationalism. And finally, 4) I argue that Egyptian Jews demonstrate an attachment to Egypt in both its modern incarnation and biblical past. Egyptian attachment is the common thread that pulls together the writers in this book and directs attention to their most profound grievance; namely, nonrecognition, the egregious injustice of being summarily judged to be foreigners in their native land. As Yves Fédida says: "And we didn't feel like strangers in Egypt. We were at home. My father was born here. I was born here. It was my country."[4] The writers in this book prompt the questioning of a view that has painted Egyptian Jews as a foreign people—opportunistic, disloyal, and disengaged. Attentive to their efforts to make known their story, I read the works as expressions of resistance against being uprooted from Egyptian history just as they were from the land of Egypt itself.

Egyptian Jews living in the first half of the twentieth century were never more than a small minority among Egyptian minorities. Yet, by all accounts, like their biblical forefathers Jacob, Joseph, and Moses, many had contributed in remarkable ways to Egypt's prosperity. In a modern Egypt determined to compete on the world stage, an Egypt that promoted entrepreneurial activity, Egyptian Jews were industrious participants. They reached out to commercial interests across the Mediterranean and east of the Nile. From the first decades of the 1800s to the first three decades of the 1900s Egypt witnessed unprecedented economic growth and population expansion. It modernized and expanded its military, institutional, and urban infrastructures. At first under Muhammad Ali, it opened channels to the global sphere and became incorporated into the world economy more completely than ever before. "Between 1870 and 1890 workers from the Balkans, Italy, and Spain flocked to Egypt, North Africa, and various parts of the Eastern Mediterranean and Anatolia." Some settled for long periods and others were seasonal.[5] Between 1860 and 1914, the populations of Cairo and Alexandria grew exponentially, necessitating the expansion of the cities themselves, which tripled in size. Egypt's success in competing commercially on a global scale was due to the aggressive application of financial instruments (Khuri-Makdisi, 3). This allowed Egypt to build canals, expand railways, develop new ports, and enlarge existing ports. It built a fleet of steamships. It embraced new technologies like the telegraph and dramatically improved the reliability of its postal services.[6] It was also during this period that an ambitious urban development program transformed a mostly medieval Cairo into "Paris on the Nile." The most consequential of these projects—of consequence to Egypt's enormous growth and, paradoxically, to its fall—was the construction of the Suez Canal, which opened in 1869. It was because of it that Egypt was able to compete for commercial traffic and to expand its markets and further attract people from around the Mediterranean, Europe, and Asia. But the project was handicapped by corruption at every level, attributable to both Europeans and Egyptians. Besides the increasing debt associated with the Suez Canal project, the Egyptian government under Ismaïl Pasha continued to build up the mercantile, urban, and communications infrastructure. This was done with the encouragement of the British and the French. European powers had nothing to lose and everything to gain from an indebted Egypt. Between 1865 and 1875, Egyptian debt tripled. The country had to declare bankruptcy in 1876. This debt burden, in addition to the Urabi rebellion, became Britain's specious justification for its military occupation of Egypt in 1882, a de facto takeover that was slow to loosen its grips on the country.

Its debt notwithstanding, by the 1880s and well into the 1950s Egypt was regarded by most accounts as the most prosperous, modern, and promising country in the Middle East. Over the nineteenth century, there was a fifty-fold expansion in its foreign trade (Cole, 107). Egypt's population more than doubled, fueled by an upsurge in immigration. The French demographer Daniel Panzac estimates that the Egyptian population rose from about 4.5 million in 1800 to 5.4 million in 1846; and to 7.8 million in 1882 (Cole, 57). The addition of millions of inhabitants did not merely expand Egypt's population; it transformed it. The cities of Tanta, Mansura, and Damanhur, newly linked to the Mediterranean by rail, experienced between 80 and 170 percent growth in the decades between 1850 and 1880 (Cole, 112). Cairo and Alexandria grew dramatically; they were the cities of choice for immigrants—newly arrived Jews, non-Jews—and Egyptians leaving the countryside for the cities. For example, between 1897 and 1907 "the number of Cairo's residents who had been born outside Egypt increased from roughly 35,000 to 75,000; Alexandria witnessed a similar expansion of its population. From 1897 to 1917, the foreign percentage of the population grew from 14.5 to 19 percent."[7] In Alexandria, significant population growth occurred in the second half of the nineteenth century. From 1848 to 1897, the overall population of the city more than tripled. And between 1847 and 1927, it multiplied more than five times (Reynolds, 24). It is estimated that between 1800 and 1957, the period most relevant to this work, "The Egyptian population grew more than fivefold, from 4.5 million to 24 million people, but the population of the country's largest city, Cairo, expanded twelvefold" (Reynolds, 23–24). With demographic expansion came a change in the ethnic composition of the Egyptian population. This was accompanied by changes in social dress, mores, and language, which, as Nancy Y. Reynolds has argued, "reinforced visibly and experientially" the modern orientation Egypt was undertaking and influenced the discourse over Egypt's identity in the first half of the twentieth century. Ilham Khuri-Makdisi rightly points out that the changes that took place between 1870 and 1920, collectively referred to as the "era of globalization," "occurred in tandem with local, internal reconfigurations triggered by both state and society. Concomitantly the specter of foreign interference and dominance, which peaked with the British Occupation of Egypt in 1882, magnified some of these processes and set off its own tremors" (Khuri-Makdisi, 3). These dramatic changes created structural inequalities that resulted in discontent as well as great expectations. In the words of Yoav Di-Capua, they "ignited the sensitivities of the already diverse urban population," and became the source of contestation.[8] In Egypt, this "discontent," as I argue later, found popular expression in the identitary discourses of nationalism.

Both Jews and non-Jews tended to come to Egypt from the northern, southern, and eastern shores of the Mediterranean. "The number of foreigners grew from 10,000 in 1850 to 125,000 in 1900."[9] A Mediterranean country harboring a dynamic and open society, Egypt was the pole of attraction for immigration and migrations starting in the nineteenth century and well into the twentieth. Its modernization efforts and booming economy, particularly in contrast to that of its neighboring countries, drew to its cities workers, craftsmen, entrepreneurs, and political refugees at a time when the use of passports and nationality documents was not standardized (Khuri-Makdisi, 5). As for Jews, in the mid-1800s, they numbered about 6,000 to 7,000 persons in a population of about 5 million.[10] Between 1897 and 1917, the population of Jews is estimated to have more than doubled; from 25,200 to 59, 581.[11] In 1948, it is estimated to have been around 80,000. Among the Jews living in Egypt in 1948, about 5,000 had Egyptian nationality; 30,000 had foreign nationality, and 40,000 were stateless (Shamir, 34). At the turn of the twentieth century, the indigenous community of Jews constituted anywhere between 30 and 50 percent of the Jewish population.[12]

The categories of indigenous Jews and newcomers or immigrant Jews has framed the discussion on Egyptian Jewry both in Egypt and in the West. It has contributed to the widely held view that Egyptian Jews had "shallow roots" and lacked loyalty to Egypt.[13] Having been singled out as such, Egyptian Jews were framed "as refugees exploiting the generosity of their hosts. Even after one or two generations they were still regarded as intruders" (Shamir, 40). This view is rooted in popular Egyptian nationalist discourse and in the discourse of Egyptian scholars working in the second half of the twentieth century who were motivated politically to advance Arab nationalist ideology. In his examination of that body of work, Thomas Mayer has shown that these scholars regarded the Jewish community "as something basically alien and mostly European," ignoring the fact, he writes, that this community "had an indigenous foundation and that even among those Jews who were not originally from Egypt there were a good many who came (like many Muslims and Christian families) from Arab and East Mediterranean countries."[14] These Egyptian scholars, Mayer recognizes, regarded the Jewish community as "a servant of wider Jewish and Zionist interests," adding that in their work "Jewish efforts to integrate into Egyptian society are seen as deceptive. The Jews are blamed for exploiting the honesty and hospitality of the Egyptian society in order to promote their own economic ambitions and to assist their brethren in Palestine to establish a Jewish state on Arab territory" (Mayer, 207).

Indigenous and Newcomers

The conventional categories indigenous and newcomers are overdetermined categories that distort realities on the ground by amplifying difference, creating an abstract dichotomy. How is indigeneity conferred? And at what point does a "newcomer" stop being a newcomer? Like the concept of origin, the notion of indigeneity is a politically malleable construct. Its history is imperialist, its impulse hegemonic, and its effects invariably divisive, even violent. Rightly or wrongly, it serves to satisfy an ideology. The idea of indigeneity is particularly problematic in the case of Egyptian Jewry, where estimates of the number of indigenous Jews range widely from 15 percent (Krämer's figure) to 80 percent (Fargeon's).[15] It is important to keep in mind, as I explained above, that nineteenth-century Egypt saw a dramatic increase in its population. The Jewish community was formed, as Joel Beinin explains, "by a distinctive process of historical accretion" (Beinin, 2). But what exactly is meant by the indigenous population of Egypt? Its demographic expansion due to the arrival of Jews and other peoples is not a phenomenon unique to the nineteenth century. It has been an ongoing process for thousands of years during which Egypt served as the hub of commercial activity for the entire Mediterranean region. Egypt is a Mediterranean country and Jews are a Mediterranean people, as S. D. Goitein's work on the Geniza documents has shown.[16] It was one of the wealthiest provinces under the Roman Empire and the most prosperous under the Ottomans. It attracted many peoples from throughout the Mediterranean, and did so continuously. Egypt drew Jews and non-Jews to its cities. It is not surprising, therefore, that a significant Jewish community was present in Egypt without interruption for more than 2,000 years. Jews lived in the Nile Valley, in Egypt's deserts, and on its Mediterranean shore at least since the destruction of the First Temple in 586 BCE when the Judeans, accompanied by a reluctant Jeremiah, fled to the "land of Egypt." They had a significant presence in Alexandria, Cairo, Tanta, and other Egyptian cities at the time of Alexander the Great (356–323 BCE). In Ptolemaic Egypt (323 BCE–30 BCE), a large, acculturated, and visible community prospered. One of its achievements was the translation of the Bible into Greek. Centuries later, in Egypt, during the Roman and Byzantine empires Jews continued to be represented in all walks of life and in significant numbers. A large Jewish community existed in Egypt when it was captured by the Arabs between 639 CE and 642 CE. Like the Copts, they interacted with the new rulers throughout the following centuries. They lived alongside them and negotiated terms of coexistence for their communities. It is a fact of history that these communities, both Jewish and Coptic, were at times strengthened and at other times weakened. For example, during the Fatimid period (969–1171) and the Alawiyya Dynasty of Muhammad Ali (1805–1952), Egypt had a vibrant and engaged Jewish community. At other times, due to restrictions targeting the Jewish and Christian minorities, the community's influence and its well-being diminished. Ottoman rule in Egypt from the sixteenth to the nineteenth centuries was "reasonably good" for Jews and, conversely, under the Mamluks (1250–1517), it was not uniformly bad.[17] How can we talk about indigenous Jews in a country traversed by diverse populations, of Jews and non-Jews, for hundreds and thousands of years?

And yet conventional American academic discourse on Egyptian Jewry leans heavily on the distinction indigenous/newcomers (i.e., foreigners). In this binarism, indigenous Jews are described as a homogeneous group that has not changed over time. Newcomer Jews, meaning those who arrived in great numbers in the middle of the nineteenth century during Egypt's vast expansion, are, however, still considered to be newcomers in the first part of the twentieth century. In addition, a most cursory examination of this binarism would not fail to note that it sets up newcomers as prosperous, entrepreneurial, Westernized, multicultural, multilingual, and dismissive of Arabic language and culture; whereas indigenous Jews, in contrast, are poor, backward, partial to Arabic culture, do not speak French, and are unable or unwilling to Westernize. In short, the binary is based on social categories of the up and down sort: superior/inferior, wealthy/poor, educated/uneducated. I suggest that emphasis on the distinction indigenous/newcomer distorts the image of the Jewish community and is misleading. The conventional view asserts that the larger of the two groups comprises the newcomers, 85 percent of Egyptian Jews according to Krämer. As such, newcomers are considered to be more representative of the character of Egyptian Jewry. The newcomers serve to define the *ethical* and *moral* character of the community taken as a whole. The indigenous population is marginalized and made out to be insignificant both qualitatively and numerically. The effect of this differentiation strips away from Egyptian Jews their claim to be *of* Egypt, attached to Egypt as to one's homeland; it sets them up to be foreign elements who are apt to be disloyal. As I suggested, what is remarkable about the discourse on Egyptian Jewry in the West is how closely it follows the view adopted by the politically motivated discourse of Egyptian public officials and scholars. The unquestioned distinction indigenous/newcomer in contemporary thought on Egyptian Jewry mirrors the efforts of Muslim nationalists in the late 1920s to exclude Egypt's Jewish population from legal Egyptian citizenship. Shimon Shamir argues that public officials discovered that the most effective way to decline Egyptian nationality to undesirable minorities was to frame the requirements so narrowly that the so-called "unabsorbable spilled over to the treatment of groups whose roots in the region were indisputable" (Shamir, 57). The result was that "the whole Jewish community was projected in the image of its most foreign elements" (Shamir, 57). Once classified as foreign, it is not hard to focus grievances upon them and mobilize popular animus toward them.

I suggest that by the time Egyptian Jews were forced to leave the country, beginning in the second half of the 1950s, the distinction between indigenous or "local" Jews and newcomers was at best specious. Most if not all had been born in Egypt; there would have been at least one generation separating newcomer families from their first native-born child. Indigenous Jews and their newcomer Jewish compatriots mingled and frequently intermarried. In the space of one generation, most would have found it possible to set aside certain regional customs, different cuisine preparations, foreign or peculiar idioms and accents, and would have found these and other singularities if not endearing, then pretexts for playful teasing and put-downs. After the first generation, if not before, Jewish newcomers and locals could be said to share some things and not others and yet still consider themselves to be of one family. Rare were the families that did not overlap or intertwine ethnic and historical provenance. At the turn of the century, it was not uncommon to find individuals (often young men but women as well) and families immigrating to Egypt from Baghdad, Aleppo, Izmir, or Tunis with the expectation they would reunite with remnants of their families dating back decades or generations. The Jewish community in Egypt was old and had dealt with many waves of Jewish immigration. It had a communal structure and networks of relations that by all accounts were able to bring together Jews from different territories and religious congregations. This was as true in earlier times in Egypt as it was in more recent history. For example, in the eleventh century when Egypt was home to two major congregations, one that followed the Babylonian Talmud and another the Palestinian Talmud, and even though each community struggled to preserve its character, differences did not polarize the overall community. An indication of this is that when Jews from the Maghreb arrived in Egypt, and were mainly followers of the Babylonian Talmud, "Maghrebis could be found in both congregations."[18] Reflecting on this, S. D. Goitein writes:

> It is natural that such competition [between the two Talmuds and, hence, congregations] would sometimes lead to friction between the leaders of the congregations or even between their members. But according to our documents, the two congregations appear throughout the classical Geniza period as belonging to one community. Witness the fact that the public chest was administered in common. As a rule, donations were made and fines stipulated or imposed for the benefit of the two synagogues in equal shares. (Goitein, 96)

The resilience and flexibility of the Jewish community is demonstrated in another example. When Sephardi Jews arrived in waves in the fifteenth century during the Spanish expulsions, it did not take long before the existing Jewish communities and these new immigrants found common ground. At first, the newcomers "organized their own congregations, courts, and charitable institutions; however, despite the new divisions, the overall organization encompassing all Jewish groups remained intact" (Bareket, 131–132). This was also the case when Ashkenazi Jews fleeing pogroms in Russia and Poland arrived in the seventeenth and twentieth centuries, and then later when they fled the Nazis. And it was the case in 1914 when between 11,000 and 12,000 Jews of the Yishuv arrived in Egypt after their expulsion from Palestine by the Ottoman Turks. The Yishuv are the Jews who lived in present-day Israel during the Ottoman empire. Each time Jewish immigrants came to Egypt, whether under duress or by choice, the community accommodated them; and their interactions changed *both* the local Jews *and* the newcomers. During these times, Jewish communal autonomy continued, and presented a unified front. Egyptian Jews had been interacting, trading, and intermarrying with other Jews for centuries. Egypt was during most of its history a hospitable place, and Egyptian Jews had this cultural trait ingrained in them such that it colored their dealings with Jewish and non-Jewish newcomers alike. It is not surprising that their disposition would extend to their diverse coreligionists in whom they recognized a common bond in Judaism. Improvised social mixing was the norm. Twentieth-century Alexandria and Cairo did not invent Egyptian cosmopolitanism. As Tobie Nathan remarks: "Modern societies did not invent mixed communities; they only accelerated their frequency."[19]

Finally, before their expulsion, the long history of the Egyptian Jewish community intertwined with the history of other Egyptians. To the extent that any Egyptian minority could make such a claim, Egyptian Jews were, *culturally* speaking, Egyptians. I say culturally and not legally because nationality is a modern phenomenon. It is a judicial category that emerged in Egypt during the two decades before and after the turn of the twentieth century. William Hanley's far-reaching work on the history of nationality in Alexandria demonstrates that the phenomenon of nationality, both as legal doctrine and legal practice, has always been "contingent and strategic."[20] It was then, as it is now, Hanley argues, "a legal fiction" (Hanley, 17). Nationality is "a latent quality that only becomes real when individuals are tested by concrete circumstances," he writes (Hanley, 6). It was difficult for Jews to acquire Egyptian nationality, whereas it was an entitlement conferred upon most Muslims even when they did not reside in Egypt. The exclusionary practices of Egyptian public officials became more pronounced in the 1930s when nationality laws were being solidified, presenting intractable problems for Jews unwilling to renounce Judaism. Even so, Egyptian Jews shared the same cuisine, listened to the same music, saw the same films, attended the same operas, walked the same streets, laughed at the same jokes: they worked, interacted with, and lived in the same neighborhoods and in the same buildings with other Egyptians who were part of the same socioeconomic class. Compared to one of the largest minorities, the Greek community in Egypt, and the numerous Armenians and Italians born and residing in Egypt, Jews of every socioeconomic stripe were far more likely to speak Arabic and engage in the same activities as the majority Muslim population. Before Arab nationalists redefined Egypt and began to demonstrate hostility toward the Jewish community, Egyptian Jews, for the most part, perceived themselves as Egyptians. Like many other Egyptians in liberal Egypt, they aspired to lead modern lives and adopted the model of secularization that many Muslim elites followed from the time of Muhammad Ali's reforms. In the nineteenth and twentieth centuries, Enlightenment values and the pursuit of modernity were standards many people around the world aspired to and worked to incorporate into their societies. The end of the Jewish community came about because Egyptian Jews could not fit into a collective project that, as Yoav Di-Capua rightly observes, "stresses the nation/Egypt and not individuals—the public and not the private" (Di-Capua, 228) and whose understanding of citizenship "emphasized commitment to the heritage of Islam" (Di-Capua, 228). In her excellent study on the cookbook memoir genre and the cases of Claudia Roden and Colette Rossant, Nefissa Naguib explains what she perceives as a paradox in the complex discourse of Egyptian Jews. Naguib writes that Roden's and Rossant's books strongly communicate the feeling of "having possessed an Egypt that they lost and which they are able to reclaim only through memories of the comforts and feelings of home that they project on 'their' Egypt."[21] She continues: "There is a sharp contradiction between their former inability to think of themselves as Egyptians, when they were actually living in the country, and the professed nostalgia of the exiled" (Naguib, 50). By stressing a certain Egypt, Naguib is not far from resolving the "contradiction" she and others perceive as duplicity in the identitary discourses of Egyptian Jews. Naguib recognizes that "the message" the works of Roden and Rossant confirm is, to put it simply, "that life in Egypt initially was good but then turned bad" (Naguib, 50). In the experience of many, as Levana Zamir puts it in the documentary film entitled *Starting Over*, the world of Egyptian Jewry changed. Almost overnight they began to be treated like criminals and usurpers. This sea change in the lives of many Jewish Egyptians is portrayed in the works of the writers I examine in this book.

The Intellectual Climate: Egyptian Territorial Nationalism

From roughly the 1890s to the mid-1930s, a period marked by liberal ideas in business and in the broader national ethos, Egyptian Jews had reasons to believe they were part of a modern Egypt. The high-water mark of collaborative and inclusive interaction between Muslim Egypt and its minorities was reached in the 1920s. The espousal of liberal ideology in Egypt was not limited to the elites; it was shared by the middle and popular classes. It was in this dynamic setting that the Egyptian Jewish community thrived. Family names like Curiel, Cicurel, Cattaui, Menasche, Mosseri, Suares, Aghion, Smouha, and Chemla—to name only those who became remarkably successful—contributed to Egypt's modernization efforts. These entrepreneurial families and their less well-heeled compatriots worked in various sectors of the economy. Besides their prominence in banking and as brokers, merchants, and distributors, they helped to build and develop Egypt's urban centers, railway, hospitals, schools, and department stores. Wealthy members of the Jewish community served on commercial courts, in Mixed Tribunals; they held membership in the Egyptian Chamber of Commerce, founded associations, were involved in philanthropic work, and participated in the liberal Wafd government. There were artisans, jewelers, seamstresses, and tailors. In the 1920s and 1930s, Jews occupied a pivotal position in the film industry. There were celebrated Jewish actors like Leila Mourad, Nagua Salem, and Beshar Wakim; directors and producers like Togo Mizrahi, the Frenkel Brothers, and Robert and Raymond Hakim; leading film distributors like Zaki Bonan of Behna Films, Jacques Cohen of International Film, and Elie Israel of Mathatheia Films.[22] In addition, Jewish men who came of age in the 1940s and 1950s joined the ranks of a rising professional class, the *effendiyya*. This class comprised educated men who practiced professions such as law, medicine, engineering, pharmacy, and journalism.[23] In this upwardly mobile urban society most Jews could be counted among the striving middle classes: those who hoped to improve and make more secure their lives and the lives of the families in their care. Among Egyptian Jews, some were *fellahin*s who cultivated the land, and others were overseers who administered it. There were also poor Jews who lived in urban enclaves like the various *hara*s. The history of Egyptian Jewry in the last two decades of the nineteenth century and the first three decades of the twentieth attests to their diversity and to the Jewish community's confidence, strength, and vitality. They were, as David Maslowski so rightly says, "A minority on the rise" (Maslowski, 35).

With the exception of Jews born in the late 1940s and early 1950s, like Paula Jacques and André Aciman, Egyptian Jews knew Egypt at a time when it was undergoing a renaissance. It was a time that held forth the promise of a secular harmony between the Muslim majority and the country's many minorities. It may well be as Joel Beinin suggests that liberalism represented a false promise (Beinin, 38). But the period before the turn to radical nationalism was a defining moment for Egyptian Jews. As Dario Miccoli has shown, and as the works of both Jacqueline Kahanoff and Edmond Jabès concur with, Jews were interested in asserting their belongingness to Egypt. They looked to history to confirm their lineage there. In 1925 they founded the Société d'Etudes historiques juives d'Egypte, wrote books, became involved in cultural activities that focused on Egyptian history both ancient and modern.[24] The discourse of modernity, which I take up below, was seductive to many Egyptians and not only to Egypt's minorities. Ziad

Fhamy's work demonstrates that contemporary discourses on modernity, cultural liberalism, and republicanism were not the sole purview of the elites and the educated public.[25] Liberal ideas reached the wider public through newspapers, cafés, theaters, music halls, and film. This new Egypt not only felt new; it was new and it was forward looking. It promised inclusivity, access, self-determination, and dignity. This period is referred to by cultural historians as Egypt's "Liberal Age" and the movement that characterizes it is referred to by some as Egyptian "territorial nationalism." The level of confidence Jews felt during this period, between the two World Wars, showed itself in the interest to define themselves with respect to Egypt. It is a period that the majority of Egyptian Jews consider the truest expression of Egypt's identity and the most faithful representation of the Egyptian character and its aspirations. They felt that it was this liberal Egypt that was hijacked by Arab and Islamic nationalisms.

By the 1920s, Egypt had seen tremendous economic and political change. Politically, it had witnessed the dissolution of the Ottoman Empire, the end of the Caliphate (1924), and the prospects of an end to British rule (1922). The Egyptian Constitution was adopted in 1923. It granted equal rights to all Egyptians, without distinction of race, language, or religion (Shamir, 33). And the Wafd government enjoyed wide popular support and served as a concrete illustration that these fundamental changes had entered the system and carried institutional legitimacy. Minorities were to be an integral part of Egypt, and this concept reassured religious minorities. As Fahmy has shown, this transformation and the resultant confidence in Egypt's future inspired optimism among large segments of both the elites and popular classes. This was evident in the press and in political discussions among Muslims, Christians, and Jews well into the 1930s and the first half of the 1940s. These changes motivated Egyptian public intellectuals to examine what made Egypt and Egyptian culture distinct among nations. And it led them to define, or redefine, Egyptian identity.[26] Egyptian territorial nationalists stressed Egypt's unique geography, topography, climate, and the distinguished history of its Pharaonic past. The discovery of the tomb of Tut-Ankh-Amon in 1922 further reinforced the sense of Egypt's uniqueness and its glorious history. As Israel Gershoni and James Jankowski have argued, Egyptian intellectuals rested the foundation of this new Egypt on four principal images. The first demonstrated that the environment of the Nile Valley determined the national character and distinctive personality of Egyptians, which made them unique. The second stipulated a collective history, continuous since Pharaonic times and stretching into the future. The third posited the Pharaonic heritage as the only authentic national heritage. And the fourth, "was a *cultural image* proving that Egypt had an independent national culture separate from that of the Arab and Muslim legacy ... derived from the environment and history of the

Nile Valley" (italics in text; EIA,131). Importantly, Egyptian territorial nationalism was informed and reinforced by three distinct models: 1) Western liberal and secular concepts and practices, marked by the deterministic and positivist philosophy of Ernest Renan and Hippolyte Taine in particular; 2) the Turkish nationalist movement's break with historic Islam; and 3) a tradition within Islam itself, the movement called *shu'ubiyya* that "glorified ancient and non-Arab people and ideas" (EIA, 102–103). The *shu'ubiyya* movement emerged in the ninth and tenth centuries as a response by Persian Muslims to what they saw as the growing Arabization of Islam in Iran. The liberal constitutional government of Egypt challenged religious fundamentalism. This changed the rules of the game and allowed more people to get involved. Given that religious identities were set aside, Jews, Copts, and Syrian and Lebanese Christians found ways to participate in the Wafd government. Nationalist and secular, the Wafd's base seemed both broad and deep. Fittingly, it attracted a number of Jews.[27] The popularity and staying power of the liberal movement was sustained for many years even in the face of the steady rise of Arab and Islamic nationalisms in the 1930s and 1940s. As Gershoni and Jankowski point out: "Liberal ideas about both politics and society continued to be expressed with considerable vigor by Egyptian intellectuals and publicists" in the years preceding World War II.[28]

The concept of Egyptian territorial nationalism did not emerge full-cloth on the eve of the 1919 Revolution. Much of its foundation was laid earlier by writers, intellectuals, and statesmen like Ahmad Lutfi al-Sayed (1872–1963), Muhammad Husayn Haykal (1888–1956), Tawfiq al-Hakim (1898–1987), Salama Musa (1887–1958), Abbas Mahmud al-Aqqad (1889–1964), and Taha Hussayn (1889–1973), to name a few who lived to witness the Arabist sea change. Most of these men had in common a deep-seated belief that Egypt's natural environment was evidence that it belonged in a category apart, one that distinguished it from Western Asia and North Africa. For example, Muhammad Husayn Haykal believed that "the Egyptian personality (its *shakhsiyya*) was a genuine, well-defined independent phenomenon; as such it deserved to serve as the basis of a distinct Egyptian identity" (EIA, 38). Lutfi al-Sayed argued that to gain independence and enjoy fully its benefits, Egypt must protect and preserve its Egyptian identity. Egyptians loved Egypt exclusively, he insisted, and were loyal to their territorial homeland (EIA, 14). Liberal thinkers maintained that the roots of the Egyptian people went back to Pharaonic times, quoting Herodotus, "Egyptian intellectuals held that Egypt was 'indeed the gift of the Nile' and could be understood only as a unique national entity with its own geography, history, and culture." Furthermore, they "assumed a correlation between the realization of Egyptian authenticity and the attainment of modernity . . . a progressive, dynamic nation-state marching inexorably into the modern age" (EIA, 130). As a whole, Egyptian territorial nationalist intellectuals rejected the notion that modernity was a Western concept. It rose, instead, out of Egypt's Pharaonic heritage.

The Nile held a central place in their framing of Egyptian identity. For Haykal, the Nile and the Nile Valley constituted an independent entity. Separated from other countries by a desert in the west, a desert to its east, and the sea in the north, it was an almost completely closed system protected from sudden and irregular shifts of weather, and it was geographically homogeneous. Tempered by a moderate climate, the Nile Valley, he wrote, was "free of external influences." The great river reflected (mirrored) the Egyptian people whose dominant character, Haykal held, is marked by gentleness, benevolence, moderation, and, regrettably also, he added, by rigidity and conformity, which translated for him into the absence of a desire to change (EIA, 37). Similarly, for Muhammad Ghallab, Egyptology proved conclusively that Egypt was a nation that emerged from the banks of the Nile and among the mountains surrounding it. "There is nothing to link her with the Asians, nor any common nexus tying her to the Nubians, nor strands of kinship connecting her to the North Africans" (EIA, 116). For some of these writers and thinkers, the Nile and its valley were sufficient determinants of Egyptian identity. Other territorial nationalists included the Mediterranean Sea to provide a fuller image of Egypt's identity. Without undermining the country's Pharaonic past or the importance of the Nile in shaping Egyptian identity, Salama Musa, Muhammad Sharaf, and Muhammad Ghallab, to name only three, believed that Egyptian identity was most closely related, in both spirit and history, to the Indo-European race and to Hellenic-Mediterranean-Western cultural and intellectual traditions (EIA, 115–116).

As concerns Egypt's Arab heritage, the vast number of territorial nationalists took the position that Egyptians were not Arabs. This was not an uncommon view. As Jessica M. Marglin points out, "hardly anyone in the Middle East was calling themselves an Arab before the late nineteenth century, except perhaps Bedouins."[29] Like Muhammad Farid, many argued that Egyptians and Arabs represented two different races (EIA, 18). They maintained that Arabs are a "foreign" people and described both the Arab spirit and its heritage as "irreconcilable with the 'age of renewal' underway in Egypt since 1919" (EIA, 100). They pointed out that Arabs were those people who lived in the Hijaz, Arabia, Syria, and Lebanon. Tawfiq al-Hakim called on his fellow Egyptians to eradicate "non-Egyptian components" in Egyptian life; the most prominent were, al-Hakim claimed, its "Arab components." Along the same lines, Hafiz Mahmud, a member of the Liberal Constitutional Party, proclaimed that the only Arab element Egyptians have in common with Arabs is their language: "We are Arabs merely because we speak Arabic" (EIA, 99). He pointed out that during the revolution of 1919 when Egyptians fought against the British Empire, they were inspired to rise up when reminded that they were the children of the Pharaohs, that Egypt was the Mother of the Pyramids, and when the names of Ramses and Thutmose were invoked. It was not "the ruins of Arabia" that inspired them (EIA, 100). Lutfi al-Sayyid in the years before World War I had compared the nation to a living organism and to a family whose membership must not be limited to those born in it. The Egyptian community, he wrote, is made up of "ethnic Egyptians" and "other new elements of foreign origin who have made Egypt their permanent residence and the theater of their activities so that it has very quickly become the repository of their wealth and their home for the present and the future" (EIA, 13). But even he held strong anti-Arab sentiments and referred to Syrians as intruders (EIA, 16). Ibn Khaldun, admittedly the most respected historian of the Arabs and an Arab himself, argued that Arabs and Egyptians were different peoples (EIA, 103). And Sa'd Zaghlul, the leader of the 1919 revolution and the Wafd—the first popularly elected government in Egypt—"the symbol of this new Egypt, a man of the countryside who had remained truly Egyptian"—was anti-Arab (EIA, 84). Zaghlul "paid no attention either to the Arab dimension of Egypt or to a possible connection between Egyptian and Arab nationalism" (EIA, 50). The liberal movement's unequivocal repudiation of the emerging Arab movement whose anti-foreigner and anti-Jewish positions were made amply clear helped reinforce Jewish patriotism and Egyptian identity.

Like many in Egyptian society, Egyptian Jews were inspired by the discourse of Egyptian territorial nationalists to see themselves as an integral part of Egypt. Though there were still signs of antisemitism and anti "foreign" sentiments, they believed these were constrained. They took Egypt's liberal orientation as a sign of the future. It inspired them, for example, to identify with Egypt's political struggle against the British. On the whole, Egyptian Jews were hostile toward the British, a sentiment that was complicated when, during World War II, the British stood guard and defended the Middle East and North Africa from the Axis powers. In the early years, before the war, Egypt's liberal position inspired Jews, as it did other Egyptians and many of its minorities, to participate in civic activities. A number of Jews found in public life and in government service the possibility of contributing to the Egyptian nation. The Jews of Egypt were active "throughout the spectrum of Egyptian public life" (Stillman, 54). They served regularly in parliament for the Ittihad Party. Joseph Aslan Cattaoui was a member of the commission who drafted the Egyptian Constitution, and was also part of the Legislative Assembly during the Protectorate years. He was elected to parliament, and served as minister of finance in the government of Ziwar Pasha in 1924 and as minister of communications in 1925 (Stillman, 54). Léon Castro and Félix Benzakein were equally engaged in the Wafd government. It bears repeating that for Egyptian Jewry, the Liberal Age *was* Egypt. Many viewed the Arab and Islamic nationalisms that followed as unfortunate aberrations. Finally, it was the image of this liberal Pharaonic Egypt they fastened onto and remembered in the years after their expulsion.

In "'Radical' Nationalists, Fundamentalists, and the Jews in Egypt or, Who is a Real Egyptian?" Gudrun Krämer refers to the proponents of Egyptian territorial nationalism as "Westernized intellectuals" who held "so-called 'liberal'" positions.[30] It is not wrong to suggest that territorial nationalists were influenced by Western concepts or that their ideas were not liberal enough, strictly speaking. But it is injudicious to overlook the fact that, as I have pointed out, liberalism was motivated by a paradigmatic slant in the region toward openness, connectedness, and modernity led in part by the emergent Turkish revolution, and by a well-grounded tradition within Islam itself, namely, the *shu'ubiyya* movement (EIA, 103). Both Ziad Fahmy and Ilham Khuri-Makdisi have rightly challenged the deeply entrenched notion that "nationalism was disseminated predominantly by European-educated intellectuals" (Fahmy, xi). The West did *not* have everything to do with both the successes and the problems that beset Egypt. Western ideas had an impact on the way Egyptians understood and carried out the "modern" project. But these ideas were reworked, made to fit, and were transformed. It is, I believe also, inappropriate to conclude that Egyptians, whether members of the educated elite or the popular classes, did not engage with issues concerning them about politics, social rights, the environment, human nature, and other existential subjects. Egyptians had agency and could be counted on to engage with ideas. Among other factors, a newspaper and coffee-house culture thrived that facilitated such engagement (Fahmy). Khuri-Makdisi writes: "it is not a matter of importing but of adapting, and adaptation cannot take place outside of local frameworks that give meaning to novel concepts, or local spaces and institutions. . . . Adaptations also obviously have to fit into intellectual structures of meaning" (Khuri-Makdisi, 9). On a slightly different tack, responding to the stereotypical view that Egyptian Jews imitated Western culture, Shimon Shamir points out:

> It is true that the Jewish elite, including some of the oldest families in the community, developed a European cultural orientation, and it permeated the middle class as well. But that was a trend of the times discernible in Muslim and Coptic Social circles as well, and did not *necessarily* eradicate the Middle Eastern (or at least Mediterranean) roots of the social and cultural norms prevalent among the Egyptian Jews, who were predominantly Sephardic. (My italics; Shamir, 57–58)

Ideas are not the sacred possessions of a culture that controls them as with a patent, but are protean and reconfigurable. In the preface to the first volume of *Cultures of the Jews: Mediterranean Origins*, David Biale examines a fifteenth-century silver casket created by an Italian Jewish craftsman, Jeshurum Tovar. The casket, Biale observes, was intended as a wedding gift for a Jewish bride. It combines Renaissance decorative motifs, Hebrew inscriptions, and Jewish symbolism. Italian and Jewish cultural materials, he remarks, mix organically. In this and other examples of cultural syncretism, Biale asks, "How should we label such adoption of non-Jewish culture?" Was Tovar adopting Renaissance motifs for Jewish purposes? Was the meaning altered and, if so, how? These are the same questions that must be asked when we try to understand how Egyptians, both Jewish and non-Jewish, interacted with Western culture on Egyptian soil. The question is not how poorly they imitate and what moral value to assign to imitation. Imitation is not the issue. Biale is right when he argues in the case of the Renaissance Jewish silver casket that chasing after who stole, borrowed, or disfigured a motif, an idea, or a language is at best reductive. It speaks to an illiberal teleology framed around supremacy, origins, and exclusion. He writes:

> Jews should not be seen as outsiders who borrowed from Italian culture but rather as full participants in the shaping of that culture, albeit with their own concerns and mores. The Jews were not so much "influenced" by the Italians as they were one organ in a larger cultural organism, a subculture that established its identity in a complex process of adaptation and resistance. Expanding beyond Renaissance Italy to Jewish history as a whole, we might find it more productive to use this organic model of culture than to chase after who influenced whom.[31]

It is important to keep in mind that traffic between countries and territories along the Mediterranean was multidirectional during both ancient and modern times. Europeans came to Egypt and Egyptians went to Europe. When Egyptians came back, they brought ideas with them. In his fascinating work on migrations in the eastern Mediterranean, examining in particular Cairo, Alexandria, and Beirut around 1860–1914, Ilham Khuri-Makdisi shows how these cities functioned like hubs that connected to parts of the world by "webs of people, information, capital and commodities"; circulation was multidirectional and across social divisions (Khuri-Makdisi, 9). Examining movements from the countryside in Egypt, Lebanon, and Syria to large cities as well as across the ocean, Khuri-Makdisi observes: "It was not only peasants who were on the move, but also artisans, craftsmen, white-collar workers, and countless others who converged on Beirut, Cairo, and Alexandria in search of employment" (Khuri-Makdisi, 5). Jews were among these migrants. Like the migrants Khuri-Makdisi describes, they were not only entrepreneurs seeking to enrich themselves. They worked in various sectors. They were mobile, traveling and immigrating to countries where they believed they could make a living or improve their lives. This phenomenon of intense multidirectional mobility, Khuri-Makdisi argues, needs to be framed in terms of human agency, as an intrinsic part of the region's economic and cultural character. It is a mistake to view the incorporation of these populations into the global network as merely a reaction to foreign interference and dominance

(Khuri-Makdisi, 3–5).³² Egyptian Easternists in the 1920s, proponents of the idea of Egypt as part of the East, advocated that the best way to strengthen Egypt was to be receptive "to the best in the West" (EIA, 259). Non-Westerners, Khuri-Makdisi writes, "felt confident they could assemble their own visions of social and world order, borrowing, adapting, synthesizing, perhaps plundering ideas from 'the West and the rest' and melding them with local practices and ideas to produce what might strike us today as a radical package marked by contradictions and limitations" (Khuri-Makdisi, 3). Individuals who went looking for work in cities in Egypt, Syria, Lebanon, and abroad in America and Brazil came back with ideas and possibly capital. When some of them returned, they brought new methods of doing things, which they adapted according to their needs and tastes. But even before they came back, they sent remittances to families who shaped their countries. Thus they created new family patterns, transformed some peasants into members of the middle classes, and established entirely new villages.

It is indeed more productive to view cultural interaction between Egyptians and Westerners in terms of Biale's organic model of cultural adaptation. The writers I focus on in this book and the Egyptian experience they reflect display a sophisticated understanding of what it means to live in a multicultural milieu. The operative premise in their works is that syncretism, Levantinism, and the operations of historical and cultural transmission are the sine qua non of vigorous cultures. Ada Aharoni gives a simple and to-the-point expression of this stance. Without a shadow of conflict, conceit, or submissiveness, she writes that in Egypt, before the end, "Jews enjoyed the thriving cultural activities in Cairo and Alexandria where one could watch performances of such theaters as the Old Vic and the Comédie Française. But life was not totally Europeanized, for Um Kulthum and (the Jewish) Leila Morad were no less popular. In Jewish homes there was usually a mixture of European culture, Jewish traditions, and oriental customs. For the Jews, Egypt became a land of cultural choice."³³

The End of Liberalism and the Beginning of Memory

In their book *Confronting Fascism in Egypt*, Israel Gershoni and James Jankowski write that "With Egypt's transformation into a revolutionary republic in the 1950s and its adoption of a formally socialist economic orientation in the 1960s, many liberal structures and institutions (the press, political pluralism, an independent academy, a capitalist economy) were undermined or destroyed" (Fascism, 54). The collapse and near extinction of the Jewish community began with the assertion of Arab and Islamic nationalist movements. Pan-Arabism's turn toward its Arab neighbors and its exclusionary ideology was a radical shift. The tripartite attack on the Suez Canal quickened the demise of Egyptian Jewry. The enforcement and increased pressures of policies restricting employment, the arbitrary revocation of licenses, the application of sequestrations, confiscations, and the nationalization of businesses (1961–1962), and the failed wars against Israel—all these events and policies combined to guarantee that no Jewish presence of note would remain in Egypt for the first time in millennia. The community of 80,000 was forced out. Many were summarily expelled in 1956, 1957, and 1967. Others came to the conclusion that there was no chance of a reversal taking place. The economic, social, and existential hardships became unbearable for the remaining Jews, and was particularly challenging for families with children. The social and political animus against the community kept mounting, until by 1968 there were only about 1,000 Jews left in the country. As of 2015, the number of Jews living permanently varies wildly between 13 persons (Haroun) and 100 to 150 (Douer).[34] Pan-Arab nationalism was effectively the end of the road for Egyptian Jews.

For Jacques Hassoun, the past is a project of active transmission. He calls on each generation to interpret for itself the past in terms that are meaningful to it in its own time. He writes: "It is precisely because we are different from those who preceded us and different as well from our descendants who will most likely follow a road clearly different from ours, that I find fascinating the adventure that constitutes transmission. . . . And yet . . . it is also precisely in this series of differences that we inscribe what we have to transmit."[35] And every generation, Yosef Hayim Yerushalmi points out, passes the burden of meaning to a future generation that has "accepted [it] as meaningful."[36] In the work of remembering, we enter into a dialogue that continues through the ages. This model of an active *not-forgetting* is exemplified by the writers I examine in this book. Magda Haroun, the president of the Jewish community of Egypt, expressed the same imperative in an interview conducted in 2015. "Unfortunately," she says, "we won't have any weddings, but we will be acknowledged, and I will fight until the end that our presence is *acknowledged in history*" (my italics).[37] By engaging vigorously with Egypt, they wrestle to construct, reconstruct, and heal their fractured Egyptian identity. At the same time, their collective work pitches a challenge to Egypt not to forget that Jews had lived for millennia among them. It asks Egyptians to consider also that just as the great Exodus of Pharaonic times was a defining moment in the history of Judaism, so might the Second Exodus serve as a defining moment for Egypt.

Less than a decade after their expulsion—beginning some time in the late 1960s and gaining momentum particularly after the Peace Treaty between Egypt and Israel (1977–1979)—Egyptian Jews began the burdensome undertaking of transmitting to their descendants a remarkable episode in Jewish history, no less remarkable for being also the founding narrative of the Jewish people. Egyptian Jews living today in the diaspora should easily recognize that they are, in the words of Tobie Nathan, "the last of the Mohicans."[38]

Chapter 1 examines the psychoanalytic works of Jacques Hassoun and their contributions to the understanding of Egyptian Jews and immigrant communities. It begins by looking at Hassoun's work concerning immigrant and minority communities, examining his thinking regarding the operations of adaptation, among them "transmission," "contraband," and political activism. I examine Hassoun's concept of the One (*le Un*), the pre-linguistic order, anterior to the mother, which Hassoun identifies as the site of the impulse to exclude the Other. I pay attention to his theories on the "stranger" and his unsympathetic view of ethnic group-identity, a view I attempt to reconcile with his own activities on behalf of Egyptian Jewry. I situate Hassoun's notion of the mother tongue in the context of immigrant and French-speaking communities. I go over Hassoun's family background, his education, and political activities in Egypt and describe his work on behalf of the Egyptian Jewish community. I conclude with an examination of his novel, *Alexandrias. A Novel*. Chapter 2 explores Jacqueline Kahanoff's principal works. It takes into view her novel, *Jacob's Ladder*, and other fictional works, essays, and the subject of Levantinism. I read the novel as a critique of Europeanization and an affirmation of Jewish belonging in Egypt. I discuss rootedness as key to Levantine identity, examine the role French culture and the Alliance Israëlite Universelle played in the lives of Egyptian Jews, and I argue that Kahanoffian Levantinism is an aesthetics and a politics. Chapter 3 examines Egypt as subject matter in Edmond Jabès's monumental *Book of Questions* and his subsequent works. I review the role French language and culture played in Egypt's intellectual life, Jabès's criticism of France in the 1960s and 1970s, the roots of his family in Egypt, and Jabès's politics. Chapter 4 examines Paula Jacques's novels from the perspective of Jewish Egyptian attachment to Egypt, resistance to displacement, the role of France in the perpetuation of Jewish Egyptian culture, and the Jewish Egyptian approach to Israel. I examine in Jacques's work the anxiety of being without nationality, the relationship between Jews and Muslims in Egypt, the images of Ashkenazi and Egyptian Jews, and explore Jacques's representations of Jewish Egyptian experience in Egypt, France, and Israel. Chapter 5 looks at André Aciman as exhibiting an example of the psychological pressures experienced by the generation of Egyptian Jews born after 1945 when Egypt took the Arab turn. I focus attention on Aciman's attachment to Egypt, his representations of Jews and Arabs in both Egypt and the United States, and I highlight the significance of his "Open Letter to President Barak Obama." Finally, the epilogue leans on the work and words of Tobie Nathan to reflect on the Passover story from the perspective of Second Exodus Egyptian Jews.

Notes

All translations from the French are my own.

1. "C'est ainsi que, dans l'exil, j'explore avec d'autres écrivains en exil, à travers eux, une Méditerranée du Sud qui fut cosmopolite, une Méditerranée juive et musulmane, aujourd'hui orpheline des Juifs qui l'ont habitée avant l'Islam. Une histoire parfois joyeuse parfois cruelle raconte cela. Des histoires individuelles se souviennent d'une autre fois." Leïla Sebbar, *Une enfance juive en méditerranée musulmane* (Auvergne: Bleu Autour, 2012), 9.

2. See discussions on Mediterraneanism developed in the works of David Ohana; Julia A. Clancy-Smith; W. V. Harris; Peregrine Horden and Nicholas Purcell; Sharon Kinoshita; Gil Z. Hochberg's nuanced reflections on the "Mediterranean Option"; and the criticism of Ian Morris, Michael Herzberg, and Sharon Rotbard.

3. Benedict Anderson, *Imagined Communities* (New York: Verso, 2006).

4. The French text: "Et nous ne nous sentions pas étrangers en Egypte. Nous nous sentions chez nous. Mon père était né là. J'étais né là. C'était mon pays" (my transcription and translation). Found in Elliot Malki's film *Starting Over Again: A Jewish Egyptian Story*, directed by Ruggero Gabbai (Milan: Forma International Production, 2015). Further references to this film will be included in the text as (Starting Over).

5. Ilham Khuri-Makdisi, *The Eastern Mediterranean and the Making of Global Radicalism, 1860–1914* (Berkeley: University of California Press, 2013), 148. Further references to this work will be included in the text as (Khuri-Makdisi).

6. James R. Cole, *Colonialism and Revolution in the Middle East: Social and Cultural Origins of Egypt's 'Urabi Movement'* (Princeton, N.J.: Princeton University Press, 1993), 54. Further references to this work will be included in the text as (Cole).

7. Nancy Y. Reynolds, *A City Consumed: Urban Commerce, the Cairo Fire, and the Politics of Decolonization in Egypt* (Stanford, Calif.: Stanford University Press, 2012), 24. Further references to this work will be included in the text as (Reynolds).

8. Yoav Di-Capua, *Gatekeepers of the Arab Past: Historians and History Writing in Twentieth-Century Egypt* (Berkeley: University of California Press, 2009), 21. Further references to this work will be included in the text as (Di-Capua).

9. Racheline Barda, in *Encyclopedia of Jews in the Islamic World*, edited by Norman Stillman (Leiden and Boston: Brill, 2010), vol. 2, 132–142, 134. Further references to this work will be included in the text as (Barda).

10. Ehud R. Toledano, *State and Society in Mid-Nineteenth Century Egypt* (Cambridge: Cambridge Middle East), 2003.

11. Shimon Shamir, "The Evolution of the Egyptian Nationality Laws and their Application to the Jews in the Monarchy Period," in *The Jews of Egypt: A Mediterranean Society in Modern Times*, edited by Shimon Shamir, 33–67; 51 (Boulder, Colo. and London: Westview, 1987). Further references to this work will be included in the text as (Shamir).

12. For a discussion on the numbers of indigenous Jews in Egypt, see Shimon Shamir's thoughtfully considered argument (ibid., 49–51). Shamir disputes both Gudrun Krämer's figure and Maurice Fargeon's. Krämer places the number of indigenous Jews at 15 percent of the overall population (Krämer, *Jews in Modern Egypt*, 14) and Fargeon at 80 percent (Shamir, 65). Shamir and Joel Beinin put the figure at 50 percent by the turn of the twentieth century. See Joel Beinin, *The Dispersion of Egyptian Jewry: Culture, Politics, and*

the Formation of a Modern Diaspora (Berkeley and Los Angeles: University of California Press, 1998), 38. Further references to this work will be included in the text as (Beinin).

13. The chief proponent of this view is Gudrun Krämer; her study on Egyptian Jewry is the preeminent work of reference on the subject. The following encapsulates her position: "They were non-Muslims, predominantly non-Egyptian and, in spite of all protests to the contrary, of non-Arab origin. They were largely of European culture and French-speaking. There were among them leading representatives of the foreign-dominated economic system, protégés of the British, committed royalists, and also socialists, communists and Zionists.... Like all other minorities, they had profited greatly from industrialization and Westernization under European control which had given them a share in the national economy out of proportion to their actual numbers" (Gudrun Krämer, "'Radical' Nationalists, Fundamentalists, and the Jews in Egypt or, Who Is a Real Egyptian?" in *Islam, Nationalism, and Radicalism in Egypt and the Sudan,* edited by Gabriel R. Warburg and Uri M. Kupferschmidt, 354–371, 366 [New York: Praeger Special Studies. Praeger Scientific, 1983]). See also Gudrun Krämer, *The Jews in Modern Egypt 1914–1952* (Washington: University of Washington Press, 1989). It is notable that Krämer's narrative mirrors the views of Egyptian scholars writing in Egypt in the 1970s at a time when anti-Jewish views were not only encouraged but expected. See the critique of Krämer and Michael Laskier by Ruth Toledano-Attias in "La Dénationalisation des Juifs d'Egypte," in Shmuel Trigano, *La fin du judaïsme en terre d'Islam* (Paris: Denoël, 2009), 51–85. Toledano-Attias argues that both Krämer and Laskier sidestep the antisemitic motivations of the Egyptian government and the Egyptian masses with subtle rationalizations. She asks rhetorically: "Who needs subtly crafted arguments to tell us that Egyptians were not antisemitic?" ("Que valent les raisonnements nuancés qui affirment que les Egyptiens n'étaient pas antisemites?" Toledano-Attias, 84). She continues: "Even if an organized antisemitic program did not exist, the assessment of Gudrun Krämer and Michael Laskier, who believe there was no antisemitism in Egypt, must be viewed with skepticism" ("Le jugement de Gudrun Krämer et de Michael Laskier, qui prétendent qu'il n'y avait pas d'antisemitisme en Egypte, doit être reçu avec réserve même s'il n'y a pas eu de programme de persécutions organisé."; Toledano-Attias, 85).

14. Thomas Mayer, "The Image of Egyptian Jewry in Recent Egyptian Studies," in Shimon Shamir, *The Jews of Egypt,* 199–212, 207.

15. See Note 12.

16. S. D. Goitein, *A Mediterranean Society: An Abridgment in One Volume,* revised and edited by Jacob Lassner (Berkeley: University of California Press, 1999). Further references to this work will be included in the text as (Goitein).

17. The term *reasonably good* is from Michael Winter, "Egyptian Jewry during the Ottoman Period as a Background to Modern Times," in Shamir, *The Jews of Egypt,* 9–14, 9.

18. Elinoar Bareket, in *Encyclopedia of Jews in the Islamic World,* edited by Norman Stillman (Leiden and Boston: Brill, 2010), vol. 2, 126–132, 128. Further references to this work will be included in the text as (Bareket).

19. "La modernité n'a pas inventé les mélanges; elle a accéléré leur temps," in Tobie Nathan, *Ethno-roman* (Paris: Grasset, 2012), 379. Further references to this work will be included in the text as (Ethno-roman).

20. Will Hanley, *Identifying with Nationality: Europeans, Ottomans, and Egyptians in Alexandria* (New York: Columbia University Press, 2017), 7. Further references to this work will be included in the text as (Hanley).

21. Nefissa Naguib, "The Fragile Tale of Egyptian Jewish Cuisine: Food Memoirs of Claudia Roden and Colette Rossant," in *Food and Foodways* 14, no. 1 (2006): 35–53, 50. Further references to this work will be included in the text as (Naguib).

22. David Maslowski, "Les Modèles culturels des juifs d'Egypte de la fin de la domination ottomane (1882) jusquà la révolution des officiers libres (1952)" M.A. Thesis, Université de Paris 1 (Panthéon-Sorbonne), 2012–2013. See Maslowski's fascinating analysis of the Egyptian film industry; he uses the example of the film industry to frame the dynamic interplay, the vicissitudes and trials, between the Jewish community as a whole and Egyptian society. Further references to this work will be included in the text as (Maslowski).

23. In his *Working out Egypt: Effendi Masculinity and Subject Formation in Colonial Modernity, 1870–1940* (Durham, N.C.: Duke University Press, 2011), Wilson Chacko Jacob maintains that the *effendiyya* is a performative category, a "new structure of feeling," and a self-fashioning. It constructs its identity from cultural values derived from both East and West.

24. See Dario Miccoli, "Moses and Faruq: The Jews and the Study of History in Interwar Egypt 1920s–1940s," *Quest. Issues in Contemporary Jewish History* 4 (November 2012), http://www.quest-cdecjournal.it/focus.php?id=319.

25. The view that the dissemination of liberalism reached the popular classes in the 1920s is reflected in Ziad Fahmy's *Ordinary Egyptians: Creating the Modern Nation through Popular Culture* (Stanford, Calif.: Stanford University Press, 2011). Further references to this work will be included in the text as (Fahmy). Fahmy challenges the idea that the 1919 revolution was undertaken by the elite political and intellectual classes. He examines the early years of the discourse on territorial Egyptian national identity through popular culture; what he says on the subject applies equally to the decade following the revolution. On this subject, also see David Maslowski, who writes that "In the years between 1920 and the beginning of the 1930s . . . a cosmopolitanism coming from a foreign milieu and from the local elites, spreads to the more popular classes of Egyptians and also extends to middle class foreign subjects, particularly Greek and Italian" ("Durant les années 1920 et le début des années 1930 . . . la culture cosmopolite qui émane des milieux étrangers et des élites locales gagne des couches plus populaires que ce soit chez les égyptiens, ou chez les étrangers issus des classes moyennes, surtout grecques et italiennes."; my translation; Maslowski, 135).

26. Israel Gershoni and Jason P. Jankowski, *Egypt, Islam, and the Arabs: The Search for Egyptian Nationhood, 1900–1930* (Oxford: Oxford University Press, 1987), 80. Further references to this work will be included in the text as (EIA).

27. Norman Stillman, *Jews of Arab Lands in Modern Times* (Philadelphia: Jewish Publication Society, 1991), 53. Further references to this work will be included in the text as (Stillman).

28. Israel Gershoni and Jason P. Jankowski, *Confronting Fascism in Egypt: Dictatorship versus Democracy in the 1930s* (Stanford, Calif.: Stanford University Press, 2010), 4. Further references to this work will be included in the text as (Fascism).

29. Jessica M. Marglin, "Mediterranean Modernity through Jewish Eyes: The Transimperial Life of Abraham Ankawa," *Jewish Social Studies* 20, no. 2 (2014): 34–68, 37.

30. Gudrun Krämer, "'Radical' Nationalists, Fundamentalists, and the Jews in Egypt or, Who Is a Real Egyptian?" in *Islam, Nationalism, and Radicalism in Egypt and the Sudan*, edited by Gabriel R. Warburg and Uri M. Kupferschmidt, 354–371, 354 (New York: Praeger

Special Studies, Praeger Scientific, 1983). Further references to this work will be included in the text as (Radical).

31. David Biale, *Cultures of the Jews: Volume I. Mediterranean Origins* (New York: Schocken, 2002), xvii.

32. As Gershoni and Jankowski write: "In sum, the British often influenced and sometimes even controlled the specifics of Egyptian policy making in the period of the parliamentary monarchy, but they did not do so consistently, and frequently the degree of their control over the Egyptian state was less complete than has generally been assumed" (EIA, 237).

33. Ada Aharoni, "The Image of Jewish Life in Egypt in the Writings of Egyptian Jewish Authors in Israel and Abroad," in Shamir, *The Jews of Egypt*, 192–198, 196.

34. Most sources agree on these figures given by Michael Laskier: between November 1956, the beginning of the systematic expulsion, to the end of 1957, between 23,000 and 25,000 Jews left Egypt. Out of a population estimated at 80,000 in 1948, there were between 8,000 and 10,000 Jews remaining in 1960. By the end of that year, at the beginning of 1961 about 7,000 Jews remained; among them 2,000 to 3,000 were in Alexandria and about 3,000 to 4,000 were in Cairo. By the end of 1968, 1,000 Jews remained. In September 1970 there were no more than 300 Jewish persons. See Alisa Douer, *Egypt. The Lost Homeland: Exodus from Egypt, 1947–1967. The History of the Jews in Egypt, 1540 BCE to 1967* (Berlin: Logos Verlag, 2015), 263. After 1970, it is not clear how the number of Jews living permanently in Egypt is derived. It varies wildly between 8 persons and 150. See note 37 below.

35. Hassoun's text: "Ce qui me semble passionnant dans cette aventure que suppose la transmission, c'est justement que nous sommes différents de ceux qui nous ont précédés, et que nos descendants suivront le plus vraisemblablement un chemin sensiblement différent du nôtre . . . Et pourtant . . . c'est bien dans cette série de différences que nous inscrivons ce que nous avons à transmettre." Jacques Hassoun, *Les contrebandiers de la mémoire* (Paris: Syros, 1994), 14; my translation.

36. Yosef Hayim Yerushalmi, *Zakhor: Jewish History and Jewish Memory* (Seattle: University of Washington Press, 1989), 109.

37. The president of the Jewish community of Egypt, Magda Haroun, reported thirteen members to *Time Magazine* on September 21, 2015. The interview took place during Rosh Hashana celebrations at Cairo at Shaar Hashamayim Synagogue. Haroun explains that she is the youngest member of the community, at age sixty-three. Of the thirteen members, none are men, and three are in Alexandria. See *Time Magazine* online: http://time.com/4041832/cairo-jews-population-egypt; the interview was conducted by Jared Maslin. Further references to this article will be included in the text as (Haroun).

38. Interview with Patrick Cohen on *France-Inter*, September 11, 2015; https://www.franceinter.fr/emissions/le-7-9/le-7-9-11-septembre-2015.

CHAPTER ONE

Jacques Hassoun
Return to Egypt

> Remember the day when you came out of the land of Egypt
> all the days of your life.
>
> > Deuteronomy 16:33

> You leave Egypt. You leave the family. You can't go back.
> You have to move forward . . . You play the cards that are dealt you.[1]
>
> > Maurice de Picciotto

THE MOST ELOQUENT of Jacques Hassoun's works, *Smugglers of Memory* (*Les Contrebandiers de la mémoire*; 1994) argues that most of us feel the need to pass on our heritage to future generations. We are compelled to state *who* we are and *where* we come from, the moment we leave our place. Mostly, says Hassoun, it is not we who volunteer but others who want to know. He writes:

> In the Arab-Muslim world, we find ourselves daily facing the injunction to tell our story, give our genealogy, identify our clan. For example, when two people who do not know each other meet, and immediately after the customary salutations, the question that is always asked is: "What is your *asl?*," a word that means attachments (tribal and religious) and, at the same time, affiliations and membership in a specific ethnic class or mind-set.[2]

This injunction to state who we are and where we come from, explains Hassoun, is oftentimes the harbinger of a crisis. We give out this information to defend our heritage and to make sure our ancestors are not forgotten and that we and our children are counted. This impulse to pass on our history is what Hassoun calls *transmission*. Transmission is a desire. It is also a process. It represents the ontological drive to connect, communicate, and be counted. Already in Deuteronomy, Hassoun reminds us, we read: "Ask your father and he will tell you your story. Ask your ancestors and they will tell you your past." This commandment confirms for Hassoun that the imperative to transmit is written in history (CM, 10). Deuteronomy was composed after the Jewish people returned from the First Exile in Babylonia. This was a critical period. For Jewish leaders at that time, the imperative was to establish the premises upon which Jews were to continue as a people. They had to find ways to tighten the links that had loosened after the destruction of the kingdom of Judah (CM, 11). Several generations born in exile were returning to their ancestral home. The concern was that these Jews born in exile had grown up in an environment that was intellectually, economically, and socially superior to the place into which they were moving. There had to be good reasons for them to want to reclaim that heritage. A good story needed to be told, explains Hassoun: "The idea was to illuminate the present through the telling of a grand story, one that would take on mythical proportions so as to prepare a future for the planting of new roots" (CM, 12). The act of transmitting is an adventure that, when brought to term successfully, enhances our appreciation of the present and our sense of freedom. Passing heritage down from generation to generation, Hassoun argues, involves creatively weaving the past with the present in every new generation. The success of transmission depends in interesting ways upon "sneaking" information through from one generation to another. He writes:

> It is precisely because we are different from those who preceded us and different as well from our descendants who will most likely follow a road clearly different from ours, that I find fascinating the adventure that constitutes transmission . . And yet . . . it is also precisely in this series of differences that we inscribe what we have to transmit. (CM, 14)[3]

For Hassoun, heritage does not refer to a specific body of experience but to the way this experience is shaped at the moment it is recalled when we think about it, speak about it, and transmit it to others. Transmission is an aesthetic remodeling of the heritage it works to preserve (CM, 17). "The story of us" that heals Rachel Gaon in Jacqueline Kahanoff's novel, *Jacob's Ladder*, and Elliot Malki's film *Starting Over Again*, is the story we all owe our descendants.[4] Hassoun explains:

> When all is said and done, *transmission* is a treasure that each one of us constructs from elements supplied by parents and the environment. Reconfigured by chance encounters and by events we have overlooked, these elements become, over the years and in contact with day-to-day life, fundamental components both of the subject and for the subject. (Italics in text; CM, 81)[5]

To this dialectic between ourselves, our heritage, and contemporary society that constitutes transmission, Hassoun introduces the compelling notion that without transmission the individual will not be able to integrate in society. Transmission is essential to the well-being of individuals and groups. It defends individuals against a society that sees them—that will always see them—as outsiders and excludes them from the dominant scene. Hassoun was a militant psychoanalyst whose practice focused on immigrant children and children who were born in France to immigrant parents. His observations led him to an understanding that the most vulnerable children were those who did not know their family history. In *Smugglers of Memory*, he presents case studies focusing on a Polish child of immigrants, a child from Egypt, displaced children from rural parts of France, victims of the Algerian war of independence, and others to argue that each of these cases demonstrates that it is impossible for children to feel they are an integral part of society unless they can articulate what they know or think they know about their past. This framing of one's heritage may not always be carried out in discursive language, says Hassoun. But it must somehow or other represent a breaking of the silence. The immigrant or outsider must conceive a language to envisage and reconstruct his or her family history. He writes:

> We see all the time in clinical practice that such silences are responsible for much of the suffering and disorders experienced by the children of deported Jews, the children or grandchildren of survivors of the Armenian Genocide, the descendants of torture during various wars of independence, in short, all those who experienced History in its extreme ferocity. . . . Orphans of language, they suffer from the impossibility of mourning conclusively and of constructing a family narrative that helps to launch them into the future. (CM, 24–25)[6]

Without successful transmission and without exposing children to the history of their people, particularly when they are a minority, children will not be able to integrate their past with the present. They will likely experience a sense of alienation. Hassoun embodies the Jewish and Marxist imperative: know your history. Even the most pluralistic of societies, Hassoun believes, will at some point resort to divisiveness and exclusionary practices. This is not because integration was built on faulty lines, he argues, but because ideologies of exclusion are ever present in all social and political bodies. They are ineradicable. Minority populations suffer when they ignore their history and seek comfort in the delusions of not-knowing. All is deemed perfect until a crisis in the social body occurs: "In times of wretched divisions—think of the Dreyfus affair or the rise of Nazism and Fascism in Central Europe—what seemed until then incontrovertible and what seemed to have offered the subject a sense of inviolable wholeness reveals itself to be a monstrous lie" (CM, 33).[7]

For this reason, if for nothing else, children of immigrants and immigrant parents themselves must know their history. Failing to communicate one's history to the next generation puts at risk the well-being of subsequent generations. Hassoun writes that even several generations later, we find individuals who are still unreconciled, still apt to consider themselves born in exile (CM, 37). He adds, to be clear, that these people are not suffering exile from some mythical long lost "promised land"; rather, they believe exile occurred to them personally before they were born (CM, 37-38). How can the perpetuation of exilic melancholy be mitigated? This is the question Hassoun addresses directly in *Smugglers of Memory*. He identifies the immigrant problem as a problem of adaptation, which is to say it is a problem of reconciling one's past attachments with a new set of cultural directives. To adapt and be able to integrate means that equilibrium has been attained. It does not mean that an individual has left the past behind and has accepted a new state. As for assimilation, always a hot topic when Jewish identity is discussed, Hassoun is adamant that it does not work. Assimilation cannot work, he argues, because people are predisposed to exclude others at the slightest sign of a crisis.

In *Smugglers of Memory*, Hassoun does more than advocate transmission as a critical practice for successful adaptation. He demonstrates how this can be achieved. He observes that the person who succeeds in adapting in exile has found a device, a ruse. That person has fashioned an identity in the present by reframing the past, by interpreting their heritage in such a way as to have made both the present *and* the past intelligible and, ultimately, acceptable personally. That device or ruse is constituted uniquely in the form of a language. We are not always conscious of passing on something in our history. These unconscious languages (both verbal and nonverbal) are reservoirs of affect and information about us and our ancestors. When we speak, move, gesture, or write, we signal our belongingness. These figures of belongingness are passed down from generation to generation. Hassoun writes: "Is it not difficult, even impossible, to find the appropriate words to evoke the homeland of one's parents or grandparents, to transmit the essence of their past?" He continues: "The difficulty we face is understandable: the past—like a sudden gust of wind—stuns us while *beckoning that we make out what it is*. But how can we know what it is when the forms of that past inherently resist transmission?" (italics in text, CM, 54).[8] The device or ruse that allows immigrants and other outsiders to transmit their past and the rich affects that accompany remembrances are what Hassoun calls the languages of contraband, smuggled languages. These languages are embedded in our words, gestures, in the tone of our voice, and even in our silences. They are identifying traits that we smuggle in with us when we cross borders. These may be cherished traits or simply traits that are part of our identity. No matter how special or ordinary, we do not want to lose them or have them taken away from us. These languages are what we sometimes call *style*. The trick is to pass something we are attached to *as* something else. In the process of moving across borders, something is likely to be lost or altered. As Hassoun explains in the discussion on transmission, the past does not repeat itself but confronts the present and is changed by it. He argues that the metaphor of the smuggler and smuggled makes clear the *modus operandi* of immigrants and minorities. They use languages in which are embedded what they desire, what they once desired, and what they have appropriated (stolen) from different sources. For Hassoun, smuggling is a vital concept and practice. It is not just an idea; it is a call to action:

> Furthermore, I *owe it to the truth* to state the following: let us not be afraid to be smugglers because this is the way we will be able to relay our history. Let us face the fact. The idea of a transparent and fixed language is a delusion. We are all Exiles, transmigrants who have burned their ships behind them. Our past will never again be recovered intact. . . . We are from this place and from another, from the present and from the past. Unfailingly. (Italics in text; CM, 42–43)[9]

Reclaiming Egypt

Jacques Hassoun spearheaded the movement in France that gave the Jewish diaspora from Egypt a sense of itself as a people with a distinct history. His efforts spurred collective self-reflection, which in turn gave this community of Egyptian Jews an understanding of the social and historical factors that had changed the course of their lives. Twenty or so years after their exile some began to pose the question: Were we strangers in Egypt or did we have ancestral attachments to this land and culture? This is the perennial question Jews in biblical times and modern Egyptian Jews endeavor to answer. Hassoun organized the narrative of that people's presence in Egypt and gave it shape by making explicit the relation between Egyptian Jews and Egyptian-Arab culture more broadly. He argued that Egyptian Jews, regardless of their political status when they lived in their native country, were Egyptians. Throughout his work, he reminds his interlocutors that even Jews who were not born in Egypt are Egyptians. As he explains during an interview, he is Jewish because he is Egyptian and Egyptian because he is Jewish.[10] The rootedness of Jews in Egypt is asserted in the works of many Jewish Egyptian writers. In her poignant and sublime book *Egypt, Return* (*Egypte, Retour: Récit*, 2007), the photographer and writer Carole Naggar traces evocatively her protagonist's connectedness to Egypt, where for millennia "the water of the Nile and the blood" of her ancestors ran together and "their skin took on the color of the sand." For two thousand five hundred years, her ancestors were tied to Egypt "by all the fibers of their being."[11] Naggar's protagonist returns to Cairo to visit the graves of her "grand-parents, her great grand-parents, her great-great grand-parents, and their parents" (Naggar, 21). She "invents ruses" and "rituals" that are meant to refresh with her own presence the history of her people. The attachment to Egypt comes at the cost of heartbreak and doubt. Does the protagonist leave all this history behind her and turn away? "Enough already," she says, "enough scratching these roots inflamed by memory" ("Assez! Suffit de gratter ces racines de mémoire"; Naggar, 30). Before leaving, will she replace the plaque on her grandfather Elie's gravestone, ensuring that his name remains visible "or leave Elie's grave without a name?" (Naggar, 33). Has Egypt preserved something of the "fragrance" of its Jews from "before the breakup?" or have "the sands covered them in forgetfulness, the deserts closed in and erased their trace, and the Nile like a mirror serene and impassive will not be bothered to remember" ("Ou bien le sable de l'oublie a tout recouvert. Ou bien le désert s'est refermé sur nos pas, a recouvert nos traces, et l'eau du Nil, a peine troublée, recoule comme un miroir qui ne se souvient pas"; Naggar, 126). This is the bind served to the children of Egyptian exiles by a long, complex, and monumental history.

The dedication in Naggar's book is made in Hassoun's memory. She writes: "This voyage was taken without him. Without him it would not have been taken." Hassoun's contribution to the return to Egypt cannot be overestimated. True, the project to reconnect the Jews of Egypt with their past there was a collaborative endeavor. But Hassoun's efforts gave the project direction, depth, and intellectual coherence. As a protagonist in the May 1968 upheavals in France, Hassoun had experience as a leader. He was learned, professionally accomplished, and gregarious. And he was by all accounts charismatic. He was therefore in an excellent position to lead the Jews of Egypt to reconnect with their past and their culture. When relations between Israel and Egypt improved in the late 1970s, it became possible for Jews to visit Egypt more easily. Hassoun personally led many of them quite literally to the site of memory. Assisted by friends, he organized trips with groups of his compatriots. Some were returning for the first time since they had left; others were the children of exiles, often in their thirties and forties, who could not remember Egypt.

The motivation behind the effort to connect with a complicated Jewish past came from Hassoun's personal circumstances and worldview. It also came from his experiences as a trained psychoanalyst. As I indicated, Hassoun worked with immigrants. In postwar France, many communities experienced dislocation. There were immigrants from other former colonies as well as from Egypt; immigrants from Western and Eastern European countries; displaced individuals and families migrating from French villages and farms to urban centers. Both his theoretical and clinical works focused on the trauma of immigration, particularly as it affected children. Hassoun was drawn to their issues. He believed that psychoanalysis was particularly suited to articulating how individuals coped with new conditions, related to new groups, and navigated through an environment that tended to be unsympathetic to them. Tobie Nathan, a contemporary fellow Egyptian Jew and psychoanalyst himself, explains in his memoir—an intellectual biography he describes as an "ethno-novel"—that in the 1960s many Jews outside the mainstream of French intellectual life took up psychoanalysis as a way to understand themselves and establish themselves in French society.[12]

Similarly, Adam Phillips suggests that psychoanalysis is a language that makes it possible to talk about loss, about dislocation, about the cost of losing everything in order to survive. He writes:

> Psychoanalysis is first and foremost a psychology of, and for, immigrants (people who can never quite settle); not a Jewish science as Freud feared, but an immigrant science for a world in which, for political and economic reasons, there were to be more and more immigrants. The human subject that Freud will describe in psychoanalysis will be a person with little autonomy, subjected to forces he can for the most part neither control nor understand.[13]

Psychoanalysis was, at least originally, a science for outsiders, remarks Phillips (Phillips, 159). In France in the 1960s and certainly during the 1968 uprisings, psychoanalysis was undergoing a radical reconsideration of its function as a practice of healing. It took a skeptical view of its increasingly institutional framework. Hassoun was active in shaping this discourse and changing psychoanalytic practice at the ground level. Jacques Lacan, Félix Guattari, and André Green are perhaps the best known to American intellectuals, but there were others, too, who were redefining the practice of psychoanalysis. Nathan writes:

> I still wonder about the passion that took hold of young children of immigrants born abroad, who like their parents were compelled to adapt as quickly as possible to an unfamiliar world. Basically, psychoanalysis was to us, a small group of young immigrants, what boxing was to Italians thirty years ago; or what rap and slam are today to the children of the suburbs: a short-cut toward gaining a foothold in the active life of society. Psychoanalysis had barely begun in France. . . . Everything was yet to be. For us immigrants, to become expert in a new discipline in its early stages was to be thrown right into the game, to become part of the action. It helped us catch up on many years of backwardness. (Nathan, 23–24)[14]

Jacques Hassoun was born October 20, 1936 at number 1, Place Albert in Alexandria and died on April 24, 1999 at the age of sixty-three. He was born to an observant Jewish family. They spoke Arabic at home, although his mother also spoke French. When he arrived in France in December 1954, at the age of eighteen, he spoke French fluently as well as Arabic and Hebrew. He wrote in French. Like many aspiring men and women living in large cities in Egypt, Jews and non-Jews alike, the choice to speak a particular language was a decision made along cultural lines. Speaking French signaled that one belonged to the milieu of the cultural elite comprising educated Egyptians aspiring to live a modern lifestyle. In pre-Nasser Egypt, to be without French or another European language such as Italian or English, for example, risked compromising one's professional and social advancement. But one also understood and spoke Arabic simply because it was all around—it was the language of day-to-day life.[15] To *not* speak Arabic would have to be the result of deliberate avoidance, either a self-imposed avoidance or one imposed by parents on their children. Jacques Hassoun was educated in a French school, the Lycée de l'Union Juive pour l'Enseignement, founded in 1925 by notables of the Jewish community of Alexandria to provide Jewish children with a rigorous and progressive education. The school closed its doors in 1957 after the Suez War. It was known for having particularly talented teachers who left their mark on students like Hassoun. Education at the Lycée was both secular and Jewish: students were taught Hebrew as well as Jewish history. The take on Jewish history was not biblical but historical and intellectual. The school had an active intramural newspaper. There were after-school clubs where politics and other heady subjects were discussed. Politics, political theory, feminism, psychoanalysis, and relevant topics of the day were debated and positions adopted. It was common, even expected, that students would join a political movement.[16] Hassoun prized the Lycée and credited it with forming his intellectual character. His education mirrored that of children in the French Republic. But Hassoun also read Jean-Paul Sartre, Simone de Beauvoir, and Marxist thinkers. These writers were not part of the traditional French curriculum but were discussed in the clubs that met every Friday at the Lycée. Hassoun attributes to Beauvoir's *The Second Sex* his awareness in his early teens of the abject condition of women. He points out that Beauvoir's work was important in yet another way; it was instrumental to his understanding that a critique of the Other is part of a larger strategy to undercut the hegemonic discourse of Western culture. This discourse, Hassoun recognized early on, promoted sameness with determination and resourcefulness. This hegemonic impulse at the heart of Western culture is something that Hassoun critiques in regard to social organizations. The rejection of comprehensive ideologies finds parallels in Kahanoff's notion of Levantinism and Nathan's ethnopsychological approach. It was also due to Beauvoir that Hassoun came to theorize on the "distracted mother," a subject that has distinguished him in Lacanian psychoanalysis. In Egypt, to sum up, French education marked Hassoun's learning and his intellectual development. This was the case for many Jews and non-Jews aspiring to be successful and modern.

In the 1930s and 1940s, many young Egyptian intellectuals were attracted to communism. Jews were not an exception.[17] It was the order of the day to defend Egypt against the British occupation and to do so from within the communist movement. As André Cohen and Raymond Stambouli explain, the political position of young intellectuals was part of the fight against the British. Stambouli points out in a documentary film: "We were all, more or less, communists and nationalists. Jacques was steeped in this atmosphere."[18] From the 1930s to the 1950s, many saw in communism and, especially in Marxism, the path to overturning imperialism and emancipating the poor. It was in the name of a free and egalitarian Egypt that these activists risked prison. We see this activism dramatized in several of Paula Jacques's novels.[19] These activists considered themselves Egyptians fighting for the cause of their country. Tobie Nathan observes that many young people joined the Communist Party, hoping to get closer to "the people." However, they did not find "the people" in the Communist Party—they found them in mosques dominated by the Muslim Brotherhood. Egyptian Jews who were attached to Egypt (and many were, says Nathan) did one of two things: they could leave Egypt or convert to Islam. Not surprisingly, among those who stayed, many converted.[20] Nathan offers a powerful example of this radicalization in the character of Nino Cohen in his novel *This Country That Is Like You* (*Ce pays qui te ressemble*; 2015). A Jewish intellectual, brilliant and sensitive, Nino turns savagely against his family and his religion in the name of Egypt and the Egyptian people.[21] For some, like Nino, communism combined seamlessly with radical nationalist ideology. Zionism was often thought of as a form of betrayal to Egypt.

Hassoun himself was associated briefly with the Dror movement, a Marxist-Zionist youth organization. In March 1953, Dror was dissolved and its members joined HADETO, the largest communist faction in Egypt and a clandestine association. HADETO is an acronym for al-Haraka al Dimuqratiya li al-Taharrur, known in English as the DMNL or Democratic Movement for National Liberation. Hassoun joined the organization along with eight other Jews from Alexandria. The group's goal was to liberate Egypt from British domination.[22] He was arrested in November 1953 at the age of seventeen, legally a minor, and was brought to trial in early 1954 (Pérez). André Cohen, who was arrested along with Hassoun and six others, describes him in the film as very young looking, a kid really, with a lot of nervous energy. They were detained for twenty-four hours and then transferred to the military prison in Cairo, where they were placed in solitary confinement for a month. André Cohen describes the windowless cells, lit by electric lights that were never turned off. The prisoners did not see or meet each other during this time. Cohen also reports that one day, without explanation, they were transported in chains to a military prison in Alexandria, where their treatment was less rigid than it had been in Cairo. The Egyptian court sentenced them to a year in prison and incarcerated them in the prison for foreigners. The lawyer for the group was the well-known Félix Benzakein. They were released after six months.

Hassoun was expelled from Egypt without his family in December 1954. He was barely eighteen years old. His case was not unique—many young Jewish men and women, many as young as age sixteen, were imprisoned and later expelled without their parents. Often their parents were not even alerted. Hassoun relates the story of his expulsion as an example of a perverted, twisted, covenant between himself and the Egyptian officer who released him from prison. In the exchange, the officer informed Hassoun that the only way he could stay in Egypt, the only way he could be "reinstated" as a resident, was for him to agree to first being expelled. Only after that could he be "reinstated."[23] Hassoun took the bait and did what he was advised. As Hassoun tells the story in Paula Jacques's *Magnetic Nights* (*Nuits Magnétiques*), "I said if that's the case, expel me!" Only later did he realize that he had been duped. Thus he had become, in his own words, responsible for willingly arranging his own expulsion, an act he had wished to avoid in the first place. Upon leaving Egypt by ship, Hassoun remembers standing on the deck, looking down below at his parents and his sisters Rachel and Claudette, who were in tears. He adds: "I always knew I would come back."[24] And he believed it to be true until the 1956 Suez War broke out and he and other Egyptian Jews realized there would be no return. Of course, some eventually did return as visitors after the Camp David Accords of September 1978 between Egypt's President Anwar Sadat and Israel's Prime Minister Menachem Begin.

The Immigrant and Progressive Politics

Upon settling in France in 1954, Hassoun began his medical studies in Montpellier and soon after joined the Communist Party (PC). He also joined the Rome group, the émigrés movement for Egyptian Jews led by Henri Curiel. He remained active with the group until 1968. He also joined several other political groups on the Left, including Voies Nouvelles, Débat-Unir, and Voies Communistes. Later, he would join a number of others. Hassoun held that participation in political circles was strategically and existentially important for him and for similar immigrants. He argues that the best way to establish new roots is for a young immigrant to join a political party and particularly a Leftist party; he felt that progressive groups connected him to what he, and others in the 1960s and 1970s, referred to as international collaboration. Political participation is what *makes* a French citizen. In this way, groups on the Left provide access to citizenship. Engaging in civic association and in Leftist politics also allows young immigrants to contextualize their family's history and to see this history as part of the larger struggle. Hassoun argues:

> This is to say, that all these organizations, all these meetings gave immigrants an opportunity to place their mark on the unfolding history of France. Political engagement allowed them to be part of France's history without the fear of betraying their own history to the extent that Left leaning organizations promoted internationalism as the ultimate goal and guarantee.[25]

Hassoun makes an important point here in asserting that immigrants who engage in the politics of the Left will discover that they do not need to reject their own past and heritage in order to forge a new life. Involvement in the political process provides an education, a way of thinking about the world. What is true of France, for example, is true more generally. He writes: "It is all about bringing these pages from history into the present, updating them by highlighting their international ramifications rather than their limited French context" (Vive, 132–133).

Hassoun stresses that political discourse is advantageous in yet another way. It prevents the immigrant from responding emotionally to conflicts and mitigates internal conflicts and external frictions. Political discourse can be counted on to provide reasoned arguments and a framework within which one might process experiences. As such, political engagement rescues young immigrants transplanted in a new environment from responding provocatively to both their heritage (family and ethnic culture) and their minority status. If immigrants cannot find a way to engage ideologically and work productively on the inevitable difficulties inherent in their status as an outsider, they will surely react in more extreme and violent ways. To respond emotionally is to risk turning the *crossing* from one culture to another into a violent clash of cultures. Emotionally, the immigrant is naturally given to pit tradition (the old country and its culture) against the new country and the present. When children are involved, they run the risk of being pitted against their parents. If the child's response to the conflict drives him or her to introversion, the psychic damage can foster perpetual melancholy. Responding affectively is risky and dangerous.

Militancy inspired by Leftist ideology offered Hassoun the opportunity to join others in a common defining struggle, the struggle to align French institutional practices with the values of modern life founded on the principles of open access, transparency, and the leveling of distinctions—the heritage of 1968. Marxism allowed Hassoun in the early years to come to terms with Judaism and Egyptian culture. It provided him with a system and an ideology that enabled him to understand his father and to cope with his heritage. As a psychoanalyst, Hassoun took as a fundamental principle that the father, both the actual person and the imaginative and mythic construct, determined the success or failure of the child's entry into the world. He writes:

> I come from an Arabic-speaking milieu, which in Egypt meant an environment that was religious and very modest. Incidentally . . . the language one spoke mostly determined one's position in society. . . . However, through a series of coincidences, starting with my participation in a Zionist left (Dror) movement, one of whose branches joined the Israeli Communist Party, I had the opportunity, very young, to be introduced to Marxism. (Vive, 128)[26]

Political activity acts as a mediation. It repositions the father.[27] For Hassoun, the actual father in society is considered a relic and an embarrassment: "He is seen by everyone in the society as barbaric, ridiculous, a failure" (Vive, 132). It is important, therefore, that the father's place be mediated and that he be saved from himself, that he be made safe for his offspring in order to allow them to thrive in the new country. If the immigrant boy/girl cannot identify with the father and his past, they will be "adrift" ("en état de dérive"). For Hassoun, Marxism was the way out. It was instrumental in saving him and his/the father.

Hassoun explains that in Egypt this Marxist journey was shared by other ethnic groups such as Muslims, Greeks, Armenians, and Copts. It was through Marxism that they were able to enter the modern world (Vive, 129). And later, Marxism allowed them all, he writes, "to cross over from our native countries to the countries that welcomed us" (Vive, 129). In May 1968, Hassoun broke with the Communist Party but continued to participate in Marxist causes, notably the Bastille group that secured psychiatric help for people of modest means. Hassoun was also among the first to send teams of psychiatrists into nursery schools. In the years following decolonization culminating in the May 1968 rebellion, psychoanalysis and Marxism worked hand-in-hand. Hassoun writes: "From that time forward, the psychiatrist, without losing sight of his traditional role, had to join the revolution (this was the thing to do)."[28]

In 1979, Hassoun, André Cohen, Ibram Gabbai, Emile Gabbay, Raymond Stambouli, and other Jews from Egypt who had been active in the French branch of HADETO founded the Association to Safeguard the Cultural Patrimony of the Jews of Egypt or ASPCJE (Association pour la Sauvegarde du Patrimoine Culturel des Juifs d'Egypte). When Henri Curiel was assassinated in 1978, this group of friends, who had been gathering unofficially, decided that it was important to reference Curiel's origins. On his tomb, they placed a wreath that read "Des amis juifs d'Egypte" (Jewish friends from Egypt).[29] In December 1978, they organized a conference at the Rachi Center in Paris. Hassoun recalls that in the 1970s, it was fashionable to reconnect with one's roots. The first gathering was attended by nearly four hundred people, mostly Jews from Egypt living in France. The proceedings were published in a book entitled *Getting to Know the Jews of Egypt* (À la rencontre des Juifs d'Egypte, 1984). A year later, in December 1979, the organization was founded. Its stated goal was to "reclaim its history"; to connect with Jews from Egypt throughout France and across the world; to pass on their rich heritage to future generations; and to reflect on the role they played in Egypt in many domains: finance, industry, business, journalism, literature, music, and film. The idea behind ASPCJE was to record this history. But the idea was also to register the attitude and worldview, the *zeitgeist*, that distinguished the Jews of Egypt in the minds of the founding members. The charter emphasizes that the organization "remains committed to the values they held when in Egypt, the values of universality, cosmopolitanism, and cordial entente with all religious communities." These principles describe the political and philosophical positions that Hassoun held to the end of his life.[30]

Return to Egypt: "I always knew I would come back"

Hassoun returned to Egypt on several occasions, beginning in 1977. He made three trips between 1977 and 1978 and visited again in 1983 and 1993. His last visit was in 1997. On most of these trips, he was in the company of a group of Egyptian Jews and the children of Egyptian Jews many of whom had never been to Egypt. His visit on February 17, 1993 was recorded and broadcast in Paula Jacques's *Nuits Magnétiques* in June, 1993 and rebroadcast in 1999 to commemorate Hassoun's death. The broadcast was the brainchild of Jacques, who describes it as "Seven Days and Six Nights or the Time of a Return to the Homeland." Jacques likened Hassoun to "Moses leading his people home" (Nuits).

On this trip, Hassoun explains why it took so long for many Jews to return to Egypt even after they could visit. Twenty or thirty years after their expulsion, Hassoun explains, most Egyptian Jews were still too disturbed from that shock to think of returning. Edmond Jabès and Tobie Nathan are only two examples among many others who could not imagine going back. The psychology of rejection is intricate and singular. Some returned. Others could not bring themselves to do so. When asked in 2015 why after writing extensively on Egypt Nathan has not returned, his answer is simple and cutting: "I will go when I am invited back."[31] One hears on the tapes of *Nuits Magnétiques* Hassoun's reactions to once again seeing places and things he had left long ago. He is particularly upset that the Jewish names on buildings, street signs, and gravestones have been expunged. Erasure of names and of the Jewish presence in Egypt is a recurrent theme in the works I examine in this book. How does it feel to have one's heritage irremediably expunged from the history of one's native land? The writer and performer Rachel Cohen who was traveling with Hassoun and the group from *Nuits Magnétiques* has written eloquently of Hassoun's impressions during this visit. She recalls his distress at seeing the erasure of names in the Bassatine cemetery, Bassatine is the Jewish cemetery in Cairo dating back to the ninth century. Cohen writes: "Jacques, the name, names have disappeared. You can't stand it. Headstones are missing. If there is no name, we are done for."[32] Hassoun's grandfather was buried in Alexandria, at Chatby Cemetery. Hassoun's desolation at Bassatine is not only in regard to his immediate and personal family; it extends to the entire Jewish community. When Hassoun made the despairing comment to which Cohen alludes, he was reacting, much as Carole Naggar and Paula Jacques do in their work, to what he saw as the attempt to erase the traces of the Jews of Egypt on Egyptian soil.

Le Passage des étrangers (*The Strangers' Crossing*) and the "Reign of Clones"

Through history, and particularly during the wave of nationalistic politics in Egypt, from the late nineteenth to the mid-twentieth century, the Jews of Egypt had a difficult time asserting their status as Egyptian nationals. As I explained in the introductory chapter, the phenomenon of nationality was new at the turn of the twentieth century. No laws defined who was legally an Egyptian until after the dissolution of the Ottoman Empire. In the 1920s, mostly Muslims were considered Egyptian nationals. A small number of Egyptian Jews were able to obtain Egyptian nationality. Most of them remained stateless (*apatrides*), a dreaded status for it offered no legal protection. In the late nineteenth century and into the 1930s, some sought and were granted citizenship from European countries willing to count a few stateless Jews among their subjects. These countries expected their "adopted" Jews to defend European interests in Egypt.[33] Still, for a Jew living in Egypt at that time, it was by no means clear whether it was better to claim citizenship of a foreign power or to remain stateless and therefore unprotected. You were damned by Egypt either way. From the 1930s onward, Egyptian Jews were subjected to a concerted political and religious effort on the part of the Muslim majority to exclude them from civic, political, and economic life. Statelessness, discriminatory policies, and the imminent threat of dispossession and displacement created a state of perpetual anxiety, a heightened sense of insecurity that is reflected in the works of the writers in this book. For clinicians like Hassoun and Nathan, such anxieties sharpened their understanding of the suffering of the immigrants they treated in their practices. In his writing, Hassoun returns again and again to the compulsion to exclude, which he considers to be a universal human trait. He develops the subject of exclusion both analytically and anecdotally. It is particularly in *The Strangers' Crossing* (*Le Passage des étrangers*; 1995) that he explores the syndrome in depth.[34] The work is a bold examination of the psychological, social, and political motives that underlie the impulse to single out a stranger. Hassoun examines this compulsion in terms of psychological suffering and physical violence. *The Strangers' Crossing* offers a model for individuals, communities, and governments to follow in order to restrain what he calls this most "savage" impulse, namely, the compulsion to exclude. In many respects, Hassoun's book draws our attention to the condition of minorities in many societies, Jewish and non-Jewish alike. Yet the work is a manifestation of Hassoun's single-minded concern to defend Jewish Egyptians' claims to their Egyptian heritage, to assert the legitimate place of Egyptian Jewry in the history of Egypt.

In *The Strangers' Crossing*, Hassoun argues that the stranger is a construct. It emerges in the imaginary of individuals and societies when they perceive a threat, and it functions as a device to help strengthen solidarity among members and preserve the group from whatever it perceives as endangering them. In short, the stranger is seen as necessary for the group's survival (PE, 13). Hassoun argues that the stranger is often indistinguishable, "almost-same" (*presque-même*) from the "excluder": "anxiety is not caused by what is perceived as foreign and heterogeneous, but by what seems too-familiar, as in the nightmares of our childhood. The almost-familiar is disturbing precisely because it is not exactly the same, is almost different, is almost the same" (CM, 50).[35] The more the stranger and the excluder resemble each other, the more anxious individuals become and the more violent their reactions. Hassoun offers as an example the Spanish persecution of the *conversos* who were pursued precisely because they were not easily distinguishable from the Spanish ruling class. He also offers the example of Jews in Nazi Germany who were "nearly invisible" in German society. The same, he adds, can be said of violence against Protestants in France and England. It is often the most indigenous who, in times of crisis, have been labeled strangers (PE, 15).

For Hassoun, the stranger is a concept before it is attached to an individual. As a concept, the stranger catalyzes the return to the *One* (le *Un*), to the presymbolic order. The emergence of the stranger in a society, he observes, is a manifestation of the desire to be one-and-the-same as the Origin. The stranger is the alibi for a regression to the most primitive, most basic existence. In this presymbolic state, the subject basks in the pleasures of sameness. It is this sensation, fantasized or experienced and remembered, that the excluder aspires to return to when he singles out and tracks down the immigrant and the outsider. Hassoun argues that the world the excluder wants to recapture here is totalitarian. The excluder longs for the absolute he believes exists. Hassoun dubs that desire as a desire for the "reign of clones." This totalitarian impulse is so deeply ingrained in the psyche of individuals, and therefore so dangerous, that modern societies have had to institute civil rights laws to protect people against the hate crimes it fosters. These laws are essential and are constantly challenged because the desire for the *One* is so irrepressible. He writes:

> And nothing, I repeat, nothing from time immemorial seems to change this in the slightest. It is fully deployed in the imaginary order. So we can safely postulate that if history repeats itself, it does so because the compulsion to exclude, separate, and reject exists at the heart of the subject's desire. Exclusion is a remedy that societies in crisis rediscover periodically and that they apply thinking it will solve all their troubles. (PE, 20)[36]

The drive to separate, classify, and dissociate from the stranger, Hassoun suggests, is a burden on the excluders themselves, leading them to perpetual melancholy and, often, to violence. The drama of the excluders is that in their desire to return to the *One* they must give up a great deal. They are in a perpetual state of unease because they do not know what they have lost in pursuit of the *One*. Their inability to identify what they have lost results in melancholy. The melancholy subject, Hassoun explains, suspects that the *One* is *not* recoverable; that it is lost for good; and that, possibly, it never did exist. Unable to return to the *One*, the subject is haunted by that loss; melancholy inhabits its very being. Hassoun writes:

> The excluder is by definition a person whose existence is threatened. He is shocked that he even exists. Armed to the teeth with certainties, he is half crazed by melancholy as he strives doggedly to conjure up the ideal of homogeneity, to blind himself to its lack, to string together into the *One* a series of clones, a series threatened by that inevitable misfit which puts into question the *One*'s very existence. (PE, 42)[37]

Melancholy constantly reminds the subject of his tainted existence, his fundamental indignity.

Hassoun makes a compelling argument when he criticizes progressive societies who misguidedly and paradoxically promote separation and exclusion, believing they accord the Other due respect, understanding, and solidarity. Not all differences, he points out, are exclusionary; ideological and religious differences can be exclusionary but are not necessarily so. However, divisions based on ethnic and racial grounds *are* essentially and necessarily so. This is because ethnic and racial distinctions, he submits, rely on superficial signs of belonging (skin color, country of birth, cultural practices, and pronunciation), all of which are features that reduce identity to physical and cultural signs that some people naïvely believe to be significant (PE, 68–69). Emphasis on these types of differences, Hassoun argues, undermines the social contract. The narratives these groups invent to justify exclusionary practice may differ between people and groups but the root cause remains the same. The root cause is a desire to return to the *One*, the apolitical and illusory oneness of being. Racial and ethnic classifications exacerbate social tensions by policing a cover-up instead of addressing grievances directly. In addition, this triage fosters a risky fundamentalism built on chauvinism. Hassoun's antipathy toward politically correct discourse should not lead us to conclude that he does not understand the reasons for its appeal. He recognizes that the elevation of racial and ethnic identity is not surprising given the pressures these groups face. He concedes that even in liberal societies, where laws have been traditionally designed to protect individuals, minorities are not secure. The bottom line for Hassoun is that any form of exclusionary practice is misguided, dangerous, ineffective and morally objectionable regardless of who does the excluding. "All those who do . . . can't resist engaging in the deeply ingrained behavior that demands that the *Other* be clearly marked and labeled . . . whether it is to protect or to exclude him, no matter the reason, by signs that, nevertheless and always, differentiate and exclude" (PE, 19).[38] Whatever the avowed reason for labeling someone or some group, the labeling sets them up for "extreme distinction" and, correlatively, for extreme generalization, meaning that they have lost some of their uniqueness in the process. These losses, argues

Hassoun, outweigh any benefits the group might derive from accentuating its ethnic and racial solidarity. He insists, as I have suggested, that it is only through political reforms and social activism that minorities—that is to say those dubbed as strangers in the midst—have a chance to thrive. Admittedly, laws can be challenged and overturned, but laws, he points out, have proven to be effective in limiting exclusionary practice.

Hassoun's resistance to ethnic and racial distinctions is explained further by his suspicion that group affiliation thwarts the political process by substituting in its place fidelity to the group. He writes:

> So I am tempted to distrust that feeling (a feeling that is both old and new). It is a feeling that strings together in the imaginary a whole range of desires, in the realms of both the social and the personal. It ties these desires together in a *bundle* (the Italian word for bundle is *fascio*) under the heading of belongingness. And it favors this at the cost of political action (trade union struggles, class struggles . . .). This shift in focus in favor of ethnicity or belonging and away from political action is a trend today. It is a sign that society has embraced the *illusion* of an apolitical social order. (My italics; PE, 57)[39]

We can debate with Hassoun whether or not ethnic and racial groups necessarily eschew the political. But it is hard to deny his point that both represent a defensive move inward and a backing off from the struggle for justice across class divisions. Hassoun's Marxism is hard core. Psychological well-being, the imperative of a cosmopolitan hygienic, we could say, depends on the successful connections we are able to maintain with others outside our group. Connections are a struggle. Classifications based on race and ethnicity are regressive and founded on illusion, lack of clarity, and fatalism—the belief that nothing can be done to change the way things are. Hassoun asks rhetorically:

> Is falling back on one's ethnicity not an attempt to stop time and prove that a group can resist all outside influences?
> Is this not a way to dismiss geography and deny socio-cultural divisions? And all for the glory of a relic, the desire for the *One*?
>
> And finally, is it not true that the feeling of belongingness emerges on the scene only when a group is estranged from its own history which it ignores and therefore experiences as mysterious? (PE, 61)[40]

The impulse to divide society along racial and ethnic lines is a fetishization of Origins. The problem, says Hassoun, is that the fetish blocks the truth. It does not advance it. It deepens schisms instead of mending them: "As a result, we have a radical failure to adapt. . . . What up to that time served as a link, a hyphen if you will, falls apart. What is left is a schism, or a desire for the ineffable and impossible return to the Origin. The effect is a dizzying feeling of belongingness"

(PE, 67).⁴¹ Moreover, racial and ethnic groups are fodder for those in a position to exploit them. Hassoun argues that such groups, in effect, accept and, by so doing, reinforce social inequalities:

> Ethnicity, this impertinent avatar for the political, implies the erosion of the social contract and the principles that support it. Instead, it promotes an imagined ideal of community. Whereas politics responds to a whole set of practical issues to protect the interests of this or that social class, the hapless goal of ethnicity is to mark distinctions and oppose itself to other classes. In this, they are like corporations . . . artificially constituted groups that mix together the privileged and underprivileged to the greatest glory of those in power who find very clear benefits in this new arrangement, this new decoupage of social space. (PE, 80–81)⁴²

When divisions based on race and ethnicity are front and center, the problem of inequity is not seen for what it is. It is not configured as a class problem, Hassoun argues. These divisions fail to account for what he refers to in English as the "up or down" variety of distinctions. What takes place is a form of club mentality of the "in or out" coterie instead of the "up or down" richer/poorer sort. Under such an arrangement one asks who is "in" and who is "out" instead of asking who in this society as a whole occupies the economic and socially advantageous positions. The problem as Hassoun sees it is that this arrangement makes it very difficult to fight against social inequalities from within the group (PE, 69). The ethnically or racially organized society is riven internally both in its politics and in its psychology. Group identity fans the flames of exclusionary impulses; it consoles only in the short term. By the same token, racial and ethnic distinctions provide the dominant group with a larger target for the return of the repressed held in check with difficulty by, among other things, forms of political correctness. Hassoun speaks of "these dangerous recesses of fundamentalism that, in the open, under everyone's eyes show a sympathetic side but behind closed doors attest to a ferocious sense of entitlement always susceptible of pouncing, of returning—a *lynching mentality*, long repressed, ready to erupt at any moment" (italics in text; PE, 69–70).⁴³ In short, Hassoun is vigorously against any movement that retreats into itself at the expense of reaching out toward others and engaging in productive debate about how to live together, a debate that takes place in an atmosphere in which the marking of degrees of sameness or of difference is irrelevant. He writes:

> To disengage as subject, as citizen, as member of a class battling against other classes; to do this in order to connect instead to a matricial ethnicity is the same, isn't it, as succumbing to the poisonous charms of a pleasure whose source and support is nostalgia, the desire to create a *pathetic geography* [the term is from Vladimir Jankelevitch] that would *transform* urban or cosmopolitan spaces into places of exclusion and devotion. Isn't this what it's all about? (Italics in text; PE, 70–71)⁴⁴

The Fiction That Is the Jew of Egypt: "Thus, the Egyptian Jew would be pure fiction . . ."[45]

Given Hassoun's repudiation of ethnic group identity, how might we understand his preoccupation with his own origins as a Jew from Egypt? In his embrace of the Jewish heritage of Egypt, is Hassoun not also participating in what he has described as the fetishistic, illusory, and regressive search for ethnic belongingness and totalitarian homogeneity? In his desire for the father's name to *not* be erased, is Hassoun not driven by the same impulse as those who pursue the *One*, who long for a return to the *Paradise Lost of origins*? Finally, is he not extending in perpetuity the melancholic state to his fellow Egyptian Jews who accompany him in this return to Egypt? I will address these questions by looking at specific works by Hassoun.

The Strangers' Crossing opens with the issue of antisemitism framed in the context of his personal story of exclusion: "I was born in a foreign country" ("Je suis né à l'étranger") (PE, 9). This country, he continues, is *not* France but Egypt. Egypt, he explains, looked upon him and his ancestors as strangers. He explains that, like many Egyptian Jews, his family was considered "almost-without country" (*presque-apatrides*). It is not clear to me what the "almost" refers to. As I pointed out, significant barriers were applied to Egyptian Jews under Nasser's Pan-Arab policies that, when it did not expel them forcibly, made it nearly impossible for them to be participate in the economic and political life of the country. In a manner of speaking, Hassoun's work on Egypt and his psychoanalytic work with immigrant communities were attempts on his part to deal with the exclusionary practices to which Jews were subjected and, beyond that, to construct a narrative for a return, a possible reinscription, of Egyptian Jews into the larger history of Egypt. I suggest that Hassoun's project is part of an effort to compel Egypt to admit into the historical record the history of the Jewish community it excluded. More than this, by returning to his origins, by reconstructing the terrain of his cultural and ethnic identity, Hassoun takes control of that narrative and shapes it. By promoting the historical presence, he degrades the terrain of nostalgia. Furthermore, in recognizing his responsibility as a psychoanalyst, a doctor, a clinician whose aim is to heal, we can see that in this return to Egypt Hassoun was conducting a group psychoanalytic intervention, an attempt at least at a group cure.

The Strangers' Crossing is interspersed with vignettes. The first recounts a trip he took to Egypt in 1978. On the way to Luxor, Hassoun writes that he noticed a group of peasants watching tourists disembark. He overheard one of them, an especially harsh-looking peasant, a *fellah*, say: "May Allah destroy the homes of the strangers!" ["Allah Yékhreb Beit el-aganeb!" ("Qu'Allah ruine la maison des étrangers!")] (PE, 17–18). Hassoun, surprised and troubled, asks him: "Who is the stranger?" ("Qui est l'étranger?") . . . "Min houa el-agnabi?") (PE, 18).

The peasant, Hassoun observes, was just as confounded by this question as Hassoun himself was surprised in hearing himself ask it. This event, this "strange adventure," returns to Hassoun vividly again and again in the course of sixteen years. This sort of memory is what Freud called a screen memory, a seemingly banal event remembered periodically and that, when analysis is made of it, turns out to mask (screen out) something distressing that remains unresolved—here, this something is the vexing question: "Am I or am I not an Egyptian?" Hassoun asks himself somewhat rhetorically: "Did the peasant understand the meaning of my question? Did he realize that I myself was one of his compatriots and that my great-grandfather dressed just like him, that he spoke the same language as he did? And, to top it off, that my great-grandfather most likely shared his same views and prejudices? *May Allah destroy the homes of the strangers / Who is the stranger. . . ?*" (italics in text; PE 18–19). In the heat of this paradoxical moment Hassoun catches a glimpse of the magnitude of his question. At first, he reflects on this question: is he, Hassoun himself, the stranger, the man who was forced into exile and who is returning home? Or is the *fellah* the stranger, the person who has stayed behind while the world moved on? The question hangs in the air, resonating with both Hassoun's perplexity and his annoyance with the curse uttered by the peasant. It seems impossible to break the impasse and to answer the question. As he reflects on this question, others come into view: who exactly is a native? From what source does that person draw power? He recognizes that both he and the fellah are Egyptian natives. At the same time, he recognizes that the sense of entitlement the native born possesses is not based on legal status, per se. It is rooted in a human impulse to exclude. Indigeneity, like the "mother tongue," as I discuss later, have very little purchase in Hassoun's thought. I believe this odd event and the questions it raised moved Hassoun to devote a great deal of his energy to clarifying and making known the story of the Jews in Egypt. As he explains in an interview: "I had to practically reconstruct for myself the category of Egyptian Jews; I had to create associations with others, and I had to finish with this story of the Egyptian Jew in order to finally see all the different aspects of my identity reconciled" (Beinin, 271).

I argue in this book that Edmond Jabès, Jacqueline Kahanoff, Paula Jacques, and André Aciman, like Hassoun, are all similarly driven by the compulsion "to make known"—Jabès's words—the story of an injustice perpetrated on them and their compatriots. When a person is sent packing from the only place they knew as home, their sense of self, the ground upon which they built their world, slips away. As immigrants now, they must assert that *self* before anything more is asked. Listen to my story, we hear the immigrant call, listen so I might figure out how I go on from here. In probing the past, Hassoun is anxious to establish a sense of continuity between the *fellah* and his own ancestors. He seeks to establish his Egyptian identity not in order to stress its differences from the rest of the

Egyptian people but in order to make known his history *as* an Egyptian among them. He writes in the introduction to *A History of the Jews of the Nile* (*Histoire des Juifs du Nil*; 1984) that he and the other authors who collaborated on the book wanted "to vouch for the existence of the Jews of Egypt" (HJN, 12).[46] He writes: "This book is dedicated to all those who are not aware of the dramatic history of this community. But it is also dedicated to Egyptians—Copts and Muslims— who might try to forget that at their side many had lived who we call today—and who, to this day, call themselves—*Egyptian Jews*" (italics in text; HJN, 12).[47] Hassoun points out in the same book that in writing about the history of the Jews of Egypt, its authors wanted to put an end to rampant nostalgia. The focus on historical facts and research are helpful ways of preventing homesickness, regret, and feelings of unworthiness, all of which are symptoms of nostalgia. As in a novel or a film, *A History of the Jews of the Nile* opens with thirteen brief descriptions of men and women, all Jews from Egypt in various settings. We see them in Paris, the suburbs of Paris, Milan, Lausanne, Zagazig, Montreal, Alexandria, Melbourne, and Marseille. We are in 1956, 1957, 1965, 1972, and 1978. These men and women represent different social milieus but share one thing in common: they and their ancestors were Jews who lived in Egypt at some point in the past *twenty-five centuries*. They are Egyptian Jews. They lived in any number of places in Egypt from Elephantine to Domyat to Rachid, from the shores of the Mediterranean, from Alexandria to the Sinai peninsula. The point to be made, Hassoun asserts, is that Egyptian Jews, like any other religious or ethnic group, had many incarnations in the course of changing times and circumstances. They are, he argues, in all their diversity, unquestionably *of* Egypt. He writes:

> It would be foolish to speak of a Jew from Egypt in any transhistorical, immutable sense. The Jews of Egypt integrated, absorbed cultures and invasions, schisms and heresies, those that *their country*, Egypt, had suffered and those their community had known.
>
> Thus the Jew of Egypt is a fiction, a poetic license born of dispersion and of distinctiveness. On *his native land*, this Jew was plural. Plural in time. Plural in the society of which he was part. (My italics; HJN, 10–11)[48]

Within this sober perspective, Hassoun advances the hypothesis in *The Strangers' Crossing* and *Smugglers of Memory* that a return to the past can only be successful with the agency of the father. By father, as I suggested earlier, Hassoun can mean the real person or *actual* father, or the *imaginary* father, or yet again the *symbolic* father. To avoid the entanglements of psychoanalytic discourse and still give a sense of Hassoun's conceptual framework and terminology, I will use a very crude shorthand to refer to the various functions of the *father*, taking care to make the referent clear in context. Hassoun incorporates the father, particularly the name of the father, to inscribe his own identity as an Egyptian Jew with roots stretching back in history. We find this emphasis in his attachment to names, quite literally the name written on a surface, visibly there for all to see. Jewish names that are disappearing from the site of memory are a source of tremendous sadness, as with the disappearance of Jewish names on the headstones at Bassatine, for example. In Paul Pérez's film, *Jacques Hassoun: de mémoire* (2008), we hear Hassoun explain his own name. The surname Jacques, we hear him say, means Jacob and Israel; Jacob is named Israel after he wrestles with an aggressor who demands to know Jacob's identity; Jacob becomes twisted and limping during the encounter and is then transformed into Israel, straight and upright. The name Hassoun, he goes on, alludes to the Arabic words *hass* and *sah* and the Hebrew word *noussah*. He explains: "HASS is the Arabic word for feeling which also brings to mind the Arabic word SAH, meaning clarity. The Hebrew word NOUSSAH means the search for the truth in the text." In the recordings we have of Paula Jacques's *Magnetic Nights*, we hear Hassoun's deep disappointment and his agitation as he searches for the street that carried his family name in the Old Jewish Quarter. In calling on the father, and the name of the father, Hassoun is appealing to history. The traumatized individual needs history to ground him in order to face a world in which his existence is denied. The return to Egypt is *not* a return to origins, to the "the mythic history of the Jews in Egypt" (PE, 55). Such a return is a death wish (PE, 71). Those who imagine a return to origins act as if nothing had changed, nothing took place. They are delusional. As Hassoun puts it, this attachment to the myth of one's origins does not conform to geopolitical and sociocultural realities. It cannot, therefore, help the exile come to terms with his past (PE, 69). In contradistinction to this position, I will show in the chapters devoted to the works of Jacqueline Shohet Kahanoff and Edmond Jabès, how and why they find a return to the biblical and mythic Egyptian past of the Jewish people to be necessary, restorative, and self-affirming.

Hassoun accepts the basic Lacanian premise that the possibility of knowledge and the foundation by means of which the subject can address the world are attributed to the symbolic order and to the function of the father. It is thanks to the father that the subject enters the world. According to Hassoun, the question the subject asks the father *unknowingly* is, "How can one be a stranger to him whose name was given to us? How can one be a stranger to one's father?" (PE, 97).[49] If the father is not/cannot be a stranger, it is because, for Hassoun, he always accompanies the subject in his journey. And both the subject and the father gain strength, heal the wounds of exile, when they undertake the journey together. The father lives on as a result of his own efforts to pass down a shared heritage but, also, and crucially, through the efforts of the subject, his progeny, whose responsibility it is to keep the exchange between them going. To put it differently, the subject sutures the wound of expulsion from which both of them suffer with the help of the father. I believe that Hassoun's "return to Egypt," leading the diaspora to look squarely at its Egyptian roots, can be understood as his attempt to heal the father's wound(s), restore the Jewish past. By way of illustration, I call attention to three vignettes or "moral tales" that Hassoun relates. In the first, a woman he calls Giulia visits Egypt, a country she left at the age of thirteen. Once there, she barely recognizes the sites and feels only indifference. However, days later, upon visiting the building in Alexandria where she grew up, she notices the benches in the corridors on each floor of the building. They were placed there when her family lived in Egypt to help her father rest as he climbed the stairs because he suffered from heart problems. Seeing the benches, she starts to cry. The second vignette is divided into five parts. Each describes a scene that takes place in a different city around the world, in Essen, Leningrad, San Francisco, Athens, and New York's Harlem. In the first, an elderly father inquires about the synagogue of Essen. His son responds impatiently that the synagogue of Essen has burned—this is a lie told by the son only to dismiss the question; he can't be bothered. In the fifth and closing part, we come to understand that the elderly father has died. Hassoun describes the son as confused and distraught. He visits the site where he expected the synagogue to be. It is not there. The son's guilty lie induces psychosomatic blindness—the synagogue *is* there; he just does not see it. On the road once again, we see him tear something to pieces, a letter or perhaps a photograph. Hassoun explains that this gesture suggests that memories are not always carried in words and images; they are expressed through the body and, symbolically, in the name of the father and the memories we keep of him. The synagogue of Essen had not been burned. But for both the father (now gone) and the son it will remain the site of their symbolic reunion. The third vignette relates two famous episodes described by Freud. One is the anecdote where Freud's father tries to impress upon his young son how much better his son's life is compared with his. He describes his encounter on the street with a Christian man who angrily knocks the father's hat to the ground and screams at him: "Jew, get off the sidewalk." Sigmund asks his father: "And what did you do?" "I picked up my hat," Jacob answers. This humiliating incident revealed his father's vulnerability and lack of courage. The other episode Hassoun describes is Freud's elaborate account and examination of his visit to the Acropolis when he was forty-seven years old. Standing there and seeing the site with his own eyes, Sigmund is shaken up by the words he hears himself saying: "So all this really does exist, just as we learnt at school!" Freud understood some years after the event that his reaction, his expression of disbelief that the Acropolis really existed (that it was not some fiction too good to be true) combined with the story of his father's hat, was a manifestation of a compounded sense of guilt at his own success. Even though the imperative had been to exceed the father, he could not help feeling pain at the thought he had betrayed and humiliated him. Like Freud, Hassoun maintained that no entry into the world is possible without the father's involvement and no psychoanalytic cure can be successfully carried out without wounding him (PE, 116). The three vignettes telescope the critical role played by the father, and more pointedly by his name. Hassoun underlines: "Mourning the father can also come about when we have destroyed images we have attached to him in order to appropriate the only thing a child can take from his father, his name" (PE, 121).[50] Hassoun likens these three vignettes, these three "journeys," to stations on the road to the proverbial Promised Land. It is the journey that gives the Israelites the Law. The generation that went out of Ancient Egypt, he reminds us, was not the generation that entered the Promised Land. Similarly, the three vignettes follow the itinerary of a lost generation for whom the father is wounded, isolated, and existentially threatened to be cut off from history.

In a manner of speaking, all exiles, and particularly first-generation exiles, Hassoun explains, will not enter the Promised Land nor can they go back from where they came. This is the drama Hassoun-psychoanalyst evokes in a powerful passage in *Strangers' Crossings*, where he explores imaginatively, by way of metaphors and images, ways to address his exiled compatriots and relieve their suffering. He tells them, for example, they will not be alone in the wilderness because the motherland will follow them like a shadow: "This shadow is our image, the image we have of our motherland, the image of this benevolent guardian, father-mother, without whom we cannot begin to live" (PE, 122).[51] Having introduced the image of a beneficent being, Hassoun pulls it back, as it were. The first-generation immigrants who came to him as patients seeking help would find this image of a beneficent motherland if not troubling at least inappropriate. They were, after all, disowned by the motherland, this entity "without whom" they "cannot begin to live." He qualifies the image and writes that the shadow of the "mother-land" ("mère-patrie") accompanied them in France like a "dead body shrouded in darkness" ("le deuil d'un corps dont il ne resterait plus que l'ombre") (PE, 122). Hassoun finds in this dramatic address to exiles the right note to address honestly their suffering. He diagnoses the problem. The root of their suffering, and his, is that they do not know their own history. He acknowledges the psychic burden movingly in these words:

> Fashioned by exile, we have become a shadow of ourselves. We trip on a lost language and an odd name. Our elders are silent about why we had to leave our lives behind. Our fathers cannot tell us anything about our history.... The knowledge we have of our history is wavering. Our anxieties are irritating to others and annoying, not to say, humiliating to our descendants. (PE, 122)[52]

Hassoun took on the role of teacher and healer, of the parent and, psychoanalytically speaking, of the father who accompanies his children on part of their journey. The purpose of passing down this heritage is not to fan feelings of resentment or to sound the sirens of ethnicity and "of savage nostalgia" (PE, 123). Rather, as I have explained, Hassoun takes on the preservation and the safeguarding of the cultural heritage of the Jews of Egypt in order to make their history better known, to inscribe this history in the Egyptian narrative, and in this way to help heal the wounds of his compatriots. He acknowledges in *Smugglers of Memory* that everyone suffers exile. Most people are exiled from themselves and from their history. But he states his specific concern unambiguously: he, personally, is interested in and moved by any individual, Jewish and non-Jewish, who is subjected to exclusionary practices. He is interested in and moved by all those whom society has designated as strangers in their midst (CM, 20). In *The Same Book* (*Le Même livre*; 1985), containing his correspondence with the Moroccan writer Abdelkebir Khatibi, Hassoun writes that "the roots of neurosis, the kind that is particularly damaging in children, derive from the fact that all of us have forgotten that our fathers were once-upon-a-time children."[53] A return to Egypt is thus a way to save one's own father, oneself, and to save one's community from the dehumanization, humiliation, and alienation that society reserves for immigrants and other outsiders.

Minorities Trafficking in Language

Hassoun takes it as a fundamental tenet that the unconscious is structured like a language and that human beings traffic in and through language. As a clinician, he sees language as a tool. The language we choose or avoid using is a sign of the complicated terrain that must be negotiated between ourselves and others. What is on the line is how we adapt both socially and psychologically, how we are able to integrate. All negotiations are accompanied by anxiety. These are particularly tense for minorities and immigrants. And the choice of which language to use is a tricky thing. It is both personal and political. And it is always of consequence. Hassoun could maneuver in three languages and was attentive to the ramifications of language choice. In the correspondence he kept from 1981 to 1984 with Abdelkebir Khatibi, Hassoun asks: "To what language do I belong?" It is as if he were asking: Where do I come from? Who am I? He writes Khatibi: "I envy you the ability to write in Arabic. I am condemned—against my deepest wishes, but also, by some innate inclination—to write French in Arabic or in Hebrew. The result is strange stylistically" (ML, 15). French was Hassoun's primary language for most of his life, for speaking and especially when writing:

> My French—which at first was imposed on me—is a relationship to language that is *impossible to change*. It is a traumatic event in my life. It is still deeply unsettling. The day I understood that I could *change* the impossible, that it was a good idea to change it, my style became the sharp tool I used to work over the devastation and humiliation I was feeling. My "style" took over and overtook the trauma so that I could see and think outside of it. (Italics in text; ML, 95)[54]

In other words, he discovered he had the power to transform his relationship to a language that had been imposed on him by cultural imperialism. He discovered that style was a weapon that could shape and transfigure. Georg Garner writes: "Jacques Hassoun had some style. He knew it. He banked on it."[55]

Hassoun asks, if I have three languages is it because I am from three countries—three different spaces. Yes, he answers: Egypt because it is in my "body and blood," France which is "in my language and my attachments," and a space we might call "Juderia, Hara, Mellah, ghetto or Carrara, a place that from Cordoba to Venice, from Baghdad to Sana'a, from Aleppo to Salonica, from Jerusalem to Vilna extends the geographical boundaries of *Heimatlosland* and masterminds an insane game of Chutes and Ladders" (ML, 143). The person living in exile is afraid to be singled out as a stranger, and, therefore, he looks for language to save him from that (ML, 149). Exile does not begin when the child or the adult leaves the motherland, says Hassoun; it begins "when the language and dialect our ancestors spoke are forgotten, scorned, whispered, when we are ashamed of them and also when we are aroused by them" (EL, 65).[56] Children born in exile need to find ways to silence the voices that exert pressure on them to, on the one hand, *not* speak their native language and those who, on the other hand, whisper that their native language, and particularly that their mother tongue, is *special*; that their mother tongue is who they really are, is their true identity. But the mother tongue, according to Hassoun, is not a single thing with a single overwhelming charge. It is plural. It is made up of other languages, not all of them discursive (EL, 73). "What do I mean by mother tongue? Simply this: a language, called *lalangue*," a language "that is both unique and ordinary. It accompanies us throughout our life, manifests itself in all sorts of social interactions and intellectual pursuits; and it is there when we play and when we love" (EL, 73).[57]

The mother tongue is not central to his conception of language. It is no more and no less significant than any other language. The mother tongue is, in his words, ordinary ("quelconque"). Notwithstanding his interest in undermining it, he nonetheless assigns to it a special status. When we speak in our supposed mother tongue, Hassoun says, we can generally say more about our feelings, sensations, scents, and sounds than with languages we have learned. This makes it in a certain way special but, he cautions, it is important that the mother tongue not be regarded with excessive reverence. The mother tongue is the language or languages we do not remember having learned. It is oral and writing is *not* its manifestation. While he deemphasizes the oral and somatic discourses, he elevates writing, which he describes as the site of a disruption that takes place when the child is unable to express himself.

Some of the most compelling discussions about language, writing, and the mother tongue are in his book, *Language in Exile: Fragments of a Mother Tongue* (*L'Exil de la langue. Fragments de langue maternelle*; 1993). He examines both the ontological and cultural dimensions of language, affirming that language is plural and language choice is fraught with social and political ramifications. He points out that in clinical practice he has witnessed individuals so stuck on a language that the very thought of speaking another made them silent, made them suffer. These suffering individuals were asking the impossible question Hassoun himself had asked Khatibi: What am I doing when I choose one language over another? Who am I betraying? Whose side am I on? Hassoun saw the psychological damage caused by such linguistic investment. He recognized that suffering comes from many directions. In certain cases, it becomes extreme when "the subject finds himself at the confluence of two or three languages, all of them equally cherished, and then one of these languages, possibly more than one, shows itself to be adorned in the accoutrements of the degraded and degrading dominant culture."[58] The subject can also suffer from a generalized sense of unworthiness that is attached to his language. It is as if he could hear others say, "You are your language and your language is worthless" (EL, 84). Hassoun dramatizes here and elsewhere the powerful feelings we attach to certain languages. Yet, in asserting that languages are plural and that the mother tongue is just another language, he is advocating a less passionate investment in the languages we use. The difference between Khatibi's views on language and Hassoun's is striking. Khatibi's position, like that of Tahar Ben Jelloun and other Maghrebi francophone writers, is complicated by the French colonial experience such that he can only write "from the irremediable and from a traumatic trace" (ML, 98). In contrast, Hassoun's relationship to language, French and Arabic, remains close to his heart, opportunistic, artisanal, and playful. He could say, as he does in the quote cited above from *The Same Book*, that he is deeply unsettled by the fact that French has imposed itself upon him. But his response to French language's imperialism is to imagine himself overpowering it, doing what he wishes with it.

Alexandrias. A Novel (*Alexandries. Roman,* 1985)

Having concentrated my attention so far on Jacques Hassoun the scientist, clinician, historian, and scholar, I now ask how this Hassoun aligns with him as a novelist. Novels are exploratory modes of thinking that bring into relief the imaginary of writers, the mindset that informs how they perceive and construct the world. Fiction exhorts writers to let their guard down, to not fuss with loose ends like contradictions and invalid arguments, and to allow unruly impulses and designs to see the light of day. I have argued in this chapter that, through his efforts on behalf of his compatriots, Hassoun worked out a conceptual framework for helping them through the difficulties of exile. I have also suggested that in his analytic work and in communicating their history, he maintains an optimistic outlook. He asserts, for example, that immigrants can integrate in a host society through political engagement; that one's heritage can be smuggled into the future and thus foster continuity and novelty to new generations. He demystifies the issue of the mother tongue by advancing that it is plural and can have several incarnations during our lifetime; and he asserts that languages are available for our self-construction. By focusing on the history of Egyptian Jews, Hassoun makes their history and exile intelligible; and by connecting this history to the greater history and cultures of Egypt, he secures the community's identity. He is positive and affirmative in yet another way: he psychoanalyzed some of his compatriots and other immigrants suffering from the trauma of exile, wrote about the process of healing, and took groups to Egypt to experience their ancestral home firsthand. His energy and dedication are evident in his efforts to preserve the heritage of Egyptian Jews. He battled for them and with them to that end.

I now turn to his fictional work, his novel *Alexandrias. A Novel*, and suggest that in it we discover a different Hassoun, one who makes us regret that he did not write additional novels. Hassoun understood that through the agency of the novel, he could put into play different possibilities and points of view. He describes *Alexandrias* as a novel about memory inspired by four women. He writes:

> Giulia, Marie-Sol, Léa, Amina . . . women who have set off memories and brought them to rest here. These women do not exist apart from each other. Each one of them brings from a different place the thread that together will weave the history of our exile.
>
> This memory made up of what is remembered and what is forgotten through the ages and across space, I will call *Alexandrias. A Novel*.[59]

Hassoun asks that we confront memory in exile not as an integrated narrative, a narrative with a single perspective. Rather, as Michael Rothberg has shown and as Colette Wilson has stated about *Alexandrias*, memory is made up of scenes both remembered and forgotten; forgotten memories are these feelings, gestures, and words that return to us like a sign of recognition we can never be certain that we can trace to our past.[60] In this novel, we have the portrait of a community captured novelistically at the very moment it recognizes that its existence has come to an end. At the same time, it comes to the equally troubling realization that its distinctly Egyptian character will also not survive the diaspora. There is a lot of material here for art to handle. In a style at once bare and evocative, *Alexandrias* expresses the experience of loss. It dramatizes the battles the characters wage against nostalgia, exclusion, and melancholy. It also highlights the emotional investment involved in revisiting the story of a Jewish community now dispersed around the world. This is a contemplative novel which invites the reader to enter the world of the dispossessed for a glimpse of the way they might experience their situation and face their future.

The novel is divided into eight chapters, an epigram, and an acknowledgment page. Each chapter presents a character who addresses a reader, most of whom are anonymous. A few of the chapters take the form of a letter. Others are narratives with a distinctly oral character; one chapter is a diary entry. The chapters are fragments of a larger story, the story of expulsion. Each of the eight chapters can be described in the words of one of the characters, Sedaka Raoul, as "the remains of a text torn to shreds by history" (A, 128). A few characters make cameo appearances in different parts of the novel. As the reader moves from one chapter to the next, there is a growing awareness that many of the characters know each other, have heard of one another, move in the same circles—or did at one time. Colette Wilson has aptly likened the structure of the novel to a musical fugue. She writes: "As in the contrapuntal musical form, each narrating voice in *Alexandrias* picks up the theme and makes it her/his own. Each chapter or episode throws further light on what has gone before and looks forward to future developments and recapitulations of different aspects of the lives of the characters and the history of the Jews more widely" (Wilson, 106). Wilson adds further that in the novel the fugue is not only a structuring device: "The fugue also functions in its literal sense relating to the flight from one's usual environment, from the Latin fuga, as well as in its psychological sense, that is, in relation to the loss of one's identity" (Wilson, 106).

Alexandrias is a novel about dislocation and loss. It draws the reader into the heart of the issues at stake when one leaves a way of life behind under duress. In some narratives, the reader is witness to a difficult choice that is made in a time of crisis. In others, he or she is present as characters review and assess the aftermath of challenging circumstances.

I begin with "The Travel Journal of Sedaka Raoul Viterbo" ("Le Journal de voyage de Sedaka Raoul Viterbo"). The story is a haunting reflection on the decision that one man, Sedaka Raoul, had to make in deciding whether to leave or remain in Egypt. The question the story poses is whether Jews should have stood their ground in Egypt instead of caving in to pressures and allowing themselves to be expelled from their native land. The action unfolds as an internal monologue by Sedaka Raoul, a doctor from Bab el Louk, an upper-middle-class neighborhood in Cairo.

Sedaka Raoul is a character straight out of a novel by Dostoyevsky. He is ravaged by guilt. He is also perfectly lucid. He tells of how he watched many of his compatriots flee Egypt while he, unlike them, stood his ground. He only contemplated leaving once, he confides, when his club, a club to which he belonged for decades, rescinded his membership. He was reinstated six months later, he hastens to add. But the event had unsettled him enough that it had made him think about possibly leaving Egypt once and for all. It had set him thinking, more broadly, about how the Jew through history was fated to wander.

What disturbs Sedaka Raoul more than being excluded from the club—after all, he was reinstated—is the thought that the cancellation of his membership was the reason, the sole reason, for him to contemplate leaving. That he would be moved to leave because of such a trivial incident, an incident that implied he enjoyed a privileged lifestyle, mortifies him. He keeps this thought a secret and shares it only with Marie-Sol, the only other Jew besides himself to remain in Egypt after their fellow Jews have left. Is Hassoun suggesting that the Jews' expulsion from Egypt is analogous to expulsion from an exclusive club? I do not think so. Nowhere has Hassoun trivialized the Jewish exodus from Egypt in these terms. Nonetheless, it is an idea the story presents and that we are invited to consider.

The action of "The Travel Journal of Sedaka Raoul Viterbo" revolves around the board game Chutes and Ladders, where each square represents a country around the globe. The game is a representation of the wandering Jew. We follow Sedaka Raoul on this game board as he moves from square to square according to the roll of the dice. On each square, he visits a place where his compatriots are living. He goes to Paris and its suburbs, Melbourne, London, Khartoum, Abidjan, Montreal, Amsterdam, Milan, Brussels, Barcelona, Malta, Athens, Brooklyn, Denver, San Francisco, Los Angeles, Saõ Paulo, Caracas, Singapore, Tokyo, Cape Town, Salisbury, and countless other cities. Sedaka Raoul goes everywhere except Israel. He writes:

> For a time, I was tempted to go to Israel. There, I supposed, I would find Jews who believed they could put an end to exile by creating roots they thought permanent; or who came to Israel because they lacked the means to go elsewhere. But I had the feeling that if I were to go to this country, I ran the risk of finding myself in a script that was not meant for me; on a square that would eject me right out of the game and into a warped space whose distortions I imagined to be horrifying. (A, 124)[61]

Something about visiting Israel made him feel uneasy, even "horrified." What was it? Why is Israel a problem? Is it because, as he says, landing on its square means the end of the game? If so, what difference does it make whether the game continues or stops? It is clear that the game of Chutes and Ladders is an allegory of Jewish history and of the fate of the Jews as eternally displaced. But the nagging question is why it is important for Sedaka Raoul that the game should continue? Hassoun does not help us and neither does Sedaka Raoul. The reader is left alone to interpret a decision Sedaka Raoul tells us was binding: "My decision was final, even though it seemed to me to have been taken somewhere else and by another. Another me" (A, 125). It is as if Hassoun is suggesting that the Jew can only recognize himself as destined to always wander in exile.

I propose reading this allegory of the wandering Jew as Hassoun's reflections on Israel as a political space and an existential choice. Hassoun was an early Zionist who, later, like many French intellectuals on the Left, became critical of

Israel for its treatment of the Palestinians. I think that in "The Travel Journal of Sedaka Raoul Viterbo" Hassoun is registering a response to Israeli politics that reflects his dissension. It should be noted that the round of Chutes and Ladders that Sedaka Raoul plays does not end with this dissenting view. The next square takes him to Khartoum instead of Israel. There, he checks out a synagogue built by one of his ancestors. The end of the story, and the last square played in this game, finds him back in Egypt. This round of the game was an excursion, he says; he had just been out for a spin. Will the game continue with possibly a different ending? If Hassoun were here to give an answer, I expect it would be, "Who knows"? History tells us that societies are dynamic and that political situations are unstable. Sedaka Raoul might decide to visit Israel the next time around.

We have in this work one of Hassoun's most moving and explicit expressions of the damaging psychological consequences of displacement. Sedaka Raoul is bitter about the fate of the Jews. He minces no words to express the grinding ambivalences in his own feelings about being a Jew: "I hate our fate with all my being—even if day in and day out I rely on it to form my worldview. But I am also very bitter against all the people who did not know how to hold on to this land no matter the hardships they would endure" (A, 126–127).[62] In this rant, Sedaka Raoul exposes the raw nerves of his pain and despair. At one point, he brings up the story of Job as interpreted by St. John Chrysostom. Disheartened, he asks himself why his community did not suffer with dignity, as did Job, who was also driven out of his home and suffered so much. Might they not have taken to heart his example and accepted their suffering instead of going into exile? If they had resisted, would they not have attained greater stature, instead of being humiliated and diminished time and again? Why do they simply leave "without any fuss" when things get hard, he complains bitterly (A, 126). If they did not resist enough, he asks, are they not therefore responsible for their exile? The reader can take this remark to mean that Sedaka Raoul, or Hassoun for that matter, is proposing that Jews follow Job's example and not leave even under pressure. I take the question to be rhetorical, to reflect one line of thought and to express Sedaka Raoul's despair. But perhaps not. We see similar resistance expressed in Paula Jacques's works. True, Sedaka Raoul is bitter that, in his view, Egyptian Jews, like Jews around the world, have simply left when pressed. But, equally true, he is revolted that the majority always demonizes and pursues minorities, giving them little choice. He writes in his diary: "To secure their national identity, will the majority always evict minorities, always suspect them of consorting with the devil disguised as the stranger who comes from the dark recesses out there?" (A, 126–127).

In *Alexandrias. A Novel*, Hassoun reflects on the hold our past has on us and the compulsiveness with which we attend to it. He explores this obsession in "Giulia." In this epistolary narrative we find out that Nathan, a character who reminds us of Hassoun, had once been passionately involved in uncovering the history of his people. We also understand that he had stopped doing this. He writes Giulia about the folly of the enterprise:

> To be utterly oblivious to one's desires and whims is crazy. But the opposite is also crazy. The opposite, which is to say, the desire to reconstruct and relive the twists and turns of one's history and the history of one's ancestors; to take that reconstruction and the desire that spurs it on to the point of nausea; to submit this enterprise to ceaseless hounding, and to think you can survive with impunity after that. There will always be one piece of the puzzle missing or an extra piece to be used by someone who, in his exile, will try to compose for his own benefit a document where this or that event will be subjected to his ruses. (A, 16)[63]

Nathan seems to be convinced that his endeavor is foolish. He writes Guilia from Manhattan that in this city everyone is obsessed with their past, "this Babylon where exiles come to start a new life" (A, 13). These "mutants," Irish, Jewish, or whatever pursue every lead possible to bring their ancestors back to life one last time, he says (A, 14). He advises Giulia to resist this quest, which he describes as the hunt for "ghoulish ghosts" (A, 15). He follows this warning by confessing that he recognizes himself in this type of seeker. But he is cured, he reminds her: "You know as far as I am concerned that I've been there and back" (A, 15). We are made clearly aware, subsequently, that Nathan is not cured. He ends his letter to Giulia in order to chase a lead: "I need to run. I am simply too curious" (A, 16). His obsessive character is evident in his protesting too much against it when he immediately adds: "Please believe me" (A, 16). Do we have in "Giulia," this opening chapter of *Alexandrias*, a self-critique meant to undermine his own project of rescuing his heritage? Is he claiming that this project is a personal obsession and that it is mad? In the work I examined earlier, Hassoun is very clear about what we must do about our ancestors: we must face them, rediscover our heritage, and reconstruct it in the image of the present to serve future generations to connect and reconstruct their heritage. I believe that in "Giulia" Hassoun is offering, for our benefit, an insider's perspective on the complex feelings and ruses involved in pursuing a meaningful narrative of the Jewish Egyptian community. The story percolates with questions. Is it possible? Is it worth it? Am I the one to do it? Am I sick or living the good life beyond trauma? Will I ever know?

In "Léa," Hassoun offers another perspective. Léa addresses her young nephew from Jerusalem where she was born and to where after a lifetime in Egypt she has returned. The young man is her nephew by marriage, and the narrative is a plea in the form of advice from a wise aunt. Léa's pleas and advice echo many of Hassoun's own thoughts in works like *Smugglers of Memory* and *The Strangers' Crossing*. For example, she implores her nephew to not succumb to nostalgia and the temptation to fetishize the past. She reminds him of the cousin who refused until the end of her life to believe that the moon she was looking at from the top floor of her Manhattan apartment was the same moon that shone upon the Nile. She reminds him also about his cousin Gabr who, no longer in Egypt, observed Shabbat using the Egyptian time zone as his guide; he refused to accept a higher authority than the authority of his native village, she explains. She tells him: "I wish for you that you are not struck down by the same illness." She adds a warning and a concern that her nephew not delude himself into thinking he knows why Egyptian Jews were expelled from Egypt (A, 66). She tells him that their fate was sealed the moment they left their language, Arabic, and their villages for the big cities and for foreign countries (A, 66).

Léa also expresses her pessimism about the possibility of preserving their memory. She tells her nephew that even the most tenacious and fervent efforts will not forever preserve his community (A, 66). Regardless, she adds quickly, the children should know about it: "Now that the elders have left the scene, all you can do is teach the children their history and bits and pieces of our lore in the strange languages that you have adopted" (A, 66).[64] The past will not, indeed it cannot, be retrieved in all its integrity. "In any case," she muses, and here we are reminded of Hassoun's reflections in *Smugglers of Memory*: "who can presume to know beforehand what he passed on? A person deprived of reason or a dictator, that's who. Two revolting figures of authority" (A, 67).

In the chapter entitled "Alexandria" a narrator who is a descendant of Jewish *fellahin* (peasants), addresses an anonymous reader. He introduces the reader to *Lui*, in English *Him*,[65] a fellow Jew whose perspective on Alexandria is Rimbaldian, which is to say poetic and phantasmagoric. *Lui* describes Alexandria as a divine goddess ("aimée divinisée") with hair and limbs that span from the shoreline to the old city and the markets of Alexandria. The narrator informs the reader that this account is not pure fiction (A, 112). Fiction and nonfiction are intricately woven in the text. We recognize the lycée Hassoun attended; his family circumstances; and we learn that upon entering school he felt ashamed to speak Arabic; and we review his itinerary, a Jew born in Alexandria who returns two decades later. We can relate these details of *Lui*'s life to Hassoun's own. But we learn more than factual details. The narrator is intimate with *Lui*, whom he refers to sometimes as "the child." He knows a lot about him, about his ideas and feelings. But the narrator is not *Lui*. We have, in "Alexandria," versions of what it feels like, what it looks like, and what it means to be, as Hassoun was later, a witness to the unraveling of a community and of a way of life.

The narrator tells us that *Lui* regretted not knowing anything about the Jewish *fellah* of Egypt. This was an Arabic culture, the narrator tells us, Jewish and Arab (A, 102). In addition, we find out that it was many years after he had left Egypt that *Lui* understood that French culture in Alexandria had been imperialist. Before then, French culture seemed an organic and inseparable part of Alexandria (A, 99). We find out that it was after he left Egypt that *Lui* realized the degree of his attachment to his Jewish Egyptian identity. He came to identify with this group of people "whose quick and open manners, whose way of talking, and whose beliefs and convictions echoed fundamentally his own" (A, 104–105).[66]

In a knowing way, the narrator conveys *Lui*'s profound melancholy. He tells us *Lui* finds Alexandria changed since he had left twenty years earlier. He had expected to see, feel, hear, and love it the same way. But he does not. He does not recognize its feel and touch. Having ceased to be her "long suffering troubadour" (A, 109), the city for him is now a present and living reality (A, 110). It is not the "divine goddess" he remembers from his childhood. *Lui* can now, presumably, find pleasure in this new Alexandria. This dissonance has a virtue: "Today he seems to understand and take an uncanny pleasure in accepting Alexandria as it is with its history and its people" (A, 110). But this note of detachment is not convincing. The melancholy it encloses is thick and palpable. This new Alexandria in all its liveliness does not blot out from view the evidence of the still unfolding extinction of the Jewish Egyptian community, which is painful to see for both the narrator and *Lui*. In one of the most moving passages in the novel, *Lui* reflects on their humiliation:

> Thus he was able to return and rejoin his people in their extreme isolation on the road to extinction.
>
> Their end was not accompanied by the noise and fury of genocide or by the brutal destruction of war. The end came slowly like a long drawn-out wasting away of something.
>
> Who finds interesting an old man languishing in agony? It isn't exciting or heroic. It is just tiring, unpleasant, inappropriate. It interests no one. (A, 105)[67]

In *Alexandrias*, Hassoun makes up for the indignity shown the Jews of Egypt by constructing a novelistic universe where their story is given due consideration, where he reveals the issues at stake, and evokes the *inner life* of the community. It does not prescribe what should be done to feel better. Due to his intimate knowledge of the situation and his literary artistry and sensibility, this beautiful novel is a testament to just how deep and varied Hassoun's production is. Hassoun's rich and original theoretical work, his work with patients, his militancy on behalf of immigrants and minorities, and his efforts to organize, articulate, and bring to the fore the history of the Jews of Egypt: all these efforts and successes have secured Hassoun a remarkable reputation. But his work deserves more attention. To begin with, it needs to be translated and placed in the perspective of Jewish studies, where it clearly and rightly belongs.

Notes

I use the following abbreviations and editions of Jacques Hassoun's work. All translations of his works, including titles, are my own.
(A) *Alexandries. Roman* [*Alexandrias. A Novel*]. Paris: Editions de la Découverte, 1985.
(AR) *Alexandrie et autres récits de Jacques Hassoun* [*Alexandria and Other Writings by Jacques Hassoun*]. Paris: l'Harmattan, 2001.
(CM) *Les Contrebandiers de la mémoire* [*Smugglers of Memory*]. Paris: Syros, 1994.
(EL) *L'Exil de la langue. Fragments de langue maternelle* [*Language in Exile. Fragments of a Mother Tongue*]. Paris: Payot, 1979.
(HJN) *Histoire des Juifs du Nil* [*A History of the Jews of the Nile*]. Paris: Minerve, 1990.
(ML) *Le Même livre* [*The Same Book*], Jacques Hassoun & Abdelkebir Khatibi. Paris: Editions de l'éclat, 1985.
(PE) *Le Passage des étrangers* [*The Strangers' Crossing*]. Paris: Austral, 1995.

Other Works of Jacques Hassoun used in passing in this chapter:
La Cruauté mélancolique. Paris: Flammarion, 1995.
"Glossaire," in *Juifs du Nil*, 2nd edition. Paris: Editions du Scribe, 1984.
Jacques Hassoun extraits d'une oeuvre. Paris: l'Harmattan, 2009.

1. In Elliot Malki's film *Starting Over Again: A Jewish Egyptian Story*, directed by Ruggero Gabbai (Milan: Forma International Production, 2015). Further references to this film are included in the text as (Starting Over).
2. Hassoun's text: "Dans le monde arabo-musulman, nous retrouvons quotidiennement . . . cet impératif de se réclamer une histoire, d'une généalogie, d'une appartenance: ainsi quand deux personnes inconnues se recontrent, immédiatement après les salutations d'usage, une question est constamment posée: 'Quel est ton asl?', terme qui veut dire tout à la fois rattachement (tribal ou religieux), adhésion et appartenance à tel mode de pensée ou à telle ethnie." Jacques Hassoun, *Les Contrebandiers de la mémoire* (Paris: Syros, 1994), 11. Further references to this work are included in the text as (CM).
3. Hassoun's text: "Ce qui me semble passionnant dans cette aventure que suppose la transmission, c'est justement que nous sommes différents de ceux qui nous ont précédés, et que nos descendants suivront le plus vraisemblablement un chemin sensiblement différent du nôtre . . . Et pourtant . . . c'est bien dans cette série de différences que nous inscrivons ce que nous avons à transmettre" (CM, 14).
4. See chapter 2 on Jacqueline Kahanoff. Further references to this work are included in the text as (Kahanoff). See also Elliot Malki's film *Starting Over Again*, cited above in Note 1.
5. Hassoun's text: "Car somme toute, la *transmission* serait ce trésor que chacun se constitue à partir des éléments livrés par les parents, par l'entourage, et qui, remodelés par des rencontres hasardeuses et des événements passés inaperçus, s'articulent au fil des ans avec l'existence quotidienne pour jouer leur fonction principale: celle d'être fondatrice du sujet et pour le sujet" (italics in text; CM, 81).
6. Hassoun's text: "La clinique nous enseigne quotidiennement que de tels silences jouent un rôle primordiale dans la difficulté de vivre que rencontrent les enfants des dépor-

tés juifs, les enfants ou petits-enfants de survivants du génocide arménien, les descendants des torturés lors des guerres d'indépendance, bref tous ceux qui ont côtoyé l'Histoire dans sa plus extrême férocité. . . . Orphelins d'une parole, ils souffrent dans leur chair d'un deuil impossible à effectuer et d'une difficulté à bâtir un roman familial qui leur permette de se projeter dans l'avenir" (CM, 24–25).

7. Hassoun's text: "Mais qu'advienne le temps de la déchirure, le temps de l'affaire Dreyfus ou de la montée du nazisme et des fascismes centre-européens, et c'est alors que ce qui semblait aller de soi, qui semblait aussi faire partie intégrante du sujet, allait se présenter comme l'expression d'un énorme mensonge" (CM, 33).

8. Hassoun's text: "N'est-ce pas cette difficulté de trouver des mots pour évoquer le pays natal des parents ou des grands parents qui rend constamment impossible la transmission de ce que fut son essence même? D'où la difficulté logique à laquelle nous sommes confrontés: ce passé est un appel à la transmission—comme on dit un appel d'air—et dans le même temps la forme même que prend cette *pulsion invocante à savoir*, interdit que cela fut transmis (italics in text; CM, 54).

9. Hassoun's text: "Aussi, *je dois à la vérité* de déclarer: ne craignons point d'être des contrebandiers. C'est à ce titre que nous arriverons à transmettre. En acceptant que le purisme de la langue, son immuabilité, soit un leurre. Exilés, nous le sommes tous tels des transhumants qui ont brûlé leurs vaisseaux. Nous ne retrouverons jamais intact notre passé. . . . Nous sommes d'ici et de là-bas, d'aujourd'hui et d'autrefois. Indéfectiblement" (italics in text; CM, 42–43).

10. In the interview transcribed in Joel Beinin's book, Hassoun explains: "I had to practically reconstruct for myself the category of Egyptian Jews, I had to create associations with others, and I had to finish with this story of the Egyptian Jew in order to finally see all the different aspects of my identity reconciled." Joel Beinin, *The Dispersion of Egyptian Jewry: Culture, Politics, and the Formation of a Modern Diaspora* (Berkeley and Los Angeles: University of California Press, 1998), 271. Further references to this work are included in the text as (Beinin).

11. Carole Naggar, *Egypte, Retour. Récit* (Paris: Nahar Misraïm, 2007), 37. Further references to this work are included in the text as (Naggar).

12. Tobie Nathan, *Ethno-roman* (Paris: Grasset, 2012). Further references to this work are included in the text as (Nathan). All translations of this work are my own.

13. Adam Phillips, *Becoming Freud: The Making of a Psychoanalyst* (New Haven, Conn.: Yale University Press, 2014), 30–31. Further references to this work are included in the text as (Phillips).

14. Tobie Nathan's text: "Je m'interroge encore sur cette passion qui s'est emparée de jeunes enfants d'émigrés, eux-mêmes nés à l'étranger, soumis à l'urgence de s'adapter à un monde qu'ils ignoraient. Au fond, la psychanalyse a été pour notre petit groupe d'enfants d'émigrés ce que fut la boxe pour les Italiens des années 30; ce que sont aujourd'hui le rap ou le slam pour les enfants des banlieues: un moyen de plonger sans retard dans les profondeurs de la société. La psychanalyse démarrait à peine en France. . . . Tout était à construire. Pour nous autres, migrants, nous spécialiser dans une pensée dont on percevait les premiers balbutiements, c'était être tout de suite dans le coup, rattraper en quelques années notre retard existentiel millénaire," Tobie Nathan, *Ethno-Roman* (Paris: Grasset), 23–24.

15. Irène Fenoglio, "Egyptianité et langue française," in *Entre Nil et Sable: ecrivains d'Egypte d'expression française* (1920–1960), edited by Marc Kober, Irène Fenoglio, and Daniel Lançon, 15–25, 24 (Paris: Centre National de Documentation Pédagogique, 1999).

16. Jacques Hassoun, *Alexandrie et autres récits de Jacques Hassoun* (Paris: l'Harmattan, 2001), 34–35. Further references to this work are included in the text as (AR).

17. See Victor Segré, *Un Aller sans retour: l'histoire d'un communiste juif egyptien* (Paris: L'Harmattan, 2009) and Avraham Bar-Av (Bentata), *17 Sheikh Hamza Street, Cairo* (Lexington, Ky., 2016). The Hebrew version of the novel was published in Israel by Rimonim in 2011. See also Beinin, note 10 above.

18. Film of Paul Pérez, http://www.dailymotion.com/video/x21bycy_jacques-hassoun-de-me-moire_shortfilms. The film was produced in 2008. All transcriptions and translations are my own. Further references to this work will be included in the text as (Pérez).

19. *La Descente au paradis*, *Kayro Jacobi, juste avant l'oublie*, and *Un Baiser froid comme la lune* are three novels by Paula Jacques in which communist or Marxist activism are represented as misguided and naïve.

20. Tobie Nathan, *Café Littéraire du mercredi—Tobie Nathan—Ce Pays qui te ressemble*, https://www.youtube.com/watch?v=dt9zhRN2FeQ.

21. Tobie Nathan, *Ce Pays qui te ressemble* (Paris: Editions Stock, 2015). Nathan follows Nino's intellectual and political evolution throughout the novel. In the end of the book, after the violent repression of the Muslim Brotherhood in 1965, Nino opens a café in Cairo frequented by intellectuals. He will remain unmarried until his death. Further references to this broadcast will be included in the text as (CR). All translations are my own.

22. Joel Beinin's chapter "The Communist Emigrés in France" in *Dispersion*, 142–178 provides useful information on the participation of Jews in the formation of the communist parties in Egypt and the adherence of many Jews to Marxism.

23. Jacques Hassoun, "Glossaire," in *Juifs du Nil*, 2nd edition (Paris: Editions du Scribe, 1984), 266. Also in *Alexandrie et autres récits de Jacques Hassoun* (Paris: l'Harmattan, 2001), 34.

24. Paula Jacques, *Nuits magnétiques*: "Sept jours et six nuits ou le temps d'un retour au pays natal," Radio Broadcast on *France Culture* June 1993; rebroadcast June 1999. Tapes available through *France Culture*, Paula Jacques, and myself. Further references to this broadcast will be included in the text as (Nuits). All translations are my own.

25. Hassoun's text: "Tout ceci pour dire que tous ces groupes, tous ces lieux de rencontre permettaient à tout ce que la France pouvait compter comme immigrés, de s'inscrire avec leur histoire dans l'histoire du pays de France en train de s'écrire, sans crainte de trahir ce dont ils étaient les porteurs, dans la mesure même où l'internationalisme représentait pour eux la garantie ultime." In "Vive l'internationale. Entretien avec Jacques Hassoun par Hélène Vignobles," in *Jacques Hassoun extraits d'une oeuvre* (Paris: l'Harmattan, 2009), 125–134, 130. Further references to this work are included in the text as (Vive). All translations of this work are my own.

26. Hassoun's text: "Je viens d'un milieu en grande partie arabophone, ce qui voulait dire en Egypte un milieu particulièrement religieux et fort modeste. Soit dit en passant . . . la ligne de cassure sociale passant le plus souvent par l'engagement dans telle ou telle autre langue. . . . Or, par une série de hasards, il s'est trouvé qu'à travers mon adhésion à un mouvement sioniste de gauche (le Dror) dont l'une des tendances ensuite a rejoint le Parti communiste israélien, j'ai eu la possibilité, très jeune, de rencontrer la théorie marxiste" (Vive, 128).

27. Hassoun uses Lacanian categories when he refers to the *father*. The father for Hassoun is all three functions serving at different times or in combination: the *father* might be the real father, the imaginary construct, or the symbolic function. Hassoun diverges from

Lacan in considering Lacan's "real father" not as a psychic place where language is absent. Rather, Hassoun thinks of it as the actual, biologically determined flesh and blood figure perceived by the child and, later, the man.

28. Jacques Hassoun, "Psychanalyse et antipsychiatrie. Folles histoires," in *Jacques Hassoun extraits d'une oeuvre* (Paris: l'Harmattan, 2009), 146.

29. ASPCJE published a journal, *Nahar Misraïm*, in which Hassoun published many articles. The journal ran three issues a year from 1980 to 1989 and then again from 1999, after Hassoun's death, to the present. Beginning around 1990 the organization floundered. *Nahar Misraïm* was reactivated expressly as an homage to Hassoun after his death on April 24, 1999. It was at that time too that, after a period of relative inactivity, ASPCJE resumed its function under the direction of one of its founding members, André Cohen. ASPCJE today raises money for the restoration and upkeep of the Bassatine Cemetery in Cairo and the Eliahou Hanabi Synagogue in Alexandria, to mention principal concerns. It publishes novels, essays, and memoirs about the Egyptian diaspora through its press, Editions Nahar Misraïm. It holds regular conferences with invited speakers and organizes a monthly reading and discussion group that draws speakers of importance to the Sephardic community. In addition, it collaborates and retains a strong presence among other world Jewish organizations concerned with the Jews of Egypt, in France and outside France, notably, the important organization Nébi Daniel that plays an important role in the funding efforts to restore synagogues and religious artifact in Egypt; under the leadership of Yves Fédida, it has worked tirelessly to recover the official records of the Jewish community. In addition, ASPCJE participates in the wider Jewish context in France, Israel, and abroad.

30. ASPCJE website: http://aspcje.fr/notre-association/objectifs.html.

31. Tobie Nathan, interview with Jean-Pierre Elkabbach on Bibliothèque Médicis, Public Sénat; https://www.youtube.com/watch?v=Iv6enTbzSkU.

32. Rachel Cohen's text: "Jacques, le nom, des noms n'existent plus. Tu ne supportes pas. Des stèles ne sont plus là. S'il n'y a plus de nom, c'est foutu." Rachel Cohen, "Bamia. Mémoire d'enfance, le retour en Égypte avec le cousin," in *Lettres de l'enfance et de l'adolescence* (Paris: Eres, 2002/4), 111–118.

33. See Norman Stillman, *Jews of Arab Lands in Modern Times* (Philadelphia: Jewish Publication Society, 1991); Shimon Shamir, *The Jews of Egypt: A Mediterranean Society in Modern Times* (Boulder, Colo. and London: Westview Press, 1987), and Gundrun Krämer, *The Jews in Modern Egypt 1914–1952* (Seattle: University of Washington Press, 1989). For a succinct summary on this subject, see Racheline Barda's entry, "Egypt," in the *Encyclopedia of Jews in the Islamic World* (Leiden and Boston: Brill, 2010), vol. II, 135–137.

34. Jacques Hassoun, *Le Passage des étrangers* (Paris: Austral, 1995). Further references to this work are included in the text as (PE). All translations of this work are my own.

35. Hassoun's text: "l'inquiétude n'est pas liée à l'étranger ou à l'hétérogène mais au trop-familier des cauchemars de l'enfance, au presque-familier de ceux qui sont d'autant plus inquiétants qu'ils ne sont pas tout à fait semblables, presque différents, presque semblables" (CM, 50).

36. Hassoun's text: "Et rien, rien de siècle en siècle, ne semble venir apporter la moindre modification dans ce dialogue tout entier imaginaire, spéculaire, de telle sorte que nous pouvons postuler que si l'histoire se répète, c'est constamment à l'endroit du désir d'exclure, de séparer, de rejeter . . . remède que des sociétés en crise redécouvrent périodiquement et qu'elles tentent d'appliquer à tous leurs maux" (PE, 20).

37. Hassoun's text: "Aussi pourrions-nous définir celui-ci comme un être menacé dans son existence, étonné d'exister, bardé de certitudes qui, du lieu de son ensauvagement mélancolique, ne cesse de tenter de créer de l'homogène, d'effacer le manque, de suturer le *Un* d'une série menacée dans son existence par celui qui, différent, semble menacer sa raison d'être" (PE, 42).

38. Hassoun's text: "les uns et les autres . . . se heurtent à une tradition: celle qui exige que l'*autre* soit clairement défini par ses insignes . . . pour être protégé ou exclu, mais toujours distingué" (PE, 19).

39. Hassoun's text: "Aussi suis-je tenté d'éprouver quelque méfiance à l'endroit de ce sentiment (ancien-nouveau) qui réunit sous l'enseigne de l'*appartenance*, un *faisceau* (en italien *fascio*) d'imaginaires sociaux et individuels qui tendent à venir prendre le devant de la scène sociale en lieu et place de la politique en acte (luttes syndicales, clivages de classes . . .). Ce déplacement de l'investissement du sujet au profit du groupe, de l'ethnie ou du sentiment d'appartenance, semble venir s'inscrire aujourd'hui à l'ordre du jour des *illusions* apolitiques" (my italics; PE 57).

40. Hassoun's text: "Le repli sur l'éthnie ne tente-t-il pas de figer la dimension temporelle afin de maintenir intact le mythe d'un groupe supposé pouvoir résister à toute influences extérieures? / N'est-ce pas une manière de nier la géographie et de dénier les clivages socioculturels pour la grande gloire d'un reliquat, hypostasié en lieu premier et dernier du désir? / Et enfin, le sentiment d'appartenance ne fait-il pas irruption dans la vie sociale dès lors qu'un groupe subit l'histoire comme un exil intérieur d'autant plus énigmatique qu'il est méconnu?" (PE, 61).

41. Hassoun's text: "Il n'y a plus qu'une désadaptation radicale. . . . Dès lors, ce qui fait passage ou trait d'union s'effondre, pour laisser la place à un sentiment de schize ou à une aspiration vers l'ineffable d'un impossible retour, propre à créer un sentiment vertigineux d'appartenance" (PE, 67).

42. Hassoun's text: "L'ethnicité, cet avatar grimaçant du politique, témoigne de l'éclipse du lien social et de la pensée qui le sous-tend au profit de l'imaginaire communautaire. Là où le politique s'adresse à un ensemble qui défend les intérêts de telle ou telle autre classe sociale, la pensée de l'ethnie est celle—immonde—qui crée des clivages propres à constituer des ensembles inter-classistes. Semblable en cela aux corporations . . . ces groupements artificiels mêlent les notables aux défavorisés pour la plus grande gloire du pouvoir en place qui trouve dans ce nouveau découpage de l'espace social des avantages certains" (PE, 80–81).

43. Hassoun's text: "ces funestes replis communautaires dont le côté cour expose les illusions consolatrices, tandis que le côté jardin cache tout à la fois la férocité d'une exclusion toujours susceptible de faire retour, mais aussi celle du mépris social et de *la loi de Lynch* qui, refoulés, peuvent à tout moment éclater" (italics in text; PE, 69–70).

44. Hassoun's text: "Se désappartenir comme sujet, comme citoyen, comme membre d'une classe sociale confronté aux autres classes sociales pour choisir d'adhérer à une ethnie matricielle, n'est-ce pas succomber aux charmes vénéneux d'une jouissance qui aurait pour support *la géographie pathétique* d'une nostalgie qui *fabrique* en lieu et place des espaces urbains, des lieux d'exclusion ou d'adoration?" (italics in text; PE, 70–71).

45. Hassoun's text: "Ainsi le juif d'égypte serait une fiction. . . ." Jacques Hassoun, *Histoire des Juifs du Nil* (Paris: Minerve, 1990), 11. Further references to this work are included in the text as (HJN).

46. Hassoun's text: "Il s'agit pour nous de témoigner de leur existence. Ce témoignage, nous l'avons souhaité multiple. . . . Cette diversité n'est-elle pas d'ailleurs à l'image de l'histoire égyptienne, à l'image de l'histoire de l'ensemble de ses minorités?" (HJN, 12).

47. Hassoun's text: "Aussi ce livre est-il dédié à tous ceux qui ignorent la vie passionnée de cette communauté, mais aussi aux Egyptiens—coptes et musulmans—qui seraient tentés d'oublier qu'à leurs côtés avaient vécu nombreux ceux que l'on continue à appeler les *Juifs d'Egypte*, et qui continuent à se désigner comme tels" (italics in text; HJN, 12).

48. Hassoun's text: "Il serait inepte de parler d'un Juif d'Egypte transhistorique, immuable. Les Juifs d'Egypte ont intégré, absorbé les cultures, et les invasions, les schismes et les hérésies. Ceux que *leur pays*, l'Egypte a subis. Ceux que leur communauté a connus. Ainsi le Juif d'Egypte serait une fiction, une license poétique née de la dispersion d'une minorité. Sur *sa terre natale*, ce Juif était pluriel. Pluriel dans le temps. Pluriel dans la société dans laquelle il s'inscrivait" (my italics; HJN, 10–11).

49. Hassoun's text: "Comment peut-on être étranger à celui dont on a hérité le nom? Comment peut-on être étranger à son père?" (PE, 97).

50. Hassoun's text: "Le deuil du père peut aussi passer par la destruction des images qui le concernent pour garder vivant le seul élément qu'un enfant puisse s'approprier: le nom" (PE, 121).

51. Hassoun's text: ". . . cette ombre est notre image, l'image portée de notre mère patrie, l'image de ce père-mère tutélaire et bienveillant sans lequel/laquelle nous ne saurions vivre" (PE, 122).

52. Hassoun's text: "Constitués dans l'exil de notre histoire, nous sommes devenus l'ombre de nous-même, nous nous heurtons à l'énigme d'une langue perdue, d'un patronyme aberrant, nos anciens sont muets sur ce qui nous a poussés à quitter nos enracinements passés, et nos pères ne peuvent rien nous révéler de notre histoire que nous imaginons glorieuse . . . notre sang est métissé, notre savoir sur notre histoire chancelant. Cette inquiétude est en elle-même irritante pour les autres et agaçante sinon humiliante pour nous-mêmes et nos descendants" (PE, 122). I have barely scratched the surface of this profound and beautifully written book.

53. Jacques Hassoun and Abdelkebir Khatibi, *Le Même livre* (Paris: Editions de l'éclat, 1985), 80. Further references to this work are included in the text as (ML). All translations of this work are my own.

54. Hassoun's text: "[M]a langue française—qui me fut d'abord imposée—est une langue *irrémédiable*, elle est un évenement traumatique, un bouleversement des racines. Le jour où j'ai compris qu'il convient de *transformer* l'irrémédiable, mon 'style' est devenu l'incisif d'une phrase qui doit accueillir la décomposition et l'humiliation pour témoigner au-delà du trauma" (italics in text; ML, 95).

55. Georg Garner, "Fin-de-Siècle, Paris: Actualités d'un malaise," in *Che vuoi? Revue de Psychanalyse* (Paris: l'Harmattan, 1999), No. 12, 52.

56. Hassoun's text: "l'exil commence quand la langue ou le dialecte parlés par les ancêtres sont oubliés, dédaignés, chuchotés dans la honte ou la jouissance" *L'Exil de la langue. Fragments de langue maternelle* (Paris: Payot, 1979), 65. Further references to this work are included in the text as (EL).

57. Hassoun's text: "La langue maternelle? C'est tout simplement celle qui nommée *lalangue*, incomparable et quelconque tout à la fois, nous accompagne dans les différentes manifestations de notre vie sociale ou ludique, intellectuelle ou amoureuse" (EL, 73).

58. Hassoun's text: "le sujet se trouve au confluent de deux ou trois langues, que l'une d'entre elles au moins se présente comme aussi chérie que les autres mais portant en elle la culture dominatrice ou avilie/avilissante". Jacques Hassoun, *Fragment de langue maternelle. Esquisse d'un lieu* (Paris: Payot, 1979), 25.

59. Hassoun's text: "Giulia, Marie-Sol, Léa, Amina . . . ces femmes sont à la fois sources et aboutissements de la mémoire. L'une n'existe pas sans l'autre et en elles se renouent les fils dispersés de l'histoire d'un exil. Cette mémoire d'oubli qui se joue des lieux et du temps, je la nommerai: *Alexandries. Roman.*" Jacques Hassoun, *Alexandrias. A Novel.* (Paris: Editions de la Découverte, 1985), 7. Further references to this work are included in the text as (A). All translations of this work are my own.

60. Michael Rothberg, *Multidirectional Memory. Remembering the Holocaust in the Age of Decolonization* (Stanford, Calif.: Stanford University Press, 2009). Colette Wilson, "Multidirectional Memory and Exile in Jacques Hassoun's Polyphonic Novel *Alexandrias. A Novel*," *Journal of Romance Studies* 13, no. 2 (Summer 2013): 94–115. Further references to Colette Wilson's work are included in the text as (Wilson).

61. Hassoun's text: "Un temps, je fus tenté d'aller en Israël retrouver ceux qui avaient pensé mettre fin à leur exil en y créant un enracinement qu'ils croyaient pouvoir être éternel, ou ceux qui n'avaient pu, faute de moyens, poursuivre leur périple plus loin. J'ai eu le sentiment qu'à me rendre dans ce pays je courais le risque de faire irruption dans un scénario qui n'était pas le mien, dans une case qui m'expulserait hors du jeu dans un espace qui serait le fruit d'une distorsion aux effets que j'imaginais effroyables" (A, 124).

62. Hassoun's text: "Je hais cette fatalité de tout mon être, même si jour après jour je compose avec elle au point de lui donner quelque assise idéologique. Mais grande est ma rancoeur aussi vis-à-vis de tous ceux qui n'ont pas su s'accrocher à cette terre, quel que soit le prix qu'ils auraient eu à payer pour leur persévérance" (A, 126–127).

63. Hassoun's text: "Etre dupe à ce point de ces désirs et de ces errances me semble aussi fou que de croire pouvoir reconstituer tous les méandres de son histoire et celle de ses ascendants, de vivre ses désirs jusqu'à leur faire rendre gorge, jusqu'à leur arracher le mot de la fin, et de pouvoir ensuite survivre impunément à cet exercice. Il est toujours une pièce manquante, une pièce en trop dans un puzzle, qui permet à l'exilé d'écrire pour son seul usage un traité du savoir-vivre avec lequel il ne cessera de ruser" (A, 16).

64. Hassoun's text: "Maintenant que les anciens sont sortis de la scène, peut-être pourriez-vous simplement enseigner à vos enfants notre histoire et quelques bribes de notre savoir dans les langues barbares que vous avez adoptées" (A, 66).

65. Hassoun does not capitalize the third-person pronoun *lui* as I do here. I made the decision to capitalize in order to make my explanations easier to follow.

66. Hassoun's text: "Ce groupe éclaté de personnes dont la langue, les croyances et les convictions trouvent un echo passionnel en lui" (A, 104–105).

67. Hassoun's text: "C'est ainsi qu'il y eut un temps possible de retour et de retrouvailles avec l'extrême isolement de sa nation en voie d'extinction. Cet épuisement ne s'est accompli ni dans le bruit et la fureur d'un génocide ni par une destruction brutale, guerrière, mais par une lente et interminable usure. Qui s'intéresse à un vieillard qui ne finit pas de se consumer dans une longue agonie? Ce n'est ni exaltant ni héroïque. C'est tout juste lassant, gênant, indécent. Ça n'intéresse personne" (A, 105).

CHAPTER TWO

Jacqueline Shohet Kahanoff's Egypt
A View from the Nile

> All this was Cairo. And home.
> *Jacob's Ladder*

Jacob's Ladder (1951), Jacqueline Shohet Kahanoff's novel, chronicles the life of a Jewish clan living in Egypt between the two World Wars. The novel is also about Egypt under British imperial rule and the threat it represented to Egyptian society as a whole. When on more than one occasion the young protagonist, Rachel Gaon, expresses her support for nationalist demonstrators by repeating "Egypt for the Egyptians," she speaks as an Egyptian Jew.[1] She is aware, as her father makes clear and her English governess cautions, that the expulsion of the British from Egypt spells the end of Egyptian Jewry. Nothing good for Egyptian Jews would come out of British retreat. Yet, throughout the novel, Rachel battles the British for Egypt's autonomy, for its soul. At the Passover Seder, reflecting on Pharaoh's expulsion of the Jews, she asks: "Is it wrong that I should love Egypt as my country?" (J, 238). Her mother, Alice Gaon, responds: "It happened so long ago.... People just live their own lives, in their own time, and that's quite good enough" (J, 238–239). *Jacob's Ladder* addresses head on the question of Jewish Egyptian identity. The first part of this chapter examines how Kahanoff describes the pressures of negotiating this identity under the gaze of a sinister imperialism and a budding Arab nationalism. The second part explores the concept of Levantinism throughout her work.

Jacob's Ladder is a *bildungsroman*. It is the saga of two Jewish families living in Egypt in the first half of the twentieth century. The two families, the Gaons of Baghdad and the Smadjas of Tunis, are presented in the context of an

Egypt in crisis. The British occupation has forced a traditional society to question its values. The novel explores ways of being all at once Jewish, modern, and Egyptian. The storyline follows a child, Rachel Gaon, from about five years of age into late adolescence. When the novel ends, she is nearly seventeen. Through her consciousness we are afforded a look into interwar Egypt. From her perspective we see the adult world, and we watch as decisions are made, family concerns expressed, and political events unfold. Kahanoff's literary tour de force is her creation of an omniscient narrator who is positioned so close to the child-character that we suspect her to be Rachel's adult self. Kahanoff pulls off this conceit without turning Rachel into an unrealistically precocious character and, most importantly, without diminishing the authority of the narrative voice.

In the course of the novel, Rachel learns to negotiate multiple familial, religious, and cultural loyalties. At the same time, the reader learns a great deal about Egyptian Jews and their practices at the turn of the twentieth century. We are witness to forms of British domination, the value of French language and culture, the conduct of commercial activity at that time, the intractable conflicts between generations, and the cultural differences between Mizrahi and Sephardic Jews. Like most family sagas, *Jacob's Ladder* is expansive, so I will take time here to sketch out a few characteristics that make up this world.

The novel features at least three generations and brings together two families and their extended relations. The elders are in their late eighties and nineties (Jacob, the patriarch, is one hundred years old at the end of the novel), their children are in their forties, fifties, and sixties at the beginning of the book, and their grandchildren Rachel and her younger brother Daniel are about six years apart. Kahanoff describes how the family spends its money, who cared for the children, and where they attended school. She writes about holidays and how they were celebrated. She evokes their lifestyle and describes where they live, how they dress, where they find enjoyment, what they eat, and the values they place on their experiences. She allows the reader to follow Rachel's family, Alice and David Gaon, as they rise from the middle to the upper middle class of Egyptian society, as they move to the Garden City district from downtown Cairo, and vacation away from the crowded neighborhoods in Alexandria to a villa with a tended garden farther away. Kahanoff pays close attention to Rachel and certain other characters as they develop their perspectives on life and politics. Besides being about coming of age, *Jacob's Ladder* is a novel of manners. The novel dramatizes encounters between different social and religious groups like Jews, Muslims, Christians, Irish Catholics, and the English; and between people from different walks of life within these groups. It shows how traditionalist, Europeanized, rich, middle-class, and poor Jews interacted with Muslims and Christians within shared social and economic spaces. In interwar Egypt, enthusiasm for modernity finds support particularly among the urban middle class. It is reflected in their leisure activities and their passion for commerce. Business is given considerable attention in the novel.² Both the Gaons and the Smadjas are business people; they came to Egypt to modernize and strengthen their commercial interests, or as Jacob Gaon the Baghdadi puts it, to "rekindle" his business in the East by "the trade winds from the West" (J, 6). We follow discussions of inflation, mechanization, when, what, and how much to import, the reasons behind strikes, their unusual occurrences, and ways to avoid them. There is much talk about modern retail practices as opposed to traditional practices, about the expanding market for luxury goods in Egypt and about the new class of buyers.³ We learn about Suez shares and their value over time (J, 406). In short, the novel represents a slice of life at a specific time in history, the year 1919 to around 1932. Kahanoff, like Dickens, Balzac, and Zola, is sensitive to the textures of that experience. *Jacob's Ladder* is an invaluable source of information for the reader, offering us opportunities to observe closely the material, social, and political realities that make up that world.

A "fine line in the Sand." Battle at Alexandria

In 1951, when *Jacob's Ladder* was published simultaneously in London and New York, the battle Egyptians were waging against the British was both political and cultural. It consisted for Egyptians in *un*doing the psychologically perverse work of British supremacist ideology whereby Egyptians were treated as inferiors in need of a European hand. Kahanoff's novel is engaged in this undoing and is most usefully read in this light. It is a critique of Western hegemonic culture and a full frontal attack on the British occupation of Egypt. The character who embodies British dominance in Egypt is the Gaon's British governess, Miss Nutting, who enters the family's employ when Rachel is ten years old. Rachel's project, from roughly the second part of the novel, is to force her back to England. This critique of imperialism is a dominant subject from the beginning of the novel. The patriarch Jacob Gaon is questioning his earlier assumption that in marrying East and West he was offering his family the best of both worlds. He bitterly contemplates the disaster:

> In anguish, I search among my grandsons, the few who are here, and find them strangers to me. Where I thought the new way of life would enrich us, I see my grandsons corroded with doubt and secret shame, living like beggars in a new world, when they should have so much to give. The vision which guided my life fades away, and I see it only as a vain illusion. (J, 68)

Jacob describes his son, David, as a man living "in exile, lost in a new world" (J, 68). Jacob is correct about David, Rachel's father. He lives in Egypt as in exile from his Arab roots. In Egypt, or rather in modern Egypt, he is compelled to speak French and live like a European. How can he relate to those who are closest to his heart in a language that is foreign? "A native tongue was like a home, he thought sadly, and his Semitic heart lived in exile, unable to find the fitting French expression, and because words betrayed him, Rachel must think his love betrayed her" (J, 12). David's fear of losing his child because he does not speak French is justified. Rachel, still a toddler, treats him like a "foreigner," throwing herself at her uncle Moses instead because Moses "exercised his scanty French" on Rachel and she, in recognition, clapped her hands in delight (J, 102). David explains his daughter's rejection this way: "Rachel should not be blamed if, after years in the hands of alien women, she saw her parents through the contemptuous eyes of a stranger" (J, 113). David embodies some of the most desirable qualities of any character in the novel. He is generous, successful, loving, gracious, and wise. He does not slavishly conform to European standards. He gets along with all sorts of people, enjoying conversations with modest vendors as well as prosperous businessmen. He "knows the chiefs in almost every hamlet, and speak[s] their language, even their dialects" (J, 11). This sense of ease is possible because he can communicate in Arabic. Baghdad and Egypt are not worlds apart. But the West is. It is only when Rachel catches diphtheria and nearly dies that David is able to express himself in French. He tells her their story, "the story of us," relating Jacob's departure from Baghdad to Egypt: "He spoke hesitantly, hoping that his French would not fail him, but as he went on, the immense urgency of his desire to help loosened his tongue" (J, 335). On that night, David finds "the gift of his tongue" (J, 337).[4] The story gives Rachel strength and saves her life. The novel is structured along the lines of before and after the expulsion of the governess from the Gaon's home and from Egypt. After Rachel hears the "story of us," the story of her family's roots, the ancestral heritage, she recovers the confidence to confront the British governess. The governess had used all the tools in her arsenal to destroy Rachel's self-confidence and make her feel inferior. Referring to the governess, Rachel explains to Daniel, her brother: "she thinks everything in Egypt is dirty, and must be washed in some smelly disinfectant. Soon, we'll be coming to the beach with a barrel full of lysol, and pouring it around us when we swim, or who knows, perhaps she'll want to boil the sea, to kill all the germs" (J, 355–356). The British assault on Egyptians is not only political, Kahanoff suggests. It is psychological.

The novel can be read as a thinly veiled allegory of the drama facing Egypt. The ten-year-old Rachel is given the responsibility to hire the governess and bring her to Egypt. From their first meeting, Rachel is aware that the governess is wicked. While the family is still in Saint-Tropez and before she is hired, she has the audacity to say to Rachel, even as she is accepting the position: "I may have to work for your parents' money, but my parents wouldn't have invited them to tea" (J, 257). Yet Rachel, knowing what she knows, approves Miss Nutting accompanying them to Egypt: "It made her dizzy to think of home, where the River Nile, brown, rich, and muddy, flowed past her window, and that she, of her own accord, had let the enemy into her paradise" (J, 257). Rachel's decision can be explained in psychological terms. Masochism is a feature of Gothic literature, and it is evident that Rachel is drawn to the mysterious and arrogant woman. More interestingly, I think, Rachel's decision serves as a dramatic transposition of Egypt's nefarious 1882 decision to allow Britain to take over the governance of Egypt. The battle between Rachel and the governess is fought over cultural values and self-determination. Miss Nutting applies her formidable psychological arsenal to impose herself and shape Rachel. Rachel resists her throughout and, in the end, wins the battle. Kahanoff has created a character, a Jewish girl, to represent Egypt and the Egyptian spirit. Rachel is Egypt.

The event that leads to her victory crystallizes in the episode involving a Muslim Egyptian family on the beach at Alexandria. It takes place after her father tells Rachel the "story of us" and, following his example, Rachel's mother, Alice, and her grandmother, Hnina, tell Rachel their own family stories. Now cured, Rachel plots the governess's expulsion from the shores of the Mediterranean. She mounts a "counter-crusade" against the British "invader" "during which her world invaded Miss Nutting's and utterly destroyed it" (J, 359). How Rachel defends her family and defends Egypt from the British invaders presents the colorful drama of the second half of the novel. The tide-turning action goes like this: Fifteen-year-old Rachel, along with her younger brother, Daniel, the governess, various relatives of the Smadjas branch are all at the beach. It is summer in Alexandria and the children are enjoying the freedom denied them in Cairo. Rachel has just recovered from diphtheria and has learned about her family's past, how the Gaons from Baghdad and the Smadjas from Tunis came to Egypt at the turn of the twentieth century. The family is staying in a villa but they also occupy a cabin on the beach where they spend the day. The cabin next to theirs is occupied by a family of Muslim Egyptians, a young mother and her three children. The father is "a renowned judge" (J, 363). Like David Gaon and most heads of families, the judge stays behind in Cairo occupied with work and only comes to the beach on weekends to join his family. When he does, he and David have friendly chats. Rachel's mother, Alice, is "appropriate" though "cold" toward the young family. To Rachel's distress, Alice mocks the Muslim mother behind her back. The governess, however, is horrified by their proximity to the Gaon's cabin. She treats the family with contempt, not unnoticed by the Muslim mother. The governess instructs Rachel and Daniel to pay no attention to the family and to decline any invitation to play. Rachel is fascinated by the mother and children, moved by their openness and their amiable manner and the easy way they relate to each other. But she is not totally accepting of the way they live. She finds them rough around the edges. At this point in the novel, Rachel is still trying to figure out what is acceptable and good and what is not in human behavior. For example, she absolutely hates the way the governess treats the Muslim family; her sense of superiority toward them fills Rachel with rage. And yet, paradoxically, she feels uneasy that her father is chummy with the Muslim father. She wonders about her contradictions but cannot yet explain them.

The Muslim family aspires to be modern in the European manner, just like Rachel's mother. The Muslim mother speaks French, sends her daughter Zeinab to a French school, the Sacré-Coeur, and wants to take advantage of the present company so that Zeinab can practice French with Rachel: "[S]he spoke in French, pleased to show that she also was becoming Europeanized and educated" (J, 360). Seemingly, the family had not accomplished a satisfactory transformation. The mother is dressed inappropriately for the beach. She wears "black stockings rolled down over her garters below her bouncing thighs and dimpled knees." Her son wears "striped pajamas" out in public. He pees on the beach. Rachel notes that, to the amusement of his mother, the young boy performs artful arabesques on the sand where he pees (J, 357). Then, abruptly and twice in one day, tensions erupt in this zone between the two cabins. The first incident takes place when the governess, always alert to the slightest sign of influence on the Gaon children from the Muslim family, thinks she just saw Daniel picking at his nose, a habit she observed in Zeinab. She snaps at him and startles him. He is doubly confused when she asks, not rhetorically: "Did I see you picking your nose?" When he answers her: "Did I? I didn't notice, Miss Nutting, really I didn't" (J, 361), she presses on stiffly: "That only makes matters worse." She then proceeds to take the heavy spade he was playing with and, in front of all assembled, she "brought it down two or three times across his knuckles" and sent him off with the heartless command: "Go back and play now" (J, 362). Although she had struck him before, it was clear to both Daniel and Rachel that the governess had never "struck him so viciously" (J, 362).

The tension between the two cabins intensifies. A metaphorical line in the sand is drawn between them. That line "tore Rachel apart" (J, 364–365). She is not sure who is in the right. She had asked herself in similar circumstances: "Why did she feel ashamed when she fought Miss Nutting, and ashamed when she did not?" (J, 299). Surely, she thought to herself, one can object to certain behaviors without feeling that one was betraying the whole person, the whole culture. The young Muslim mother nursing her baby in the open expressed a tenderness and a joy that spoke to Rachel: "There was a sense of abundance about the woman both sweet and violent, so powerful that it could never be harnessed by things like tidiness, decency, and good manners" (J, 358). She is appalled by the governess's galling self-confidence. The battle Rachel wages is for the dignity of the Egyptian people, Jews and Arabs alike. Her observations, like her actions when she offers flowers to the demonstrators hollering "Egypt for the Egyptians," suggest that Rachel understands culture as inherently political.

The second critical event takes place later that same day, as the Gaon children and the judge's family roam around in the zone between the two cabins. The Muslim mother, noticing that Rachel is coveting a sticky candy her kids are enjoying, offers her a piece. Rachel accepts it in full view of the governess who, as soon as she sees this, orders Rachel to throw "that filthy thing away immediately" (J, 365). When, not heeding her, Rachel "continued to nibble" on it, the governess "reached over and slapped the candy out of her hand" (J, 365). With everyone between the two cabins watching, Rachel not only picked up the candy, but dusted the sand off and bit into it, whereupon, the governess slapped her face for having blatantly disobeyed, and Rachel in turn "slapped Miss Nutting hard, across both cheeks" (J, 366). Reflecting on this while the drama is unfolding, Rachel measures the absurdity of the situation: "It seemed incredible that so much meaning could be attached to a piece of dirty sugar, that so much of what she would think of herself in the future depended on her eating it" (J, 365). Back home after the "battle on the beach," the governess acknowledges to Rachel that she has lost the battle and that she plans to leave, but not before she has let Rachel know that although she has won the battle *and because* she has won it, Rachel has, in effect, lost the war (J, 367). Miss Nutting, mounted on her high horse, offers the girl some cruel advice: "Perhaps you can't and won't understand what I am going to say. Don't waste your life chasing after dreams. Some things are lost never to be found again" (J, 367). The governess is referring to more than lost traditions. She is alluding to the fate of the Jews in Egypt after the British leave. This is a reality Rachel is not prepared to confront just yet. So, Rachel responds with: "I don't know what you mean" (J, 367).

Miss Nutting fails not because her project to modernize Rachel was entirely objectionable to the Egyptian way of life. Rather, it fails because she wanted nothing less than to expunge all trace of her Egyptian character. The governess degraded and mistreated Egyptians. As Rachel tells her: "If you had only scolded us about those sort of manners, I wouldn't have hated you . . . but you made everything that belongs to us look stupid and ugly, and then I didn't know what to do" (J, 367). Britain's exploitation of Egyptians is dramatized in an episode where an outraged David accuses the governess of criminal usury. The governess proposed that Rachel borrow money from Daniel and set an outrageous rate of return. When the story is told around the family, one of the uncles compares the terms set by the governess to Britain's egregious abuse of Egypt: "We laugh, but isn't Miss Nutting's conduct typical of Great Britain? She lends to profligate nations, and kindly charges five hundred per cent so that the naughty children may learn to manage their finances wisely. It was to secure payment of a debt that the English first set foot in Egypt. . ." (J, 285).

Throughout the novel, in the allegory Kahanoff lays out, Britain is presented as cruel, arrogant, and profiteering. Unlike the French, who at least offer an enlightened culture, the British give nothing in return.[5] In this allegory, Egypt is presented in two ways. On the one hand, the country is described as having abandoned its responsibilities to the Egyptian people and handed them over to the British (as Alice does to Rachel). On the other hand, Kahanoff presents Egypt as naïve—easily conned or simply innocent.

Hassounian Transmission . . . Egyptian Jewish Identity

After the showdown at the beach between Rachel and Miss Nutting, the governess announces her departure. Rachel has successfully expelled her from Egypt. Having realized the measure of her victory, Rachel slips out of the house and for the first time in her life goes alone to the beach without an adult. She stands on the cliff, looking at the ships on the horizon, at the shores of the Mediterranean, like "a sentinel protecting her shore and the *world behind it*. She has cast out the invader. She had won the battle . . . now she and her world were safe. She did have a world, and it couldn't change, not Rachel's world, not ever again" (my italics; J, 370). The "world behind it" is Egyptian culture, Egypt without the Europeans. When Rachel's mother calls her to come home, "Defiantly she picked up a stone, rubbed smooth by the sea, and flung it at the distant line of ships behind which the other world lay" (J, 371). This is not the end of the story but the beginning of the next stage. Rachel will be redefining both Egypt's identity and her own. She says in the same scene: "That world wasn't like Humpty-Dumpty who fell and could never be put together again" (J, 371). But Rachel is not ready just yet to put it together. First, she needs to figure out how. She thinks to herself:

> Everything would be as it was before Miss Nutting had come. No, before Nanny had come [the good Miss O'Brien, the Irish nanny]. No, before Mamma had gone away to England. No, before Rachel was born. It would be again the world Grandmother Gaon had lived in. Rachel started at the realization that she had not known that world, and *quickly pushed away the thought*. She would be exactly like her Grandmother Hattouna had been. Then Rachel thought irritably, *no*, after all, even when she was very old, she wouldn't wear a wig, or dress like an Arab, or take snuff. (My italics; J, 370–371)

We follow Rachel's consciousness as she measures and corrects her position. Something is not quite right about a return to how things were before the governess came. True to the Hassounian model of transmission, Rachel understands that she must bring up-to-date traditions and a way of life that used to be.[6] She will not wear a wig, dress like an Arab, or take snuff. But she will engage with her heritage. And it will strengthen her.

After the governess's expulsion, Rachel throws herself into the society of Egyptian girls who are her age. She wants to know how other Egyptians live. She befriends girls from the Muslim and Christian bourgeoisie. Her parents support her and give her room to explore that world. And we watch as she uneasily does that. The universe Kahanoff creates is an organic world where change is possible and desirable but not easy.

Throughout the novel, Rachel battles to assert her Egyptian identity and to integrate it with her Jewish identity. Her parents David and Alice and her grandparents on both sides were not born in Egypt. But in every respect they act in ways that suggest that Egypt is their home. The Mizrahi clan, the Gaon family, is more conservative and more attached to Jewish religious practice and to Arab Egypt than the Sephardic branch. The Smadjas are less observant, more liberal, and more receptive to European culture than are the Gaons. They speak French and enjoy lighthearted banter. This is not so on the "grave" Baghdadi side. Rachel emerges from both branches a modern iteration, a new model, who exemplifies the modern Egyptian Jew. At the end of the novel, Rachel's education is complete. The young woman who greets her guests at the Passover Seder at the end of the novel is Jewish, Egyptian, and modern. *Jacob's Ladder* is a coming-of-age novel. Transformation is its central theme and transmission its operating system, as it were. Most characters undergo a transformation. This includes the two characters, Jacob Gaon and Alice, who appeared least likely to change.

Jacob's Egypt . . . Rewriting the Biblical Canon

Jacob's Ladder opens with a vivid description of the house of Gaon. Jacob, at its head, ruled his family with a firm hand. A man of few words, grave, and autocratic, he is not inclined to express his love for his children and wife. He is portrayed as a particularly inflexible man who does not tolerate dissent. When Jacob arrived from Baghdad, the neighborhood in Cairo where he and his wife Hattouna lived was a place of mutual respect: "Moslems and Jews sent servants bearing gifts to his neighbour on religious holidays, where everyone lived by the peace handed down to him by his forebears, obeyed an ancient order and accepted the fortunes and misfortunes of life and the will of God, women still lived in the seclusion of their own quarters" (J, 4). Unlike his sons, Jacob does not wear European suits. He wears a cotton robe (a *galabeya*), and his food is served on a brass tray placed low on the floor. He eats "in biblical simplicity," tearing bread, dipping it into his bowl, and scooping out the food with it (J, 66). He speaks Arabic with a Baghdadi accent. He is in his mid-eighties at the beginning of the novel. Toward the end of the book, after he has set aside business matters to prepare for his death, Jacob reveals a depth of character and a nuanced interpretation of life that strikes those around him as uncharacteristic and radical. Did he all these years, the narrator muses, "grandly play" the part of the patriarch, certain about everything? Has Jacob changed his opinions or is he simply revealing an aspect of his personality he possessed all along? (J, 8). The fact is that Jacob *does* undergo a transformation. What is remarkable, I would point out, is that after

Rachel's illness and the subsequent expulsion of the governess, the novel itself takes a turn, changes tack, and seems stylistically to breathe more freely. It is *as if* after the expulsion of the British subject matter the novel responds by exploring new, looser, and more generous ways of relating. There are in *Jacob's Ladder* pages and pages of beautifully composed descriptions of the Nile in front of the family's Garden City apartment. Kahanoff's touch is exquisite. Like the paintings of Mahmoud Saïd of feluccas on the Nile, they are *not*, as some might be tempted to say, pastiche postcard-like evocations of an exotic Egypt and its Nile intended for tourists. While it is certain that all descriptions are a priori intertextual, Kahanoff's scenes of the Nile unfolding before the readers' eyes, both at close range and from afar, are animated by a sensibility informed by direct experience, by intimate knowledge of the places they evoke. These tableaux are reflections of Kahanoff's wistful remembrance of common-enough actual scenes of the Egypt of her time. They express Rachel's rootedness to Egypt and, by the same token, Judaism's roots in Egypt. Like the Egyptian territorial nationalist movement I discussed in the introductory chapter, Kahanoff looks to the history of Egypt and to its geography to define Jewish Egyptian identity.

I am focusing here on the changes Jacob, Alice, and Rachel undergo. But changes occur in other characters as well. Donia, the Christian servant, runs away with Hassan and takes her daughter Angèle from the Gaon family; Hnina Smadja blossoms in front of Rachel's eyes, and the reader's, as she reveals her lineage; Samuel Gaon reconsiders his approach to Europeanization. Looking at Jacob, it is unquestionable that his portrayal suggests that for Kahanoff change is important and necessary. He is now tolerant of change and lives in the present without losing sight of the past:

> He spent a good deal of time on the balcony, dozing in the fine winter sunshine, while Rachel wondered what might be his thoughts as he faced the Pyramids and the Nile. Was he not Jacob, who had brought Israel back to the land of Egypt, where it grew in numbers and in wealth? And did he hope that this time the story would have a happier ending? (J, 419)

With the governess out of the picture, Rachel is free to look at Egypt through Jacob's eyes. This scene is particularly important because it evokes both the present, the pleasures of the here-and-now, as well as the Egyptian ancestral past. Egypt is incontrovertibly her home and the home of her ancestors. Unlike the biblical Jacob, Jacob Gaon leaves Jerusalem where he had traveled to die and returns to Egypt.[7] He revises the biblical narrative, bringing it up to date. Upon his return from Jerusalem to Egypt, he seems rejuvenated, happier, more philosophical, and more open with his family. The once rigid patriarch goes so far as to give David and Alice a progressive Hassounian lesson. When Rachel's parents express concern about her difficulties adapting to an Egypt without the governess, Jacob tells them that Rachel "must be free to accomplish her own destiny" and to "find her own truth" (J, 421). It is the same kind of answer he gives David about Daniel, the young boy who with his fair complexion and artistic temperament seems least like a Gaon. In his advice about Daniel, we measure the distance Jacob has indeed traveled. He seems perfectly at peace with the idea that family, like country and religion, are not immutable; the past must keep up with the present. Jacob's answer to David and Alice's concerns about Daniel suggest that he now privileges looser ways of relating to others, including family members. He says: "Daniel is the seed the wind scatters far away. But if the seed bears fruit, does it matter in which man's garden?" (J, 422).

True to his new tenet, Jacob trusts Rachel to carry the Gaons into the future. Fittingly, on the last Passover with her grandfather, Rachel is now about seventeen years old, and she takes over the responsibility of the Seder preparations. Interestingly, the person who instructs her is not Alice—her mother is ignorant of the tradition. It is Jacob's Muslim servant, Ahmed, who does. At first Ahmed refuses. But he too adjusts his perspective and recognizes in Rachel the new face of the Gaons and with that, perhaps, the new face of Egypt. In these last pages of the novel, as Rachel opens the door for her guests, she looks not "elegant but dignified." Change does not represent a break with the past. On the contrary, Kahanoff, like Hassoun, insists that change is necessary to preserve the past. Looking at her guests assembled around the table, Rachel notes the continuity from generation to generation.

> She saw them all as they were, but also *as in a vision*, possessed by the strange sensation that the scene before her eyes was a repetition of something that had happened in the same manner, with the same people, long, long ago, in a place she knew well, though she could not recapture its name.
>
> This was the Seder, that had always been and always would be, the indestructible family, assembled round a table to give thanks for its survival, for its daily bread, for life itself. (My italics; J, 426)

Rachel alludes to the *indestructibility* of the union between Judaism and Egypt. She sees her family around the table "as they were, but also as in a vision," sensing that the scene before her eyes had happened "in the same manner, with the same people," a long time ago, "in a place she knew well" (J, 426). Rachel achieves this moment of high "dignity" and solidarity with her Egyptian ancestors precisely because, like her ancestors before her, she knows how to move the past forward. By making the past thrive in her own time, Rachel succeeds in asserting the fact that she is irrefutably *of* Egypt. She is Jewish because she is Egyptian and she is Egyptian because she is Jewish, to reframe a line Hassoun gave in an interview.[8] Rachel's attachment to the past, to traditions, and her fascination with the history of her people in Egypt are the same interests and activities that nurture transmission in Hassounian terms. But they also reflect a contemporary fascination with historiography.[9]

Understanding Alice

Middle-class Jewish mothers in interwar urban Egypt were responsible for raising the social status of their family. It was their responsibility to ensure that their children grew up to be successful men and women capable of sustaining a middle-class lifestyle. Mothers were also the guardians of sociability. European-style sociability, manners, dress, and language-use distinguished the cultivated upwardly mobile modern Egyptians from Egyptians who, like the *Hara* Jews reviled by Alice, were perceived as "backward." Behavior and appearance were keenly monitored. Mothers, with governesses and nannies in their employ, policed them. A mother's principal role was to advance the family educationally and socially; the father's was to advance its economic well-being. In a society that prized advancement, where progress was rapid, and where so many seemed headed for a higher position on the ladder to success, the status quo could only mean decline.

Kahanoff's naturalistic portrait of Alice as she evolves from the daughter of Tunisian immigrants to a well-to-do wife and mother reflects the lives of many women of Alice's socioeconomic background. These women understood what was at stake and behaved accordingly. They aspired to join in what they considered, and many people around the world at that time agreed with them, to be a change for the better. Their championing of modernity was not an expression of abject subservience to European culture. These women were confident that they were participating in a progressive and lasting movement. This new age declared itself in the Egyptian press, in its Constitution, and in popular forms of entertainment such as cinema, theater, and café and music culture. Modernity gave Egyptians, and particularly Egyptian women, a sense of optimism. This perspective was not unique to Jews in Egypt; the Muslim woman on the beach in Alexandria has the same mind-set. To understand Alice, and the many women like her that she stands for, it is important to examine their lives in the context of Egypt's modernization project. As far as Jewish women were concerned, women like Alice were enlisted, directly or indirectly, to mediate the cultural "regeneration" of Egyptian Jewry. This project was defined and promoted by the Alliance Israëlite Universelle (AIU) in the nineteenth century. By the first part of the twentieth century, it had not only gained acceptance in the Jewish community; it was an applied doctrine. Its ideology was perceived as progressive at a time when, as I suggested above, throughout most of the world progress was deemed desirable, inevitable, *and* European. Many of these women were educated in the schools of the Alliance or, later, in the Lycée Français network. As Aron Rodrigue explains:

> Since the *Alliance* sought to spread its message across the full spectrum of the Jewish population, it was deeply concerned about the status of women and attached a great importance to the education of girls. . . . The education imbibed in these schools opened many vistas for Jewish women and sometimes led not only to individual social mobility but to the transformation of their status.[10]

The experience of women and, eventually, of the mothers of the AIU gave these women and their families confidence that they were doing the right things for their families. Paméla Dorn Sezgin writes that the role of women changed "almost overnight." They became European culture bearers, transforming them "into agents of change."[11] Rodrigue points out that "it is undeniably true that the educational programs in the *AIU* schools heightened awareness of the newer versions of Jewish existence . . . obtained in Europe, and thus led students to *reevaluate* their place and belief-system in their own communities" (my italics; Rodrigue, 176). The Alliance's influence was significant. It was, perhaps, even the sole factor in the reevaluation of what it meant to be both Jewish *and* modern. The majority of women and their families did not adopt radical, all-or-nothing positions, with respect to Western ideas. Rather, as Rodrigue suggests, and as we see in the case of Alice: "Most adapted the new to the old, creating a fluid and flexible traditionalism" (Rodrigue, 179). Dario Miccoli points out that Pierre Deschamps, founder of the Mission Laïque Française, aimed at: "perfecting the *indigènes* by harmonising the two cultures and respecting the indigenous one through a deep understanding of French culture" (italics in text).[12] In this period of rapid social change, women like Alice brought to the domestic arena a way of thinking and a way of life they learned about in these schools. This meant mainly the need to use French, to hold high regard for Enlightenment values, and to adhere to the belief that French culture was exceptional. It bears saying here, as Rodrigue argues, that as Jews imbued with the history of expulsion from Spain, Egyptian Jews, both women and men, understood that their success in the Ottoman world was attributable *not only* to their knowledge of Muslim rule but, also, to their connection to Europe. Jewish women in Egypt, be they Sephardic, Mizrahi, or, as was often the case, a fusion of both, knew that change (progress) did not mean the relinquishing of one's own worldview and traditions. It meant taking from both to create individuals able to, as Alice says, "live their own lives, in their own time" (J, 239). They did not simply accept what they were told.[13] Sezgin suggests that the educational program of the Alliance Israëlite Universelle was designed to "remake students into modern citizens of the countries in which they lived with a decidedly pro-European and 'rational' outlook" (Sezgin, 226). In the process, Sezgin observes, the AIU created Jews who were decidedly ambivalent about their character. This is true. Kahanoff is attentive to this ambivalence and illustrates it in sharp detail throughout the novel. Rachel, Alice, David, and even Jacob are ambivalent about their culture. But Kahanoff also shows them working out these issues. That's what people do. In his discussion of André Nahum, Ammiel Alcalay points to the fact that the position of "in-betweeness" expressed in Nahum's work "was often turned into a positive attribute by women writers such as Jacqueline Kahanoff and Andrée Chedid."[14] In-betweeness *is* a position and a legitimate space in the imaginary of people. Feelings of ambivalence are not unique to "colonized" societies. Admittedly, Kahanoff suggests, the Egyptian Jewish imaginary leaned on a Europeanized narrative of modernity and progress. But she also shows that it is equally true that the Egyptian Jewish imaginary was constructed less on the idea of reproducing Europe on the southern shores of the Mediterranean than on creating a new variety of culture made of both East and West. Rachel and Jacob's Egypt is a new iteration informed by an enlightened, imaginative, and critical Levantinism. It is something to keep in mind that in its bylaws, AIU directives stipulated that its role was to educate, build character, and eradicate "bad habits." It did not foster denigration of country. Frances Malino rightly points out that Alliance teachers and their students were spurred to "love country" and work toward the common good: "With these 'virtues,' the Alliance believed, less fortunate coreligionists would be better prepared for citizenship in their own countries."[15] It was part of the curriculum that, among other subjects, students learned about "local and universal history" (Malino, 58).

It is easy at first blush to dislike Alice. She seems overly invested in appearances and manners. And the anxiety she manifests in her desire to be appropriately modern and to seem European is discomfiting. Tortured by the imperative to raise her children correctly, and believing European culture to be superior to Egyptian culture, she puts enormous effort into Europeanizing her family. She is sincerely befuddled that the advice given to her by Miss O'Brien, the Irish nanny she employed before Miss Nutting, is the same as the advice her parents give her. And she is surprised, not to say disturbed, that O'Brien likes Tunisian food and enjoys the company of her parents (J, 171). Alice believes the values and manners she learned at school and in books are valuable, worth passing on to her family. She tells the governess: "I want my children to have fine manners, to be Europeans, at home in any society. *I can't do that for them*, but you can do it for me, better than anyone else" (my italics; J, 281). Alice reads a lot and takes book discussions seriously. But the strength of Kahanoff's portrayal of her is to show her as a complex person, a thinking and feeling character, involved in an ongoing process of discovery and adjustment.

Alice is exemplary of AIU education. She is open-minded and values progress and reason. She is a secularist indifferent to religion and averse to superstition. One of her solid attributes is, in fact, her lack of dogmatism. In that, Kahanoff attributes to her a characteristic of Levantine identity. Her husband pleads with her to put a blue stone on Daniel to ward off the evil eye. And although she does not believe in its power, she agrees. She is horrified, as is Rachel, when the rabbi who is called to Rachel's sickbed wishes to offer a sacrifice of a chicken over her head according to a Jewish tradition. Yet she allows this to take place and pleads with Rachel to allow it. It is noteworthy that, notwithstanding her fear of "appearing" Arab, Alice seems to place more importance on hygiene than she does on racial, ethnic, and religious differences. She hires an Arab wet-nurse for Rachel and refuses to hire one for Daniel only after she discovers Arab wet-nurses drink "helba," a drink that leaves an unpleasant odor behind. She adamantly refuses even to consider a Jewish woman from the *Hara*, saying they are poor and dirty (J, 177–178). Instead, she hires Amina, a poor but "dignified" dark "Syrian Christian . . . clean, strong, healthy, honest" (J, 180). Alice is intelligent, assertive, and loving. She takes care not to offend and humiliate those who do not share her views. She admires European culture and is trying to get a job done, as she tells the governess. At the beach, she mocks the candy man's French poem and his accent. But she is careful not to do this within earshot of the man. She explains to Rachel that she is not mocking him but is only finding him amusing. She looks down on the Muslim mother at the beach but tries not to show her feelings in public. To be clear, I am *not* arguing that Alice's indirectness excuses her for harboring unpleasant views of people and for thinking Arab culture is backward. But I am suggesting that, true to her Levantine character, she is not dogmatic and, as I argue later in my discussion of Levantinism, Alice makes sure to separate her private thoughts from public display. True, she is not like her husband who harbors no classist feelings and befriends the Muslim family and all sorts of people, peddlers and businessman alike. But neither does she follow the governess blindly. I think it useful to point out that throughout the novel Alice keeps her distance from the governess. She also stands up for her principles. Alice knows who she is. She and the governess exchange books and have discussions about serious matters. But this interaction is a two-way street. A closer examination of the conversations between them, on books and other topics, reveals that Alice is neither obsequious nor pandering. Far from it. She stands up for her principles when the governess reproves her for showing too much familiarity toward Amina. When she asks Amina to join the family for dinner, the governess bluntly objects, saying to her mistress: "I'm sorry to disappoint you, Mrs. Gaon, I've never yet been asked to sit at a table with a native wet-nurse, and see no reason to start now" (J, 263). Alice does not accept this. She blushes but answers forthrightly: "'Amina is a friend of the family on a visit, she'll eat in the dining-room with us.' She turned to the woman, much embarrassed, and said in Arabic: 'Come, Amina, you'll feed the boy [Amina's son], then have lunch with my husband and me'" (J, 263–264). Alice's anxieties stem from a desire to spare her children the kind of difficult life she led. European culture appeals to her. It does not change who she is but *how* she lives. She is a woman who is discovering as she goes along what she wants and what she does not.

When the reader first encounters Alice, she is standing beside her husband at his parents' home in Abassieh, an old district of Cairo. Her father-in-law Jacob sees her as he would a stranger. And she herself feels like a stranger among the Gaons. Jacob thinks to himself: "Standing beside her husband, she appeared squat, *unfinished*, but this was as it should be, the old man thought, because of all his sons, David most needed a sturdy wife" (my italics; J, 3). Kahanoff presents Alice to the reader as such, unfinished, a work in progress, as it were. The child of immigrants to Egypt from Tunisia, Alice was, and remains, the sole person on whom Nathan, her father, relies. When they are side-by-side, he seems the child and she the adult. Nathan is incapable of making any decision without her. She has never let him and the rest of the family down. On the contrary, she has ably and consistently shouldered her parents' and siblings' problems in this new country. There is an episode occasioned by Alice taking a trip to England on business with David where Nathan expresses his concern about living without her. He recounts, tears in his eyes, and in the eyes of the family assembled, just how important Alice has been and is for the family:

> "Our first year in Egypt, when business was bad, and Hnina [Alice's mother] gave birth to Sandra, and nearly died, wasn't it Alice who helped little mother take care of them? And who did the cooking, the mending, the ironing, to save us the wages of a maid? And who read the business letters for us, and explained them? Wasn't it Alice?" ... Nathan swept on, tears rolling down his eyes. "And you children, didn't Alice wash and dress you, and get you ready for school every morning, and help you with your homework?" ... "Stop, Papa, please," Alice said weakly, much shaken to be reminded of all she had shared with her father.
> And still Nathan went on, "Alice, my girl, didn't she always come back from school the first in her class? I'd find her doing her homework after midnight, bent over her books, with a candle burning to save electricity, and she was up again at six every morning! Oh, Alice, my darling, to see you go tears my heart! Part of it is always with you. I don't know what I'll do without you if we have any troubles while you're away."
> Alice flung herself into her father's arms, crying in her turn, "Oh, Papa, my Papa, this is so hard!" while he stroked her brown hair. (J, 34–35)

The Smadjas are "incorrigible sentimentalists" (J, 47) and *Jacob's Ladder* is a sentimental novel. In this immigrant family, as in most immigrant families, parents and younger siblings depend on the eldest or more dependable daughter, and Alice has always come through. They continue to rely on her long after the initial need has passed. Alice is generous. She is also sensitive and aware of the fine line she must keep between doing too much for them, and thereby taking time away from her husband, and not doing as much as she could. When soliciting David's financial help to assist them, she is careful not to take advantage of his unquestioning generosity and devotion. Helping her parents is a delicate affair that she manages wisely, thoughtfully anticipating their needs. When she moves to posh Garden City, she arranges for her family to move next to her. She is intelligent, strong, and resourceful. She is far from being the proverbial pampered woman of the fictions she reads. A Smadja and a Sepharade, Alice is light-hearted. She considers her Mizrahi in-laws too serious. Rachel, it turns out, takes from both worlds: "Alice could see in Rachel that ancient strength of women, a quality Ajila (the Tunisian) and Hattouna (the Baghdadi) had equally possessed" (J, 424).

Jacob's Ladder . . . A Matrilineal Society

A feminist, Kahanoff portrays both Mizrahi and Sephardic women in *Jacob's Ladder* as strong and independent. But she also attributes strength to others. From the servants to the women who run the homes, women are shown to be responsible, able, and forward-looking. Kahanoff recalls the restrictive conditions under which older women like Hattouna Gaon lived in Baghdadi society and shows Alice to be a respectful daughter-in-law who sincerely admires her traditional Mizrahi mother-in-law. Hattouna is the foundation on which Rachel models herself, a solid starting point and a springboard. The Smadja's side is also endowed with strong women, including Mamma Zeiza, Ajila, and Hnina. Rachel's grandmother, Hnina Smadja, Alice's mother, credits her own father, a learned man, a Dante scholar, and a loving father for making certain that she learned to read and write (J, 344). And because he did, Hnina tells Rachel, she always held her head high. Rachel learns from Hnina about her impressive great-grandmother, Mamma Zeiza, a Tunsi, who spoke only Arabic. Hnina is eager to introduce her granddaughter to her Tunisian side of the family and to instruct her about class divisions among Tunisian Jews and their contact with modernity: "I must tell you," she says:

> In Tunis, there are three kinds of Jews, the *Tunsis*, who are the natives, the *Granas*, who came from Spain a long time ago, and the *Ghornayim*, the most refined and wealthy, who were treated as Europeans, not as natives. They looked down upon the *Tunsis*, although they do it less to-day, now that everyone gets a French education. (J, 344)

Mamma Zeiza, Rachel's Tunsi great-grandmother learned to speak French, albeit a broken French, from her children who learned it in school. At the age of sixty, Mamma Zeiza had insisted that one of her grandchildren in Tunis teach her to sound out the alphabet and to write. She cannot read but she can write. "Her letters are funny, she writes as she speaks—very Tunisian," Hnina points out (J, 347). Her language is "a mixture of French and Tunisian words running together, obeying only one rule, that of Mamma Zeiza's pronunciation." Rachel is "astounded that the old woman could express so much with so little at her disposal" (J, 345–346). This was how, observes Hnina, she was able to write letters to her family, keeping them close to each other and to her. Rachel understands that, in the end, and "by the sheer power of her will and pen, old Mamma Zeiza had made them all, including Rachel, out of her own substance" (J, 348).

The lesson Rachel draws from the women in her family is that one should live one's life to its fullest potential. This means, above all else, having the prescience, willingness, and strength to transgress, adapt, and coerce tradition into making needed changes. She also learns, and here we hear the voice of Kahanoff alluding to her own writerly project, that writing keeps families together. It should not escape our attention that in telling the story of Mamma Zeiza, Kahanoff is reflecting on her own role as the writer of this family saga. Writing about a Jewish Egyptian family at the turn of the century means reaching out across time to others, ancestors and descendants alike. Kahanoff suggests in "A Letter from Mama Camouna" that these stories reveal to us that families are bound together by their history, and that history does not change all that much. She writes: "It's always the same caravan crossing and recrossing. Perhaps memories are like water in a well, that well Rachel uncovered for Jacob when he came to his Uncle Laban. Perhaps that is when it all started, and since then it is only the means of transportation that have really changed."[16]

As Hassoun has argued, children of immigrants who are reluctant, as Alice was, to face their history end up hurting themselves. In her ardent desire to spare Rachel and Daniel the kind of life she lived, Alice was at the same time liquidating her own past and theirs. David's telling of the "story of us" is not only Rachel's cure; it is also Alice's. Both mother and daughter acknowledge their histories and are better equipped to face life. From that point in the narrative, instead of rejecting her immigrant past, Alice faces it. Before she tells Rachel her version of the "story of us," she explains to Rachel why she was reluctant to share it with her. Exposing her vulnerability, Alice says: "Rachel, you know how much I've always wanted you and Daniel to be the finest of children in the world . . . but I was always a little afraid that you wouldn't be interested in my life, and might even stop loving me. It's good to share them with you. Now I feel you are my closest friend, Caline, *benti*" (J, 343). This is the first time, Rachel had "heard the word *benti* [Arabic for 'my daughter'] cross her mother's lips" (J, 343). Alice then tells Rachel her story. In the process, Alice realizes just how salutary that is: "She felt something released in her as all the memories of her own childhood, so carefully locked away, flooded over her in a great rush, giving her back not the feeling of cramped, over-burdened days, but a sense of pride and richness in a duty well-performed" (J, 342). Rachel becomes aware that the hardships her mother suffered during her childhood were the reason "why her mother had entrusted her and Daniel to a governess, and attached such importance to having one. She lost her resentment, and felt a protective tenderness for her mother" (J, 343). It is striking that the Alice we see at this point in the novel is a *child* Alice to her *adult* daughter. The child–parent relationship between Alice and Rachel echoes Alice's relationship with her father, which I described earlier. As a result of David's cure, Alice is able to free herself and be the child she was not given the opportunity to be. In the last scene of the novel, mentioned earlier, we have a dramatic representation of Rachel's own apotheosis. Kahanoff describes Rachel as she opens the door of the Gaons' residence to receive her guests for the Passover Seder. She receives them together with her mother. Standing to receive them, Rachel seems to unfold in front of all as the future matriarch, combining the strengths of the Smadjas and the Gaons, both her Sephardic and Mizrahi heritage, in a new iteration.

Levantinism

For a Levantine society to function more or less well, and it is always a "more or less" proposition, Jacqueline Kahanoff suggests that it must be clear in that society that "personal pasts," "specific identities," and "particularistic" identities are protected.[17] In both fact and perception, private life and communal attachments must be made secure. Levantinism is a concept, a politics, and an aesthetics.[18] It provides an opportunity for relational networking where confrontation has been structurally neutralized to create the conditions necessary for members of a diverse society to live together. Practically speaking, it is an arrangement, more often implicit than not, between diverse people who live and work together. Kahanoff suggests in *Jacob's Ladder* that for Levantinism to work, given that differences will always exist and that they *are* desirable, two conditions must be met. Levantinism proceeds from the premise that in mixed societies significant differences exist between people; if these differences are not taken out of circulation, so to speak, they inevitably compete with one another and violence ensues. The first condition, therefore, is to recognize differences among groups without attempting to modify, exclude, or erase them through assimilation. The second condition is that the integrity of the group, its values and its imaginary, must be allowed to develop as it deems fit in the privacy of its communal networks and institutions. Levantine organizations are secured by the strict separation of private and public realms.

In an essay entitled "Afterword: From East the Sun" (1968), published for the first time by Starr and Somekh, Kahanoff suggests that "deep-rooted habits," personal histories, must be allowed to exist if nations aspire to create solidarity among people. She criticizes the hegemonic culture of Zionism. And in "Israel: Ambivalent Levantine," she opines that "Israel 'wins' if it becomes the model of a well-integrated Levantine country, which refuses neither side its inheritance in creating its own values."¹⁹ Tobie Nathan echoes Kahanoff's view and expands on it. Without using the term *Levantine*, he describes how it worked in Egypt:

> At that time, Egypt was a multi-cultural country. There were many communities.... There was the Jewish community, of course.... These were communities! Communities that lived together.... That is, they lived together without mixing. They knew one another. They knew one another in their difference. From time to time, they would mix. That was always a spectacle. And when they did mix it was a huge thing. It was grand—these were *events*! The world today wants to believe that in order to be together we have to be alike. That's a mistake. People who believe that are wrong. *To be together, we have to be different.* We must be different from each other. The world I am describing here, Egypt knew it, lived it. (My italics; my translation and transcription)²⁰

Kahanoff insists in "Afterword," that the Levant needs to be modernized "while remaining respectful of its diversity" (AES, 254). The result, she proposes in the same essay, is that "together we may form an association of modern people, attached to their own respective pasts but not enslaved by them. *The past can be reinterpreted* in order to bring people together in a more modern, livable, workable, bearable framework" (my italics; AES, 258). The past in the eyes of Kahanoff and Hassoun is a source of vitality and not mere fodder for nostalgia. As she illustrates in *Jacob's Ladder* and as Hassoun has argued throughout his work, the past is the necessary foundation for new, reinterpreted, successful beginnings. For Kahanoff, Hassoun, and Nathan, it would be disastrous for individuals and groups to relinquish "deep-rooted habits" in the service of a hegemonic ideology. Histories cannot be silenced nor roots destroyed. In a world as vastly interconnected as the one we live in, Nathan argues, immigrant populations are only an Internet address, phone call, or flight away from their native country—from any country. Personal histories and languages will not disappear and cultures will not be monolithic. Like agglutinative languages, Nathan asserts, we will see strings of cultures, cultures attached to each other with slight or no modification, with no concern as to what is dominant or minor (Nathan).

In a remarkable passage in *Jacob's Ladder*, Kahanoff describes how a dynamic Levantine city appears. The scene in the novel takes place during a year "when all calendars miraculously converged, giving Moslems, Jews, Catholics, and Greek Orthodox their sacred festivals at nearly the same time" (J, 235). The narrator describes the streets of Cairo animated by the movement of people, each belonging to a different social and religious group. Kahanoff evokes colorfully dressed crowds, with men, women, boys, and girls dressed in both modern and traditional clothes. She follows the movement of vehicles, carts, donkeys, and European cars as they make their way in encumbered streets. She describes the market stalls and fancy storefronts overflowing with merchandise. All the while, she takes care to draw the reader's attention to the divisions that delimit the public and private: "Rachel felt she could burst from the wonder which flowed through her city. In mosque, church, synagogue and home, *each lived his own religious passion*, but in the streets, people lived in a common frenzy, by which Egypt welded their diversity into a unity peculiar to itself" (my italics; J, 235). In interwar Egypt, it was not uncommon for events to bring people of different religions and social milieus together. People worked alongside each other and celebrated in the streets together.[21] Teachers complained there were not enough days to cover the curriculum because "there were so many Feast Days, Moslem, Christian, Jewish, without counting special ones, like Boxing Day, and when the King opened Parliament, and when the Sacred Carpet arrived from Mecca and was taken in procession to the mosque of El-Riffai, all blue and gold" (J, 227–228). It is not only where religion is concerned that the private and public are kept apart. The huge wedding reception of the Gaons and the Padovas, in chapter 8 of the novel, is a brilliant dramatization of this environment. The guests in attendance are as diverse as Cairo itself. Besides Sephardic, Mizrahi, and Ashkenazi Jews, there are Muslims, Christians, and Copts. There are traditionally dressed Egyptians, Egyptians dressed in European attire, and European people. One finds rich people, middle-class guests, and less well-to-do others. Conspicuously, guests keep to their own groups and do not mingle. Rather, it is the host, Samuel Gaon, who circulates among them. He goes from group to group, welcoming each and introducing members of his family to them. These diverse groups could be identified by the separate rooms they occupy, by their manners and the language they speak—Arabic, French, English. In this Levantine Egypt, to manage differences, to avoid being overwhelmed by the variety of discourses and approaches, and to sustain sociability the public and private realms are kept distinct. Attempts to mix public and private, outsiders and insiders, represent a challenge and a risk. In the words of Nathan, mixing is bound to result in "high drama" ("Et c'était toujours un drame.") (Nathan).

In a Levantine society where differences abound, personal histories need to be robust. Levantine societies are not immune to confrontation and to the risk of assimilation and dissolution. Each community must therefore strengthen its roots, probe the depths, and preserve its history. For a Levantine society to work, individuals must be armed with their history and with self-confidence, necessary ingredients to keep grounded and make one be true to one's heritage. Depth, roots, and cores are dominant images in Kahanoff's work. There is something of the same appeal to roots in Edmond Jabès's aphorisms, in his notion of the book, and in his experience of the desert. There is also this same fascination in Tobie Nathan. In Nathan's novel *Ce pays qui te ressemble*, for example, an extraordinary force and source of vitality, an ancestral core ("noyau"), exercises its influence over events and the course of life.[22] Kahanoff writes in "Afterwords: From East the Sun" that roots are proof of identity: "The Jewish people are native here [in Israel] no matter how long they were absent before returning; their roots are here" (AES, 245). Roots that are hidden deeply may not be visible to others. Yet they connect with others in the same network and make themselves felt by them. For example, in "A Letter from Mama Camouna," Kahanoff's cousin Amy comes to visit with her family from Manchester, England. At first, the two cousins are distant, but then the narrator points out: "It was fascinating, this extraordinary resemblance we came to discover, not so much in looks but rather as something very deep in our natures, which made us react exactly the same way and share the same likes and dislikes" (L, 29). There is in Kahanoff's fiction a tendency to sense affinities between people. Rootedness, for Kahanoff, is critical in the economy of the Levantine subject. Tamra, the eponymous character of Kahanoff's unfinished novel, clings to Egypt and thinks of it in terms of rootedness. Myth, history, blood, and culture are organically tied together and are deeply embedded in the ancestral land of Egypt, not merely in its soil. Her roots, says Tamra, "unlike those of the fellahin who were molded from the very loam of the Nile, ran *invisibly* below the surface, far, *deep*" (my italics; T, 79). In the imaginary of Kahanoff, and in the imaginaries of other Egyptian Jewish writers such as Jabès, Hassoun, and Nathan, rootedness in Egyptian soil imposes itself with the power of a fact. Kahanoff calls roots "the memory of oneness."[23] This affirmation, the "memory of oneness," is a memory that depends on the knowledge, and the feeling, that individuals share with their community a core identity that binds them together, as by the roots. Kahanoffian Levantinism rests on this affirmation. Is there an ideal Levantinism, a fantasy of its most dazzling incarnation? Kahanoff suggests there is. One day "the old deep-rooted habits" will surface and "without extinguishing the old religious and communal" identities, they will forge new ones (AL, 211). Ideally and hopefully, she seems to say, "core memory," personal histories, and intense particularities will come out into the open while still preserving their distinct character. To build on the metaphor, there are root systems that exist on the surface of plants, and some of them create new plants. Kahanoff puts a fine point on this metaphor in "To Live and Die a Copt" (1973), when she states that Egypt's problems stem from a failure to establish "a culture that was both deep-rooted and at the same time open to the world."[24]

The episode of the pilgrimage to Matariah in *Jacob's Ladder* offers a view of how an inspired Levantine society might appear. It is a powerful example of Levantine aesthetics. Not surprisingly, for the feminist Kahanoff this society is represented by women. At Matariah, east of the Nile outside of Cairo, near Heliopolis, the narrator tells of a pilgrimage made uniquely by women to the tree where Mary, Joseph, and Baby Jesus were said to have stopped on their flight to Egypt. To reach the spot, women made the journey "through the green valley," in carts, cars, and donkeys. The landscape evoked is maternal and fertile: the dirt road skirts the Nile, passes by small "villages huddled under their shade, as in the arms of a mother, with naked children playing, women pounding grain in stone mortars. . . . All around were cotton fields, with pods just breaking to show their white wealth" (J, 329–330). At the tree, women gathered to pray, each in her own tongue, for the fulfillment of her wish. This "ancient rite" is not observed uniquely by Christians. It is celebrated by all faiths and all classes of women. Matariah is a place of joy, prayer, and sisterhood. Personal histories, private lives, are so very near the surface. But the line is not breached. Women inquire about each other using broad generalities to wish each other good luck: "Clusters of women surrounded the tree, most of them Moslems and Copts, but also those of all Egypt's religious sects, and they smiled as they told each other: 'My sister, may your heart's desire be fulfilled'" (J, 330). Kahanoff suggests that whether it is between groups or between members of the same group, people from different ethnic, religious, and economic groups can and do connect honestly and sincerely. The women at Matariah engage in a fulfilling common Levantine experience.

Fragile and susceptible to the threat of hegemonic pressures, Levantine societies are most stable when they have safeguards to minimize confrontation. I suggest that in both fiction and essay Kahanoff locates this safety zone in what she refers to as *manners* in the sense of a code of responsible social behavior. Manners are principles of civil behavior designed to make those we address feel at ease and safe. They are a form of hospitality, we also see in Edmond Jabès. Manners are managed by rules designed to avoid even the appearance of confrontation. Manners provide an approach to others in their difference. They are a form of sociability and a poetics based on the conviction that coexistence depends on a code of behavior intended to police and neutralize encounters. Kahanoffian Levantinism, I suggest, is a form of sociability, a relational aesthetics, and a codified social practice for managing overt differences. It relies for its success on elevating the status of manners to a moral philosophy.

Kahanoff writes in "Afterword: From East the Sun" that "because of its diversity, the Levant has been compared to a mosaic—bits of stone of different colors assembled into a flat picture. To me it is more like a prism whose various facets are joined by the sharp edge of differences, but each of which, according to its position in a time–space continuum, reflects or *refracts* light" (my italics; AES, 247). Both reflection and refraction suggest that an image is sent *away from* the source image; reflection and refraction do not allow light to penetrate. They keep to the surface. Quite apart from her representation and celebration of Levantine sociability, as I described it above in the episodes of Matariah, the Gaon wedding, and the streets of Cairo celebrating the convergence of calendars, the word Levantinism itself appears in *Jacob's Ladder*. In that novel, written almost two decades earlier than this remarkable essay, it carries a negative charge. It suggests danger and shadiness. But we also detect in the novel a suggestion that Kahanoff is examining the conventional view of Levantinism, identifying its parts, thinking about what is missing from it, what is wrong about it, and perhaps, also, what is needed to make Levantinism a workable option. She uses the resources of imaginative discourse (literature) to feel her way to some sort of illumination. In the novel, Rachel uses the word Levantine to denote Cairo. She calls Cairo at one point "the Levantine City, Babel of conflict and confusion" (J, 316) and uses the word again when she visits her grandparents' home "in the lane" outside the European section of Cairo for the last time; and as she does, she closes her eyes "to savour and remember its silence, so that it should not be engulfed in the clamour of the *Levantine city*" (my italics; J, 407). The word *Levantine*, here, is used in its conventional negative sense; a clear distinction is drawn between Cairo, a Levantine city, and "Ancient Egypt," the land of the Pharaohs, the Jews, and the *fellahins*. The riverboat episode in chapter 20 helps to highlight this distinction. The riverboat is called *Happy Days*. Rachel and Daniel are walking by the banks of the Nile when they are struck by the mysterious beauty of the colorful stained-glass windows adorning the riverboat's foredeck. In their fantasies, the boat is a special boat that transports people away from Cairo and to the interior of Egypt. Rachel tells Daniel: "The people on the boat see the desert, and all the temples and old cities in it, for days, and days, and all the time the squares of coloured light travel with them" (J, 316). She tells him that these passengers see Ancient Egyptians and they see the *fellahin*. In this allegorical fantasy, Egypt is inhabited by various peoples (colored glass). They are different, separate, yet held together (as in a stained-glass panel). Each color is welded to the others, all together creating one effect and moving together, aiming in the same direction and heading toward the same place. In "Wake of the Waves" (1962), she evokes the Mediterranean as a force that pulls together the Levant into a whole. Reflecting on her compatriots in exile, she writes: "Our wanderings were still bounded by the margins of the Levant, and the routes crossing it were like the corridors that connect rooms in a familiar house."[25] The riverboat on the Nile and its passengers are heading in the same direction, away from Cairo and toward deep Egypt, and this is good. *Happy Days* could be said to serve as a representation of felicitous Levantinism. But the allegory does not stop here. Kahanoff couples *Happy Days* with the figure of a sinister magician. On the same walk on the banks of the Nile, while the children are still fantasizing about the riverboat, they encounter a magician. He is dressed in colorful garb and on his belt are attached many mirrors that sparkle in the sun. At first the children are fascinated by him. They are mesmerized by the sparkling mirrors. They are literally drawn to his charms (in his bracelets and rings). Unlike the stained-glass windows of the riverboat, the mirrors suggest something false and dangerous, with a dazzling surface. The narrator establishes without the shadow of a doubt that the magician is treacherous. He is wicked and lures children with the promise of false things. Donia the servant, who is accompanying the children, warns them to not approach him: "They steal children and then they sell them. . . . Once you're in their clutches, it's finished, no one sees or hears of you ever again." Once the magician catches someone, they are forever changed. Donia says: "Not even the police can find you, because they change your face and voices so that no one can recognize you" (J, 318). Spooked by Donia's interpretation, Rachel "turned to look at *Happy Days* once more, thinking *not* of its bright lights shining on the water, but of the dark, creepy silence inside" (my italics; J, 319). The magician functions as a warning. A Levantine society fascinated by surface effects and unconcerned with its roots and its history is a sinister society. Rachel is attached—rooted, as it were—to Egypt. Egypt is the bond that pulls together past and present and establishes continuity between the ancient and the modern nation: "As she watched the boat, everything Rachel had learned at school about Ancient Egypt was tinged with magic, seen through the squares of dancing light *Happy Days* reflected on the Nile. . . . The Egypt she lived in melted into the past, and the dead stone gods became alive" (J, 317).

The coupling of *Happy Days* and the magician in the same episode suggests to me that in the process of writing, Kahanoff was thinking about what it means to live in a Levantine society and perhaps even to suspect that for an honest, confident, and effective Levantinism to take root personal histories, "the memory of oneness," and past attachments are fundamental. A Levantinism without roots, that is without attachment to place, to ancestors, and to history is, like the images projected by the magician, a lurid, promiscuous, and risky thing.

"To Remember Alexandria" . . . Israel and Levantinism

In her short story "To Remember Alexandria" (1976), Kahanoff poses the following question: Can Levantine culture be reproduced on Israeli soil and, more pointedly, should it? Is Levantinism at its core a corruption of society that leads to its untimely demise or is it, on the contrary, a dynamic, productive, and desirable social framework? As is often the case in Kahanoff's fiction, characters serve to dramatize a concept, creating opportunities for working out compelling issues. The protagonist, Antonia Ferrar, a forty-something woman, is battling breast cancer. Unable to return to her native Egypt, Antonia travels to the shores of the Mediterranean near Caesarea in northern Israel, hoping to see for the last time the same sunset she used to see from Alexandria. Since her expulsion from Egypt, she has lived in Italy where the sunsets do not look like Levantine sunsets. Which brings us to the question, can Levantinism be duplicated in Israel? Published in 1976, "To Remember Alexandria" is an open-ended exploration of the options facing Israel. Walking along the road, Antonia is spotted by a young Israeli pilot named Josh. He is fascinated by her and both fall in love. He calls her sometimes *Alexandra* and at other times *Antonia of Alexandria*, suggesting that she is emblematic of Alexandrian Levantine culture. As they get to know each other, he asks Antonia to describe *her* Alexandria (his emphasis). She answers with a tinge of melancholy that Alexandria was the flower, perhaps the last flower, the Levant produced, suggesting that, like the author herself, "it didn't have the time to flower before being destroyed" (A, 219). The parallel between Levantinism as a corruption of cultures and Antonia's breast cancer is obvious. Antonia expects Josh to find their love objectionable: "*You* should find it repulsive" (italics in text; A, 228). He does not.

When Antonia first addresses Josh, he strikes her as the embodiment of Israel; he is strong, arrogant, and lacking nuance. As she gets to know him better, he surprises her. She discovers that this Israeli pilot and an Ashkenazi Jew to boot has read Durrell's *Alexandria Quartet*. In other words, he is cultured. The suggestion is that, like Josh, post-1967 Israel might indeed be less provincial and dogmatic now that Israel's geography has forced it to engage with others in the region. Perhaps there is a chance, as Josh's attraction to her suggests, that Levantinism could take root in Israel. It is striking, given Kahanoff's investment in the idea of Levantinism, that what is in *doubt* in the story is the desirability (not merely the workability) of a Levantine society for Israel. Will Israel's expanded cultural horizon—no longer limited to its founding ideologies, namely, Zionism and European culture—continue to thrive? Or will Israel, instead, weaken and become feeble through precisely the sort of Levantinism Antonia embodies? If Josh does not find Antonia's cancer "repulsive," it is because in this story, figuratively speaking, he is willing to try anything for the sake of Israel's future, including the Levantine option. Upon discovering that Josh is not the narrow-minded positivist she expected him to be, Antonia remarks: "But you all look so—healthy, so sure of yourselves, so cocky, never doubting . . . I couldn't imagine . . . people here might be more complex than they appear" (A, 220). "And I wondered," she tells Josh, "if Israel would take over where Alexandria left off. Israel is hard and vital, where we were not. Really believes in its survival, where we perhaps did not. The Levant must always be saved by one of its minorities, against itself" (A, 219). The problem, I suggest, is that Antonia is unable to imagine Levantine culture on Israeli soil.

In the course of the story, Antonia learns more about the new Israel from Josh, and he, in turn, learns what it is to be a Levantine. During their discussion over the Six-Day War, she reveals to a shocked Josh that she supported *both* Israel and Egypt in the conflict. She confides to him that she suffered equally when she imagined either country destroyed: "In June 1967, I thought God had to be, simply had to be with Israel. I don't know where God is anymore, why there must be such terrible retribution hanging in the balance, for either people or both. Must there be again the Ten Plagues over Egypt for Israel to be Israel because Pharaoh is still Pharaoh? I flee from the confrontation . . ." (A, 223). For a Levantine like Antonia, confrontation is not only painful—it is also an existential risk. Her sympathy for Egypt, Antonia is quick to reassure Josh, does not extend to other

Arab countries or, for that matter, to Western empires like France and Britain. True to Kahanoff's viewpoint (as an Egyptian territorial nationalist), Antonia explains to him that Egypt is unique in the Middle East. She tells Josh: "neither Syria, nor Lebanon, nor Iraq has mythical dimension, while Israel and Egypt do" (A, 223). On this both she and Josh agree. Fittingly, Kahanoff has Josh say to Antonia: "It was as if I recognized you, had known you before, Antonia Ferrar. Don't ask me to explain" (A, 226).

When the story opens, Josh is ruminating over the state of Israel, its Jewish children, indigenous populations, and its ancient history. Looking at the Mediterranean landscape where he grew up, he muses: "Asia Minor, really, neither Europe nor the East, but the place where they endlessly confronted one another, repulsion and attraction inextricably mixed" (A, 213). He recalls that as a child looking at young Arab boys at play and at work, he saw them as "alien, wild, yet native—native in a way kibbutz youngsters could never be, for their parents were pioneers from Russia and Poland who had come to redeem their ancient homeland" (A, 213). When he later meets Antonia, Josh acknowledges to her that he is, like other Israelis born in Israel, "fascinated by—how shall I say—not the Arab-Moslem world, so much, but by all that happened here, that is beneath, behind, and around us" (A, 220). He is fascinated by ancient roots, and by their history. He continues: "We seek the traces of our past, but it turns out mixed with those of so many others! . . . What you call the Levant stirs *beneath the Israel our parents created*. . . . It's a dimension we lack, which tempts, fascinates, repels, intrigues" (my italics; A, 220). He concludes with a comment that betrays both optimism and dread, explaining to Antonia that after the 1967 war, after the reunification of Jerusalem, only two positions are now possible for Israel. On one hand, there is the model of Masada and self-destruction and, on the other, the Levantine model. In other words, there is self-annihilation or an invitation to "compose differences." He continues: "The Jerusalem we call reunited is an unresolved confrontation not only between Arab-Moslem and Jew, but between the Levant and Israel. The temptation is within us, always to be overcome. You are on the other side of the coin—that Mediterranean world *we* once belonged to. Will you visit Jerusalem with me, Mrs. Ferrar? Antonia Ferrar of Alexandria" (my italics; A, 220–221). By using the first-person plural, Josh has reached deep, very deep down into his Jewish ancestral past and recovered his Mediterranean roots. He is thus transformed, has seen the light thanks to her. Antonia agrees to go with him to Jerusalem but when the time comes, and because the Yom Kippur war has erupted, the trip to Jerusalem does not take place and he dies.

If Levantinization is a dying or dead flower and Josh is killed during the Yom Kippur War, is it because he discovered his Levantine roots "beneath the Israel" his parents created? What does it mean that both Josh and Antonia die? And what is Kahanoff suggesting when in the closing scene of the story, Josh's red-headed young daughter is running toward her mother? What do we make of Josh's widow, the child's mother, swearing stubbornly to erase any memory of Antonia and remember only Tel Aviv? Not Jerusalem, the contested plural city. Does their death suggest metaphorically speaking that the fate of the new Jerusalem, new Israel, rests precariously between two equally problematic models, Masada and Levantinism? Kahanoff stops short of endorsing a Levantine option for Israel. The ending leaves us to ponder the dilemma, like all good literature does; it leaves us to deal with the confrontation in our own time. One thing is clear, "To Remember Alexandria" reinforces Kahanoff's notion that a special bond, both historical and mythic, unites Israel and Egypt. Gil Z. Hochberg is right to argue that Kahanoff presents "an alternative to Zionism's ethnonational separatism," that she brings together "West and East but also the past . . . and the present."[26]

With the notable exception of "Afterword: From East to Sun" (1968), Kahanoff"s discussions of Levantinism, are tentative. Why is that? In her essay "What About Levantinization?" (1972), written four years before "To Remember Alexandria," we are left at the end of the essay with the sense that perhaps Kahanoff's idea of Levantinism is "both a traumatic outcome of colonialism and a means of recovery," as Hochberg aptly puts it in a slightly different context (Hochberg, 53). The essay, or afterword, "Afterword: From East the Sun" is stunning in its handling of the question of Levantinism. It is indeed visionary. It evokes the past as a source of strength and intimates a felicitous future. The text has a confessional tone without being apologetic. According to Deborah Starr and Sasson Somekh, it was written "in 1968 as the introduction to a planned collection of essays in English. It is regrettable that when a book of Kahanoff's essays was published in Hebrew in 1978 under the same title [*From East the Sun*] this essay was not included."[27] I can only wonder why, for it contains Kahanoff's most penetrating and confident thinking on Levantinism. She asserts, without a trace of dogmatism, that "reconstructing a pluralistic Levant may offer a workable . . . framework in which people have the right to be free, different, and equal" (AES, 247), and she uses the example of Greeks and Jews to reassure those who are concerned that Levantinization will absorb and assimilate into extinction peoples and cultures. Greeks and Jews, she argues, have existed for centuries in the Mediterranean. It is in the history and geography of the Levant that the constant shuttling back and forth has not erased its people's particularities (AES, 251). In a passage at the end of the "Afterword" in Starr and Somekh's *Mongrels and Marvels*, Kahanoff calls on Israel to rethink Levantinism as the robust social practice that she knows it to be. Without going on the defensive, as she tends to do in some of her essays, she addresses Israel and its future, asserting that Zionist ideology must "relate itself to the history" of the region (AES, 256). She writes: "Hence, we might rewrite the story of Ishmael and Israel—and of their respective mothers— to give it a happier opening onto the future" (AES, 256). The essays that precede

"Afterword," Kahanoff herself concurs, were mostly of the "old order." She has turned the page. "Were I to write this book today, it would be different, *less hesitant, more assertive*" (my italics, AES, 244). The experience of the Six-Day War would explain the optimism. By 1972, or earlier, that optimism seems to have dissipated, replaced by the raw feelings of despair. "What About Levantinization?" (1972) is an angry, barely contained, denunciation of the Israeli people and Israeli culture. And "To Remember Alexandria" (1976) with its two tragic protagonists paints a future for Israel so bleak that even the appearance of a child at the end of the story cannot lift the sense of doom.

A decade or more after her death in 1979 at the age of sixty-two, Jacqueline Kahanoff's role in bringing attention to Levantinism as a social practice has been recognized by a number of cultural critics. Chief among them is Ammiel Alcalay whose role in raising Kahanoff's profile and boosting Levantinism to a category with historical, political, cultural, and literary dimensions has been critically important. Kahanoff did not invent the term Levantinism and she may not have been solely responsible for shifting its definition away from one with disparaging connotations to a more constructive one. But she has helped move the discourse of cultural critics toward a more positive consideration of connectivity, exchange, and circulation. To be sure, Kahanoff has contributed to the dialogue taking place in Israel since the 1970s asserting Levantinism's potential for working through some of the thorny issues of multiculturalism (S, xxvii). As Gil Hochberg has argued, Kahanoff's Levantinism might indeed offer the best terms for peace between Jews and Arabs (Hochberg, 54). I have argued that Kahanoffian Levantinism is not a social theory but an aesthetics, a way of doing things. It addresses others in their difference, establishes the importance of rootedness in community, and safeguards the separation of private and public while, at the same time, it encourages open, neutral, and decentered relational activity. By sometimes affirming Levantinism and at other times problematizing it, I think Kahanoff asks that we take it as an opportunity for thinking about new more vibrant, more mindful, and less contentious social configurations. As such, Kahanoffian Levantinism is an always provisional and experimental practice.

Notes

I use the following abbreviations for Jacqueline Kahanoff works:
(J) *Jacob's Ladder*
(A) "To Remember Alexandria."
(AES) "Afterwords: From East the Sun."
(AL) "Israel: Ambivalent Levantine."
(L) "A Letter from Mama Camouna."
(T) *Tamra* (unfinished novel).

Works of Jacqueline Shohet Kahanoff used in this chapter:
"A Culture Stillborn," in Deborah A. Starr and Sasson Somekh, *Mongrels and Marvels: The Levantine Writings of Jacqueline Shohet Kahanoff* (Stanford, Calif.: Stanford University Press, 2011).
"A Letter from Mama Camouna," in Deborah A. Starr and Sasson Somekh, *Mongrels and Marvels: The Levantine Writings of Jacqueline Shohet Kahanoff* (Stanford, Calif.: Stanford University Press, 2011).
"Afterwords: From East the Sun," in Deborah A. Starr and Sasson Somekh, *Mongrels and Marvels: The Levantine Writings of Jacqueline Shohet Kahanoff* (Stanford, Calif.: Stanford University Press, 2011).
"Childhood in Egypt," in Deborah A. Starr and Sasson Somekh, *Mongrels and Marvels: The Levantine Writings of Jacqueline Shohet Kahanoff* (Stanford, Calif.: Stanford University Press, 2011).
"Israel: Ambivalent Levantine," in Deborah A. Starr and Sasson Somekh, *Mongrels and Marvels: The Levantine Writings of Jacqueline Shohet Kahanoff* (Stanford, Calif.: Stanford University Press, 2011).
Jacob's Ladder (London: Harvill Press, 1951).
"To Live and Die a Copt," in Deborah A. Starr and Sasson Somekh, *Mongrels and Marvels: The Levantine Writings of Jacqueline Shohet Kahanoff* (Stanford, Calif.: Stanford University Press, 2011).
"Wake of Waves," in Deborah A. Starr and Sasson Somekh, *Mongrels and Marvels: The Levantine Writings of Jacqueline Shohet Kahanoff* (Stanford, Calif.: Stanford University Press, 2011).
"What About Levantinization," in *Journal of Levantine Studies* Vol. 1 (Summer 2011): 13–22.

1. Jacqueline Shohet, *Jacob's Ladder* (London: Harvill, 1951), 364.
2. See Nancy Reynolds, *A City Consumed: Urban Commerce, the Cairo Fire, and the Politics of Decolonization in Egypt* (Stanford, Calif.: Stanford University Press, 2012).
3. Along with Reynolds's work, see the dissertations of Gina Rauf, "Cities of Hope and Despair: Reimagining Cosmopolitanism" (Harvard University, 2009) and Amr Tawfik Kamal, "Empires and Emporia: Fictions of the Department Store in the Modern Mediterranean" (University of Michigan, 2013).
4. It would be useful to explore why David is suddenly able to speak French. Kahanoff's complicated relationship with language deserves closer attention. Gil Hochberg has reflected on Kahanoff's discomfort with the Arabic language and has diagnosed the problem as a "complex and enigmatic relationship to Arabic," the result, she suggests, of an "inner colonialism" (Permanent, 239). I pose the question of language choice more generally in the hope that it addresses another question along with it: Why did Kahanoff write in English and not in the impeccable French she knew equally well? And what about Hebrew? If it is true that Kahanoff resisted speaking Hebrew (not only resisted writing it), what accounts for that?
5. See chapter 3 on Edmond Jabès for a discussion of the rivalry between French and English, France and Great Britain, and the tendency among Egyptian Jews to favor the French and feel hostile toward the British. We find this pattern also in the works of Paula Jacques, as I show in chapter 4.
6. See chapter 1. Jacques Hassoun, *Les Contrebandiers de la mémoire* (Paris: Syros, 1994).

7. See the epilogue of this book for some insight into the penchant among Jewish Egyptian writers to reinterpret canonical narratives of biblical Egyptians.

8. Joel Beinin, *The Dispersion of Egyptian Jewry: Culture, Politics, and the Formation of a Modern Diaspora* (Berkeley and Los Angeles: University of California Press, 1998), 269.

9. See Dario Miccoli's "Moses and Faruq: The Jews and the Study of History in Interwar Egypt 1920s–1940s," *Quest. Issues in Contemporary Jewish History* 4 (November 2012), http://www.quest-cdecjournal.it/focus.php?id=319.

10. Aron Rodrigue, "Alliance Israélite Network," in *The Encyclopedia of Jews in the Islamic World*, edited by Norman A. Stillman, vol. 1, 171–180, 176. (Leiden: Brill, 2010). Further references to this article will be included in the text as (Rodrigue).

11. Paméla Dorn Sezgin, "Jewish Women in the Ottoman Empire," in Zion Zohar, *Sephardic and Mizrahi Jewry* (New York: New York University Press, 2005), 216–235, 227.

12. Dario Miccoli, *Histories of the Jews of Egypt: An Imagined Bourgeoisie, 1880s–1950s* (London and New York: Routledge, 2015), 61.

13. Critics of the Alliance are many. I address them indirectly in my examination of Alice. For a thoughtful argument on the resistance to the French colonialist project in the Maghreb, see Joshua Schreier in his book, *Arabs of the Jewish Faith: The Civilizing Mission in Colonial Africa* (New Brunswick, N.J.: Rutgers University Press, 2010). The French thought Algerian Jews were capable of being "regenerated" and went about putting in place systems meant to help them reach the goals set. The record of Jewish resistance to French policies has not been sufficiently pointed out. Schreier writes: "The civilizing project was thus interpreted, shaped, and sometimes even executed by the local Algerian actors it was originally intended to transform" (3). He argues further that, unfortunately, few historians and cultural critics have called attention to disagreements between "the colonialists" as to policies and even fewer have examined what these disagreements suggest.

14. Ammiel Alcalay, *After Jews and Arabs: Remaking Levantine Culture* (Minneapolis: University of Minnesota Press, 1993), 213. Further references to this study will be included in the text as (Alcalay).

15. Frances Malino, "Prophets in Their Own Land? Mothers and Daughters of the Alliance Israélite Universelle," *Journal of Jewish Women's Studies & Gender Issues*, no. 3, Motherhood (Spring–Summer, 5760–2000): 56–73, 57. Further references to this study will be included in the text as (Malino).

16. Jacqueline Shohet Kahanoff, "A Letter from Mama Camouna," in *Keys to the Garden: New Israeli Writing*, edited by Ammiel Alcalay, 18–39, 33 (San Francisco: City Lights Books, 1996).

17. Jacqueline Shohet Kahanoff, "Afterwords: From East the Sun," in Deborah A. Starr and Sasson Somekh, *Mongrels and Marvels*, 243–259, 247–251.

18. Gil Z. Hochberg makes a compelling argument in 'Permanent Immigration': Jacqueline Kahanoff, Ronit Matalon, and the Impetus of Levantinism," *Boundary 2*, 31, no. 2 (Summer 2004): 219–243. She argues that the "Levant is *above all* a space of literary production, one that is explored along 'numerous surprising meetings,' such as in the literary collaboration between Jacques Hassoun, an Egyptian Jewish writer living in Paris, and Abdelkebir Khatibi, a Moslem Moroccan writer from Rabat" (my italics; 226). Hochberg is right to suggest that literary discourse is a rich and powerful medium for communication, experimentations, and for surprising revelations. I agree also that it fosters intercultural and open exchanges. By an aesthetics of Levantinism, I include behaviors that have little to show us in terms of tangible material production, literary or otherwise. It is a way of

approaching the other in their difference, accepting that differences are impenetrable. I believe that for Kahanoff Levantinism is a pedagogy (it is teachable) and an aesthetics (it can be expressed in various ways). It is an artful mode of carrying on, of carrying oneself, that is alert to opportunities to engage with others *as* others. Tobie Nathan reiterates the Kahanoffian imperative when he suggests that when we meet a stranger, an immigrant, a refugee, we ask: "Who are you that we are not?" ("Qui êtes-vous que je ne suis pas"), letting them explain what and how much they want to share with us. An aesthetics of Levantinism would be less apt to get involved in communication that seeks to penetrate the essential difference of the other. It seems to me that literature can work either way. It can probe and it can also keep to the surface.

19. Jacqueline Shohet Kahanoff, "Israel: Ambivalent Levantine," in Deborah A. Starr and Sasson Somekh, *Mongrels and Marvels*, 193–212, 211. Further references to this work will be included in the text as (AL).

20. Tobie Nathan, "Rentrée Littéraire 2015," https://www.youtube.com/watch?v=FY-DYARHi9U. Further references to this clip will be included in the text as (Nathan).

21. In *The Eastern Mediterranean and the Making of Global Radicalism, 1860–1914* (Berkeley: University of California Press, 2013), 156–157, Ilham Khuri-Makdisi argues that recent studies have shown that in Alexandria and Cairo worksites employed a mix of indigenous, immigrant, and migrant workers of various ethnicities. Interestingly, he writes: "it was employers themselves (and mostly European employers) who created the two categories of foreign and indigenous labor by favoring the former over the latter." But these categories, such as "local and foreign, foreign and less foreign, etc." were categories in flux.

22. Tobie Nathan, *Ce Pays qui te ressemble* (Paris: Stock, 2015).

23. Jacqueline Shohet Kahanoff, "Childhood in Egypt," in Deborah A. Starr and Sasson Somekh, *Mongrels and Marvels*, 1–13, 10.

24. Jacqueline Shohet Kahanoff, "To Live and Die a Copt," in Deborah A. Starr and Sasson Somekh, *Mongrels and Marvels*, 128–135, 133.

25. Jacqueline Shohet Kahanoff, "Wake of Waves," in Deborah A. Starr and Sasson Somekh, *Mongrels and Marvels*, 136–152, 137.

26. For a truly compelling examination of the "Levantine Option" for Israel, see Gil Z. Hochberg, *Jews, Arabs, and the Limits of Separatist Imagination* (Princeton, N.J.: Princeton University Press, 2007), 52. Further references to this work will be included in the text as (Hochberg).

27. Deborah A. Starr and Sasson Somekh, *Mongrels and Marvels: The Levantine Writings of Jacqueline Shohet Kahanoff* (Stanford, Calif.: Stanford University Press, 2011), 243. Further references to this work will be included in the text as (S).

CHAPTER THREE

Edmond Jabès
Egypt Recovered

For Saul Israel

I have always found myself without a place, without a sense of belonging. But the image of a place for me is the image of Egypt.[1]
 Edmond Jabès

It does not matter what country excites your imagination. It does not matter what its shores are like. What will always matter to you is your country, your shores.[2]
 Edmond Jabès

EDMOND JABÈS IS a major figure in French intellectual letters. His works are a meditation on exile, hospitality, and the Jewish condition in the aftermath of World War II and the Holocaust at a time when Europe was grappling with grave ethical issues and complicated social problems. France, in particular, was contending with the influx of thousands of Jews from the Middle East and North Africa.[3] Jabès and his Jewish Egyptian compatriots were among those who arrived in increasing numbers from 1956 to 1967. Upon its publication in 1963, his *The Book of Questions* (*Le Livre des questions*) was recognized immediately by intellectuals, philosophers, and literary critics as a substantive contribution to the discourse on the shattered state of Judaism in the world after the war. It received serious attention from major thinkers of the second half of the twentieth century, among them Jacques Derrida, Maurice Blanchot, and Emmanuel Levinas. Its highly original form and the density of its meaning altered the way literature was viewed. *The Book of Questions* injected into postmodern literature a high level of contemplation, expressions of feelings, intimacy, and warmth.

Sarah Hammerschlag has rightly attributed Derrida's turn to the literary to his encounter with Jabès.[4] And Edward Kaplan has stated rightly that Jabès's *Books* "have received extraordinary attention because they are both post-modern and traditionally humanistic."[5] From the beginning, *The Book of Questions* and subsequent works have been viewed principally through the lens of the Holocaust and European suffering. This chapter attends to the presence of Egypt in that work. Without compromising the place the Holocaust occupies in it, I argue that from *The Book of Questions* onward Jabès's work is marked by his experience of exile from Egypt. This perspective has not received the attention it demands. His concerns for his compatriots both Egyptian and North African, the love and reverence he feels for the Egyptian landscape, his attachment to Egyptian people and culture, and his own history as an Egyptian Jew: these issues occupy a significant place in the work Jabès wrote after his exile.[6] As with Jacqueline Kahanoff, Jabès's Egypt is Mediterranean and Nilotic, and he evokes biblical Egypt as source and continuous site of the Jewish people. "The pharaohs barely belong to the past," he declares.[7] Jabès's work reflects, recirculates, and revives the history of Judaism with roots going back millennia to Moses, the flight from Egypt, and forty years of wandering in the desert. Without undermining the European context, Egypt past and present is the place from which Jabès begins his meditation on the Jewish condition and seeks to rebuild Jewish solidarity, which had been severely strained by Nazism and Arab nationalism.

Jabès left Egypt in July 1957. He was forty-four years old. In Egypt, he lived in full view of the Nile, facing the island of Rhoda where it is said Pharaoh's daughter found Moses among the reeds, saved him, and loved him as her own. The story of Moses, Passover, and the Jews wandering in the desert are vivid narratives in the imaginary of Egyptian Jews. In the work of Jabès, this story functions as the emblem of the Jewish condition made more real than emblematic, because it was lived. Jabès's personal experience is the reality from which he draws to address the state of Judaism in disarray after the Holocaust and the expatriation of nearly a million Jews from Arab lands. Personal histories matter a great deal to poets. One of Jabès's imaginary rabbis and one of his alter egos says:

> "Yesterday was me," Reb Basra had written, "and tomorrow will still be me. So you may feel free to question me on human suffering and joy as well as on the morning and evening of the world. It is always the story of my life and death that I will tell you.". . .
>
> "Can we remember a place where we have not been, a face we have not come near, an object we have never held?" Reb Zaoud asked Reb Bécri. (BR III, 79)[8]

As Jabès writes in the first pages of *The Book of Questions*: "One can only remember oneself" (BQ, 61). The memory of the Holocaust focuses Jabès's thinking and deepens it, to be sure. His personal history of exile grounds this reflection in experience and gives it integrity. Derrida has aptly recognized that in *The Book of Questions* "a powerful and ancient root is exhumed, and on it is laid bare an ageless wound (for what Jabès teaches us is that roots speak, that words want to grow, and that poetic discourse takes root in a wound)."[9]

Edmond Jabès: Background

Edmond Jabès was born in 1912 to a prominent Sephardic family from Cairo's affluent milieu. The same year, the celebrated Jewish Egyptian journalist, satirist, and playwright Yaqub Sanua, or Abou Naddara as he was also known, died in Paris. Sanua was sent into exile in France in 1878 for advocating resistance against the British in Egypt. "Egypt for the Egyptians," Sanua said. It was not uncommon for Egyptian Jews, young idealists, and intellectuals like Jacques Hassoun, Léon Castro, and Elian J. Filbert to support and even work actively on behalf of nationalist movements of independence against the British. Political engagement was an important part of Jabès's adolescence and early adulthood. He was barely seventeen years old when he and his father were summoned to the Italian consulate and threatened with expulsion if Edmond persisted in writing articles against the Italian regime. This did not deter him. In 1934, Jabès, his brother Henri, along with a few others organized the League of Youth against Racism and Antisemitism (La Ligue des Jeunes Contre le Racisme et l'Antisémitisme). Jabès continued to be politically engaged after his marriage, in 1935. For example, he and his wife were involved in the reception of refugees fleeing Germany.[10] During the war, he collaborated with the British in the fight against the Axis powers and in July 1942 the British evacuated him and other activists to Palestine, where he was stationed for ten months. He explains that the British took this action to protect them from Rommel's advancing army in Egypt (Dialogues, 23). When in the 1950s Gamal Abdel Nasser emerged on the political scene, Jabès supported the movement for Egyptian independence without giving a thought to the possibility that Nasser's regime would spell the end of the Jewish community in Egypt (Dialogues, 22). In short, Jabès was not the kind of intellectual who preferred to remain in his ivory tower even if he was devoted to literature, actively participated in the literary life of Cairo, and had decided to make a career in writing. In 1930s Egypt, with the rise of fascism, Nazism, and communism, literature and politics went hand in hand. In 1944, Jabès, the brothers Raoul and Henri Curiel, and a few others founded the important Groupement des amitiés françaises.[11] Groupement's aim was to restart cultural exchange between Egypt and France, which had been curtailed during the war. The group published a literary magazine and invited writers from both sides of the Mediterranean to contribute original work. It was the meeting place of Egyptian intellectuals. Between the 1930s and early 1950s, French literature, art, and philosophy enjoyed a tremendous international reputation. Groupement presented readings, lectures, discussions, and debates. Jean Cocteau,

André Gide, Albert Camus, Henri Michaux, Paul Eluard, Philippe Soupault, and Roger Caillois were among the many writers who visited and signed Groupement's *Livre d'or* (Golden Book). The center also sponsored French-related art exhibits and concerts. Jabès was active in Groupement until 1952. In 1956, its offices were forcibly shut down by the government; its library and *Livre d'or* with its signatures and other documents were sold (Lançon, 255). In his examination of the Egyptian experience of modernity, Yoav Di-Capua describes the dynamism these "intellectuals without frontiers" created in the 1920s and 1930s in Egypt.[12] These men and women, both Jewish and non-Jewish, represented for a period of time what it meant to be modern, Egyptian, and cosmopolitan. When he was living in Egypt, Jabès's personal contributions to Franco-Egyptian entente earned him in 1952 the title of Chevalier de la Légion d'Honneur. Later on, living in France, he was the recipient of numerous awards. He was among the four writers, along with Camus, Sartre, and Levi-Strauss, to present his work at the 1967 World Exposition in Montreal. He was awarded France's prestigious Prix des Critiques (1972), the Prix des Arts, des Lettres et des Sciences de La Fondation du Judaïsme Français (1982), and the Prix Pasolini (1983). In 1986, he was named Officier de la Legion d'Honneur and in 1987, he was awarded the coveted Grand Prix National de la Poésie, and the Citadella Prize. Starting in the 1980s, Jabès received invitations from universities throughout the world to lecture and give readings; and colloquia were organized in his honor. When he died in Paris on January 2, 1991 at the age of seventy-eight, he was a respected French writer and intellectual.

The Jabès family traces its roots in Egypt to the early nineteenth century (Jaron, 27). His wife's family, named Cattaui, was an affluent and influential Cairene family also dating back to the nineteenth century. Jabès described his background and that of his wife in a 1990 interview: "Both my wife and I issue from very well-established bourgeois Sephardic families. My father was a banker and my wife's family, which was very religious, were prominent and influential in the Jewish community" (Lançon, 22).[13] The Jabès family ran the successful Banque Isaac Léon et fils d'Elie A. Jabès. Jabès himself opened a brokerage firm after his marriage in 1935. He later left it to join the firm of his father-in-law René Cohen, also a stockbroker. As Jaron explains, working in finance "occupied Jabès during the entirety of his professional life in Egypt, and his importance to the financial institutions of the country grew steadily. In fact, in the final months of his residency there, he worked as vice-president of the stock exchange and watched the work of generations of Egyptian economists crumble" (Jaron, 28).

The Jabès family had Italian nationality. In 1882, after the Urabi Pacha rebellion, fearing continued political instability, his paternal grandfather did what many Egyptians did at that time to protect his family and their interests: he solicited the citizenship of a country that would offer him protection in exchange for securing a foothold and defending its interests in Egypt. Shimon Shamir explains that the British did not grant their nationality to many, Italians were more generous, and the French gave preference to Jews of North African origin. By 1929, all were phasing out the granting of passports.[14] Jabès explains in an interview that until 1923–1929, no laws defined Egyptian citizenship: "Only the Muslim, even if a foreigner, was considered Egyptian." One's religion determined one's nationality. "Jews and Christians who had been residing in Egypt for centuries were automatically excluded" (Dialogues, 21). This is why, he explains in all simplicity, "our family all of a sudden became Italian" (Dialogues, 21). As members of the Egyptian Jewish community, the Jabès family was involved in Jewish philanthropy. His grandfather built a small synagogue, the Reb David Ibn Abi Zimra, in the Mousky section of Cairo. It was also known as the Jabès synagogue. The synagogue had three "beautiful" Torah scrolls dating back to the seventeenth century (Dialogues, 19).[15] Jabès makes references to these Torahs in his work. After his grandfather's death, Edmond Jabès took over from his uncle and administered the affairs of the synagogue. He was also responsible for the Jewish community school founded by his wife's grandfather. The school educated approximately two thousand children free of charge. They were taught in French and received secular instruction (Dialogues, 19–20). The Jabès family were Cairene and their activities reflected those of the greater Cairo Jewish community (Jaron, 36). Judaism constituted a significant aspect of Edmond Jabès's ethnic identity, the same way that other minority populations at that time distinguished themselves from one another. Like most of the many minorities who had lived for generations in Egypt, "the Jabès family was set apart from but not excluded from the Muslim Arabic-speaking Egyptian majority" (Jaron, 18). Edmond Jabès attended synagogue during major holidays and he and his wife were actively involved in the social and religious life of the Jewish community.

The French Language

Jabès spoke French and Arabic fluently. Like many members of the upper and middle classes in Cairo and Alexandria, both Jewish and non-Jewish, he mixed French and popular Egyptian seamlessly. French held an elite status because it was the language of instruction and of culture. But it did not replace Arabic. French was not the most important language, but neither was it negligible, explains Irène Fenoglio.[16] In her study on the Egyptian Francophone language, Fenoglio, a linguist and researcher at the CNRS (Le Centre National de la Recherche Scientifique) specializing in the history and generative study of Egyptian French, describes "the rich sociolinguistic complexity of Egypt" in the first half of the twentieth century. Arabic, she argues, was ubiquitous; it was the basic language of communication (Nil, 30), understood and spoken by all but a few. The situation was different for writing and reading. Writing and reading in Arabic was limited to those who studied it in school. Alongside Arabic, there existed groups who spoke French, Greek, Italian, and English with varying degrees of proficiency. These groups were not numerous, but the effect that this multilingualism had on the fabric of the whole society was profound.[17] Fenoglio explains that the usage of French "became natural" (Eclosion, 37). Of the languages spoken alongside Arabic, French was the language of prestige; its culture was deemed superior. The high regard for French was a global phenomenon in the latter half of the nineteenth century and the first part of the twentieth. The sentiment was not unique to Egypt or to France's colonies. Jabès explains to Marcel Cohen the high regard with which French language and culture were held: "even Egyptians of Muslim origin who belonged to the bourgeoisie sent their children to foreign schools." He continues: "Was it because foreign languages were sacrificed in [state] schools? Was it because in the foreign schools the curriculum and the teachers were better? Whatever the reasons," Jabès points out, "the fact remains that for a long time Egyptian families preferred to send their children to the French schools." He adds:

> Wasn't France the country of human rights? Since Napoleon Bonaparte French influence had remained strong in Egypt. With Egypt under British mandate, one can understand for example that the children of one of the leaders of the Wafd, the great nationalist party, went to the Lycée Français. A lawyer, he himself had studied in France. Everybody knows of the rivalry between France and England. To give a French education to one's children was, in a way, to show one's *hostility towards the occupying power*. (My italics; Dialogues, 22)

Jacob's Ladder, as I have shown in chapter 2, is an elaborate dramatization of those feelings. Fenoglio makes the compelling claim that French in Egypt did not grow against the grain of Arabic culture. Rather, it grew against English. Nancy Y. Reynolds confirms this view in her marvelous *A City Consumed: Urban Commerce, the Cairo Fire, and the Politics of Decolonization in Egypt*. She writes: "Many Egyptian nationalists preferred French language and culture to English . . . as a sort of anticolonial protest against the British overlords. The use of French, especially after the 1867 *World Exposition* in Paris, became in Egypt (as elsewhere) its own autonomous cultural mode, reflecting an interest in France but not necessarily a desire for French rule or hegemony."[18] English was taught in British schools and in government schools as the second language of instruction. The perception was that English was useful for careers in government, in civil service administration, and foreign affairs (Nil, 18). "English was at that time," writes Fenoglio, "simply a means whereas French constituted a direct way to participate in a different cultural experience, an opportunity to engage in literary creation" (Nil 23). It was French, not English, that produced in Egypt what Fenoglio aptly describes as "a significant literary and artistic production of remarkable quality" (Eclosion, 35).

Jabès was educated in French schools. He first attended the Collège Saint-Jean-Baptiste de la Salle (1917–1924) and then the Lycée Français de Bab el-Louk (1924–1929), where he received his baccalaureate. In 1927, the director of Lycée Bab el-Louk described with pride the composition of his school:

> In this Lycée, sitting at their desks, we have nearly a thousand children representing fifteen nationalities—350 are Egyptians, 135 French, as many Greeks and Italians—and six different religions: Greek Orthodox, Muslim, Catholic, Protestant, Jewish, and Copt. Under the aegis of the French language and French civilization, they are united in brotherhood in an independent Egypt and serve as an example of perfect friendship and tolerance. (Eclosion, 34)

Students in French schools in Egypt repeatedly heard words like tolerance, equality, and brotherhood uttered in the same breath as the term *France*. In the end, they believed France embodied these ideals. It was on such idealism that they constructed their fantasies about an enlightened France. This view marked most of them, as it did Jabès. However, France was to be a source of great disappointment once they immigrated to that country and interacted with the French people, as I explain later and as Paula Jacques's work makes clear. Upon completing his baccalaureate, Jabès attended the Sorbonne and worked on a License de Lettres (1930–1934). He did not complete the degree but returned to Egypt, married, and began his dual career as a stockbroker and a writer.

A Writing Career before *The Book of Questions*

By the early and mid-1940s, Jabès had written and published a large number of poems, essays, and reviews in French-language literary reviews. His first book of poetry, *Les Illusions sentimentales*, written when he was seventeen years old, was published in Paris by Figuière. It brought him a certain degree of celebrity on both sides of the Mediterranean and gave him access to Parisian literary salons "like that of Madame Rachilde, where," Jabès admits, "there were senators, deputies, academicians, who sent me letters. I was read at the Comédie Française by one of the great actors."[19] In 1936, he published another book of poetry, *L'Obscurité potable*, in Paris with Guy Lévis Mano, a respected private press that specialized in poetry. It published the works of Paul Éluard, Philippe Soupault, and of other avant-garde poets (Jaron, 93). Other works followed in Paris in the 1940s.[20] In 1947, Pierre Seghers published *Chansons pour le repas de l'ogre*, a fascinating and understudied work, and in 1948 Mano published the equally compelling *Trois filles de mon quartier*. He had other Parisian publications in the early 1950s. Seghers, for example, published *L'écorce du monde* in 1955 and included some of Jabès's poetry in several anthologies and reviews.[21] I mention these early works written in Egypt and published in France to say that when Jabès arrived in Paris in 1957 he may not have been a well-known writer, but he had important literary connections. He was certainly not a novice when the prestigious Gallimard

Press published the groundbreaking *The Book of Questions*. After he arrived in Paris in 1957, Jabès continued to publish in highly regarded French journals and literary magazines such as the *Mercure de France, Les lettres nouvelles*, and *La nouvelle revue française* (Stoddard, 300). His most important publication before *The Book of Questions* was the anthology *I Build my Dwelling (Je bâtis ma demeure)*, published in 1959 by Gallimard.

Judaism in France after Auschwitz

It is a common reflection of Jabesian criticism that Jabès wrote in Egypt as if he were in France and that he wrote in France as if he were in Egypt. When he arrived in France as an exile from Egypt, France was a known entity for him. He had studied there, visited on numerous occasions, and had friends on whom he could call. Still, it was traumatic to arrive as an immigrant expelled from his homeland, without the expectation of a return. It changed his way of thinking and writing. As he explained to Paul Auster:

> I don't think I would have written *The Book of Questions* if I had remained in Egypt. It took this break in my life for *my experience in Egypt, my experience of the desert*, to enter my writing the way it does. These books came into being as a result of this break. . . . as a result of my having to leave this country because I was a Jew. One day I was told, this is it, you have to leave. Fine. This was *a little drama* for me and my family. On a personal level it was quite serious, of course, but on the larger, human scale, as part of the history of Jewish suffering, it was nothing more than *a little drama*. But there I was, neither a practicing Jew nor a Jewish believer, forced to leave because I was Jewish. (My italics)[22]

The "little drama" remark belies a deeper wound. Jabès recounts that a day or two after he arrived in Paris he saw near the Place de l'Odéon a graffiti that spelled out in black and white: "Death to the Jews. Jews Go Home" ("Mort aux Juifs, Jews Go Home"). This event, Jabès explains, rattled him to the core. It forced him to face for the first time in his life what it really meant to be a Jew in the world; and to accept the reality that a Jew had no "place." It took these words to make him realize he could never write as he had before. As he puts it: "A few graffiti on a wall were enough for the dormant memories in my hand to take over my pen, for my fingers to determine what I see" (BQ, 26).[23] The words "Death to the Jews, Jews Go Home," were written on a public wall more than a decade after the Holocaust. Jabès was shattered. How was it possible that in France—after the Enlightenment—such prejudice persisted? He had a difficult time understanding how such hatred could be displayed openly without anyone being moved enough to erase it: "That evening, all of this came back, breaking over me like a wave of nausea. Nothing seemed to have changed. France, in which I had invested so much of myself through its culture, seemed all of a sudden to reject me" (Dialogues, 41–42). At that very moment, the ground beneath him seemed to give way and he saw himself as a foreigner. The black and white antisemitic graffiti illumined painfully the exilic condition of every Jew. Jabès explains to the journalist Madeleine Chapsal that this experience made him not only confront the Jewish condition as it revealed itself after the Holocaust, but forced him to take it on, "to own it," so to speak (Jaron, 2).[24]

The first years in France were difficult for Jabès. He had lost everything in Egypt and had to support his family while also trying to resume his writing career. His own personal trauma and the drama of other Jews forced out of Egypt and North Africa were compounded by what he saw as the heavy toll the Holocaust had exacted on Jews and on Judaism. During these years, Jabès recalls, he was emotionally and intellectually bereft. "I was living in such intellectual turmoil," he explained to Marcel Cohen (Dialogues, 52). Sandrine Szwarc, Seán Hand, and Sarah Hammerschlag have written thoughtfully about this period, the late 1950s, when right after the war, and several decades following that, French intellectuals, and particularly Jewish intellectuals, could see that Judaism was damaged and Jewish life devastated. They felt it necessary to confront the Shoah and with it Judaism, Jewish life, and Jewish identity.[25] French Jews lived a cruel irony. France was the first country to have granted emancipation to Jews in 1791, soon after the revolution. Under Napoleon, the nation created the Central Consistory (Consistoire Israélite), an institution that administered the affairs of the community. However, French support for the Nazi regime served as evidence that antisemitism had not diminished since the Dreyfus Affair. For many intellectuals, the principal question was: Will Judaism survive after the Holocaust? It was the existential question debated in a number of circles, including the Colloquium of French-Speaking Jewish Intellectuals (Colloque des Intellectuels Juifs de Langue Française; CIJLF). The first colloquium was held in 1957, the year Jabès arrived in France. At first, the Colloquium was held once a year and then biannually.[26] The organizers and participants were respected Jewish philosophers, Talmudic scholars, and social scientists, among them Emmanuel Levinas, André Neher, Vladimir Jankélévitch, Albert Memmi, and Eliane Amado Lévy-Valensi. Jabès was a member of the organizing committee (Comité Préparatoire) in 1974. The publications of the *Cahiers* of the Colloquium show that he attended a few of the gatherings. What is more to my point is that the discourse on Auschwitz had emerged during Jabès's first years in France as a central preoccupation of intellectuals; Jabès would have followed these discussions and his work would be influenced by them. The Colloquium was conceived as an attempt to rethink what it meant to be a Jew in post-Holocaust France by finding in Jewish thought itself the possibilities of Judaism's future vitality. The organizers hoped to establish a framework in which to address the question put by André Neher, one of the Colloquium's key figures, namely, how a Jew after the Shoah could remain a Jew among nations. They wanted to advance a way of thinking about Judaism that would strengthen individual Jewish lives and Jewish communities everywhere. Greatly influenced by Levinas, the organizers wished to emphasize the universalist character of Jewish thought and demonstrate that Judaism was, and had always been, the prophetic voice of the West. These intellectuals felt that because Western philosophy valued universalism, the way to elevate Judaism was "to see in Judaism only what contributed to philosophical universalism" (Szwarc, 158). Other approaches to the question of Judaism's survival ensued both from within and outside the Colloquium. In the *Anatomy of French Judaism* (1962), Wladimir Rabonovitch (Rabi) argued that the future of French Judaism was to be found in a balancing act between the ethical and the practical.[27] He was critical of Levinas's and Neher's "spiritual intractability" and the "monolithic" character of their reflections. Similarly, Albert Memmi and Léon Askénazi, Tunisian and Algerian respectively, tried to steer the discourse of Levinas and Neher in the Colloquium away from philosophy and Talmudic debate and toward more pressing social issues. Askénazi, a philosopher himself and one of the group's founding members, proposed a session for the Fourth Colloquium in 1961 to address the issue of the arrival of Jews from North Africa. His proposal was accepted after what Askénazi describes as an exhausting debate.[28] Even so, the title of the session, "Encounters between Intellectuals from France and Algeria" ("Rencontre entre intellectuels juifs de France et d'Algérie"), reveals how deeply the reigning discourse resisted addressing issues on the ground. Memmi understood that this resistance was wrapped up in "subtle forms of discrimination" (Szwarc, 132) that coincided with the arrival at that point of nearly 235, 000 mostly Sephardic and Mizrahi Jews from the southern shores of the Mediterranean. Where Jabès stood in this debate is not clear from what I know. As I try to show in the following pages, what is clear is Jabès's belief that to save Judaism Jews needed to strengthen their connections to each other. The way forward was solidarity in the name of ancient bonds, ancient roots that had grown and multiplied in the Book.

The Holocaust and the Second Exodus

Living and working in France alongside survivors of the Holocaust, Jabès was keenly aware that his experience of persecution in Egypt had been very different. He felt solidarity with European Jews, explaining to Marcel Cohen that if the troops of Rommel had invaded Egypt, as Hitler had intended, "we would have had to confront the same indifference. The Oriental Jews too would have suffered the fate of European Jews. I see no serious reason to think otherwise" (Dialogues, 61–62). Jabès was always quick to point out that he and his compatriots had been spared. In Paris, he undertook to study the Talmud and Kabbalah, which he knew only superficially. He also began to formulate an idea that he made popular, that the Jew's only future and only possible home is the book; thus he invented the concept of the book *as* place. Jabès conceived *The Book of Questions* as a modern Talmudic project, secular in scope, where questions and commentaries collide. He explains how he came upon the idea that the book, the Jew, *and* the writer are tied inextricably together:

> I was neither practicing nor a believer. I'd always lived in this country which was mine, and one fine day, when I wasn't prepared for it, I was forced to leave because of being Jewish. So, that posed certain problems for me. I told myself that we do not escape a certain Jewish condition. At the moment we least expect it, things explode and, without knowing why, you're forced to abandon everything and to lead a life of exile, of wandering. Finally, little by little I realized that, since the Jew has not had a real homeland for thousands of years, since he's been obliged to leave one place for another each time, what did he do? He made the book his true home, his real territory. And you find in the books of the tradition, in the Kabbalah, in the Talmud too, a questioning of the book, because it's there that the Jew's freedom was exercised, it's in the book.... And I found that there was such a similarity between the Jew and the writer that it struck me in an amazing manner. (Weiss, 183)

Many readers saw *The Book of Questions* as a solemn reflection on the Holocaust. Berel Lang famously criticized Jabès for not naming the Holocaust in the text, for holding back its representation as a historical event, and for writing obliquely about it.[29] Lang unfairly, I believe, accuses Jabès of turning a blind eye to the hideousness of the Holocaust and for presenting it as simply another episode in the history of Jewish persecution. It is interesting to note that a considered discussion of the Shoah was also missing from the Colloquium of French-Speaking Jewish Intellectuals (Szwarc, 139). Jabès defends his decision to not write *explicitly* about the Shoah in *The Book of Questions*. Given the enormity of the subject, he explains, he could not write as if he knew what it was like to live through it. Jabès makes this decision, he says, not because he shares Adorno's view that the Holocaust is unspeakable and unrepresentable. Jabès believed, on the contrary, that writers had a responsibility to write about it and make evil known (Dialogues, 62). He is clear about this: people who witnessed it, saw it up close, and lived its horror had the duty to speak about it. As for himself, he could only write about Egyptian exile. He would reference the Holocaust in *The Book of Questions* in the only way possible for him at the time, to use Gary Mole's apt phrase, as an "all-pervading presence, an unnarrated background,"[30] or, as Nathalie Debrauwere-Miller puts it, as a "collective cry of revolt."[31] Jabès's position is clear but also complicated. He could not write about Auschwitz. But, also, as he explains in the following statement, neither could he write as if it did not happen, as if it were not a very deep wound in the Jewish psyche:

> One can't speak of Auschwitz. People imagine that I tried to speak about Auschwitz. But I've never tried to speak about Auschwitz because I've not lived

> Auschwitz. I can't talk about it. But Auschwitz is something we have, in a certain sense, all lived. This horrible, unspeakable thing, entered into the very heart of words. Words, for me, have totally changed. . . . It's not for me to testify. Elie Wiesel can testify because he was in the camps. I did not know the camps. Now that doesn't mean I don't have the right—I'm not talking about the right to talk about the camps but of the right—to say what we've all become after the camps, what language has become for me. I read a sentence, see the wound in the sentence. I see the wounded word, exactly as if I saw someone in the street, or a friend, who showed me a wound. I see that, and it has entered all my words.³²

I believe that Jabès refrains from writing explicitly about the Shoah because, as he explains above, he did not experience the Shoah firsthand. But I also believe that he could only write about it "obliquely," as Berel criticizes, because his Egyptian experience and the suffering it was causing him were still very fresh. Egypt was still his most vivid and pressing reference point in those early years. I have argued elsewhere that we can understand his reluctance in psychological terms.³³ By not overtly engaging with the Holocaust in *The Book of Questions*, Jabès, I suggested, was expressing an unconscious (because unacceptable) resistance to being upstaged by the suffering of others, bracketed by theirs. On an unconscious level, the Holocaust threatened to overshadow his own suffering and the suffering of other Jews from Arab lands. Is it possible that his exile from Egypt with all that it meant in suffering could compare to the horror of the Holocaust? Clearly, it could not. But also, psychologically speaking, how could it not? Jabès wrote about exile and suffering at a time when to be a Jew, to suffer as one, meant to be a European Jew. To be clear, I am not suggesting that in *The Book of Questions* the Holocaust is obscured or diminished in importance by Jabès's concern with his personal suffering. This is not the case nor is it the point. *The Book of Questions* is about *all* Jewish suffering. In his work Jabès asks that his own suffering and the suffering of his compatriots be heard despite the din of others' suffering. It is also a testament to his integrity that he refrains from making his own what can only be experienced by others. He writes in *Aely* that people can only feel deeply their own reality, what they experience personally: "Mine can only be recognized by me, so much my own are its lacks and certainties" (BQ II, 314). It is too easy to identify with others and usurp their space of suffering—or of pleasure, for that matter; we must take care to be ourselves. As Jabès puts it: "To be yourself, methodically, in facing others; to know yourself, *try to be known*, while facing the unknown in others" (my italics; BQ II, 320).³⁴ I call attention here to the exhortation to "try to be known." The French verb is more forceful. It literally says to "force yourself (or try hard) to be known" ("s'efforcer d'être connu"). We must make an effort to be noticed, to be known, to *make known* to others who we are and where we are from. Like Salomon Schwall (Sarah's grandfather) in *The Book of Questions*, Jabès wants to be recognized and needs to know he counts.

He asserts himself in the book: "Need for roots. Need to recognize himself, to be recognized, a creature, a plant, a presence of this soil in its whole sweep, a living element of the landscape. Need to be reborn in it" (BQ, 158).

Jabès could not write about Auschwitz in *The Book of Questions*. But he *could*, in good conscience, write about his experience of loss and exile as an Egyptian Jew on his own behalf and on behalf of other non-European Jews like himself. Jacqueline Kahanoff refers to *The Book of Questions* in this way: "Some of these imaginary rabbis bear the names of Jewish families from all around the Mediterranean basin (Acobas, Panigel, Segré, Chemtob) as if the poet were engaged in a secret dialogue with ghost-like witnesses of this Jewish past who are still alive, although it is dead." "Eddie," she asks him one day in Paris after he had left Egypt for good, "How did you come to invent those imaginary rabbis?" He replies: "I think they were always with me, but they spoke only when I learned what exile is."[35]

Yukel / Serafi . . . Seaming

To tell his story and, at the same time, to invoke the Holocaust, Jabès constructs a formal structure in which Jewish grievances are dramatized by evoking a story of exile and suffering that goes back thousands of years to the experience of the Jewish people in the Egyptian desert. He creates a character, Yukel Serafi, who represents two figures at the same time. On the one side, Yukel is the Ashkenazi Jew deported to the camps and, on the other, he is Serafi, the Sephardic Egyptian Jew or the Jabesian in the text. The first represents what Jabès knows only *indirectly*: the horror of the Holocaust. The latter, Jabès knows as directly as anyone knows himself. Yukel is the main character, the hero, the witness, and the narrator. Serafi is the author. The two are addressed separately and each is unique. Yet at moments, as I explain later, the two share the same position, connected as by a seam where the two parts are visibly distinct yet held together. For example, the father of Sarah Schwall, Yukel's betrothed, is an Ashkenazi Jew (Moses Schwall), born in the south of France. Her mother was born in Cairo (Rébecca Sion). Both are destined to die together in the camps. As with Yukel/Serafi, they are connected at the seam and their fate is the same. This seam, figuratively speaking, is visible most of the time. But at times, as in the following exchange, it tears open and the two stand apart:

> Who were you, Yukel?
> Who are you, Yukel?
> Who will you be?
> "You" means, sometimes, "I."
> I say "I," and I am not "I." "I" means you, and you are going to die. You are drained.
> From now on, I will be alone. (BQ, 32–33)

Jabès is forthright: The "I" is "I, Serafi, the absent, am born to write books" (BQ, 58). The *I* is the author, Jabès. *I* is the writer who exists to give a voice to Yukel and Sarah's suffering. *I* is Jabès the Sephardic. Yukel is the "hero and narrator of the book" (BR II, 71). Jabès writes: "You are the narrator, Yukel, from book to book, from sky to sky / I am the stranger" (BQ, 123). Jabès is the foreigner; he is the outsider who has not experienced the Holocaust and was spared. From here on, I will refer to the *I* as Jabès, to make for easier reading. Jabès explains to Paul Auster that Yukel is double; he is both the narrator and the hero (Auster, 14). Yukel is also Jabès's alter ego. Jabès knows he *could have* lived and died like Yukel, but did not: "I could have been this man. I share his birth" (BQ, 68). Yukel serves an existential and formal function. He is the larger of the two, the all-important hero whose death helps make the point for the author. Because of Yukel, Jabès can now write the book and knows to locate exile at the heart of the Jewish condition. In *The Book of Resemblances*, the book about uncertainty and repetition, Jabès asks: "Yukel, is it really you? Then it's me also, and everything has to start over, be lived again, but where, under which horizon, in which generous corner of the earth, on which auspicious and willing page of the book to be composed?" (BR, 76). Yukel Serafi and Jabès are a composite figure, with this difference: Yukel (like Sarah) embodies the ineffable whereas Jabès is the word made flesh. The cries of Yukel and Sarah rise up from the ancient roots of Jewish suffering: "this scream wedded . . . to its breath and older than any of us" (BQ, 33). They offer Jabès the spiritual dimension necessary for the writer to represent his personal suffering. Because of them, Jabès is able to speak on behalf of *both* Ashkenazi and Sephardic suffering: "I, unsubdued, / closer to writing than to souls, / closer to the life of words than to my own, / closest to Sarah and Yukel / in my soul and in total oblivion. . ." (BQ, 296).

Jabès writes in *The Book of Resemblances*: "There is no thought without body. Where I speak, where I am silent, my body is the body of my thought" (BR II, 37). He attributed Max Jacob's power as a writer to Jacob's capacity to stay connected to the real, the actual, and material universe. Many don't see this, Jabès points out to Marcel Cohen. But Jacob had a passion for the concrete universe of things. "When he worked," continues Jabès, "he liked to surround himself with objects—pebbles, turned wood, stones, etc.—enjoying either their forms or textures, so as never to lose sight of the real and fall into abstraction" (Dialogues, 12). He explains further to Paul Auster: "I do believe that a writer works with his body. You live with your body, and the book is above all the book of your body. . . . we work with our bodies, our breathing, our rhythm, . . . writing in some sense mimes all this" (Auster, 15–16). This penchant for the physical and phenomenal world is fundamental to Jabès's aesthetics. But it is also, and paradoxically, construed as insufficient in itself. As such, Jabès (Serafi) is the figural representation of material presence, embodiment perceived as inevitable, but also as limitation.

Together, Yukel and Serafi form a whole. He writes in *Aely*: "The body is close, the soul is distant. Thus we are both absent and present" (BQ, 276). Yukel is essence and spirit, "thought without body," without the body of the writer, while Jabès is the body whose spirit can only enter the book by way of Yukel. At one point, Jabès asks Yukel to forgive him for taking his place, for occupying his "scream" with his own story, and for giving it form. He writes: "Forgive me, Yukel. I have substituted my inspired sentences for yours. You are the toneless utterance among anecdotal lies. An utterance like a star engulfed among stars. In the evening, only my stars will be seen, only their warm and wonderful sparkle. But just for the time of your brief vanishing. Returning, you will take your place again. Silent" (BQ, 33–34).

The utterance is Jabès's personal story that, like the story of Yukel and Sarah, is a story of dispossession that all three know intimately. The book can only be written because Yukel exists as the face of unspeakable suffering. Yukel Serafi alludes to both Holocaust suffering (Yukel/Ashkenazi) *and* Egyptian suffering (Jabès/Sephardic), joined at the seam by their Jewish fate. The seam shows. It is meant to show, as we see in the following example. Jabès says to Yukel:

> You were coming towards me. The same desire for freedom brought us closer, we walked side by side. An occasional glance assured us both that we were near each other. I tried to use your soul to make one for myself, tried to climb higher up without weakening the rungs of your suffering. I prepared myself to take on the experiences you felt. Each of them awakened a world. I saw my own face in them.—I am in my writing more anonymous than a bed sheet in the wind, more transparent than a window pane. To be free, I had to have a face and you had to lose yours. (My translation; BQ, 114)[36]

In another telling passage in *The Book of Questions*, Yukel is called upon to face up to a problem inherent in this double construction (author/narrator, narrator/ character, Sephardic/Ashkenazi, the word/the ineffable). It is a self-critique. Jabès suggests that by looking beyond the personal, the immediate pain of exile, by turning to the metaphysical dimension of a universalist conception of human suffering, Yukel has ignored the suffering of Egyptian Jews living in the present. He failed to address or reflect their pain. The complaint of exiles from Egypt goes like this:

> Yukel, you have not told us the story of the olive tree which died of no longer finding the soil of our country. You have not told us the story of the date tree which died of being at the threshold of our country. You have not told us the story of the donkey which died of no longer walking the paths of our country. You have not told us the story of the dog which died of having lost his master.
> You have told us the story of man.
> Yukel, you talked about the desert, and we looked for the date tree. You talked about Nathan Seichell, and we looked for the olive tree. You talked

about wisdom and madness, and we looked for the donkey. You talked about life and death, and we looked for the dog.
You have not told us the story of man. (BQ, 121)[37]

Yukel has failed to address their suffering. They were asking to hear the story of *their* suffering on a scale to which they could relate, and not on a universal level. Instead, they heard Yukel speak about shadows and ideas. Yukel responds to their complaint and acknowledges he has failed them: "I talked to you about man's health. . . . I talked to you about the eloquence and nudity of the word. . . . So, approaching my words made me retreat from you" (BQ, 121–122). Jabès then concludes with words that underscore the tenuousness of Yukel's embodiment in the text: "Yukel, the stranger, would be nothing on earth but the nameless and unnecessary display of an instant of the *unutterable* distress" (my italics; BQ, 123). Jabès's world *is* the olive tree, the date tree, the donkey, and the dog, suggesting perhaps that his suffering and the suffering of his compatriots from Arab lands is prosaic by comparison to the scale and mode of Yukel's and Sarah's. Jacques Derrida, whose personal story of expatriation is in many ways similar to the story of Jabès, wrote in *Monolingualism of the Other* that all of us, no matter how rooted in our "native" land and culture we claim to be, are in fact exiles, "but it does not follow that all exiles are equivalent. From this shore, yes, *from this* shore or this common drift, all expatriations remain singular" (italics in text).[38] By calling attention to the dual belongingness of Yukel Serafi—Ashkenazi and Sephardic—I am suggesting a way to recognize, pay tribute to, and "make known" the personal Egyptian side of Jabès's monumental oeuvre. In the last pages of this chapter, I will return to the Yukel/Serafi couple and point out some further nuances.

The Book, the Reader, and the Door That Is Egypt

With *The Book of Questions*, Jabès forges a literary genre that consciously breaks with French literature, defying generic categories and imitation. The form he creates is vast, open, loose, eccentric, fragmented, and chaotic. Not exactly an epic, it is nonetheless Talmudic in inspiration and, like the Talmud, it is a monumental project. Jabès describes his work in deceptively simple terms: "it's a book of *putting* into question" (italics in text; Weiss, 173). It is the putting into question of "language, death, life, everything. Roughly historicity" (Weiss, 184). He compares the process of questioning that his books invite his readers to undertake to the art of questioning we find in the Talmud:

> And since all the questions reap only unsatisfactory answers, to a certain extent, the question continues. If the Talmud is a book without end, it is because the questioning is without end. How does the Talmud proceed? By rigor and by questioning. And so you find in these books [*The Book of Questions* and *The Book of Resemblances*], for example, a question in the first one which you find formulated differently again in the third. You have to go through two whole

books before that question returns, and then it will bring a different answer. And the reason there are all these characters that I call rabbis, their voices, is to permit each one to say a thing that is sometimes in contradiction to another. Whence the flow of these characters who enter and question, question. And they question in time and outside of time. (Weiss, 188)

In the Jabesian imaginary, the book (the book he is writing and the book we are actively reading) is a dwelling in the same way the Book is the portable homeland of the Jewish people. Jabès writes: "We had a land and a book. Our land is in the book" (BQ, 255). He points out in an interview with Jason Weiss: "I think that Judaism is evident throughout the book, that true Judaism is there" (Weiss, 193). And he explains to Paul Auster that for the Jew "living out" the Jewish condition, the book has become not only the place where he can most easily find himself, but also the place where he finds his truth. And the questioning of the book for the Jew . . . is a search for truth" (Auster, 12). Jabès writes poignantly: "The sign is Jewish. / The word is Jewish. / The book is Jewish. / The book is made of Jews. / Because the Jew has for centuries wanted to be a sign, a word, a book. / His writing is wandering, suspicion, waiting, confluence, wound, exodus, and exile, exile, exile" (BQ II, 290). The book is the portable home of the Jewish people, its open road. Open, vast, unending, and ungraspable the dominant image of the Jabesian book is, like the desert, "divine mirror ground fine" (BR, 45). As Susan Handelman rightly suggests: "The identification of Jew and writer is not, for Jabès, merely a conventional analogy or apt metaphor; it is the essence of his vision. In a godless and secular century stunned by its glimpse of the void, Jabès discovers the haunting ghosts of theology long thought to have been laid to rest."[39] The book is the promised land: "O promised land all promise" (BR, 86).

Unlike his contemporary postmodernist writers who rejected the idea of deep meaning, seeing depth as a lure and false promise, Jabès's dense writing invites his readers to plumb the depths of his texts. His texts are profound. They depend on the reader, he says, on the experiences readers bring to the table during the act of interpretation. Edward Kaplan reminds us that "Jabès is neither religious nor nihilistic; he smashes only the naïve, idolatrous view that language adequately represents experience" (Kaplan, 115). Jabès admired the dense and suggestive styles of celebrated Jewish mystics who wrote in Hebrew and Arabic, noting that both the content and style of their writings led readers to consider profound matters, weighty sentiments, and thought. He held the view that Hebrew prayers were deeper and more significant than Christian prayers. Christian chanting, he suggests, begins by amplifying the words of the prayer. Then in the course of praying, as the sentiment of transcendence soars, words are little by little detached, emptied, and left behind. Hebrew chanting, which moves him more profoundly, keeps words and chant together; words, tropes, and vowels are one and inseparable. In the synagogue, Jabès explains, "it is the very words of the sacred, immutable text that let their chant be heard, allowing nothing other to be heard or seen than the word, the infinity of the letter" (Dialogues, 20). Hebrew chanting is part and parcel of the words themselves. "The Jewish chant has remained glued to the text" (Dialogues, 20). We find no sense of transcendence. Instead, we have an intense experience of the material density of the text. Hebrew chanting is "the very scream of an unbearable suffering stuck, one could say, to the word" (Dialogues, 21). Hebrew prayers manage suffering by looking inward and deeply.

The desire for depth is a desire for origins, for roots, providing it is understood that they will always be beyond our capacity to grasp entirely: "Writing means having a passion for origins. It means trying to go down to the roots. The roots are always the beginning. Even in death, no doubt, a host of roots form the deepest root bottom. So writing does not mean stopping at the goal, but always going beyond" (BQ, 325). Depth is the Jabesian book's essential character, a complex layering of affect and thought. "Writer and critic join battle against conventional meaning, against the trivialization of truth" (Kaplan, 123). In a beautiful passage I quote only partly below, Jabès suggests that depth matters a great deal to him:

> Because everything can hide within itself a certain truth.... What I try to do is to show that behind each word other words are hiding. And each time you change a word or make a word emerge from another word, you change the whole book. When I say there are many books in the book, it is because there are many words in the word. Obviously, if you change the word, the context of the sentence changes completely. In this way another sentence is born from this word, and a completely different book begins.... I think of this in terms of the sea, in the image of the sea as it breaks upon the shore. It is not the wave that comes, it is the *whole* sea that comes each time and the *whole* sea that draws back. It is never just a wave; it is always everything that comes and everything that goes. This is really the fundamental movement in all my books. Everything is connected to everything else. There is the whole questioning of the sea, the whole questioning of the ocean, in its depths, in its movement, in the foam it leaves behind, in the delicate lace it leaves upon the shore.... At each moment, in the least question, it is the *whole* book that returns and the *whole* book that draws back. (Italics in text; Auster, 24)

Meaning comes to the surface from the depths undone. The Jabesian book is not Blanchot's text, where writing seeks to abolish all trace of memory, body, and world. This is important to underscore. For Jabès, writing and reading are operations that connect human beings to history and to the phenomenal world. They are not deconstructive activities. His notion of the book is inseparable from the idea of hospitality and presence. "In fact," Jabès points out, "everything I've ever written comes out of something lived. There's never been any invention on my part, there's something lived behind it" (Weiss, 176). "And it's the accumulation of moments that makes continuity. That's part of what I wanted to show" (Weiss, 182). The book, then, is the accumulation of never-to-be-forgotten fragments of worlds, lives, generations. In the Jabesian imaginary, people, words, sounds, images, and wounds are real, obdurate, and weighty. The Jew cannot forget. In *The Book of Hospitality*, a Jew asks a wise man: "'How can I forget my past? . . . Not only has it been pursuing me since the day I was born, but, sometimes, I am convinced it will be my future.' And the wise man said: 'There are chains that only God could break. And he does not break them'" (LQ, 56). The Jew bequeaths to his descendants the book to interpret as best he can "in his day"—as it is said in Jewish commentary. The Jew does not leave his descendants mosques and cathedrals; he still remembers the destruction of the Temples (BQ, 193). The book contains the roots of a history, going back five thousand years and circling to the present, not in an act of repetition but of return. Every time the story returns, it brings something new. Beth Hawkins is spot on when, to describe Jabès's invitation to the reader to interpret the text, she writes: "*The Book of Questions* is a stunning, exhausting tribute to the power of the unanswered question. At the core of Jabès's world, the question resides, a pulsing, dynamic entity that vehemently rejects conclusions, yet promises to foster a relation between the one who asks and the one of whom the question is asked."[40] Jabès invites personal readings, requiring that we approach his text from any of its loose ends, any of its "doors," as he puts it. Ronnie Scharfman asks: "What door do we use to enter this book where we have nothing but doors and thresholds?"[41] But enter we must. To refuse is to turn our back on our people, our past, and who we are. The image of the door, recurrent in Jabès, is a rich metaphor for understanding the reading process as an ethical, personal, and genealogical imperative. Readers hold the key to the work: "I carry you, my brothers like a set of keys" (BQ, 75).[42] The principal and most obvious door to the work, Jabès instructs us, is not the most revealing. He encourages readers, if they are so inclined, to find less obvious points of entry. The reader, Jabès explains to Marcel Cohen, can easily refuse to enter through the main door, "the one that by its dimensions, characteristics and location, offers itself proudly as the main entrance, the one designated and recognized both outside and inside as the sole threshold" (Dialogues, 3). Yet the reader who takes the "wrong" door or enters a work through a side door, ignoring the writer's blueprint, has the unparalleled opportunity to surprise the work. All readings enter forcibly, Jabès reminds us; they break into the text as into a house that belongs to someone else. In any event, the reader never strays away from his own perspective: "A door towards which we would have bent our steps, moved by I don't know what lost reason, what unsatiable desire to unlearn or to founder in the abyss, will never have misled us, will never mislead us," adding this to reassure us: "This is so doubtless because, in the book, there are no visible doors, and by evoking its order, its law, I allude only to its luminous progress from page to page by author and reader, *both united* in the same adventure and henceforth accountable only for their own steps" (my italics; Dialogues, 3). The book is the home the author *and* reader build together. The hope—the expectation—is that the reader will find his or her roots and Jabès's roots tangled together in the book: "You alone will find me, because my roots are in your book" (LH, 20).

It is important for Jabès that the reader exist as an actual person and not merely as a function of the text. The book is an existential project for both the writer and reader.[43] It is in the book that Jews find each other. In this spirit, I am moved to acknowledge that my desire to highlight Jabès's Egyptian experience is informed by my personal history arising under similar conditions to leave Egypt in 1961. My father, Saul Israel, was born in Assiout in 1917, the birthplace of the great nationalist leader Ahmad Lutfi al-Sayed and of Gamal Abdel Nasser. My father was forty-four years old, like Jabès, when he left Egypt. I know that I read Jabès with my father in mind. In Jabès, I recognize the movements of his thought, sensibilities, certain experiences, and, most certainly, his gentle melancholy. Certain features of Jabès's writing feel very intimate to me. I hear in his work the inflections of people I knew while I was growing up, habits of grandparents, parents, aunts and uncles. Finally, it matters a great deal to me that my concern with Egypt-in-Jabès coincides with Jabès's own desire to "make known" his Egyptian exile. Yet, no matter our background, I believe Jabès asks that his readers meet him on *his* own soil:

> I have *The Book of Questions* in my hands. Is it an essay?"
> "No. Perhaps."
> "Is it a poem with deep wells?"
> "No. Perhaps."
> "Is it a story?"
> "Perhaps."
> "Am I supposed to infer that you would like it taken as the story of *your* rivers, *your* reefs?" (My italics; BQ, 300)

As I suggested at the beginning of the chapter, Jabès's work, from *The Book of Questions* onward, is informed by Egypt. In his imaginary, Egypt is both an experiential recent past and his heritage going back millennia. In the very same landscape, he comes face to face with "not a mythology but a foundation," to use Alcalay's apt phrase (Alcalay, 13). And both recent and ancient Egypt represent scenes of adversity. The biblical flight from Egypt, the first exodus, is repeated in the twentieth century by a second exodus. Tobie Nathan points out that the Hebrew word for Egypt is a plural noun, designating two Egypts: *Misraïm*. The word for Egypt in Arabic, however, is singular: *Masr*.[44] Why is that, asks Nathan? Why is Egypt in the Hebrew imaginary double? Nathan does not offer an answer and I find it unnecessary to go into the reasons given by Hebrew scholars. For the purposes of my argument, I find the reference to a plural or double Egypt felicitous. It helps amplify the idea that for Jabès, and for Egyptian Jews more generally, Egypt is double. It is both hospitable and inhospitable. Egypt, the cradle of civilization, "mother of the world," and the birthplace of the Jewish nation has played the part of both the good and the bad mother to Jews. In Jabès's imaginary, Egypt is the site of Judaism, a reservoir of memory. Every Jew carries Egypt with him in his wanderings. It is the screen memory of Judaism. It comes back to mind unexpectedly to remind us that we are still where we always were. Little changes. Everything for the Jew returns to Egypt. Marcel Cohen is right to say that the presence of Egypt in *The Book of Questions* is obsessive (Dialogues, 30). It is, perhaps, this measure of complicity that Berel Lang expected to see when he looked for the Holocaust in Jabès's book and found it missing. Jabès confesses: "I can say today that all my books are autobiographical" (Dialogues, 9).

The Olive Tree, The Palm Tree, and the Mediterranean Sea

When Jabès was forced to leave Egypt, he had a family, elderly parents, a career to think about, and responsibilities to carry out on behalf of the beleaguered Jewish community. Egypt was his home and his life. Its landscape, the Egyptian desert, the Mediterranean, the Nile, and Cairo formed his sensibility, composed his imaginary. The flight from Egypt in 1957, his personal humiliation, his separation from people dear to him—elderly parents, friends, relatives—affected him profoundly. As he often said, in the years following his exile, that he was hurt and confused. In France, Egypt loomed larger than ever on his mind. He longed for it, for the Mediterranean, for sunshine, and friendly faces. His alienation, desolation, and disgust with France are evoked pointedly in "The South," the story of the tailor on the rue de Pontoise in *The Book of Questions*.

How does it feel to live in a dreary and dark Paris where his own history of suffering was always met with incomprehension, if not blatant indifference? (MLN). The story begins on a gray and rainy day in Paris, "In the pleura of the world, the base of the eyes, men's hearts. Ugh. What mud" (BQ, 306).[45] In the original French, the recurrent sounds of "d," "p," and "b" evoke a sort of sputtering or spitting, as when we try to get rid of something in disgust—even with anger. On that morning, Yukel goes to a tailor to get an old jacket altered. In the shop, he sees an old man bent over a sewing machine.[46] At first, the tailor ignores him. Yukel is in a bad mood and doesn't like the man. He notices right away the man's accent: "the peculiar accent of Jews from Central Europe, in dragging, drawn-out words, barely unglued (the glue still sticky)" (BQ, 306).[47] After some waiting, the elderly man asks Yukel if he is not the author of the story of Sarah and Yukel: "The old man had questioned him with an indifference so obvious that Yukel made a concerted effort to answer him in a neutral voice."[48] Is the old man affecting indifference? Why would he? He simply doesn't care for literature. But Yukel is put off by the marked indifference ("indifférence si marquée") and responds as neutrally as he can, fearful lest he reveal his own thoughts, maybe even his feelings—of what exactly, we are not sure. This is when the tailor's wife comes in the shop and they are introduced. "'Ach,' said the woman. 'You're Jewish, like us'" (BQ, 307). She begins to tell Yukel about their deportation and their children's death, a girl and a boy, in a camp. She then asks:

> Were you in France during the war?
> —No. I was in Egypt.
> —So, you're a happy Jew; no matter how much you suffered, you are a happy Jew.
> —Enough mama, said the old man. Stop bothering the gentleman with . . . But the old women continued.
> —He's a Jew, no? He's a writer, no? (My translation; LQ, 341)[49]

The woman narrates scenes of death and suffering in the camps with marked lyrical inflection. "The South" is a rich story and the theme of indifference can be read in more contexts than the one pitting Holocaust survivors against a writer who was simply expelled—"a happy Jew." The old couple is mourning, while he is merely depressed. Were Yukel's feelings hurt because of the old man's indifference? Did the man's indifference surprise him or was he accustomed to this sort of indifference from people who compared all suffering to the suffering of Holocaust victims? When Yukel is done with business and the tailor's wife is done recounting, Yukel leaves the shop, pulled by an irresistible urge to see the Mediterranean. The story concludes on this, as does *The Book of Yukel*: "What pressing urge pushed Yukel to take a train south a few hours later? To see the Mediterranean again, listen to the lesson of the sea which keeps forever its salt and its color" (BQ, 308).

In Paris, Jabès comes face-to-face with European indifference. The tailor and his wife are indifferent to his suffering. The woman calling him a "happy Jew" is for him nothing less than a catastrophic indictment; it crushes his spirit as only a comment that is both true and false can do. With the phrase "a happy Jew," Yukel can agree entirely and disagree entirely. In post-Holocaust Europe, a non-European Jew needs to tread carefully lest others whitewash his pain with the broad brush of their indifference. By leaving Paris and taking the train to see the Mediterranean, Yukel reinforces his own history and his singularity with respect to the European cultures of the North. The Mediterranean is the cradle of his Egyptian ancestors; it is his birthplace and the place of his thriving. The Mediterranean has a privileged place in Jabès's work. He describes it in *The Return of the Book*, the third book in *The Book of Questions* cycle. The Mediterranean is pure pleasure and abandon, "morning sea, impulsive, but distracted, imaginative; amorous sea, soft; sea of swims and speed" (BQ, 328).[50] It is *least of all* a site of indifference: "In its shells, I have heard the echo of my name moaning" (BQ, 327).[51] It is not only *not* the site of indifference; it is the site of his history and his people: "The Mediterranean restored the eyes of those who came before me. This is why I want the sea to be the bond, a moving, millenary binding in the book. And this is why my dreams, in a world torn apart by departures, feel like deliverance. Run for your life! Out there, there's perhaps something for us, life."[52]

Jabès asserts his belongingness to Egypt by evoking the sea and, as in the following example, its flora, fauna, and terrain: "My trees are the flamboyant and the date tree. My flower is jasmine; my river the Blue Nile. My deserts, the sand and the flint of Africa" (BQ, 328). These evocations are tinged with melancholy, his sense of belonging veiled in doubt: "Did I have the right to call them mine because they entered through my eyes and my heart and because my lips called out for them?"[53] The heartbreak of exile, the heartbreak of the melancholy subject, is that he knows he is alone in his love, that the object of his desire, Egypt, does not reciprocate his love and has cast him away with indifference. Exile is physically wrenching and emotionally draining. This is the immigrant's story. For seven months before they could leave Egypt, the Egyptian authorities led Jabès and his family to believe they could leave any day. After seven months of hassles ("tracasseries"), they were given eight days to depart with the proviso never to return (Dialogues, 51). This was more or less the experience of thousands of Egyptian Jews, documented in their memoirs and in historical accounts.[54] They were uprooted from Egypt, some more summarily than Jabès, and dispersed throughout the world. Their dispersion is evoked most movingly in "Dedication," the opening words of *Return to the Book*:

> In the cemetery of Bagneux, *département de la Seine*, rests my mother. In old Cairo, in the cemetery of sand, my father. In Milano, in the dead marble city, my sister is buried. In Rome where the dark dug out the ground to receive him, my brother lies. Four graves. Three countries. Does death know borders? One family. Two continents. Four cities. Three flags. One language: of nothingness. One pain. Four glances in one. Four lives. One scream.
>
> Four times, a hundred times, a thousand times one scream....
>
> *(Mother, I answer to life's first call, to the first word of love, and the world has your voice.)* (Italics in text; BQ, 311)[55]

As in biblical times, the Jews of Egypt are cast off. The cruelty and humiliation of exile echoes through Jabès's work. I include here a few of the most poignant examples. In "Song," he compares Jews to dead leaves strewn on the road that are crushed, and swept away: "Sweep up the leaves / Sweep up the Jews" (BQ, 332). He then asks: "Will the same leaves regrow in spring? / Is there a spring for trampled Jews?" (BQ, 332) He evokes the brutality and humiliation that accompanies a life of wandering: "my face battered by the stones on our roads" (BQ, 45). The verb trample ("piétiner") suggests repeated physical and mental pounding. Reb Lehar says: "I am down on the ground. You stomp on me. You stomp on my eternity" (BQ, 325). But it is better, far better, to be trampled, crushed, stomped, and flattened than to be transplanted. As one of the rabbis says: "A thousand times better to be trampled grass than a flower transplanted."[56]

Jabès's *Book of Questions* cycle rests on the strength of a conviction that between its pages the Jew will find his "brothers." In the "Well" fragment inserted early on in the text, Jabès explains the source and purpose of his writing:

> *(The well I draw from is on Jewish land.*
> *My story is born in this well.*
>
> *The well I draw from is on Jewish land.*
> *My brothers sit on its edge.*
> *They have drunk of the water of their land.*
> *I bring you back this well.*
>
> *My story is born in this well.*
> *At first, it was pure cool water.*
> *My brothers have lost their well.*
> *My brothers have wept for their well.*
>
> *I bring you back this well.)* (Italics in text; BQ, 59)[57]

This prolonged parenthesis expresses Jabès's concern that we understand that his compatriots are included in the book—the Jews who expect to be sidelined. The parenthesis is unabashedly emotional, in earnest, and committed to making that point clear. The "brothers," Jabès's compatriots, both the Egyptian Jews living in biblical times *and* those living in the present, are the *source* of his work. Like him, they lost their source, their birthplace. This is not to suggest that Jabès is excluding non-Egyptian Jews. He addresses them as well. He addresses all his brothers from the place he knows best:

> "Yukel, which is this land you call Jewish, which every Jew claims as his own without ever having lived there?"
> "It is the land where I have dug my well."
> "Yukel, which is this water of our land, so good against thirst that no other water can compare?"
> "It is the water *fifty centuries* have forgotten in the hollow of our hands." (My italics; BQ, 59)

The place he knows best is Egypt. Jabès writes in *The Book of Resemblances*: "In this way Jew has been going toward Jew ever since the exodus. All the countries of Jews are the same divided homeland which they make whole again by gathering to complete the book" (BR, 86).[58] He promises in the parenthetical and italicized "Well" passage that his work will bring succor to both his Jewish Egyptian compatriots *and* to all Jews dispersed throughout the world in the name of a solidarity rooted in ancient Egyptian history. Jewish bonds are mythic, mystical, and visceral.

Inhospitable France

Jabès reflects the experience of many French speaking immigrants upon arriving in France from Egypt and North Africa. This drama is taken up, as I suggested, in several of Paula Jacques's novels.[59] I remarked earlier that Jabès was disillusioned by France. When he arrived in France as an immigrant—not as the wealthy tourist, Sorbonne student, and writer from the literary outpost of Egypt—France seemed illiberal and inhospitable. Forced out from Egypt, which labeled him a foreigner, and discovering that France too viewed him as a foreigner, Jabès felt doubly cut off. He writes poignantly: "I left a land not mine / for another, not mine either. I took refuge in a word of ink with the book for space, / word from nowhere, obscure word of the desert" (F, 79). It did not help that, as he put it: "*I gave the impression* of having sought out that integration" (my italics; Dialogues, 51). He felt deeply humiliated that French people thought he *wanted*, or preferred, to live in France rather than in his native Egypt. As he explains to Paul Auster: "it would be impossible for me to say that France is my country, that it is my landscape. . . . It is not my landscape, not my place, my true place" (Auster 11–12). But it was especially the French attitude toward users of the French language that was most cutting. Jabès spoke French fluently and elegantly. Ironically, this classical elegance was used against him to mark him as an outsider, a foreigner.[60] This French-speaking cultured immigrant, a man of the world, and a writer of some renown, felt acutely the inhospitality of the French. More than the personal affront, he found it most hurtful that the French language was used to exclude and shun his compatriots and other French-speaking immigrants from North Africa. Most of these immigrants admired France and many had French citizenship. Many still believed in the superiority of French culture, believed it to be the incarnation of the Enlightenment. They arrived in France expecting to find the hospitality that was denied them in their native country. In the following dialogue, he exposes an ugly nationalistic strain in the French people. The dialogue is introduced by the following question: "Do words change when other lips utter them?"

>—What are you doing here in my country?
>
>—Of all the countries on earth, yours is dearest to me.
>
>—Your feelings for my country do not justify your permanent presence among us.

—What do you hold against me?

—You are a foreigner. You will always be a foreigner to me. Go back to your place.

Your place is not here.

—Your country is the country of my language.

—Behind a language, there is a people, a nation. What is your nationality?

—Today, it's yours.

—A country is, first of all, a land. (My translation; LH, 51)[61]

The dialogue goes on for a while, revealing the arrogance of French nationalist feelings. Jabès is outraged at the treatment of immigrants from Arab lands: "What is the meaning *of France for the French* if not *France for France*?"[62] And anyway, he pursues, what France are we talking about? Is it not a fact, he argues, that the immigrant who is treated like a foreigner in France is the same person to whom France owes her glory and international reputation—its "rayonnement"? He offers his own example as a case in point in *The Book of Hospitality* (*Le Livre de l'hospitalité*):

> For example, in Egypt, where I was born and where I lived until I came to Paris in 1957, Egyptian minorities such as Jews (France's greatest advocates in terms of numbers), Copts, and Christians, whether of Egyptian or foreign nationality were responsible for sustaining French influence in that country. They chose French, made it a common language and made French culture a universal culture. It was a commitment based at first on an *image* of France they believed in deeply and *would have liked to keep believing in*. The image of a country founded on three words: Liberty, Equality, Fraternity. (My italics; LH, 35)[63]

These immigrants, Moroccans, Algerians, Tunisians, and Egyptians, promoted French language and culture in their native countries. *The Book of Hospitality* is a meditation on *in*hospitality, and French inhospitality in particular. Jabès's disappointment with France resonates loudly between its pages. This beautiful work, his last book, published posthumously, combines stories, meditations, argumentations, and aphorisms. He describes hospitality as the recognition and appreciation of difference: "'Come from wherever you are. / Go where you want to go. Here you will always have a bed to sleep in,' wrote a wise man. And he would add: 'Forget who you are. For that is how you earn the right to be my guest'" (LH, 56).[64] In the story that opens "L'hospitalité nomade," in *The Book of Hospitality*, Jabès makes the point that true hospitality is utterly disinterested, so disinterested that it would even refuse friendship as a sign of recognition for its hospitality (BH, 81–85). Given Jabès's feelings of resentment toward France, it should come as no surprise that he was not eager to pursue French nationality right away. It is an established fact that he could have easily received it soon after his arrival in France in 1957. He waited until 1966 to present his papers, becoming a French citizen only in 1968 (Jaron, 124).

Paradoxically, but understandably, living in France made Jabès think about Egypt more than ever. In a 1989 documentary film, filmed a few years before his death, he reflected on his attachment to Egypt.[65] He remarks wistfully (the ellipses in the two passages below mark the brief pauses that accentuate his thought as he takes measure of what he wants to say): "It's a country that has marked me deeply. It's the landscape of my childhood," adding:

> To talk about Egypt now seems a betrayal. How can forty-four years of life be recaptured? I've since turned the page. Egypt has become now, for me, a mythical country. A dream. If I . . . if I . . . had to talk about Egypt, I would speak about the fascination this country has always exercised on me. But when I was in Egypt, I didn't feel this fascination because I was living it. I was in it. I lived this thing . . . So, this landscape . . . these landscapes . . . are my landscapes, the landscapes of . . . the landscapes of my childhood. When first I opened my eyes, I saw this . . ., this . . . flat landscape. This desert (My transcription and translation).[66]

He reflects on the complications the French language created. Words matter. Language matters. Egypt was his country but it was *not* the country of the language he used to write his books. And this language, both foreign and not, made him feel he was in exile even as he was living in Egypt:

> It's a curious thing. You spoke to me once about exile. In Egypt also I didn't feel . . . [or rather] I also felt *just a little* as if I was in exile because Egypt, my country, was not *the* country of my language, the country of the language of my books, if you will. The end result is, in fact, I have always felt that I had no place, belonged nowhere. But, the image I have of a place is the image of Egypt. (My italics)[67]

This "just a little" suggests a tinge of pain; if language mattered, and it does for him, some damage to the sense of belonging can be expected. When Jabès thinks of place, of home, he thinks in no uncertain terms of Egypt. He is *of* Egypt. Both the Egypt of Moses and the Egypt he knew so well are as one in his mind. Just as a certain Paris was with him in Egypt, so in Paris he thinks of Egypt and the Nile, as he recites in the film from *The Book of Yukel*:

> This morning between rue Monge and la Mouffe (after the rue des Patriarches and rue de l'Epée-de-Bois, where I live) I let the desert invade my neighborhood. The Nile was not far. However, I have not led you to its banks where we used to walk, but to the spot where, like two young people overcome by sleep, death lies next to life. (BQ, 302)[68]

In "A Culture Stillborn," Jacqueline Kahanoff describes Jabès's apartment in Paris: "In most Jewish homes I know there are a few dearly loved relics rescued from a former life: pictures, candelabras, a rug. In Eddie and Arlette's small living room in Paris, I recognized the tapestry representing a child squatting among wild ducks half hidden among the rushes of the Nile. These tapestries, depicting Egypt's village life, had been made by the children of fellahin." Kahanoff adds: "Nothing I have ever seen is more evocative of Egypt's melancholy mud villages, barely emerging from the Nile silt, than these naïve, intensely poetic tapestries" (Kahanoff, 119–120).

The Egyptian landscape features large in Jabès's writing. He is rooted in the land and feels a closeness to Arab culture. Ammiel Alcalay relates a meeting he had with Edmond and Arlette Jabès in Jerusalem. When Alcalay arrived, there was an Egyptian film playing at the hotel: "Palestinian workers from the hotel sat on the couch watching and commenting. Neither Edmond nor Arlette could hide their delight at the black-and-white images of their former, Cairene life on the screen. Soon they were among the workers, gossiping away in Arabic about the famous stars" (Alcalay, 13). Jabès's education was French "but fairly quickly," Jabès points out in an interview, he became interested in the masterpieces of Arabic literature and thought which, "unfortunately," as he put it, he read only in translation because, as he explains to Jason Weiss: "I read Arabic, but still it was an effort" (Weiss, 181). Jabès maintained that Europeans never understood the East; they had no idea what to make of its culture but cultivated an image of it which was "completely false" (Weiss, 181). The East understood the West, Jabès explains, but it was not "deeply affected" by its culture and worldview. Speaking as a man of the East, he gives the example of the Egyptian peasant, the *fellah*, considered by Europeans to be lazy. This is an error, Jabès insists; the peasant works very hard day and night. It is simply that the Egyptian peasant has a different concept of time than Westerners. For the *fellah*, as for the nomad in the desert, "time doesn't count . . . what counts is the space" (Weiss, 178). Jabès explains further:

> There is a wisdom in the East that the West doesn't know. The wisdom of its peasants has nothing to do with the wisdom of the French peasant who is crafty, who counts his pennies. These others have an extraordinary wisdom, one would say they've traversed the centuries. And it's the landscape too that leads to that. These people have a way of thinking that's extremely deep but doesn't appear to be. (Weiss, 181)

Jabès writes explicitly and warmly about Egypt and wonders if he would be welcomed back: "Of the country I left I have kept the memory of a bed where I slept, dreamed, loved. / I shall no doubt die in the conqueror's country. But if I by chance went back to my homeland, could I again sleep there, dream there, love?" (BQ, 355).[69] In Deuteronomy, it is written: "You shall never again dwell in the land of Egypt." Yet Maimonides made an exception of it when he settled there and was welcomed. What to make of a country that welcomes and disinvites repeatedly? Egypt is an inhospitable territory for Jews and yet the Jew returns. Jabès writes: "I have lived on displacement like a capitalist on interest. Having inherited a hostile soil from my forebears. Shall I add that, for all its hostility, it was perhaps my only asset?" (F, 18).[70] The Jew returns to Egypt because Egypt is the only site from which the Jew's story can be told. He writes: "He remembered a phrase (but why did this one rather than any other suddenly pop up in his memory?), a single phrase from a forgotten story whose tone he recalled in quoting: / 'Father, which was this city of which we were guardians?'/ This city is not Paris. And yet Paris is the Capital of his [its] senses" (BQ, 305–306).[71] The return to Egypt, if only as memory, is evoked in the story of the eighty-something-year-old woman who, on her deathbed, speaks a language she had not spoken since she was a little girl (BQ, 326). Displacement and inhospitality, when meted out together, are devastating. Jabès remarks: "The absence of place, as it were, I claim as my own. It confirms that the book is my only habitat, the first and also the final. Place of a vaster non-place where I live" (BM, 171). In *Return to the Book*, he writes: "A thousand places. One place contains them all: the non-place. You live there. It is your fatherland" (BQ, 391). The book is place, to be sure. But the non-place, the place that contains them all, is loss. The book is Egypt. The return to Egypt for the Jew, and for an Egyptian Jew like Jabès, is a return to the book. The book is the repository of Jewish history and of his own personal history: "'First I thought I was a writer. Then I realized I was a Jew. Then I no longer distinguished the writer in me from the Jew because one and the other are only torments of an ancient word'" (BQ, 361).[72] In the book, Jabès can trace his existence, hear his *name* uttered by the sea—his sea, the Mediterranean. In a passage I quoted only partially earlier Jabès writes: "In the book, the colors of the sea range from the ivory of absence to ink black. The sea bathes the shores I walk. In its shells I have heard the echo of my name" (BQ, 327).[73] The sea is a strong image of self-recognition. But by far the most dominant image in Jabès's writing is the Egyptian desert.

It is curious that Jabès did not consider returning to Egypt, even for a visit. In the 1980s and in the years that followed, Egyptian exiles like Jacques Hassoun and Paula Jacques purposefully took the opportunity afforded by the 1979 Peace Treaty between Egypt and Israel to go back. Hassoun, as I discussed in chapter 1, believed that it was a necessary step for exiles and other refugees to return to see again with their own eyes the motherland that rejected them. Hassoun felt that the confrontation would be a step forward in disarming the cruelty of melancholy. When Marcel Cohen asks Jabès why did he not go back for a visit, Jabès responds first by saying he does not know why exactly, adding that the reason must be that he is afraid to be disappointed; it would be a blow to find out that the Egypt he had imagined while living in France is not the same Egypt. What if that Egypt does not really exist, that he dreamed it up? (Dialogues, 26). I have argued elsewhere that the psychology of melancholy helps explain his avoidance (MLN). I want to suggest, here, that a return to Egypt was also inconceivable structurally speaking in his own time. Like Moses, he could not go back. Once Jabès realizes Egypt stands for exile and that Jewish exile is eternal, he could not, without contradiction, return. As I suggest in chapter 2 in my discussion of *Jacob's Ladder*, Jacqueline Kahanoff gives Jacob agency to return; she gives a hopeful and defiant twist to the biblical story. Perhaps this hopefulness and this affirmation of Egyptian identity were still possible to imagine in 1954 when the novel was published. Not so for Jabès. By writing *The Book of Questions* cycle, he had constructed, or reconstructed, for himself and for his dispersed compatriots, a contemporary iteration of the exodus from Egypt. He had pieced together from the same cloth a history where Egypt and exile were, as in the biblical story, inseparable in Jewish consciousness. To return to Egypt would compromise the book, "the memorial he erected in their honor" (BQ, 325). A return might in fact cause the edifice, the memorial, to collapse under the weight of its contradiction: "You cannot build on equivocation. Only granite will do."[74]

Desert, My Desert. The Jew as Nomad

Jabès left Egypt on June 19, 1957. Like many Egyptian Jews living there during politically unstable times, he held out the hope, even the expectation, that the upheavals would subside and that Jews would be allowed to continue to live there as before. He confides to Carole Naggar and Jacques Hassoun, two compatriots, that his reluctance to leave Egypt had nothing to do with an unwillingness to give up a prosperous lifestyle but instead had everything to do with "the country itself, its people, with their wisdom and sense of humor, with the sky, with the desert, especially the desert. My desert."[75] Jabès, I suggested earlier, was fond of the Egyptian people. As an introvert, however, he was drawn to the landscape and especially to the desert. He spent time there, sometimes staying two days at a time. In part, he explains, it was a way to avoid social obligations that the small tightly knit Cairo community made necessary (Dialogues, 13). He confesses that when he felt overwhelmed by familial and social obligations, he found refuge in one of two places: a small apartment in a Muslim neighborhood of Cairo called Darb el Labbanah and in the desert at the edge of Cairo (Jaron, 92). Experiencing the desert was a way to disengage from the world (Dialogues, 13). The desert opened a space for reclaiming a deeper and more serious self. He explains that in Egypt this was the site of his depersonalization ("lieu privilégié de ma dépersonnalisation"; Dialogues, 13). Clinically speaking, depersonalization is a dissociative symptom that emerges as a result of intense and prolonged stress, trauma, and depression. It is a defense mechanism: "I went there," Jabès tells Jason Weiss, "to no longer be who I was in appearance to others in Cairo" (Weiss, 178). But it was more than social pressure that led him to seek the desert. Edmond Jabès lost his sister when he was twelve and she only seventeen. He was devastated by her death and, by his own account, never totally recovered. Her death made him see language, the words we use to speak to each other, in a wholly different way. He recalls that the words he and his sister exchanged as she was dying made words seem both piteously inadequate and, at the same time, formidably grave. The desert became for Jabès emblematic of this experience of death. At the same time, he explains, the desert brought him to writing. The desert compels you to meditate, he states; it pushes you very far deep within yourself: "Because what is writing? In writing one lifts away everything to get to a word that's more profound. Writing is also a pushing inside, and that's what the desert brought me" (Weiss, 179). The desert is both the place of origin and of death (BR II, 106); it is the site from which Judaism emerged, metaphorically, historically, and geographically. He writes in *Aely*: "Desert. All writing is first of all a wound of sand. Thus the Hebrew people had to spend forty years in Sinai in order to identify with the book. / The desert wrote the Jew, and the Jew reads himself in the desert" (Aely, 301–302).[76]

Essentially ungraspable yet real, the desert in Jabès is all at once a place, a dimension, and a process. A formidable entity, it draws unto itself all that is *and* all that was in the universe. It signifies both the beginning and the end of time. He writes: "One day the wind with all its breath will sweep the sky clear, and the desert will finally mirror the desert" (BR II, 106).[77] The visual image is as ineffectual as the metaphor is weak when it comes to communicating the desert's staggering reality. The quotation above with its sweeping invocation of the wind and desert as origin and end of the universe is *not* an image so much as an evacuation of image. The experience of the desert is anything but ocular. Jabès tells Jason Weiss: images are "the opposite of the experience of the desert." Aphorisms, on the contrary, embody the "experiences of the desert" (Weiss, 177). Jabès's signature aphorisms are the embodiment of a desert sensibility. The writer, like the Jew, is a nomad for whom words weigh very heavily: "There's a weight to words, and the weight for the Jew is very heavy, you know" (Weiss, 194). And speaking with the inflection of an Egyptian Jew who knows of desert experience and remembers his history, he remarks: "When we speak of death, for example, we speak with the memory of all our dead" (Weiss, 194). The Jew speaks "as if he had lived a life five thousand years long." For Jews, Jabès continues, "when anything happens, they remember. There's an unhappiness, oooh, that goes back five thousand years. They bring out a whole endless history, as if they themselves had lived it. And they *do* live it each time. They live an *entire* history with each event" (my italics; Weiss, 193).

In an evocative passage in *Return to the Book*, Jabès reflects on his journey from Egypt to France and on the book he has just finished writing and that we have in front of us. He relates to the reader how he came upon the mood or tonality he would use for *The Book of Questions*. He describes himself, as he imagined himself, sitting on an ancient granite block, pondering the book he has been writing for the past five summers: "It is years since I left Egypt. A succession of landings marks the repose of centuries of death" (BQ, 319). When, one day, as he was thinking about his origins, and digging deep to find them—"Writing means having a passion for origins. It means trying to go down to the roots" (BQ, 325)—two sites crystallized in his mind; one was of the desert and the other of the Nile. The first was steeped in silence and the other, also steeped in silence, was of the Nile as it flowed carrying cargoes that, to his mind, evoked "an unbroken line of red ants carrying their food." The book he would write, he decided, "ought to oscillate between these two silences" (BQ, 326). Like the desert and the Nile, *The Book of Questions* is infused with the weighty experience of Egypt.

I started by arguing that Egypt is at the heart of *The Book of Questions* and the work that follows. I tried to establish the artificial distinction between Yukel and Serafi, between Ashkenazi and Sephardic in order to drive the point that Yukel and Jabès are intertwined and yet distinct. They walk alongside each other in solidarity. The Jew from the West and the Jew from the East are both simply Jews who suffer together and suffer apart. In *The Book of Resemblances*, Jabès evokes the bonds between all Jews in this postwar moment in France and between Yukel and Jabès. Two scenes crystallize this bond. The first is from *The Book of Resemblances*. Here, Jabès refers to the inexplicable tragic death of Yukel *and* Jabès the writer: "How is it possible that the writer whose body we have just discovered could have died twice—both times, it seems, in equally tragic and inexplicable circumstances? First in the Western city he lived in, then in the Orient, amid sand?" (BR II 106). The second passage is from the last pages of *Return to the Book*. Jabès runs into Yukel. We are meant to understand that the desert and the streets of Paris converge, the desert and the book, Egypt and Paris, the ancestral past and the present; and Jabès, Yukel, and Sarah are all three pulled together tightly before the end of *Return to the Book* as the three expire in unison, their hearts ceasing to beat at the same moment: "Let my works be my three torches / and let my heart, which no longer beats in unison with my heroes', grow sober like theirs and freeze near the rendered page" (BQ, 402).[78] I believe that in *The Book of Questions* Jabès has intertwined the two strands of contemporary Jewish experience; namely, the Holocaust and Egyptian exile. If as Gary Mole has rightly put it: "Auschwitz in Jabès's texts is neither centred nor marginalized but is the locus of an alterity, a non-place which is not the negation of place but the place of vertiginous dislocation" (Mole, 298), it is because Egypt occupies that place. Egypt casts a significant presence. It is at the origin of the idea of the book as place. In Jabès, the lost Egypt is reconstituted in its modern iteration as the Place of all that was, is, and will be the Jewish people.

I have argued that Egypt occupies a significant place in Jabès's oeuvre from *The Book of Questions* onward. Represented both overtly and suggestively, Egypt animates Jabès's aphorisms and provides a landscape for his imaginary where he might connect with his past, his ancestors, the first Jews who wandered with Moses into its desert, and with present stories of Jewish suffering. But Egypt does not overwhelm the texts, as my reading by necessity makes it appear. Nor does it obscure the fact that there is far more suffering between its pages than the suffering of Jabès and his compatriots. With inimitable sensitivity and gentility, Jabès finds in his work a way to establish solidarity with other Jews, those whose suffering is immense and unspeakable, while attending to his own story and the story of his compatriots in exile with all the suffering that too entailed.

Notes

I use the following abbreviations and editions for English translations of Edmond Jabès's works:
(BQ) *The Book of Questions*, Vol. I (*The Book of Questions, The Book of Yukel, Return to the Book*). Translated by Rosemarie Waldrop. Middletown, Conn.: Wesleyan University Press, 1991.
(BQ II) *The Book of Questions*, Vol. II (*Yaël, Elya, Aely, El, or the Last Book*). Translated by Rosemarie Waldrop. Middletown, Conn.: Wesleyan University Press, 1991.
(BM) *The Book of Margins*. Translated by Rosemarie Waldrop. Chicago: University of Chicago Press, 1993.
(BR I, II, III) *The Book of Resemblances* Vol. I, II, and III. Translated by Rosemarie Waldrop. Middletown, Conn.: Wesleyan University Press, 1990, 1991, 1992.
(F) *A Foreigner Carrying in the Crook of His Arm a Tiny Book*. Translated by Rosemarie Waldrop. Middletown, Conn.: Wesleyan University Press, 1993.

Abbreviations and Editions in French of Edmond Jabès's works:
(E) *Un Etranger avec sous le bras, un livre de petit format*. Paris: Editions Gallimard, 1989.
(LH) *Le Livre de l'hospitalité*. Paris: Editions Gallimard, 1991.
(LR) *Le Livre des Ressemblances*. Paris: Editions Gallimard, 1991.
(LQ) *Le Livre des Questions I*. Paris: Editions Gallimard, 2002.
(LQ I I) *Le Livre des Questions II*. Paris: Editions Gallimard, 1997.

1. All transcriptions and translations are my own. Jabès's text: "... je me suis toujours senti sans lieu, sans appartenance. Mais, l'image d'un lieu c'est l'image de l'Egypte. Michelle Porte. *Jabès and Egypt*, film. Series: *Mediterranean Memory*, Production year: 1989. http://www.medmem.eu/en/notice/INA00055. Collection title: Océaniques, ID: INA00055,

by National audiovisual Institute–Coproduction, France Régions. Further references to this work will be included in the text as (Porte).

2. My translation of Jabès: "Qu'importe comment est le pays qui excite ton imagination. Qu'importe comment sont ses rives. C'est ton pays tout le temps qu'il te préoccupe, ce sont tes rives" (LQ, 317).

3. See Maude Mandel, "The Encounter between 'Native' and 'Immigrant' Jews in Post- Holocaust France: Negotiating Difference," in *Post-Holocaust France and the Jews, 1945–1955*, edited by Seán Hand and Steven T. Katz, 38–57 (New York: New York University Press, 2015). On the "the post-Holocaust" generation of mostly Maghrebi writers, see Thomas Nolden, *In Lieu of Memory: Contemporary Jewish Writing in France* (Syracuse, N.Y.: Syracuse University Press, 2006).

4. Sarah Hammerschlag, *Broken Tablets: Levinas, Derrida, and the Literary Afterlife of Religion* (New York: Columbia University Press, 2016). Hammerschlag examines Derrida's displacement of theology by literature, the conceptualization of which she attributes to his encounter with Jabès's works. The effects of their cultural backgrounds are outside the purview of my work. Hammerschlag does point out that in their first face-to-face meeting Levinas and Derrida discussed Jabès's *Book of Questions* and were inspired by it but that each philosopher read Jabès's work "quite differently because of the difference in emphasis each placed on his [Jabès's] Jewishness and his position as a poet" (preface x). She also recognizes in passing that the Western philosopher and the Eastern philosopher would not be expected to read Jabès in the same way. Something about Jabès and Derrida's shared Sephardic experience of expulsion and dispossession, the layered culture of the southern Mediterranean, and the dominant role that French language and culture played in their lives would be in part responsible for the work they created and the positions they assumed.

5. Edward Kaplan, "The Problematic Humanism of Edmond Jabès," in *The Sin of the Book: Edmond Jabès*, edited by Eric Gould, 115–130, 115 (Lincoln: University of Nebraska Press, 1985). Further references to this work will be included in the text as (Kaplan).

6. Daniel Lançon's literary biography and Steven Jaron's intellectual history of Jabès are both indispensable for pulling together Jabès's Egyptian experience. But missing from their work, and from most discussions of Jabès, is how Egypt and the narrative of expatriation are performed in the works; see Daniel Lançon, *Jabès l'Egyptien* (Paris: Jean-Michel Place, 1998); Steven Jaron, *Edmond Jabès: The Hazard of Exile* (Oxford: Legenda, 2003). Further references to Jaron's work will be included in the text as (Jaron) and further references to Lançon's work as (Lançon). Tiziana Carlino and Gil Z. Hochberg concur with Ammiel Alcalay that "Jabès begs to be read within the deeper and more imbedded historical texture of Levantine Jewish writing," "Desert Solitaire: Edmond Jabès, Resident Poet," in *Voice Literary Supplement* (February 1994), 13. No systematic study of Jabès's literary work has been done to demonstrate his filiation with Levantine writing.

7. My translation. Jabès's text: "C'est à peine si les pharaons appartiennent au passé" in Marcel Cohen, *Edmond Jabès: du désert au livre* (Paris: Pierre Belfond, 1980), 35. Further references in French will be included in the text as (DL). The English translation of this work is titled *From the Desert to the Book. Edmond Jabès: Dialogues with Marcel Cohen*, translated by Pierre Joris (New York: Station Hill Press, 1990). Further references to this work in English translation will be included in the text as (Dialogues).

8. Jabès's text: "Hier, c'était moi . . . et demain, ce sera encore moi. Tu peux, par conséquent, en toute liberté, m'intérroger aussi bien sur la souffrance et la joie des hommes

que sur l'aube et le soir du monde. C'est toujours l'histoire de ma vie et de ma mort que je te conterai. . . . Peut-on se souvenir d'un lieu où l'on n'a pas séjourné, d'un visage que l'on n'a pas approché, d'un objet qu'a aucun moment on n'a saisi?" (LR, 375).

9. Jacques Derrida, "Edmond Jabès and the Question of the Book," in *Writing and Difference*, 77–96, 77 (New York: Routledge, 1967).

10. Didier Cahen, *Edmond Jabès* (Paris: Pierre Belfond, 1991), 312.

11. See Jaron's *The Hazard of Exile* and Lançon's *Jabès l'Egyptien* for a trove of information about the magazine and Groupement's participants.

12. Yoav Di-Capua, *Gatekeepers of the Arab Past: Historians and History Writing in Twentieth-Century Egypt* (Berkeley: University of California Press, 2009), 112.

13. My translation. Jabès's text: "Tous deux, ma femme et moi, provenons de familles sépharades très connues, et bourgeoises: mon père était banquier et la famille de ma femme qui est très religieuse, avait un certain poids dans la communauté juive" (Lançon, 22).

14. Shimon Shamir, ed. *The Jews of Egypt: A Mediterranean Society in Modern Times*. (Boulder, Colo. and London: Westview, 1987), 33–67. See also the Introduction in this book.

15. Reb David Ibn Abi Zimra, also referred to as Radbaz, was born in Spain around 1479. He moved to Cairo in 1517 and was appointed Chief Rabbi of Egypt. To my knowledge, the Jabès family does not trace its ancestry to the Radbaz.

16. Irène Fenoglio, "Egyptianité et langue française," in *Entre Nil et Sable: Ecrivains d'Egypte d'expression française* (1920–1960), edited by Marc Kober, Irène Fenoglio, and Daniel Lançon, 15–25, 24 (Paris: Centre National de Documantation Pédagogique, 1999). Further references to this work will be included in the text as (Nil). All translations of this work are mine.

17. Irène Fenoglio, "Le Destin poétique d'Edmond Jabès dans les désécritures de la décennie blanche," in *Edmond Jabès L'Eclosion des énigmes*, 29–42, 30 (Paris: Presses Universitaires de Vincennes, 2007). Further references to this work will be included in the text as (Eclosion). All translations of this work are mine.

18. Nancy Y. Reynolds, *A City Consumed: Urban Commerce, the Cairo Fire, and the Politics of Decolonization in Egypt* (Stanford, Calif.: Stanford University Press, 2012), 68.

19. Jason Weiss, *Writing at Risk: Interviews in Paris with Uncommon Writers* (Iowa City: University of Iowa Press, 1991), 174. Further references to this work will be included in the text as (Weiss).

20. See Steven Jaron, Didier Cahen, and Daniel Lançon for detailed and meticulous datings of Jabès's early works.

21. Roger E. Stoddard, "Comment je lis Edmond Jabès: La Réponse du bibliographe," in *L'Eclosions des énigmes*, 297–309, 300 (Paris: Presses Universitaires de Vincennes, 2007).

22. Paul Auster, "Book of the Dead," in *The Sin of the Book: Edmond Jabès*, edited by Eric Gould, 3–25, 9 (Lincoln: University of Nebraska Press, 1985). Further references to this work will be included in the text as (Auster).

23. Jabès's text: "Il a suffi de quelques graffiti sur un mur pour que les souvenirs qui someillaient dans mes mains s'emparent de ma plume. Et que les doigts commandent la vue" (LQ, 30).

24. Jabès's text: "J'avais pris conscience de ma condition juive. Il fallait maintenant que je l'assume" (Jaron, 2).

25. Sandrine Szwarc, *Les Intellectuels juifs de 1945 à nos jours* (Paris: Le Bord de L'eau, 2013), 139. Further references to this work will be included in the text as (Szwarc). All translations of this work are mine. For studies on post-Holocaust French thought, French Juda-

ism, and French Jewish identity, see Sarah Hammerschlag's incisive discussions in *Broken Tablets: Levinas, Derrida, and the Afterlife of Religion* (see Note 4, above); *Post-Holocaust France and the Jews, 1945–1955*, edited by Seán Hand and Steven T. Katz (New York: New York University Press, 2015). Seán Hand's "Introduction" gives an excellent overview of conditions and debates taking place during this period.

26. For a historical overview of the Colloquium, see Sandrine Szwarc, *Les Intellectuels juifs de 1945 à nos jours* (see previous note). The Colloquium took place from 1957 to 2004; altogether there were forty. In 2016, the Colloquium was relaunched. Its organizers were Danielle Cohen-Levinas and Perrine Simon-Nahum; its inaugural topic: "Surviving: Resisting—Self-Transformation—Opening" ("Survivre: Resister—Se Transformer—S'ouvrir"). The stated aim of the Colloquium is to explore through Judaism ways to engage with problems arising from modernity, given the threat of "violence, terrorism, globalization, and a new era in politics" ("Face à la violence, au terrorisme, à la mondialisation et aux nouveaux visages du politique, les Nouveaux Colloques des Intellectuels juifs ont pour ambition, à la lumière d'une actualisation de la tradition juive, de dessiner les voies d'un nouvel engagement de la pensée et d'une réponse aux problèmes nés de notre modernité"). See http://www.paris-sorbonne.fr/programme-5398.

27. See Erik H. Cohen, *The Jews of Today: Identity and Values* (Leiden: Brill, 2011), 192.

28. For a thorough and nuanced treatment of universalism, *laïcité*, and French Jewry, see Maurice Samuels, *The Right to Difference: French Universalism and the Jews* (Chicago: University of Chicago Press, 2016). For a good historical overview of French Jewry, see Esther Benbassa, *The Jews of France: A History from Antiquity to the Present*, translated by M. B. DeBevoise (Princeton, N.J.: Princeton University Press), 1999.

29. Berel Lang, "Writing-the-Holocaust: Jabès and the Measure of History," in *The Sin of the Book: Edmond Jabès*, edited by Eric Gould, 191–206, 194 (Lincoln: University of Nebraska Press, 1985). For a very thoughtful discussion on the representation of the Shoah in Jabès's work, see Gary Mole, "Edmond Jabès and the Wound of Writing: The Traces of Auschwitz," in *Orbis Litterarum* 49 (1994): 203–306.

30. Mole, 297. Further references to this work will be included in the text as (Mole).

31. Nathalie Debrauwere-Miller, "La 'Conscience d'un Cri' dans la poétique d'Edmond Jabès" *French Forum* 30, no. 2 (Spring 2005): 97–119, 97.

32. My translation of Jabès's text: "On ne peut pas parler d'Auschwitz. Les gens s'imaginent que j'ai essayé de parler d'Auschwitz. Mais je n'ai jamais essayé de parler d'Auschwitz, puisque, je n'ai pas vécu Auschwitz. Je ne peux pas en parler. Mais Auschwitz est quelque chose que nous avons, d'une certaine façon, si l'on peut dire, tous vécu. Cette chose horrible, indicible, elle est entrée dans les mots. Les mots—pour moi—ont totalement changé. . . . Ce n'est pas à moi à témoigner. Elie Wiesel peut témoigner parce qu'il a été dans les camps, je n'ai pas connu les camps, mais cela ne m'empêche pas d'avoir le droit—non pas de parler des camps—mais de dire ce que nous sommes devenus après les camps. Ce qu'est devenu le langage pour moi. Je lis une phrase, vois la blessure de la phrase. Je vois le mot blessé, exactement comme si je voyais quelqu'un, dans la rue, ou un ami, qui me montrait une blessure. Je vois cela, et c'est entré dans tous mes mots" (Mole, 295).

33. Aimée Israel-Pelletier, "Edmond Jabès, Jacques Hassoun, and Melancholy: The Second Exodus in the Shadow of the Holocaust," *MLN* French 123, no. 4 (September 2008): 797–818. In this article I examine Jabès's attachments and the workings of melancholy. Further references to this work will be included in the text as (MLN).

34. Jabès's text: "C'est toujours par rapport à l'autre que l'on s'affirme. Face à l'autre être soi méthodiquement; face a l'inconnu des autres, se connaître, *s'efforcer d'être connu*" (my italics; BQ II, 439).

35. Jacqueline Kahanoff, "A Culture Stillborn," *Mongrels or Marvels: The Levantine Writings of Jacqueline Shohet Kahanoff* (Stanford, Calif.: Stanford University Press, 2011), 114–127, 119. Further references to this work will be included in the text as (Kahanoff).

36. My own translation of Jabès's text: "Tu venais à ma rencontre. . . . Le même désir de liberté nous rapprochait.—A peine, de temps en temps, un regard échangé attestait que nous étions l'un près de l'autre.—Je cherchais à me faire une âme de la tienne, à gravir sans faiblir les échelons de ta souffrance. Je me préparais à assumer les liens que tu avais éprouvés; chacun d'eux éveillait un vocable. Ils me rendaient mon visage.—Je suis dans mes écrits, plus anonyme qu'un drap de lit au vent, plus transparent qu'un carreau de fenêtre.— J'avais besoin, pour être libre, d'avoir un visage et toi, de perdre le tien (LQ, 127).

37. Without altering the meaning of the translation and for easier reading, I have taken the liberty of eliminating quotation marks in this passage from Rosemarie Waldrop. No quotation marks exist in the French original.

38. Jacques Derrida, *Monolingualism of the Other or the Prosthesis of Origin* (Stanford, Calif.: Stanford University Press, 1998), 58.

39. Susan Handelman, "'Torments of an Ancient Word': Jabès and the Rabbinic Tradition," in *The Sin of the Book: Edmond Jabès*, edited by Eric Gould, 55–91, 56 (Lincoln: University of Nebraska Press, 1985).

40. Beth Hawkins, *Reluctant Theologians: Franz Kafka, Paul Celan, Edmond Jabès* (New York: Fordham University Press, 2003), 156.

41. My translation. Ronnie Scharfman, *Ecrire le livre autour d'Edmond Jabès, Colloque de Cerisy-la-Salle* (Paris: Editions Champ Vallon, 1989), 285.

42. My translation. Jabès's text: "Je vous porte mes frères comme un trousseau de clefs" (LQ 85).

43. Chapter 7, "And You Shall Be in the Book," in *The Book of Questions*, Vol. I, deserves to be read in its entirety. Addressed to "A toi, qui crois que j'existe" ("You who believe that I exist"), namely the reader, the chapter communicates the centrality of the reader's activity and the force and range accorded this activity (BQ 39–45).

44. Tobie Nathan in an interview on *Café Littéraire du Mercredi* at the Institue du Monde Arabe on November 18, 2015, www.youtube.com/watch?v=dt9zhRN2FeQ&list=LL8 sK7wycKF_orQUEtyOwBAw&index=2.

45. Jabès's text: "*D*ans la plèvre *d*e l'univers, *d*ans le fond *d*es yeux et *d*ans le coeur *d*es hommes. Pouah. Quelle boue" (my italics; LQ, 339).

46. Yukel, here, is the figure of the writer, of Jabès. Yukel is his concrete and prosaic incarnation.

47. Both the French text and Waldrop's translation emphasize the "d" sounds: "cet accent particulier aux Juifs originaires de l'Europe centrale, avec des mots traînants, tirés, *d*écollés avec *d*ifficulté—la colle étant encore fraîche. . ." (my italics; LQ, 340).

48. My translation. The French text suggests indifference: "Le vieillard l'avait questionné avec une *indifférence si marquée* que Yukel s'efforça de lui répondre d'une voix neutre" (my italics; LQ, 341). Waldrop translates: "The old man had asked with such marked casualness that Yukel tried to answer in a neutral voice" (BQ, 307).

49. Waldrop translates "un juif heureux" as "a lucky Jew" (BQ, 308).

50. Jabès's text: "mer matinale, impulsive mais distraite et imaginative; mer amoureuse, mollifiée; mer du sillage et de la nage" (LQ, 363).

51. Jabès's text: "dans ses coquillages, j'ai écouté gémir l'écho de mon nom" (LQ, 362).

52. My translation. Jabès's text: "La Méditerranée a régénéré les regards qui ont précédé le mien; c'est pourquoi j'ai voulu que la mer soit, dans le livre, le lien mouvant, millénaire, et c'est aussi pourquoi mes songes, dans un monde déchiré de départs, ont le sens d'un sauvetage. Sauve qui peut! Là-bas, il y a peut-être pour nous, la vie" (LQ, 362–63). Waldrop's translation: "The Mediterranean has revived eyes before mine. This is why I want the sea to be the moving, millenary bond in the book. It is also why my dreams have the sense of a lifeline in a world torn by departures. Gangway! Down under there is perhaps a life for us" (BQ, 327).

53. Jabès's text: "Avais-je le droit de les considérer miens parce qu'ils étaient entrés en moi par la pupille et par le coeur et parce que ma bouche le proclamait? (LQ, 363). Waldrop's translation: "Do I have the right to consider them mine because they entered my pupils and my heart, and because my mouth trumpets them forth?" (BQ, 328).

54. Jacques Sardas, *Without Return: Memoirs of an Egyptian Jew 1930–1957* (Dallas, Texas: Thebes Press, 2017) is one such example.

55. Jabès's text: "Au cimetière de Bagneux, dans le département de la Seine, repose ma mère. Aux vieux Caire, au cimetière des sables, repose mon père. A Milan, dans la morte cité de marbre, est ensevelie ma soeur. A Rome où, pour l'accueillir, l'ombre a creusé la terre, est enfoui mon frère. Quatre tombes. Trois pays. La mort connaît-elle les frontières? Une famille. Deux continents. Quatre villes. Trois drapeaux. Une langue, celle du néant. Une douleur. Quatre regards en un. Quatre existences. Un cri. Quatre fois, cent fois, dix mille fois un cri. (*Mère, je réponds au premier appel de la vie, au premier mot d'amour prononcé et le monde a ta voix.*)" (LQ, 345).

56. My translation. Jabès's text: "Mieux être mille fois l'herbe piétinée que la fleur transplantée" (LQ, 157).

57. Jabès's text: (*Le puits où je puise est en terre juive./Mon récit prend naissance dans le puits. / Le puits où je puise est en terre juive. / Sur la margelle, mes frères sont assis. / Ils ont bu à l'eau de leur terre. / Je vous rendrai le puits. / Mon récit prend naissance dans le puits. / A l'origine, il était eau pure et fraîche. / Mes frères ont perdu leur puits. / Mes frères ont pleuré leur puits. / Je vous rendrai le puits.*) (italics and parenthesis in text; LQ, 65.)

58. Jabès's text: "Ainsi le juif va vers le juif depuis l'exode. Toutes les patries des juifs ne sont qu'une même patrie divisée à laquelle ils redonnent son unité, en se groupant, en se parchevant le livre" (LR, 117).

59. On this subject, see Mandel, "The Encounter between 'Native' and 'Immigrant' Jews."

60. Marcel Cohen's discussion is an example of snippy condescension. In his questioning, Cohen places emphasis on what he takes to be Jabès's quaint and odd use of French, going so far as to suggest that Jabès's style strikes a false note ("a flagrant contradiction") considering its formal, presumably radical, qualities. He adds: "We could ask if this isn't because of a subconscious desire to extend your roots, to "possess' ["d'étendre vos racines, de 'posséder'." (DL 71)]" (Dialogues, 44). Cohen submits that Jabès uses the dictionary like writers "belonging to a minority"—like Kafka, he points out—not only to take it over ["accaparer"] the French language and "make it his own" but to use the dictionary for effect and willy-nilly; he asks Jabès: "How did you come to use these words?

Do you come across them haphazardly [au hasard] in the dictionary?" (Dialogues, 45). In the 1950s and 1960s, French writers like Francis Ponge and the Oulipo group made method and practice of the dictionary. Yet Cohen sees only signs of the foreign, borrowed, and the false.

61. All translations of *Le Livre de l'hospitalité* are my own.

62. Jabès's text: "Que signifie: *La France aux Français* sinon: *La France à la France*?" (LH, 35).

63. Jabès's text: "En Egypte, par exemple, où je suis né et où j'ai vécu jusqu'à mon installation à Paris, en 1957, ce sont les minoritaires juifs, en premier par leur nombre, coptes, chrétiens, de nationalité égyptienne ou étrangère, qui ont maintenu la présence de la France, dans ce pays, faisant, de la langue française une langue commune et de sa culture, une culture universelle. Un choix qui engage totalement celui qui l'a fait et qui n'est autre, au départ, que la fidélité à *une image* à laquelle il a profondément cru et *aurait voulu, toujours, croire*. L'image d'un pays bâti sur trois mots: Liberté, Egalité, Fraternité (my italics; LH, 35).

64. Jabès's text: "'Viens d'où tu viens. / Vas où tu vas. Ici, tu as ton lit,' écrivait un sage. Et il ajoutait: "Oublie qui tu es, car, à cet oubli initial tu devras d'être mon hôte'" (LH, 56).

65. Michelle Porte, *Jabès and Egypt*, a film produced in 1989 (see Note 1).

66. My transcription and translation of Jabès in the film of Michelle Porte: "C'est un pays qui m'a beaucoup marqué. C'est le paysage de mon enfance." He adds: Parler de l'Egypte maintenant me semble presqu'une trahison. Parce que comment retrouver 44 années de vie. J'ai tourné la page depuis. Et, l'Egypte est devenu maintenant, pour moi, un pays mythique. Un rêve. Si je . . . si je . . . devais parler de l'Egypte, je parlerais de la fascination que ce pays a toujours exercé sur moi. Mais en Egypte, je ne ressentais pas cette fascination parce que j'étais dedans. Je vivais ce . . . Alors, les paysages . . . les paysages . . . sont mes paysages, les paysages de . . . les paysages de mon enfance. Dès que j'ai ouvert les yeux, j'ai vu ce . . ., ce . . ., paysage plat. Ce désert (see Note 1),

67. My transcription and translation of Jabès in the film of Michelle Porte: "Mais c'était curieux. Vous me parliez une fois d'exil. En Egypte aussi je ne me sentais pas . . . je me sentais aussi *un peu* exilé parce que l'Egypte, qui était mon pays, n'était pas *le* pays de ma langue, le pays de la langue de mes livres, si vous voulez. Ca fait que, en fait, je me suis toujours senti sans lieu, sans appartenance. Mais, l'image d'un lieu c'est l'image de l'Egypte (my italics).

68. Jabès's text: "Ce matin, entre la rue Monge et la Mouffe, j'ai laissé le désert, après la rue des Patriarches et la rue de l'Epée-de- Bois, où s'élève ma demeure, envahir mon quartier. Le Nil n'était pas distant. Cependant, ce n'est pas sur ses berges où nous nous promenions autrefois que je vous ai conduit; mais là où, pareilles à deux adolescentes surprises par le sommeil, la mort est couchée auprès de la vie (LQ, 334–335).

69. Jabès's text: "Je garde, du pays que j'ai quitté, le souvenir d'un lit où j'ai couché, rêvé, aimé. / Je mourrai, sans doute, au pays du conquérant; mais si, par chance, je revenais dans ma patrie, pourrais-je y dormir encore, y rêver, y aimer?" (LQ, 391).

70. Jabès's text: "J'ai vécu d'errance, comme le capitaliste de ses rentes, ayant, de mes ancêtres, hérité d'une terre hostile. Ajouterais-je qu'elle fut, dans son hostilité, peut-être, mon seul bien?" (Etranger, 33).

71. Jabès's text: "Il se souvint—mais pourquoi est-ce elle et non une autre qui a surgi tout à coup de sa mémoire?—d'une phrase détachée d'un récit inconnu dont il retrouvait

l'émotion, en la récitant:/ "Père, quelle était cette ville/ dont nous étions les gardiens?" / Cette ville n'est pas Paris. Et, pourtant, Paris est la capitale de ses sens" (LQ, 339).

72. Jabès's text: "J'ai cru d'abord que j'étais un écrivain, puis je me suis rendu compte que j'étais juif, puis je n'ai plus distingué en moi l'écrivain du juif, car l'un et l'autre ne sont que le tourment d'une antique parole" (LQ, 398).

73. Jabès's text: "Dans le livre, les couleurs de la *mer* passent de l'ivoire de l'absence au noir de l'encre. La *mer* baigne les rives que mes pas retrouvent. Dans ses coquillages, j'ai écouté gémir l'écho *de mon nom*" (my italics; LQ, 362).

74. My translation. Jabès text: "Ainsi, le passé participe aux métamorphoses du passé pour un avenir que l'éternité détourne du périssable quotidien. / On ne peut bâtir sur une équivoque" (LQ, 435).

75. My translation. Jabès's text: "Ce n'était pas, croyez-moi, une situation sociale, même aisée, qui m'empêchait de faire le saut, mais le pays, le peuple, avec sa sagesse et son humour, mais le ciel, mais le désert, surtout le désert, mon désert." In "Le Caire quitté," entretien avec Carole Naggar et Jacques Hassoun, in *Autrement*, no.12, "Le Caire. Mille et une villes" (Paris, February 1985) 43–47, 45. Also quoted in Daniel Lançon, *Jabès L'Egyptien*, 258.

76. Jabès's text: "Désert. Toute écriture est d'abord blessure de sable. Aussi a-t-il fallu au peuple hébreu quarante années dans le Sinaï pour s'identifier au Livre. Le désert a écrit le juif et le juif se lit dans le désert" (LQ II, 416). He also writes most evocatively: "L'expérience du désert, c'est aussi l'écoute, l'extrême écoute. . . . J'ai, comme le nomade son désert, essayé de circonscrire le territoire de blancheur de page; d'en faire mon véritable lieu; comme, de son côté, le juif qui, depuis des millénaires, du désert de son livre, a fait le sien. . . . Le désert est bien plus qu'une pratique du silence et de l'écoute. Il est une ouverture éternelle. L'ouverture de toute écriture, celle que l'écrivain a, pour fonction, de préserver. / Ouverture de toute ouverture" (LR, 200).

77. Jabès's text: "Le vent, un jour, balaiera de tout son souffle le ciel et le désert enfin se mirera dans le désert" (LR, 273).

78. Jabès's text: "Que mes ouvrages soient mes trois torches / et que mon coeur qui a cessé de battre à l'unisson de celui de mes héros, comme le leur se dégrise et se glace à proximité du feuillet rendu" (LQ, 438).

CHAPTER FOUR

Paula Jacques, Resistance and Transmission
Transplanting Egypt on the Soil of France

> No, they didn't win... the olive tree produces its most splendid fruit when it is near the end, and it will be so for the Jews of Egypt.[1]
> *Aunt Carlotta's Legacy*

> Age, it comes, it goes, it changes all the time, and my nationality also. What's so important about papers anyway? They're made of dust. Don't I know who I am?[2]
> *Light of My Eye*

PAULA JACQUES'S WORK, her ten novels to date, all concern the Jewish Egyptian community when it was under siege in the 1950s, roughly speaking during and in the aftermath of Egypt's nationalist revolution and the Suez Canal crisis. Her novels describe characters as they deal with difficult circumstances in Egypt and, later, as immigrants in France and Israel. In Egypt, they are dealing with the stresses of political uncertainty, the deterioration of the Jewish community, fear for their personal safety, humiliation, dispossession, and expulsion. In France and Israel, they face the hardships of immigrant refugees anywhere, with the added twist inflecting the experiences of many Egyptian Jews that they expected to be well received in France and Israel but they were not. This is the unsettling universe Jacques evokes.

In this chapter I focus on Jacques's work as an act of resistance, constructed in opposition to the reigning narrative of Jewish exile and perpetual wandering. Her novels foreground dramatic acts of pushing back by individual characters against the system that is seeking to evict them. Her work celebrates resistance whether it succeeds or not. Furthermore, her writing itself is conceived as a form of resistance. Jacques's stated aim is for her novels to stand as a stronghold against the forces of forgetfulness and against the deliberate efforts to erase the Jewish presence from Egyptian history. As such, she aims to reinscribe Jewish Egyptian presence into the cultural memory of Egypt. Neither Jacques nor her characters militate for an actual return to Egypt. It is too late for that. And yet there is more in her work than a striving to ensure the preservation of the Jewish Egyptian community's place in history. I argue in this chapter that in a specific way Jacques lays out a bold plan and presents an argument for the perpetuation of the Jewish Egyptian community on the soil of France, planting its ethnographical imprint, so to speak, on that country. In doing so, Jacques ensures their survival as a distinct community, a legacy of joint Egyptian and French cultures. Quite apart from the blueprint for resistance her work puts forward, this chapter examines Jacques's artful management of her subject matter. She steers clear of stereotypical characterizations and "touristy exoticism." Rather, as I explain, her writing conserves in its language and representations the liveliness, the moving presence, the way of being of a community whose attachment to Egypt her work makes amply evident.

A Model of Resistance

Paula Jacques opens her novel *A Kiss as Cold as the Moon* (*Un Baiser froid comme la lune;* 1983), with a prologue. It sets a scene. On a terrace overlooking the Mediterranean at Alexandria, the once-prosperous Del Burgo family and their friends are celebrating Passover. As Tobias Del Burgo does every year at the Passover Seder, he is relating the story of the family's origins. It tells of how his ancestors, Rabbi Saul Del Burgo and his young wife, carrying with them the Torah scrolls of their synagogue, enter Palos in Andalusia using false papers. They are fleeing the Inquisition, having arranged to sail on a ship headed for Constantinople where the Sultan Mehmet II offered safe haven to the beleaguered Jews of Spain. Waiting on the same shore is Christopher Columbus, a Marrano, alleges the storyteller. The notorious sailor contrives a ruse to help the Del Burgo family and other Jews board their ship undetected. He orders all torch lights extinguished, saying to his crew that without such lights the sun will rise with unrivaled majesty to bless their journey to the New World. The ship on which Del Burgo and his wife sail is called the *Te esperamos*, "We Await You," as in we welcome you. The novel revolves around the question of open invitations and the inclinations of some to accept and of others to turn them down.

Every Passover Seder, Tobias Del Burgo begins this story as he would a fairy tale:

> In Andalusia, the fragrant land of mimosas, two travelers arrive at the doors of Palos as the guards are about to close the city for the night. And despite the heat, the two travelers were covered in large capes. One of the travelers kept

a hood over his eyes while the other, no taller than three guavas, hid his face under a monk's habit. By the dust on their shoes, it was clear they came from very far. (Kiss, 11)

In the telling, Tobias acts out the scene to the gathering, affecting pleading gestures when asking to be admitted to Palos, a city more difficult to get into than it is for a camel to climb a tree, it is said. The person most interested in this story—although she's heard it many times—is Mélissa, Tobias's only child. She knows it so well that she has given the story a title, "The Angel of Safe Passage" ("L'Ange du passage"). She is thus referring to the episode involving the intervention of a mysterious figure who rises from the sea during the Del Burgo's flight from Spain. The legend has it that on the fateful night of August 2, 1492 as the ship was sailing toward Constantinople, a great storm arose and a frightful sea monster, half-human and half-fish or bird ("nobody knows for certain") appeared from the sea. Tobias tells of how it was caught by the Spanish sailors but then was spared by the Jews on the ship who, consulting the biblical texts they carried with them and moved by compassion, argued that the sea monster should be set free. For Rabbi Del Burgo and for the Jews on board the *Te esperamos* that night, the monster was a messenger of God. As the sailors free the sea monster, the ropes that tie it dissolve, and it turns into an angel who speaks to them in the "Jewish speak of Andalusia," saying to them that their voyage has come to an end, that Alexandria, the city of the seven hills, awaits them. They should settle there to "put an end to their wanderings and the wanderings of their descendants" (Kiss, 16). As Tobias concludes the story, all assembled at the Passover table repeat "Amen." All of them are painfully aware of the troubling parallel: The flight from Spain is about to be repeated, but this time from twentieth-century Alexandria. "They were then as we will be tomorrow . . . at death's door," says Katkout, the beadle of the synagogue, adding: "Sometimes death is better" (Kiss, 15). Katkout will choose to remain in Egypt and will die there.

A Kiss as Cold as the Moon focuses on Tobias, a good man who is easygoing, loving, and thoughtful. In his early forties, a handsome widower with a taste for the finer things in life, the head of a family business, and the main support of an aging mother, Tobias is expelled from Egypt with his ten-year-old daughter, Mélissa. He has to raise her alone, a difficult task under the best of circumstances. Mélissa is a strong-willed child who remains this way throughout her adolescence. Tobias and Mélissa will live through many hardships and indignities together. His mother, Sarina Del Burgo, the matriarch of the family, remains in Egypt to the end, like Katkout the beadle. The mother's letters to her son and granddaughter keep the reader connected to the new challenges facing the Jewish community in Alexandria. Tobias and Mélissa, first in Israel and then in France, do what they can to rebuild a home together. Life is difficult in both Israel and in

France, just as it was during their stop in Italy, straight out of Egypt. No matter where they find themselves, their sojourn is plagued with misadventures. At the end of the novel, Tobias eventually finds prosperity in the United States. Mélissa, an aspiring writer, remains in France, resisting her father's countless appeals to join him in America. This novel is about the close relationship between a father and a daughter who each slowly and not without friction construct a life apart. It is a meditation on attachment to people, places, and cultures and on the acceptance of and resistance against such attachments.

In the last chapter of *A Kiss as Cold as the Moon*, Tobias is in Paris in 1972, visiting his daughter, as he has done many times since leaving France. Tobias tries again to convince Mélissa to leave France and settle in the United States. Again she brushes him off. This time, on his way out the door of her Paris apartment—we are in the last pages of the novel—he leaves her a letter whose contents remain a mystery to the reader. The letter remains a mystery precisely because it is meant to prompt us to think about important questions, namely, what is at stake when we leave the home we have built, whether voluntarily or by force? And how does a Jew (how does anyone, really) decide when to stop looking for a safer more welcoming harbor than the hostile place one has left behind? Having taken flight from Spain, the Del Burgo family has a choice between Alexandria and Constantinople—perhaps even America, hiding in one of Christopher Columbus's ships. More than four centuries after the Spanish Inquisition, and now compelled to leave Egypt, the twentieth-century Del Burgo family is again presented with the same situation as its ancestors. Will the family go to Israel? France? America? Tobias will try all three. The prologue ends, as Tobias's story ends, with this line: "I heard this story from my late father who heard it from his father, who had it from his father. For it is said: 'where the father has been, the child is sure to follow'" (Kiss, 17). The stories fathers and sons pass down to one another are not the stories shared by mothers and daughters.

Resistance is gendered in *A Kiss as Cold as the Moon*; the women in the family provide the model for the problem of perpetual displacement, of wandering. For Tobias, by temperament a dreamer, America represents the "safe passage," or passport, that allowed Saul Del Burgo to flee Spain for the land of opportunity that Egypt and Constantinople represented at that time, hundreds of years before (Kiss, 11). In France, Tobias felt acutely the inhospitality of the French, was humiliated and called a "foreigner" by agents of the state, and was brutally beaten by a gang of thugs because he was Jewish. Consequently, Tobias has experienced enough and has recognized the signs of future inhospitality. He can turn his back on France and the culture he grew up with because, in a sense, as we see in the prologue, he faithfully follows the model of his forefathers Saul and Jacob Del Burgo. His own father Jacob is described as a collector of nationalities (Kiss, 69); Jacob even had a coat designed with several secret pockets to carry his various passports at all times. According to his wife Sarina, the coat looked ridiculous and so did he. In the family, it was called the Coat of Nations ("l'Habit des Nations") (Kiss, 70). In its lining, he placed Western passports on the right side, and on the left were passports and papers from Muslim countries such as Turkey. In the mid-1920s, when Egypt became independent, he was able "to celebrate his Egyptian citizenship" with a magnificent party, and so he placed his Egyptian papers there, on the left too: "This way, as needed, he could present the passport of the country in power" (Kiss, 70–71).[3] In his younger days, Jacob was a proud Egyptian who wore the *tarbouch*, a fez or flat-top red conical hat worn by some men in Egypt. But one day an incident on a train made him acutely aware that Jews were held in disdain by people whom he had never suspected of harboring mean-spirited feelings. He was deeply saddened by this discovery and remained paranoid the rest of his life, suspecting antisemitism everywhere he went. He hoped for and predicted that in forty years Jews would live more securely in Israel (Kiss, 71), and he rejoiced when this indeed happened. But, always fearful, he also worried that the existence of Israel would endanger the Jews living in Arab lands (Kiss, 72). For Sarina, however, Jacob was a narrow-minded coward, whose coat was emblematic of his character. He loved Egypt without qualifications and considered himself wholly Egyptian, as did she. But whereas Jacob wanted to keep his options open, Sarina was convinced that Jews could "wait it out" until the revolution came about and, as she believed, all people would unite. In her younger days, Sarina had been a political activist, a socialist-communist, with a reputation as a rabble-rouser. Tobias, in contrast to Sarina, understood his father and sympathized with his fears. At his funeral, to honor him, he wore the Coat of Nations, an act that outraged Sarina. For Sarina, and perhaps for Mélissa as well, one risks losing one's identity if one does not do battle against those who hold power. Sarina tells Tobias: "Your father was so fixated on finding the right identity that, in the process, he lost his" (Kiss, 76).[4]

Mélissa has in front of her the model adopted by Saul, Jacob, and Tobias. She also has the example of Sarina, who remained in Egypt. Mélissa takes Sarina's model and adapts it to her own circumstances. She is forced to leave Egypt with her father; there is nothing she can do about this. But she turns down the *passage* to America and remains in France, working against many odds to make a life for herself. The lesson Mélissa draws from the Del Burgo legend is that all havens for the Jews are temporary, so one has to re-create oneself where one is and when one can. Was Egypt better than Constantinople? Is America any better than France? The lesson Jacques's novels puts forward is about the futility, the danger, and the psychological harm that accompany displacement. Jacques's third novel, *Aunt Carlotta's Legacy* (*L'Héritage de tante Carlotta;* 1987) takes up this idea, which she illustrates, once again, through the journey of the female protagonist, Camélia. In this novel Jacques inserts a moral tale, the anecdote of the "Mirage Seekers" ("marcheurs de mirage"), to drive home the point (Carlotta, 88–89). In this tale, a child, stifled by the limitations of his surroundings, climbs to the roof of his house in Haret el-Barabra, a poor section of Cairo. From that vantage point, he thinks he sees pink and blue mountains way over the horizon, and he decides to leave his home and head in their direction to make his home there. As he approaches the mountains, he realizes they are not pink and blue. Turning around, he sees the pink and blue mountains elsewhere far ahead. Believing he had been mistaken the last time, he heads their way once again, and then spends his entire life going from one horizon to another, following the "call" of the pink and blue mountains. Only near the end of his life does he find himself back home at the foot of the Hara where he had started. The lesson is clearly spelled out: this man spent his life chasing a mirage and missed out on living. The moral imperative in Jacques's novels is to resist the impulse to wander and instead resist those who would force you to do so. The motley monster, half-fish or bird and half-human, like Mélissa's grandfather Jacob's ridiculous-looking Coat of Nations, is a ludicrous messenger whose invitation should not be taken seriously. Jacques puts this imperative in the mouth of the sage family matriarch Sarina Del Burgo. In one of Sarina's letters, she cautions Tobias about the futility of emigration and insists he stop pressuring his daughter to move to America. Mélissa loves France, she says, "and you want to disown it like when as a child you would throw out a dirty shirt rather than wash it" (Kiss, 323). There is in you, Sarina writes, a destructive streak: "America will not cure you of your troubles" and, alluding to the sea monster of the Mediterranean voyage, she says without mincing her words: "Think before you ruin your life and the life of your child. . . . Leave the Angel of Safe Passage in peace. Don't use him as an excuse to justify your desire to wander. If you do, his ship will lead you straight to hell. . . . Make your home where you are" (Kiss, 323–324).

Without undermining the suffering of characters who decide to leave Egypt, Jacques's novels reveal a decidedly soft spot for those who fight back and refuse to budge. They are the focus of Jacques's most passionate dramatizations. Not all resisters come out of the process winners; most, in fact, do not, and some are diminished beyond recognition. But Jacques has invented writerly characters for her novels, fictional writers, who may be viewed as surrogate authors for the novelist Paula Jacques herself. Thus the author's desire to raise the stature of resisters is paralleled by the fictional writers who lavish their own attention on them. Through their eyes, resisters are portrayed as heroic even when they act foolishly, are stubborn, and create a fuss, as do Zaki Zakein, Kayro Jacobi, and the old folks in the Home for the Aged in *Aunt Carlotta's Legacy*. These writerly characters, like Jacques herself, protect their attachment to Egypt without betraying their new home, France. The children of Egyptian Jews, most all of them immigrants in exile—Mélissa, Mona, Camélia, and Benjy—do not, and cannot, return to

Egypt. But through their writing, they can remain *with* Egypt. As with writerly characters, so with Jacques: to write the story of the past is, in a metaphorical sense, to engage in a salvage operation to bring back its lost figures—an image articulated most poignantly in *Descent to Paradise* (*La Descente au paradis*; 1995). Importantly, writing brings them visibility in the present. By dramatizing Jewish life in Egypt, and developing, deepening, and reinforcing the details of Egyptian Jews before and after exile, Paula Jacques creates the modern saga of the Jews' journey in and out of Egypt. She reconstructs their social and affective history on the Nile. Like the Torah scrolls that Del Burgo and his wife carried out of Spain, like the Torah that was carried by other Jews in other times and places to establish the continuity of the people of Israel, Jacques can inscribe her project, the legacy of the Jews of Egypt, in the larger Jewish tradition of privileging writing.

Dredging the Nile for a Sign . . .

In her ten novels (1980–2015), Paula Jacques has focused solely on Egyptian Jews. By this, I mean she focuses on characters whose origins are in this community. There are other characters from different ethnic and religious backgrounds. Several are Muslim Egyptians who have important roles, like the independent, strong-willed, and loving Zainab in *Women with Their Love* (*Les Femmes avec leur amour;* 1997) and Fouad Barbouk, the knotty police officer in *Rachel-Rose and the Arab Officer* (*Rachel-Rose et l'officier arabe;* 2006). In several novels she describes encounters between Jewish Egyptians and survivors of the Holocaust. These encounters run through her work, as I discuss later on. Jacques evokes the life of Egyptian Jews in closed and mostly humble communities such as Haret el-Yahood and Haret el-Barabra in the first decades of the twentieth century. She shows them adopting Western values, attending French schools, and living in upscale neighborhoods. She also describes their precipitous demise in the mid-to-late 1950s, and focuses on their response to political and social reversals, the way they face adversity and how they adjust to life outside Egypt. In her dramatic representations, she maintains a degree of distance to allow the voices of the Jewish community and those living closest to them to emerge and take center stage while she and her narrators step out of the light, so to speak. Yet, paradoxically, it is from the position of an insider that Jacques constructs her narratives and addresses the reader. In a 2007 interview, Jacques compared her relationship toward her characters to that of Albert Cohen: "As a rule, I love my characters very much. I watch them with a critical eye and a tender heart."[5] She confesses that it is impossible for her to ignore their plight. She is moved by them, deeply troubled by their predicament, and cannot imagine *not* writing about them. Like Sarina Del Burgo, Paula Jacques is resourceful at finding excuses not to leave Egypt. She continues to find ways to give life to the Jewish community there, seeing in its traumatic exile an inexhaustible fertile ground for her restitutive novelistic enterprise.⁶ When asked if she anticipates writing about a different subject, Jacques responds:

> I tried to write about other subjects without much luck. The subject moves me, it inspires me. When I write, I have the impression of discovering new facets each time, of deepening them. It enriches my writing and validates my efforts. And very modestly, I believe that by writing I am helping to fill the frightening void that has settled around the people, the silence that has deepened around them and erased their cultural, economic and even historical contribution to the country where they were born. (Israel-Pelletier)⁷

By writing fiction and not memoirs or history, writing in the novelistic idiom of feelings, passions, and uncertainties, and writing in the French language, Jacques has given the mostly francophone Jewish Egyptian community a readership. She has given them recognition and inscribed them in the cultural heritage of France. Thomas Nolden notes that the drive to write about one's country of origin and one's family is not typical of post-Holocaust French Jewish writers whose families had emigrated to France from European countries.⁸ But Maghrebi writers and other writers who share the heritage of Mediterranean countries with Islamic cultures, like Jacques, have brought into French literature "new subjects, figures, and stylistic forms" (Nolden, 49).

One detects in Jacques's work a pervasive anxiety that arises from the sense that the Jewish Egyptian community is disappearing without leaving a trace. This anxiety is evoked in a scene at the end of *Light of My Eye* (*Lumière de l'oeil*; 1980), Jacques's first novel. The scene takes place at the airport in Cairo as the Castro family passes through customs. Sayeda, the family's maid and governess, accompanies them to bid them goodbye. Grief-stricken, she watches as the family is harassed and their luggage is ransacked by customs agents. The agent in charge wants to confiscate the family album, reminding them that no documents are allowed out of Egypt. Sayeda begs him to hand her the album. He does and she takes it home to her parents' house in the village of El Khalifa, where she has now returned to live. El Khalifa is the door to the desert. There, Sayeda mourns the Castro family for months on end, spending long hours looking at the pictures and sighing. She invites her mother, Om' Sayeda, to share the pictures and listen to her stories about the Castro family. Her mother is not in the least bit interested. Years pass. A storm ravages the village. Cracks appear in the walls of the house. Some are rather large. To fill the gaps, Om'Sayeda, with no love lost for the "foreigners," uses the photographs to fill the cracks: "So, she pushed the photos into the fissures in the wall, tamped them in with a broom handle, and thus reinforced her house" (Cohen, 260).⁹ The result of such repair, says the narrator, is that sometimes one could make out jutting out of the cracks, here and there, a bare leg, a smiling mouth, a light eye, two hands with jewelry, a straw hat, and in the largest crack three headless children playing in the sand (Cohen, 260). With time, these fragments of a past life fall into shreds and then, little by little, turn to sand. In the last paragraph of the novel, the photographs disappear into nothing, are defaced by the elements, and become invisible: "Finally, covered with wet spots, the paper turned into rags, frayed into *grainy tears*, hung down in shreds, definitively, and then nothing more could be seen" (my italics; Cohen, 260). I suggest that in this scene, with the appearance of the fragments and their eventual erasure, Jacques constructs a visual metaphor to evoke both the fate of the Jewish community of Egypt and her narrative project, namely, to restore and make visible the passage of a community made invisible by unkind winds and indifference. The image of "grainy tears" is particularly suggestive in the way it evokes pain in concrete terms, as abrasion and laceration. The scene is at the same time a gesture of defiance against those who might forget. Like the ten books Jacques has written, the book we hold in our hands, *Light of My Eye*, makes it patently clear that the task Jacques has set out for herself is both ambitious and defiant. It is unacceptable that a community disappear into nothingness.

The struggle against the eviction of Egyptian Jews from their native soil is taken up in Jacques's fifth novel, *Descent to Paradise* (1995). This book dramatizes defiance in the face of overwhelming odds. We are in November 1943. The village of Nazlet-el-Ghana must be evacuated temporarily. The British want to secure it for a meeting between Churchill, Roosevelt, and Stalin. The entire village is willing to accommodate the British, except for Zaki Zakein, the Jew, who resists. He refuses to move out of his home, even temporarily, no matter how much they keep assuring him it is short-term. He calls the move an "expulsion," and the reader is meant to understand "expulsion" as the historical expulsion of the Jews from Egypt by Nasser's regime. Zaki repeats over and over that he is tired of being "expelled" (Paradise, 323). He is aware of the fact that his refusal constitutes an act of defiance against powerful entities like the British and the Egyptian officers who push their weight around and ruin lives. People around him, including his family, believe he has gone mad. But Zaki is a lucid man who has diagnosed his own trauma. The first time he realizes he is feeling threatened with expulsion (before the British ordered him to vacate his home), Zaki is sitting in a movie theater alone when a couple behind him ask, quite innocently and politely, if he did not mind moving over a seat so they could see better. The movie theater was not full. Zaki could have easily moved. So could they, of course. But the couple's request was the proverbial straw that broke the camel's back. Zaki responds to the request by flying into a rage and yelling at the top of his lungs: "I will not move from here, no. I will stay right here. I will never move, never, never!" (Paradise, 133). It is while lying there on the floor between the rows of the theater where he threw himself that he realizes he is having a nervous breakdown. Through to the end of the novel, Zaki resists the forces that try to expel him and remains in

Egypt—at the bottom of the Nile, as it turns out. *Descent to Paradise* is a tragedy, a moving and complex novel that does not read like an allegory, but is one.

A once prosperous stockbroker, Zaki loved his job. Born to a poor and very religious family from Haret el-Yahood, he succeeded by dint of hard work. This fairy-tale life ends when he is visited at work by a petty government officer who returns repeatedly without explaining the reasons for his visits. These visits cast a shadow on Zaki's economic affairs. Believing Zaki's business at risk, his clients stop working with him and his fellow stockbrokers cannot hire him without putting their own solvency into question. It is during these difficult times that the drama in the movie theater takes place. Shortly thereafter, Zaki moves his family from their luxury Cairo apartment to the village of Nazlet-el-Ghana where he builds a large home. Impervious to ridicule and to the objections of his family, Zaki starts a poultry business, raising chickens for the market. All he wants, he says, is to be a simple *fellah*, a farmer. So when the British order the evacuation of his village, he has had enough of being pushed around. He resists for a long time and capitulates only when his chickens are killed—probably by the villagers. Subsequently, his wife leaves him. The surrender of his home signals his fall into total madness. In the epilogue, we learn that Zaki has suffered a stroke and is abandoned to his visions on a hospital bed. Jacques describes him as if he were crucified: his arms are outstretched and his wrists are tied on both sides of the bed; with his eyes continually filled with tears, he stares blindly at a nail on the wall. But this tableau is not the closing image of the novel. His son Benjy, the sometime narrator of the novel and a future writer, takes pity on him and, without the knowledge of his doctors or anyone else, releases him from the hospital. Zaki disappears into the landscape and is believed dead by all except his wife. The village *omdey*, the mayor, orders the canal dredged to try to recover Zaki's body. To no avail. Zaki's remains are not found, which is to say, he remains in Egypt. The novel ends with the scene of dredgers looking for a sign of his remains in the Nile:

> "Nothing, there's nothing in there," the omdey kept saying. And the men who came up each time with nothing after dredging the Nile repeated: "Nothing, there's nothing...." There was nothing but nothings. Nothing wafted over the canal, the fields, crossed the village on its way to the desert where it was lost. And it was as when a lightning flash is not followed by a thunderclap. (Paradise, 337)[10]

Dredging the Nile for Zaki reveals nothing and confirms his absence. As a metaphor of Jacques's writing project, dredging suggests an anxiety, as with the disappearance of Zaki's body, that the writer-as-dredger might not be able to find anything to hold on to in the mud of the Nile. Perhaps, even more disquieting, the writer might not be able to pull together a picture to give an adequate expression of this community. In this last scene by the Nile, a scene that recalls the fragments of photographs in the desert in *Light of My Eye*, fragments of lives lived (chairs, bottles, pails, etc.) are mixed in the mud of the Nile and come to the surface as the dredgers pull their equipment. Benjy, the future writer, makes this solemn observation: "The mud knew nothing of my father" ("La vase ne savait rien de mon père") (Descent, 337). The phrase suggests the slippery, ungraspable, and difficult nature of Jacques's writing project and the anxiety associated with it. This anxiety finds many echoes in her work. In *Deborah and Those Reckless Angels* (*Deborah et les anges dissipés;* 1991), the narrator tells the reader that the people she is writing about, her Jewish Egyptian ancestors, have "disappeared without leaving a trace" (Deborah, 40). She writes: "In Cairo there is no room for them. They have faded from the memory of Cairo. Even their absence has been erased from the memory of Cairo" (Deborah, 40).[11] Jacques's objective is to keep writing even in the face of such devastating evidence.

Two opening quotations in *Descent to Paradise* address, and perhaps allay, this anxiety. The first is at the beginning of the novel and the second is inserted before the epilogue. The first is a quotation from T. S. Eliot: "In my beginning is my end. In succession houses rise and fall, crumble, are extended, are removed, destroyed, restored. . ." (Paradise, 11). And then the opening words of the epilogue, quoted from Claude Levi-Strauss, echo the first but introduce a hopeful solution. The point Levi-Strauss makes is that in the face of the certainty we have that nothing will survive in the long run: "It is incumbent on mankind to continue to work, *resist*, think and believe. It is vitally important to be brave" (my italics; Paradise, 291). Benjy, the narrator-writer, tells the reader in the first pages of the novel that Zaki's death is not an end, his disappearance is not an extinction. It is merely a temporary absence: "In my heart, the same absurd idea assures me that nothing ends, nothing begins, and *everything repeats*: the silences of my father, his frequent angry outbursts, his self-destructiveness, his obstinacy to create as much misery as possible, drop by drop, the way water drips from a bathroom faucet" (my italics; Descent, 13).[12] I suggest that Jacques's philosophical approach is based on the conviction that, as both opening quotations assert, nothing we construct about our humanity, our history, or the discourses we multiply about them, will last forever. In spite of this, she resolves to resist the forces that would silence history by continuing the work of writing. As one of the most successful autobiographical embodiments of the author, Camélia Belrespiro in *Aunt Carlotta's Legacy*, puts it: Writing is a way to resist the Jewish fate that has us dismantle one after the other the tiles of the roof over our heads (Carlotta, 48).[13] Jacques affirms the presence of Egyptian Jews as much by the content of her narratives as by their form. I want to focus briefly on *Light of My Eye* and Mona the writer-narrator to highlight aspects of Jacques's style that enliven her characters and their way of being. Mona immigrates to France at the age of ten with her mother.

The action of the novel takes place overwhelmingly in Egypt in the mid-1950s. Mona is a brooding, demanding, and insolent child, jealous of her brothers and her mother. The narrative of life in Egypt centers mostly around her. In Egypt, Mona has had many adventures, including being the Lolita to a survivor of the Holocaust. But once the novel picks up in France, the narrative stops focusing on her. Jacques switches the narrative interest and instead Mona's mother occupies center stage. We see her loneliness, her sense of loss, and her love for her daughter. Very little survives in the character of Becky Castro, Mona's mother, from her Egyptian days, and of Mona as well. In France, Mona is defined by her activity as a writer, journalist, and the one person upon whom her mother depends. She tries to remember her childhood in Cairo and solicits her mother's help to complete the picture. Throughout the novel, she pleads with her mother to talk about Egypt, about her life there, and about her father who, like Camélia's father, died in Egypt. But the mother is not forthcoming. For one thing, her sense of identity has been shaken and beaten down. She scolds her daughter for insisting she tell her story: "Why are you hounding me with questions like that?" and "Why pick me as the star?"[14] In addition, Becky does not understand the value of writing a book on Egyptian Jews. "Just who do you think would be interested in the misfortune of Egyptians?"[15] she asks Mona rhetorically. Then, throwing her daughter a bone or a bomb, she tells her: "All you have to write is a single sentence: they were chased out of paradise,—you say this and you've said it all!" (Cohen, 51). The conversation between mother and daughter continues. The mother is interested in describing her suffering. They are speaking on the phone together. Here again, the narrative focuses solely on the mother's words, as she reproaches Mona for caring more for her book than for her: "Your book is more important than your mother . . . tell me, my beauty, how much is this book going to cost you? An eye, at least" (Cohen, 51). Jacques brings to bear here a stylistic device that puts certain characters on stage, front and center. This in turn gives the reader privileged access to the way they think, feel, and speak. It works like this: the mother calls her daughter on the telephone. The reader is witness to what she says. We are only on one side of the call, the side occupied by the Egyptian mother who is alone and isolated in her apartment in a Parisian *banlieue*. Her daughter is on the other side of the line. What the daughter says is only made clear to the reader by what the mother says in response. The same is true with written communications, as in letters. The reader inhabits the side that is most in need of being heard, the person yearning for attention, the one whose voice does not reach the outside on its own—in short, the person Jacques wants the reader to take note of. These one-way conversations are tour-de-force performances by Jacques and often highlight her comic sensibility. Besides their entertainment value, they shed a singularly bright light on the person in the foreground doing the talking and writing. This person is always a member of the exiled Jewish Egyptian community and an elder. By virtue of the fact that these characters occupy the center of attention, the reader has the impression of seeing and listening to them directly. We get a sense of the sounds, inflections, and habits of speech of Egyptian Jews. The result is an intimacy that cannot be easily brushed off. By amplifying their presence and communicating both the pleasures they experience and the grievances that burden them, Jacques endows them with enormous liveliness. And by giving these characters a loudspeaker and a stage from which they might move us to care enough to know them and, for their compatriots, to remember them, she makes them eminently present and memorable.

So much is communicated in the preceding passage between Mona and her mother that is both touching and cruel. On the one hand, there is the mother's love, the mother's isolation in France, and the mother's dependence on her daughter. On the other hand, there is the daughter who hears, and probably not for the first time, the attempt to make her feel guilty. All the while she also hears her mother's love and loneliness. The daughter's conflict is heart-breaking. We sense her attachment to her mother and her desire to live her own life; her urgency to write, her exhaustion, her hopeless attempt to rally her mother behind her project. Yet Mona's predicament is not made explicit. Jacques steps back from the scene to allow the mother to occupy the center. But it is understood. Writing the tale of the family is a difficult task for the child, an immigrant of exiled parents who feel alone and betrayed by history and by life. I suggested at the beginning of this chapter that the album of family photographs, torn, mildewed, undecipherable, which become part of the desert, is a metaphor for the book Mona hopes to write and for the difficult process of writing it. Becky understands the difficulty. She tells Mona that the story of the Egyptian Jews is a hard one to tell because it is about sacrifice. And the sacrificial lamb, Becky remarks, is deeply silent. He knows "that one can't paint the wings of an angel" (Cohen, 51). Jacques's aesthetics rests on that challenge, to find a form adequate to represent the enormity of loss that individual people endure when exiled.

Writing in Exile . . .

Of all the many writers that populate Jacques's novels, the three who articulate most fully her literary project are Mona, Mélissa, and Camélia, characters from her first three novels. All three are published authors and, like Paula Jacques herself, are engaged in writing about the Jewish Egyptian community to which they remain very attached. Camélia Belrespiro, in *Aunt Carlotta's Legacy*, is the youngest of the three incarnations. She is a relatively successful author who enjoys the support of her editor. She lives in Paris not far from her widowed mother and her aunts. A significant part of the novel takes place in contemporary (1976) Egypt where Camélia has traveled in part to bury her aunt and in part to find material for her novel since she is experiencing writer's block. There are also extended flashbacks of Camélia as a child in Egypt. The Belrespiro family was expelled circa 1956, soon after the death of Camélia's father. Camélia traces the origin of the idea of writing about Egypt to when, at age nine, she was attending the *Lycée Français du Caire*, and her French-born teacher, Madame Dupoix, identified her talent for writing and prompted her to draw on her background for ideas. With her guidance, Camélia uncovers stories about her ancestors who once lived in Haret el-Barabra. The stories Camélia writes and that her teacher likes are about non-Westernized Jews, their way of life, milieu, traditions, and interests. At first, Camélia is surprised she even knows these stories. With time, she becomes aware that the stories she writes contain a mixture of stories she has actually heard and stories she imagined. She explains this in the following:

> I drew from my Jewish background . . . I returned to the Passage of the Barbarians. It was in my teacher's eyes an utterly dreadful place and terribly exotic. . . . And lo and behold, little by little, like pulling a strand of yarn from a spool, one of my ancestors would appear, *would inhabit me*, and from inside me the wretched epic of the Passage of the Barbarians would come to life. (My italics; Carlotta, 58–59)[16]

Camélia is the imaginative medium through which her ancestors take on reality and her surroundings are transformed into material fit for an epic. While Camélia is still in Egypt, her teacher helps her prepare a book of these collected stories. Unfortunately, just as the book deal is to be sealed, Nasser comes to power and Madame Dupoix is forced to leave Egypt. Shortly thereafter, Camélia and her widowed mother are also expelled. They settle in France. Years later, Camélia finds a way to publish the book. Several others follow. All are books for children inspired by traditional Jewish Egyptian culture. She even wins a literary prize. In the opening chapter of the novel—she is now twenty-six years old—and she is beginning to suspect that the stories Madame Dupoix encouraged her to write were written with the eyes of that teacher looking over her shoulder (Carlotta, 65). They were written to please the very French Madame Dupoix who liked the stories "terribly exotic" (Carlotta, 58), liked stories only good for entertaining cultural "tourists," only good for stuffing in dead people's mailboxes ("boîte aux lettres aux morts") (Carlotta, 65). When her aunt Carlotta dies in Egypt, her sisters in Paris are concerned about her burial and agree to send Camélia. Camélia is eager to see Egypt and her relatives (her subject-matter) through fresh eyes, to see them in their natural setting as they actually are in the present and without the filter that exoticized and stereotyped them. Nostalgia is not a mode that befits Jacques nor the characters she has created. As Camélia puts it: "Attachment to things from the past filled me with the sort of unease one feels at the sight of a room whose furnishings and décor are devoured by forgetfulness and dust— nothing to do with my mother who took good care of her treasures" (Carlotta,

11).[17] Camélia wants to connect with the remaining members of her community, to capture their spirit, their liveliness, and perpetuate them on French soil. And, like Jacques herself, she wants to pay tribute to their resistance, their resolve to remain in Egypt. Camélia succeeds brilliantly. She establishes this connection. Her success is made evident emblematically, both literally and figuratively, because not only does Camélia conceive a child in Cairo, but she conceives that child with her own uncle, Ponto Novo—a very feisty and seemingly indestructible specimen of a man. The baby is born in France and Camélia names the child Carlotta, after the aunt she went to Egypt to bury. Thus, Camélia transmits the bloodline of her feisty ancestors from Egypt into the present and on French soil. Camélia's desire to connect with the community as it is in the present finds its most touching evocation in two powerfully dramatized scenes. The first of these takes place at Bassatine Cemetery where Camélia and the cohort from Cairo's Jewish Home for the Aged are visiting the graves of their families and friends.

This group of elderly people from the Home are the last remaining Jews in Egypt in 1976. Camélia is introduced to them at the crucial moment when they are about to be forcibly evicted from the Home in Cairo to one in Alexandria; the term they use for eviction is "expulsion." They resist this eviction and the violence that ensues is explosive, horrifying, and deadly. The havoc they create and the trouble that they bring down upon themselves is difficult to encapsulate. Jacques brings to it her enormous writing skills. But before the elderly group learns that they will be forced to leave, Jacques describes them in the company of Camélia on their way to visit the Jewish cemetery. As the group is walking around the dusty and scorching hot cemetery looking for the graves of people they once knew, Moische the octogenarian dentist spots the grave of a member of his family and starts digging the dirt off of it on frail and bended knees. As he does so, he cries softly. The women, saddened to see him this way, try to console him and implore him to stop his tears, saying: "What's the use in crying? They've won the war against the dead. What's left for us?" But hearing the pity and surrender in their voice, Moische pulls himself up and, with a temper noticeable in his determined step and in the fierceness in his voice, he shouts: "No, they didn't win . . . the olive tree produces its most splendid fruit when it is near the end, and it will be so for the Jews of Egypt" (Carlotta, 178). The narrator adds: "He walked briskly ahead of them with strong determined steps, burning with an extraordinary passion that displayed his strength and made the tallit around his shoulders billow out in the still air" (Carlotta, 178). There is no place for pity in this resister's world. Shortly after, the motley group arrives at Carlotta's grave. The women set about scrubbing the stone, applying effort to clean it until it sparkled. As they do this, Camélia notices that Carlotta's name is beginning to slowly disappear, as the inscription was not engraved in the stone, contrary to prior agreement. It was instead painted on the surface of the stone with cheap paint. In a way, we can understand the painted name to suggest the delicate and temporary nature of the Jews' passage in Egypt, and to reflect in yet another example Jacques's anxiety about the erasure of the Jewish presence there. But the specter of this erasure is dispelled. In a phantasmatic scene that underscores Camélia's, and Jacques's, determination to resist erasure of the name and the presence, the money earmarked for the gravestone and that was thought to be already spent on an outing to the Mena House reappears, miraculously. The stone will decidedly be engraved before Camélia returns home to Paris.

A second equally poignant scene follows the cemetery scene at Bassatine when Camélia treats the group to a sumptuous meal at the Mena House. It is with the money intended for the maintenance of the grave that Camélia pays for that sumptuous meal, suggesting once more that in Jacques's universe the best place is reserved for present company.

The same ragamuffin gang of one man and three women accompany Camélia—or, more accurately, lead her—to the legendary Mena House hotel and restaurant where Camélia has invited the entire colorful group for a lavish dinner. I will not describe the scene at the Mena House, which is another literary tour de force by Jacques. These brilliant episodes in Bassatine and the Mena House, both honestly funny, poignant, and tender, are noteworthy for the portrait they give of a community, a people, that finds pleasure easy to summon even in the midst of hardship and who takes it as a matter of course that life is difficult, that roadblocks are found where least expected, that living is at times intolerable, but that things will work out. Camélia's beautiful gesture of lavishing both friendship and money on the marginalized community in Egypt—impoverished, powerless, and abandoned—her boundless kindness toward these elderly Jews, points to the importance Camélia places on them as individuals. It does so equally for Jacques, whose novels, as I try to show, are written with an eye not on the past for the purpose of nostalgic reflection, but as a reservoir of material to smuggle into the present and the future in order to perpetuate the distinctive liveliness and vitality of Egyptian Jews.

The last scene of *Aunt Carlotta's Legacy* shows Camélia's three-year-old daughter, Carlotta, nestled between her mother, grandmother, and aunts. As I suggested, the child is the living symbol of Camélia's project to reestablish the connection between her family and Egypt and to plant in France the seed of a future for the community. The family has just fêted Carlotta's third birthday. As in a pastoral, all the women are resting peacefully, bathed in a sweet post-party atmosphere. They surround the adorable child who was conceived in Egypt. Little Carlotta heralds the future. Fortunée, Camélia's favorite aunt—possibly because she still loves Egypt—is sitting on the floor, legs crossed "Turkish style," reading the "future" of the child in the cup of Turkish coffee between her hands. What does Fortunée see? "Sitting legs crossed Turkish style on the carpet, her head tilting to the side, Aunt Fortunée *smiled* vaguely as she probed the bottom of the cup and read only good things" (my italics; Carlotta, 342). The last paragraph of the novel ends with: "Only coffee grounds would tell the future" (Carlotta, 342).[18] Fortunée's reading of the coffee grounds, like the novel we have been reading, suggests that the family has been made whole. Egyptian Jews will not have vanished without a trace.

Jacques's novels evoke the energy, persistence, and dogged attachment to Egypt her characters nurture and the perpetuation of its legacy on French soil. Without breaking with the past and with Egypt, Jacques offers a model of Hassounian transmission where old histories are refreshed and made current. Baby Carlotta is *not* aunt Carlotta. A return to Egypt is not in the cards. She is her aunt's up-to-date iteration, a more livable incarnation. In transmission, Jacques Hassoun argues, the past is not duplicated. In a successful transmission, the present has wrestled with the past and integrated it. In Cairo, Camélia plays out the existential drama of the children of exile. The turmoil she experiences and the revolutions she witnesses, both political and personal, are signs of this struggle. Baby Carlotta is the symbol of that success.

The Work of Writing / A Proper Burial

The idea of giving someone a proper burial, as in the case of Carlotta and Zaki, is a significant and a difficult subject in Jacques's novels. The ending of *Deborah and the Reckless Angels* makes the point. We are at the end of April 1948, a few weeks before the proclamation of the State of Israel. Zacharie Borekitas, a resident of Haret el-Yahood, is one of several men responsible for disbursing to the poor of the community money that was sent by an American Ashkenazi philanthropist. The men responsible, including Zacharie, have been embezzling from the community funds for many years. They are criminals. But they are also angels who incarnate both goodness and immorality. Zacharie is a crook but he is devoted to his sick wife, Victoria. When Blanche Séreno, the old Jewish beggar of Haret el-Yahood curses him for his greed, he is devastated. The curse Blanche throws at his face is nothing short of catastrophic. She vows that no trace of his presence will remain. He will be obliterated; nothing will be left of him (Deborah, 41). Not long after his wife, Victoria, dies, Zacharie becomes suicidal. He injects himself with a fatal dose of morphine. Just as he is about to exhale his last breath, he begins to repent. He does not repent his crime or repent lusting in his heart while his wife was sick in bed but reproaches himself for failing to provide Blanche Séreno with a proper burial: "He would have liked to hold on to at least some of the strength that was leaving his body now . . . To go back in time . . . To change what had been . . . He felt too weak . . . *This infinite remorse was going to end with him* . . . After him, no one would dream of giving a proper burial to the old beggar thrown in the common grave" (my italics; Deborah, 247). The importance of giving a proper burial to Blanche Séreno is a thinly disguised anxiety of the writer's own concern to write the novel that preserves the trace of the Jewish Egyptian community. It is an aesthetic enterprise, and for a novelist the project rests on this difficulty: to write with an eye to introducing into a description or a portrait aspects of its alive-ness, its presence, its imprint freshly applied. In the epilogue to *Deborah and the Reckless Angels*, the writer-narrator, an Egyptian Jew herself, tells the story of the Jews of Egypt in the novel we are supposedly holding in our hands, long after all the characters in it have died. She ends with this compelling parable:

> Long ago, in our old neighborhood, there was a violinist who played with such joy and charm that we could not listen to him without dancing. And we danced every day, and the dance gave us the illusion of possessing all things, of never wanting a thing before it came to us. One day a deaf man came to our neighborhood. Since he had no idea what music might be, or what it meant to hear it, our music did not reach his ears. And his eyes saw in our dance the ridiculous agitations of a band of madmen flailing about. (Deborah, 345)[19]

To extend this metaphor slightly, Paula Jacques, an Egyptian Jew with a finely tuned ear and sensibility for her subject, can hear the music and, through her artfulness, the reader can hear it too. Her novels do help us to feel and experience the life that makes her world dance. A proper burial translates the liveliness of those who are not here to those who are watching, listening, and reading about them. The writer's difficult task is to play the music that will keep the community alive in the memory of those who lived it and for those who have only heard about it. This passage, the last paragraph of the novel, is addressed to its readers and asks if we *did* hear the music. It suggests, at the same time, that if we did not it might be because of our own limitations, our shortcomings. If we did not, it might be because we are not Egyptian Jews; we are perhaps Jews like Deborah Lewyn the Ashkenazi Jew from America who is deaf to this music. She is seemingly temperamentally incapable. Belardo Gormazzano remarks to her: "Why are you always nervous, tense, closed in on yourself ?" (Deborah, 261–262). He attributes her condition to the fact she is an Ashkenazi Jew: "Always rehashing the misfortune of persecutions, denying yourself the pleasures that God grants us from time to time. . . . What are you afraid of, Deborah?" (Deborah, 262).[20] Deborah is unable to listen to her heart, her body, and the music—let alone someone else's music. She turns down Dizzy McLean's invitation to dance at the Groppi Café-Chantant where everyone is enjoying themselves, oblivious to the political events unfolding as they dance. She cannot understand these Jews of the Nile, cannot hear their music, and cannot find pleasure in the dance (Deborah, 261).

The question Jacques asks her reader to ponder is this: is only a Mediterranean Jew or, more to the point, only an Egyptian—Jewish or not—able to hear the music in her work?

Jewish Egyptian Identity

Egyptian Jews in Jacques's novels are portrayed for the most part as having a strong attachment to Egypt. And they identify themselves as Egyptian. Even Jacob Del Burgo with his Coat of Nations is not equivocal about his affiliation and considers himself an Egyptian, wears a *tarbouch*, and is joyous when he acquires Egyptian nationality. The characters experience antisemitism and, in many cases, their lives are destroyed by Nasser's politics. Yet Egypt remains their point of reference, even as they look toward Europe and, in particular, to France to expand their cultural horizons. As it was for many Egyptian Jews living in twentieth-century Cairo, Jacques's main characters are urban, speak French—and Arabic—follow French cultural values, and attend French schools where they come into contact with native French teachers. They practice Judaism in a casual, almost secular way. But they have a strong sense of Jewish identity. As I explain in the introduction to this book, historical and political events came to a head around 1956, after the notable success of radical Arab nationalism in the 1940s and 1950s and the emergence of the modern state of Israel. These political events and the shifting social landscape they created reverberate in Jacques's novels and raise issues concerning Jewish Egyptian identity. We watch her characters in situations where they must prove their legitimate place in Egypt. Jacques's novels give the reader a window from which to watch as the Jewish community takes stock of its place in this new Egypt. We see the challenges that both Egyptian Jews and Egyptian Muslims must deal with. One of the issues Egyptian Jews in Jacques's novelistic universe face, an issue that receives some of the most incisive treatment, is the problem of convincing Muslim Egyptians that these Jews, born and raised in Egypt, are Egyptian. The common assumption shared by the majority of Egypt's population is that the Jews in their midst are foreigners. Their origin and the fact that they speak Arabic like the Cairene or Alexandrians they fully are does not alter this impression. The issue is further complicated because Egyptian Jews can have foreign names and speak a language other than Arabic. The seductive Adora Zakein, in *Descent to Paradise*, debunks the village mayor's assumption that she is Italian by saying, "Where do you get this crazy idea? Don't even mention it. We never set foot in Italy. Is there a more beautiful country than ours? I am Egyptian in heart and soul. Been one for nearly a thousand years. The Ninio-Médini family was born with the pyramids" (Paradise, 37).[21] Putting humor aside, surely she is too quick to dismiss the *omdey*, given the decidedly Italian origins of her maiden name. But she is Egyptian and feels herself to be so. Likewise, Adora's husband,

Zaki, is pained when the mayor is shocked to see him in farm attire: "Why are you shocked? I am a man! I am a fellah. You've never seen a fellah, Abdel Salam Bey?" (Descent, 41).

In 1950s Egypt, the concepts of nationalism and citizenship were still loose. This was particularly true for some members of the older generation. In a country ruled by empires for most of its modern history, one's religion and family were sufficient markers of affiliation. As these concepts became better understood and before they hardened into inexorable politics, some found ways to resist them or take them with a grain of salt. An amusing example of this push back is described in *Light of My Eye* in a conversation between Farida Benzakein, Mona's grandmother, and a civil servant. After several suspicious fires in the neighborhood damaged Farida's balcony, the man visits her at home to check the damage and file a report. He returns three times, unable each time to get the information he needs from her. Each time he comes, Farida's hospitality and his own reluctance to assert himself prevents him from getting to the point of his visit. Farida, as is customary among Egyptian Jews when they receive visitors, keeps serving him sweets as long as he is willing to eat them. And he, not aware of this custom, keeps eating because his own custom dictates he not refuse offerings of food. Even after he is finally able to question her, he cannot get her to state her nationality. In his first attempt at asking, Farida snaps in Arabic: "What do you mean! Can't you tell? I am a European from Egypt."[22] He retorts snidely: "Congratulations." Then he asks her to be specific: "I mean your nationality, what is it exactly? French, British, Greek or Italian?"—conspicuously, he does not offer Egyptian nationality as a possibility. Farida answers: "Whatever you wish, my dear. But in my heart, I am Egyptian."[23] He repeats: "Congratulations." We sense his irritation and note his sarcasm. He then tries a different tack and asks her to show him her passport. Exasperated, Farida says: "What a headache! I don't pass ports and I don't don passes. No boats, planes, trains. So, no passports either!"[24] The man is not unkind. Feeling bad for her and for himself he apologizes, saying that his job requires him to "snoop" on people and ask "indiscreet" questions; people in his position are forced to sniff around, to be "identity hounds" ("des fouineurs d'identité"). In yet another attempt, he asks her if her father's name is Maurice Benzakein. To this, she asserts proudly: "Yes, and of the purest lineage."[25] The rest of the interrogation continues just as badly. Farida responds with lies to questions she deems absurd and the man is on his way without the information he came to gather. Mona, a witness to this exchange, asks her grandmother after the man has left: "Nona, what about your age? Your papers? Is it true you don't have papers?" Farida answers her granddaughter as enigmatically as she answered the man: "The truth is where it is. It fell in the well. I lost everything in a move. As for my age, it comes, it goes, it changes all the time, and my nationality also. What's so important about papers anyway? They're made of dust. Don't I know who I am? Farida Sardaal, née Benzakein, in Cairo, on a beautiful day."²⁶ In traditional societies, as Jacques's novels reflect, the family—at one with its Jewish affiliation—remains the single most important and legitimate form of identity. Farida seems to say, as does Jacob Del Burgo, that questions of nationality belong to a different age, a ridiculous age, an age of suspicion and division. Jacques's novels bring to the fore the view that politics and ideologies of difference have put an end to Egypt's Golden Age, that time in history when relationships were not formalized and when people from around the Mediterranean came to Egypt seeking opportunities. For the young growing up in the 1950s, a new political reality presents them with ever more restrictive definitions of citizenship and raises thorny issues of identity.

El Bilad and el Watan

In Jacques, Judaism, and Israel in particular, marks Egyptian Jews as not of Egypt when by birth and in their "heart" they feel Egyptian. In *Women with Their Love*, the subject of Jewish Egyptian identity is given considered attention. The twelve-year-old Mara Louria and her maid, Zanouba, age thirty-two, highlight the issues in play. It is the fall of 1956. Mara makes up a story and tells Zanouba that she found herself in Tahrir Square during the general strike and that she was roughed up by some men who called her a "dirty Jew" and threatened to kill her "one of these days" (Women, 167). Mara asks Zanouba to explain if in the past, before the revolution, Jews were considered "foreigners" like they are today (Women, 168). Zanouba's response is that it depends. It depends on what, asks Mara? Does it depend on "identity papers"? Zanouba answers: "The wind. It depends on the wind. It blows to the right, it blows to the left and the papers fly away" (Women, 168). Mara then asks Zanouba why people call her a "foreigner" as soon as they find out her family is Jewish and what she thinks of the fact that the Koran instructs that "Muslims must drink the blood of a Jew every day to avoid damnation" (Women, 169). All this is nonsense, Zanouba answers. "The short of it," she tells Mara, is the difference between the rich and the poor—suggesting by this comment that Mara is rich and should not worry: "Your name is Mara, you go to school, you live in a beautiful house, and your messes I'm the one who cleans them" (Women, 169). Mara cannot accept Zanouba's explanation. "The short of it," Mara says, is that I am a Jew in a country that wants to kill all the Jews. She adds with a tinge of anxiety: "I am born a Jew. That's all I know. I don't know anything else. I am born a Jew and it is hopeless" (Women, 169). Zanouba, sensitive to Mara's anxiety, tries to comfort her by instructing her in the ways of Egyptian fatalism: "Why are you so worried? You talk as if God did not bring you back home safely. You are here. You are alive. Tomorrow will take care of itself" (Women, 169). Zanouba sounds like Mara's father, Nessim Louria, who counters all worries with "nothing will happen, everything will work out" ("rien n'arrivera, tout s'arrangera!") (Women, 197).

Trying to make sense of her identity, Mara writes in her journal: "I love Egypt. My country by birth and papers. But I am Jewish. I write in French, I practically can't read Arabic." She reflects on two words in Arabic used to refer to one's country, "El Bilad, the native land, and El Watan, the house attacked by a disloyal and hateful neighbor" (Women, 212–213).[27] On the one hand, there's one's native country, *el bilad*; on the other, there's the nation one identifies as one's own, *El Watan*. Mara's problem, she explains to Zanouba, is that she has more in common with the enemy—that is to say, Israel, than with Egypt. She can't help that, she says, and then adds: "I don't say this to excuse the Jews of Israel. On the contrary, I reproach them for it" (Women, 213). She is disturbed and upset that Israel has problematized her Egyptian identity. Jacques's novels show the frictions that the existence of Israel has created for Egyptian Jews, a topic I will return to later. Her characters are shown mostly to share Mara's view with regard to their Egyptian identity. Their attachment to Egypt is an attachment to *el bilad*, with which they share a common culture and a way of being. As for the *Watan*, structurally and ideologically constructed to exclude the Jew, it causes the rift and cannot be part of their Jewish identity. When Mara is told that her family will have to leave Egypt, she cries out: "Zanuba is my country, my house, my family, my ancestors, my secrets, my loves. Zanuba is my real country" (Women, 301). Zanouba is her *bilad*.

Jacques's characters defend vigorously their belongingness to Egypt and Jacques writes with an eye on establishing the rightness of this connection. Belardo Gormazzano, the head of the Jewish gang of criminals who have stolen the Jewish community's money, is warned by the American Deborah Lewyn that the Jews of Egypt must emigrate to Israel. It is amply clear, she warns, that Egypt has turned against the Jews. Unconvinced, Belardo responds: "Take out of your mind the idea that Egypt is persecuting us. I went to jail for no reason, be it, but I also came out of it, so!" (Deborah, 254). Later, Belardo tells Rachel the courtesan that he is "viscerally and exclusively" attached to Egypt and passes up the coveted opportunity to leave with her (Deborah, 291). With time, as events make it undeniably clear to him that Egypt has, in fact, turned against the Jews, Belardo is profoundly shaken. Like Kayro Jacobi, the protagonist of *Kayro Jacobi Just before Oblivion* (*Kayro Jacobi juste avant l'oubli;* 2010), Belardo simply cannot believe what has happened. The narrator, herself a member of the community—she is writing decades after the event unfolding in the novel—acknowledges the difficulty faced by those who must choose between leaving and staying when the stakes are high and the future uncertain. The narrator explains that Belardo is afraid of the "unknown and of exile—this death in life." Lest we judge him too harshly for his indecision, or fail to read in his attachment to Egypt a form of passive resistance, she dissipates all blame with the following thought:

> Who could blame a man of his age, a sexagenarian soon, for not wanting to leave, for his distrust of change? . . . he could not believe Rachel's dark vision of the future for the Jews of Egypt. It flew in the face of History. Five thousand years of existence in the Valley of the Nile, a chronicle made successively of love and acrimony, discord and peace, in short, a good marriage. All this contradicted the nasty prophecy. (Deborah, 292)[28]

A paragraph later, the narrator observes: "There are human beings who take precautions in the face of uncertainty and peril, others, weaker, hoping to be spared, act out the allegory of the three monkeys and play deaf, blind, dumb" (Deborah, 293).[29] These words are not meant to pass judgment on those who are afraid or on anyone who is slow to read the handwriting on the wall. For Jacques, to be weak is not a fault; weakness, like evil, is built into the human condition. In the same novel, one of the characters explains to Deborah that each person has an angel, a wounded angel who follows him or her. The wound that the angel carries within and from which he suffers mirrors the reckless behavior, wrong choices, or vices that the angel's double on earth suffers from. The angel takes on the pain these reckless imperfect people endure on earth. An angel guards against our feeling alone in our suffering and guilt. I believe this image of the angel's role can be used to understand one of the ways Jacques approaches her characters. She portrays Egyptian Jews as less than perfect and casts herself as the wretched compatriot whose compassion dissipates their sins. She plays a similar role as the child of immigrants who, as Jacques Hassoun theorized, carries the "wounded father" to the other side and who, in doing so, heals both of them and safeguards generations to come.

Stateless in France the Inhospitable

As I have argued throughout this book and particularly in the chapter on Edmond Jabès, France offered a great deal to Egypt's Jews when they lived in Egypt. As the narrator of *Descent to Paradise* puts it: "Every Jew harbors a love for the country of human rights" (Paradise, 46). This attachment and respect for the idea of France is partly the reason that Egyptian Jews, like Maghrebi Jews, expected that when they arrived in France as refugees and immigrants they would be received and fully recognized as compatriots or cousins-in-arms who are bound together by history, culture, and language. However, this was not the case. Their disappointment was compounded by the fear of remaining stateless ("apatride"), being left without a country to take up their cause. Leaving aside for the moment the role of Israel, being stateless was not a small matter, and given their recent experience of dispossession and expulsion, their concerns were legitimate. There is a telling and amusing scene in Tobie Nathan's novel, *This Country that Looks Like You* (*Ce Pays qui te ressemble*; 2015), that evokes both the strangeness of the concept of nationality and the rising anxiety among Egyptian Jews about being stateless. Concerned they might be reported to the police, accused of theft, and imprisoned without representation, Elie asks Poupy, the person who would be charged with committing the crime they are plotting, to explain his nationality. He asks him but half-suspects that Poupy is stateless—like "most of the residents of Haret el-Yahoud, even in these modern times"—and that, consequently, he will be treated unfairly in Egyptian courts. Poupy answers Elie's question without hesitation: I am "Egyptian! born in Cairo." That doesn't mean anything, says Elie. Do you have papers, an Egyptian passport? Poupy doesn't.

—Do you even know the name of your homeland?
—No I don't!
—Let me tell you about it. This homeland is called nothing! It is the opposite of a homeland. It is a non-homeland, an absence of homeland. I'll tell you what you are, Poupy, if you want to know. You are stateless [*apatride*] State . . . less . . . That's how one calls it! At which point everyone in the room starts repeating the word "stateless." This meant, the narrator points out, "they were nothing." And each time Poupy heard the word "stateless," he would say "Toz"! "Toz" was more a sound than a word, says the narrator. It is the sound of children when they use their mouth to imitate the sound of flatulence.

By *toz*, Poupy means, like Farida Sardaal, Mona's grandmother, that as far as he is concerned these political categories were as insignificant as foul wind ("Ces événements du monde ne sont rien que du vent . . ."). He kept repeating:

—Toz, toz and toz . . .
—Toz or not toz, Elie responded, since you are not a foreigner nor an Egyptian, nobody will defend you. You're like an animal, Poupy. Did you ever see someone come to the defense of a donkey when he is beaten by his master just to make him take a step? You can travel the length and width of Egypt, you'll never find anybody who will. So, listen, toz to you too.[30]

In the mid-twentieth century, statelessness became a political reality for many people around the world, from Hungary, Spain, the French colonies, Asia, the Middle East, and Africa. According to the 1954 *United Nations Convention Relating to the Status of Stateless Persons,* which took effect on June 6, 1960, a stateless person is defined as "someone who is not considered as a national by any State under operation of its law."[31] The *Convention* stipulates that the rights of such person are to meet "minimum standards of treatment." Jacques's novels take full account of the anxiety of statelessness. *A Kiss as Cold as the Moon* describes the conditions, the steps taken to secure legal status in France, and the emotional distress that statelessness caused. It describes the way the situation colored people's lives, affected their well-being, and determined the decisions they made. The first few chapters in the section titled "Paris, Spring 1961," are particularly instructive. They describe Tobias and others, like the Spanish immigrant and her children, trudging through the streets of Paris in all kinds of weather, waiting in long lines most of the day just to renew their temporary visa (*carte de séjour*), and the way they are addressed by contemptuous, vulgar, and unkind civil servants. Jacques describes their longing to call France their home, their need to be treated with a minimum of compassion and, lacking that, by something resembling respect. The narrator notes: "After four or five years of disappointments, stateless people still hope to become 'French from France' and Tobias, since his arrival in Paris, pursues ardently the same project" (Kiss, 29). Tobias asks himself not without irony: What does it take to be a French citizen in this country "of human rights, social security, Champs-Elysées, *Folies-Bergères*?" (Kiss, 24). The uncertainty of the status of Egyptian Jews and their hopelessness is reflected in a conversation between Tobias and his friend, Berto. Berto notes that the *United Nations Convention* describes the situation of Egyptian Jews perfectly, with one important exception: the document, says Berto, concerns political refugees. Egyptian Jews, he argues, are not political refugees. The *Convention* states that political refugees are candidates for protection because, as they hold opposing political views, returning to their country of origin would endanger their lives. This was the case for many Hungarians and Algerians, but not for Egyptian Jews. Their expulsion was motivated by religious enmity, Berto says. Tobias does not disagree. Egyptian Jews are political refugees, but, he adds, they will not be granted protection because France will never admit to calling them political refugees because to admit this would exonerate France for its "cowardly aggression" during the Suez War. Tobias, the dreamer, will hitch his star to the new world, where he can finally be a citizen. It becomes increasingly clear to him as he tries to adjust to life in France that France is an inhospitable place for immigrants and Jews. Consequently, when the opportunity to leave for America presents itself, Tobias grabs it. He leaves his daughter, the light of his eye (now an adult) to establish himself there. As he says at one point: "a political refugee will always be stateless. I want citizenship" (Kiss, 32). So even Tobias, the man afflicted with what his mother calls the "itch to move" ("la bougeotte") needs the security of belonging to a country, that a country will adopt him and protect him from those who would exclude him and persecute him. It is this fear of abandonment that motivates Gilda Stambouli who leaves her children behind in Israel to make France her home before she calls for them to join her.

In France, where many of Jacques's characters settle after their exile, Egyptian Jews are stunned that the French people consider them "foreigners" and that the government is not eager to grant them French citizenship, "la nationalité" (Gilda, 39). The narrator of *Gilda Stambouli Suffers and Complains . . .* (*Gilda*

Stambouli souffre et se plaint . . .; 2002) explains that in their desire to belong, to shed the *stigma* of statelessness, they lash out against France:

> A curse on those who administer this arbitrary system, the stateless declares. France is a far cry from this democracy extolled in books, newspapers, and in the letters of optimistic emigrants. The stateless convince themselves, *not without reason*, that it is terribly hard to be a foreigner in France, and that nothing is harder in France than the fate of the foreign Jew. (My italics; Gilda, 152)[32]

The love affair with France, its language, history, and culture is powerful. From the kibbutz in Israel where she is, Mélissa fights tooth and nail to go to France, this "Precious France, beloved country of my childhood" (Kiss, 277). Gilda's daughter, Juliette, left behind by her mother in Israel, dies in Israel unable to reach her promised land, France. It is the revelation of their lives that, once they are in France, Jacques's characters discover that France is not what they believed it to be. These French-speaking immigrants to France had been indoctrinated by their French schooling in Egypt to think of France as the embodiment of the Enlightenment, the jewel in the crown of the West, and a symbol of incontrovertible universal values, including the rights of man, equality for all, freedom of expression, and *laïcité*. After such expectations, how could the *real* France stand a chance? The following exchange between two sisters, Marcelle and Louna in *Aunt Carlotta's Legacy*, dramatizes the gap between what was expected and what was encountered and the profound feeling of betrayal Egyptian Jews felt toward France. Marcelle Sonsino bemoans the fact that her recently deceased sister Carlotta loved Egypt too much and stayed behind when she should have left for France with the rest of the family. She says: "Can you imagine preferring Cairo to Paris? That's crazy! Is anything more beautiful to behold than the extraordinary light of France over the Loire?" Marcelle's exalted comment is more than Louna can stand. She pounces on Marcelle's words: "The Loire? You, Marcelle you know the Loire . . . you celebrate France? This ball where the host and guests don't show up for the party, that's France" (Carlotta, 19–20).[33] She continues to outline the inhospitability: "You forgot? You forgot, Marcelle, that a stateless person in Paris is less than nothing, even nothing is more than the stateless? I have not forgotten and I nurse this wound. Never will I forget" (Carlotta, 20).[34] Yet Marcelle herself, when writing letters from Paris to Carlotta in Egypt, reported nothing but the most abject conditions of life in Paris (Carlotta, 22). Marcelle's nearly hypnotic reference to the light on the Loire is the disquieting effect of cultural indoctrination, suggesting the embedding of French aesthetics in the psyche of these immigrants long after their image of France has ceased to correspond to their reality. The vision is a difficult thing to shake.

The young Mona, Camélia, Mélissa, and Robie (Gilda's twelve-year-old son), all born in Egypt, are characters in the shadow of their parents' drama. Perhaps they too have been disappointed by France. In any case, and Jacques means it to be this way, the novels are not about the children—although they are pivotal for keeping the existence of Jewish Egyptians alive for posterity, as I have argued. The children, Mélissa, Robie, Camélia, Benji, and Mona are enmeshed in the story of Egypt, both the Egypt of their childhood and the Egypt evoked by their elders. They are writers who function as witnesses, confidants, and agents of transmission in the best Hassounian sense of the term.

The Land of Israel

If Jacques's characters are yearning to become citizens of a country that extends a welcome to them, what about Israel? What does Israel stand for in their lives? The relationship of Egyptian Jews to Israel depends on the character in question and at what point he or she is in life. In Egypt, most of Jacques's characters tend to see the existence of Israel, as Mara in *Women with Their Love* does, as necessary and desirable for Jews. The writer-interviewer in *Kayro Jacobi, Just before Oblivion* has the same view. She argues that given their history of persecutions, as Nazism has shown, it is imperative that Israel exist as a home for the Jews (Kayro, 252). This view is shared by Allegra Jacobi, Zaki Romano, and the young Benjy Zakein. Not all the characters in Jacques's novels see Israel this way. A few, like the young communists Bolissa in *Light of My Eye* and Nellie and Vivie in *Kayro Jacobi*, believe that Israel is an imperialist country and that Jews in Egypt are not the target of undeserved animus. The matriarch Sarina, who had been a communist in her younger days, supports Israel's existence. She criticizes Tobias for thinking that Israel is a problem for Egyptian Jews and warns him against such thinking. In the first place, it is a sin against God and, in the second place, it encourages antisemitism (Kiss, 295). Tobias, however, maintains that Judaism and Israel are two separate entities: "Israel is the country of the Israeli people. The country of the Jewish people is the Bible" (Kiss, 305).

Jacques's characters who have lived in Israel, like Tobias, Melissa, and Juliette, experience profound cultural shock there. They see Israel as a sterile and harsh country devoid of culture. They feel as alienated in Israel as they would be on the surface of the moon. Accustomed to Egyptian culture, Mediterranean and Arab, and nurtured on French culture, they never for a moment feel at home in Israel. This attitude, though, takes a radical shift in Jacques's last novel to date, *At Least It's Not Raining* (2015) which I will soon discuss. But in her earlier works, Jacques nearly always describes Israeli culture in the late 1950s and early 1960s from the perspective of kibbutz culture. Its emphasis on physical labor, military strength, and the subordination of the individual for the profit of the collective fills her characters with horror. Israel in the eyes of the urbane and cosmopolitan

Egyptians is not a livable environment. Becky Castro, in *Light of My Eye*, speaking of Israel in the 1970s, explains that when she lived in Israel with her first husband in Israel, which was then Palestine, she found it insufferable: "It wasn't like Israel now, but a land of savages. My husband would say to me, 'Don't cry, in fifty years this will be paradise.' And I would sob, 'So I'll come back in fifty years'" (Cohen, 23). To Norma Jacobi, wife of the celebrated filmmaker, even "the Israel of today" is oppressive and inhospitable. From her Tel Aviv apartment in 2007, she opines that Israelis have no sense of beauty: "Just look at Tel Aviv," she says to her interviewer, an Egyptian Jew. Norma goes on to say that in Israel nobody understands culture, the eminence of Egyptian civilization, and the remarkable role Jews played in the rise of modern Egypt (Kayro, 11). Nobody believes, least of all in Israel, that Egyptian cinema was Hollywood on the Nile, she says. Jacques's early novels portray life in Israel as Spartan and culturally barren, characterized by kibbutz culture. For Juliette Stambouli and Mélissa Del Burgo, to live without books and without personal space is unbearable. Anny Dayan-Rosenman calls Tobias and Mélissa "aristocratic crooks lost in the sunflower fields of the land of pioneers . . . ready to lie and cheat their way out of paradise and the kibbutz."[35] Tobias, trying to explain to his kibbutz friend, Judith, why he can't be happy in Israel, says: "I am not a warrior! I am a businessman, and a pacifist to boot" (Kiss, 251). And he adds: "Sometimes, Judith, we must recognize our limits and our true nature. Mine is urban, civilized. Frivolous, probably. I miss the city." She tells him in English that he is a "Jewish spoiled child" (Kiss, 251). Zoltan Gadol, a Zionist and an acquaintance from Egypt, agrees with this assessment. Despite Zoltan's crudeness and pomposity. Zoltan seems to speak the mind of the narrator and, perhaps, also of Jacques herself when he tells Tobias that Jews from Egypt are self-absorbed and oblivious to the dangers of antisemitism. Zoltan says he has seen Jews come to Israel from everywhere except Egypt. He indicts Egyptian Jews in general when he tells Tobias, "You are a stubborn man, Tobias, and a pretty selfish one" (Kiss, 203). Tobias and Mélissa plan to immigrate to France, and so Tobias tells Zoltan that he is not worried because in France, Jews are protected against persecution. Zoltan can barely contain himself:

> In France! Are you kidding me? There, like elsewhere, my friend. You'll learn sooner or later at your own expense. The *Vel d'hiv'*, the militia, the Gestapo, you know that, right? Anyway, that's your business. But you should know that we will welcome you back with open arms the day you decide to honor us with your presence. In the meantime, your trusted servants will take care of the house and clean it for you, while you bathe in luxury and live the easy life." (Kiss, 204)[36]

In *Gilda Stambouli Suffers and Complains . . .* , Gilda's thirteen-year-old daughter Juliette lives on a kibbutz near the Syrian border, and literally dies while waiting to go to France. To be sure, Juliette's death is meant to suggest the depth of despair that the child of a self-centered mother feels. But it also suggests how noxious Israeli kibbutz culture is for this Egyptian Jew who needed books and art and French culture to sustain her. Jacques uses this character to make clear just how Egyptian Jews like Tobias and Mélissa are unsuited for kibbutz life. Jacques reserves a significant section of the novel, "Ballad of the Lost Souls" ("La Ballade des égarés") to call attention to the cultural sterility of the kibbutz and the fundamental unsuitability of her two characters to lead their lives there. Tobias and Mélissa are confused by its values, including its general indifference to religious practice. For these Alexandrian Jews, raised between French and Egyptian cultures, it is France—and not Israel—that represents the Promised Land. They are barely aware that in the kibbutz they are living among Jews who experienced the horrors of Nazi concentration camps. Jacques paints the Egyptian Jews in her work as indifferent to the Holocaust. In *Gilda Stambouli Suffers and Complains . . .*, she creates a character whose cluelessness verges on the distasteful. This novel is one of the few she has written that shines a particularly cruel light on her subject. The novel takes place in Paris in 1957–1958. Gilda, the main character, a twenty-six-year-old recently widowed mother of two, is trying to build a life there before she sends for her daughter. Bertha Fromkine, a camp survivor and social worker in a Jewish aid organization that helps Jewish political refugees settle in France, dedicates herself to helping Gilda and to bringing her daughter Juliette to France. The same commitment to Gilda and her family is shown by the Lipinsky family and by the Hasidic community in Paris. Jacques has clearly juxtaposed, on the one hand, the plight of Gilda and her Egyptian cohort and, on the other, the plight of Bertha Fromkine and the Lipinsky family, survivors of the Holocaust and of pogroms in Russia. Jacques portrays the newcomers from Egypt almost uniformly as a petty group who are inconsiderate, demanding, and grotesque. The scene at the cemetery in Bagneux is a striking and not atypical example. The Egyptian Jewish community in Paris is gathered to bury an elder member. One of the members of the community, Henri Moïse, takes advantage of the situation to monopolize the podium, which he uses to berate and make demands on the representatives of the philanthropic Jewish aid organization, CASAR, who came to the funeral to pay their respects. Jacques portrays the Egyptian Jewish immigrant community as woefully unconcerned about the suffering of others even after they learn about the horrors of the Holocaust. Soraya, one of Gilda's compatriots, who is as callous as most of them, suggests an explanation for their thoughtlessness. They have all gotten a bit meaner since their exile, she comments: "That's the way it is when people don't feel at home where they are. You feel . . . like you're living outside yourself, at the door of who you are. Forced to stay outside, you can't help it, you become double: one on each side of the door. One white and the other black. You think you're white: but not at all, you're black" (Gilda, 143).[37] She offers this as an explanation and not an excuse. Jacques, like Edmond Jabès, exposes the complicated reality of competing misfortunes. As Becky in *Light of My Eyes* says to her daughter, "Frankly, I wonder who will be interested in the Egyptian misfortune. As it is, if you have a toothache you couldn't care less that your neighbor has cancer" (Cohen, 51). The pain we feel matters more than the greater pain of others. This is as true of mental anguish as it is of physical pain. And both Jacques and Jabès suggest that it would be hypocritical to pretend otherwise. Jacques dramatizes this insight to the great disadvantage of her characters.

Ashkenazi and Sephardic

With the notable exception of *At Least It's Not Raining (Au moins il ne pleut pas;* 2015), Ashkenazi Jews and Egyptian Jews clash with each other in Jacques's work. The former are perceived by the latter as excessively somber, rigid, and religious. In turn, Ashkenazi Jews consider Egyptian Jews—"orientals," as they call them— irrational, flamboyant, and manipulating. They compare them to children and patronize them accordingly. Bertha Fromkine, the social worker, describes Egyptian Jews as always in a state of "shameless anxiousness" ("névrosité provocante") (Gilda, 60). The American philanthropist's daughter, Deborah Lewyn, is regarded by the Jews of Cairo as uptight, sexually repressed, joyless, and a religious zealot. She is the emblematic figure of the Ashkenazi Jew viewed by her Sephardi/ Mizrahi counterpart. The narrator of *Deborah and the Reckless Angels*, a self-proclaimed Egyptian Jew, describes her as humorless, smug, and patronizing. More egregiously, perhaps, she portrays her as a naïve idealist who cannot begin to suspect what is in store for the newly declared state of Israel. Deborah, as I suggested earlier, is clueless about the complexity of Jewish society in Egypt and is stunned that Egyptian Jews are not eager to flock to Israel. Deborah is portrayed as a sincere person but ultimately superficial and out of touch with both the world and her body. The narrator's peremptory summary of Deborah's aspiration in the end of the novel is cutting: "Like a tourist sincerely hoping to share the experience of the locals, the young woman burned with desire to be part of the great movement that, ushering in a new messianic age, would connect this age of materialism to biblical times. So long! Have a good trip!" (Deborah, 344)[38]—a clear and sarcastic sendoff to be sure.

In closing, I will argue that in her last novel, *At Least It's Not Raining*, Jacques breaks new ground and offers possibilities for imagining the future of Egyptian Jews in Israel, of Egyptian and Ashkenazi Jews living together in Israel. In this novel, Egypt exists as an abstract principle, an attribute the two Jewish Egyptian characters, Solly and Lola, embody and that they use to reconstitute the Jewish family in Israel. The two characters are the orphans Solly, age fifteen, and his sister Lola, who is sixteen. After their parents are killed in Egypt in a car accident, they are sent to Israel under the protection of a Jewish agency. This is the first of Jacques's ten novels in which *both* the father and mother are dead, not just the father. Once in Israel, the two children fear they will be separated. In desperation, they run away to Haifa where they rent a room in the home of two concentration camp survivors, Magda Rosenthal and Ruthie Schreiber. The novel is set during the period of the Eichmann trial, when the complicated and brutal realities of the camps were exposed as was the role some Jews, like Magda Rosenthal, played in the day-to-day operations of these camps. The novel describes how these survivors were scrutinized and judged harshly. The novel also brings to the fore France's collaboration with the Nazis. To speak in psychological terms, in this novel, coming thirty-five years after her first, Jacques seems now to be able to finally imagine leaving Egypt. It is significant, I maintain, that whereas France in the earlier novels was not spared from direct criticism, in this novel the critique of France is devastating, pointed, and chilling. This criticism comes across unequivocally in the following exchange. The very francophile Lola asks the French-born Magda if she misses France. Magda answers in ways that echo the words of the Zionist Zoltan Gadol:

> France? Don't talk to me about France, please. Pure shit, that's France! France marked me with the yellow star. France rounded me up. France deported me to Drancy. France delivered me to the Germans. France is anti-Semitic to the root, Lola, and it's not from yesterday. Ein ḥadash taḥat ha shemesh, nothing new under the sun! I wouldn't go back if they paid me. And you, would you go back to Egypt? (Raining, 64)[39]

"No," replies Lola. In *At Least It's Not Raining*, both Egypt and France are displaced in Jacques's affective economy. They are, so to speak, placed in the same basket and thrown overboard, replaced by Israel. The novel, again, breaks ground with previous works and replaces the earlier image of Israel as a warrior country devoid of culture by one with potential. In this novel, Israel is a country on its way to creating a new space where Jews, artists like Ruthie and writers like Lola, can live and thrive.

The novel also reverses earlier portrayals of Ashkenazi and Sephardi/Mizrahi dissonance, describing opportunities and imaginative collaborations between Ashkenazi and Jewish Egyptians. It is through Magda Rosenthal and Ruthie Schreiber that the two children learn about the Holocaust. Living next door is a Moroccan family. Here again, the orphans learn about the plight of Jewish minorities from Arab lands now living in Israel. Lola in particular gets a chance to observe that family closely. She does not share the Moroccan way of life but empathizes with them and understands their culture in a way that Magda and Ruthie do not. A notable episode drives home to Solly the plight of the Palestinians living under Israeli rule. We are in 1959–1960. Solly sees a Palestinian roughed up by the police and recognizes in the Arab's fearful eyes something he saw in his own father's eye when, having been identified as a Jew, his father was harassed by an Egyptian officer. Jacques suggests that the two orphans are go-betweens who bridge ethnic and cultural divides. We thus have a visual illustration of the role Jacques has devised for Jewish Egyptian characters. One of the two survivors whose house the children share, Ruthie Schreiber, is a poet and musician. From the onset, she has shut herself off from everyone, keeps mostly to her room, and allows nobody to enter it. Lola, an aspiring writer who is drawn to Ruthie like one artist to another, tries sincerely to establish a relationship despite Ruthie's determination to shut her and everyone out. Eventually, the empathetic Lola succeeds both literally and figuratively in opening Ruthie's door. The novel ends with the four characters moving with Ruthie's piano, the vestige of her cultural heritage, to start life anew in a newly constructed building in the outskirts of Haifa. For all its sterility, white walls, and angular lines, this new place represents the beginning of a newly reconstituted Jewish family. There is no ambiguity and equivocation in Jacques's portrayal; they are a family. It is a fact that in this novel Jacques critiques Israeli domestic policies and describes a society that manifestly discriminates against many of its citizens, Jews and Muslims alike. But the novel also intimates a bright future for Israel, offering a new model for a fresh start inspired by the reality of Israel's composite population and by the insights of Lola and Solly, Egyptian Jews who are good at opening doors and building bridges. There is Kahanoffian Levantinism at work here, suggesting that Egyptian Jews are well positioned to help bridge the distance between European Jews, Jews from Arab lands living in Israel, such as the Moroccan and Iraqi communities, and Palestinians. The novel introduces the possibility that Israel can be, after all, a home for Egyptian Jews, a place where they can be happy. Perhaps Israel can be a country friendly toward Jews endowed with a hybrid Levantine culture, both European and Egyptian. Maybe these Egyptian Jews can be useful in ushering in a new paradigm.

Paula Jacques's work entertains at least two ambitious projects, one of which is to reinscribe Egyptian Jews into the history of Egypt, draw attention to their attachment to Egypt and their resistance against dispossession, and the other, an extension of the first, to establish the groundwork for the perpetuation of the heritage of Jewish Egyptians on France's soil and on Israel's soil. Jacques is a powerful writer whose vision, knowledge, sensitivity, and literary skills offer a unique perspective on the experiences of Egyptian Jews. To date, only *Light of My Eye* has been translated into English.[40] The rest must follow. The challenge will be to capture the inflections of the voices Jacques has recreated and to convey her lightness of touch and sharp sense of humor.

Notes

I use the following abbreviations and editions of Paula Jacques's works. Translations of texts and titles are mine with the following exception: *Light of My Eye*, translated by Susan Cohen-Nicole (Teaneck, N.J.: Holmes & Meier, 2009).

(Kiss) *A Kiss as Cold as the Moon* [*Un Baiser froid comme la lune*]. Paris: Mercure de France, 1983.

(Raining) *At Least It's Not Raining* [*Au moins il ne pleut pas*]. Paris: Stock, 2015.

(Carlotta) *Aunt Carlotta's Legacy* [*L'héritage de tante Carlotta*]. Paris: Mercure de France, 1987.

(Deborah) *Deborah and the Reckless Angels*[*Deborah et les anges dissipés*]. Paris: Mercure de France, 1991.

(Descent) *Descent to Paradise* [*La Descente au paradis*]. Paris: Mercure de France, 1995.

(Gilda) *Gilda Stambouli Suffers and Complains . . .* [*Gilda Stambouli souffre et se plaint . . .*]. Paris: Mercure de France, 2002.

(Kayro) *Kayro Jacobi, Just Before Oblivion* [*Kayro Jacobi, juste avant l'oubli*]. Paris: Mercure de France, 2010.

(Cohen) *Light of My Eyes* [*Lumière de l'oeil*]. Paris: Mercure de France, 1980). All other translations of this work are my own.

(Rachel) *Rachel-Rose and the Arab Officer* [*Rachel-Rose et l'officier arabe*]. Paris: Mercure de France, 2006.

(Women) *Women with Their Love* [*Les Femmes avec leur amour*]. Paris: Mercure de France, 1997.

    1. Jacques's text: "Quand il est près de sa fin, l'olivier donne ses plus beaux fruits et il en sera ainsi des juifs d'Egypte" (Carlotta, 178).

    2. Jacques's text: "L'âge, ça va, ça vient, ça change tout le temps, et la nationalité aussi. A quoi servent les feuilles de poussière? Est-ce que je ne sais pas qui je suis? Farida Sardaal, née Benzakein, au Caire, un très beau jour?" (my translation; *Lumière de l'oeil*, 97).

    3. Jacques's text: "Ainsi et selon les besoins pouvait-il présenter les sauf-conduits de la puissance dominante, mouvante telles les vagues déferlant au bas de la Casa Amapola" (Kiss, 70–71).

    4. Jacques's text: "A force de chercher des identités, ton père a perdu son visage" (Kiss, 76).

    5. From an interview I had with Paula Jacques, May 10, 2007 by email correspondence. Jacques's text: "J'aime beaucoup mes personnages en général, j'ai pour eux le regard dur et le coeur tendre." Further references to this interview will be included in the text as (Israel-Pelletier).

    6. At the time of this writing, 2016, Paula Jacques has informed me that she is working on a subject that does not focus on Egyptian Jewry.

    7. Jacques's text of the interview: "J'ai essayé de sortir de ce cadre, sans succès. Il m'émeut, il m'inspire. J'ai l'impression d'en découvrir à chaque fois de nouvelles facettes, de les approfondir. Là est ma richesse. Là est ma légitimité. Et très modestement, je pense combler par l'écriture le vide effrayant autour de leur place, le silence sur leur rôle, leur contribution culturelle, économique, voire historique, au pays qui les a vus naître."

8. Thomas Nolden, *In Lieu of Memory: Contemporary Jewish Writing in France* (Syracuse, N.Y.: Syracuse University Press, 2006), 48. Further references to this work will be included in the text as (Nolden).

9. Jacques's text: "Elle poussa donc les photos dans les fissures des murs, les tassa à l'aide d'un balai et s'en trouva consolé" (*Lumière de l'oeil*, 274).

10. Jacques's text: "'Rien, il n'y a rien là-dedans', disait le omdey.... Les drageurs reprenaient après lui: 'Rien, il n'y a rien.... ' Rien dominait tout. Rien passait au dessus du canal, des champs, du village pour atteindre les sables du désert où il se perdait, et c'était comme si un éclair n'avait pas été suivi du tonnerre" (Paradis, 337).

11. Jacques's text: "Au Caire il n'y a plus de place pour eux. Ils se sont effacés de la mémoire du Caire. Même leur absence s'est effacée de la mémoire du Caire" (Deborah, 40).

12. Jacques's text: "Au fond de moi, la même absurde conviction me persuade que rien ne finit, rien ne commence. *Et tout se répète*: les silences de mon père, ses fureurs, ses violences tournées contre lui-même, son obstination à se créer le plus de chagrin possible, goutte à goutte, comme on réglerait le robinet de la baignoire" (My italics; Descent, 13).

13. Jacques's text: "l'obscur devoir juif de démolir ardoise après ardoise le toit de sa maison" (Carlotta, 48).

14. Jacques's text: "Pourquoi tu m'as choisie comme vedette?" (my translation, *Lumière de l'oeil*, 59).

15. Jacques's text: "Franchement, je me demande qui va s'intéresser au malheur égyptien?" (my translation; *Lumière de l'oeil*, 59).

16. Jacques's text: "Je puisais dans le terroir juif... je retournais au Passage des Barbarins, bien calamiteux, puissament exotique pour ma maitresse.... Et voilà que l'ancêtre me revenait doucement comme on tire sur les fils d'une pelote, voilà qu'il m'habitait, et *qu'à travers moi renaissait l'épopée* misérable du Passage des Barbarins" (my italics; Carlotta, 58–59).

17. Jacques's text: "La fidélité aux choses du passé m'inspirait un malaise comparable au spectacle de décors rongés d'oubli et de poussière, encore que Maman entretint soigneusement ses trésors" (Carlotta, 11).

18. Jacques's text: "Assise à la turque sur la moquette, tante Fortunée inclinait la tête et, *souriant* vaguement à ses présages, elle sondait le fond de la tasse. / "Et il n'y avait d'avenir que dans le marc de café" (my italics; Carlotta, 342).

19. Jacques's text: "Autrefois, il y avait en notre Vieux-Quartier un violoniste qui jouait avec tant d'allégresse et de charme que nous ne pouvions l'écouter sans nous mettre à danser. Et nous dansions tous les jours et la danse nous donnait l'illusion de posséder toutes choses, de n'avoir jamais besoin d'une chose avant de la posséder. Un jour, un sourd vint en notre Vieux-Quartier. Comme il n'avait aucune idée de ce que pouvait être la musique, qu'il en ignorait jusqu'à l'existence, notre musique ne toucha point son oreille immobile. Et ses yeux virent en notre danse la dérisoire agitation qui secouait une bande de fous" (Deborah, 345).

20. Jacques's text: "toujours à ressasser le malheur des persécutions, à renier les plaisirs que de temps en temps Dieu nous accorde.... De quoi avez-vous peur, Deborah?" (Deborah, 262).

21. Jacques's text: "D'où par où l'Italie? Ne m'en parlez pas. Nous n'y avons jamais mis les pieds. Existe-t-il de plus beau pays que le nôtre? Je suis Égyptienne dans l'âme depuis presque mille ans. Les Ninio-Médini sont nés avec les pyramides" (Paradise, 37).

22. Jacques's text: "Comment, dit-elle en arabe, ça ne se voit pas? Je suis européenne d'Egypte" (my translation, *Lumière de l'oeil*, 94).

23. Jacques's text: "Comme vous voudrez, mon chéri. Mais de coeur je suis égyptienne" (my translation; *Lumière de l'oeil*, 95).

24. Jacques's text: "Quel tracas! Ni je passe les ports, ni je porte les passes. Bateau, avion, train il n'y a pas. Alors le passport non plus" (my translation; *Lumière de l'oeil*, 95).

25. Jacques's text: "Oui de source pure" (my translation; *Lumière de l'oeil*, 95).

26. Jacques's text: "La vérité dans son puits. J'ai tout perdu dans un déménagement. L'âge, ça va, ça vient, ça change tout le temps, et la nationalité aussi. A quoi servent les feuilles de poussière? Est-ce que je ne sais pas qui je suis? Farida Sardaal, née Benzakein, au Caire, un très beau jour?" (my translation; *Lumière de l'oeil*, 97).

27. Jacques's text: "J'aime l'Égypte. Mon pays par la naissance et les papiers. Mais je suis juive. J'écris en français, je ne sais pratiquement pas lire l'arabe. . . . el bilad, le pays natal, et El Watan, la maison attaquée par un voisin déloyal et infâme" (Women, 212–213).

28. Jacques's text: "Mais qui pouvait reprocher à cet homme de son âge, un sexagénaire bientôt, son immobilisme, sa défiance du changement? . . . il ne pouvait guère croire à la noire vision qu'avait Rachel de l'avenir des juifs d'Égypte. L'histoire la démentait. Cinq mille ans de présence en la vallée du Nil, une chronique faite successivement d'amour et d'acrimonie, de discorde et de paix, à l'image du bon mariage en somme, tout cela infirmait la méchante prophétie" (Deborah, 292).

29. Jacques's text: "il y a des êtres qui construisent contre les incertitudes et les périls, d'autres plus faibles espèrent échapper en contrefaisant les trois singes sourds, aveugles et muets de l'allégorie" (Deborah, 293).

30. Tobie Nathan, *Ce Pays qui te ressemble* (Paris: Stock, 2015), 210–212.

31. Convention Relating to the Status of Stateless Persons: Text of the 1954 Convention; http://www.unhcr.org/3bbb25729.html.

32. Jacques's text: "La condition de l'apatride, ils maudissent le noir arbitraire qui l'administre. La France est loin d'être cette démocratie encensée par les livres, les journaux, les lettres des émigrés optimistes. Ils se persuadent, *non sans raison*, qu'il est terriblement dur d'être un étranger en France et que rien n'est plus dur en France que le sort du juif étranger" (my italics; Gilda, 152).

33. Jacques's text: "Préférer le Caire à Paris? Folie! Y a-t-il plus beau que la lumière de la France sur la Loire? . . . La Loire? Toi, Marcelle tu connais la Loire . . . tu célèbres la France? Une fête dont le maître de maison et les convives sont absents, voilà la France" (Carlotta, 19–20).

34. Jacques's text: "Tu as oublié Marcelle? Tu as oublié qu'à Paris, l'apatride est moins que rien et rien est plus que l'apatride? Moi je garde la blessure ouverte" (Carlotta, 20).

35. Anny Dayan-Rosemann, "The Israeli-Palestinian Conflict in France: A Conflict in Search of Novelistic Representations," in *Israeli-Palestinian Conflict in the Francophone World*, edited by Nathalie Debrauwere-Miller, 81–92, 88 (New York, London: Routledge, 2010), 88.

36. Jacques's text: "En France! Tu plaisantes? Là comme ailleurs, mon pauvre ami. Partout, tôt ou tard, tu l'apprendras à tes dépens. Le Vel d'hiv', la milice, la Gestapo, tu connais pourtant? C'est ton affaire. Mais sache que nous t'accueillerons à bras ouverts le jour où tu viendras chez toi, en ta maison. En ta maison où les serviteurs auront fait le ménage tandis que tu t'adonnais au luxe et à la vie facile" (Kiss, 204).

37. Jacques's text: "C'est comme ça quand on n'est pas chez soi. Nous vivons . . . comme à la porte de nous-même. Nous n'avons pas le droit d'entrer et à la fin nous devenons deux: une de chaque côté de la porte. La blanche d'un côté, la noire de l'autre. Tu crois être blanche: rien du tout, tu es noire!" (Gilda, 143).

38. Jacques's text: "[L]a jeune femme brûlait du désir sincère, bien que touristique, de participer de l'événement qui, réalisant une nouvelle page des temps messianiques, apparentait l'ère matérialiste aux temps bibliques. Bon voyage!" (Deborah, 344).

39. Jacques's text: "La France? Ne me parle pas de la France, s'il te plaît. De la merde en barre, c'est ça la France! La France m'a marquée à l'étoile jaune. La France m'a raflée. La France m'a déportée à Drancy. La France m'a livrée aux Allemands. La France est antisemite jusqu'à la racine, Lola, et ça ne date pas d'hier. Ein ḥadash taḥat ha shemesh, rien de nouveau sous le soleil! Je n'y retournerais pas même si on me payait pour ça. Tu retournerais en Egypte, toi? (Raining, 64).

40. I am referring to the excellent translation by Susan Cohen-Nicole.

CHAPTER FIVE

André Aciman and the Mediterranean
The Staging of Egypt as Elsewhere

> In a hundred years, no one will even know my grandfather had lived or died, here or elsewhere. It's the difference between death and extinction.
> Aciman "Alexandria: The Capital of Memory"

> Where did Europe begin and end in the nineteenth century, and who was a European?
> Julia A. Clancy-Smith[1]

BORN IN JANUARY 1951 in Alexandria, André Aciman belongs to a generation of Jews who were still in Egypt a decade after the mass departures and expulsions of 1956–1957. His work on Egypt is particularly instructive for the way it describes how some Egyptian Jews felt about Egypt at a time when political animus against them was intense. There was another round of mass departures in 1961 after Gamal Abdel Nasser nationalized sectors of the economy. Aciman and his family left Egypt in April 1965 when he was fourteen years old. Like many families who had not been targeted directly, the Aciman family lived for years with one foot in Egypt and one foot out. Aciman describes his father in those years as paralyzed by indecision, unable to imagine himself uprooted. He writes in *False Papers* (2000): "Some, like us, simply waited, the way Jews did elsewhere when it was already too late to hope for miracles. We saw the city change and each year watched European shop names come down and be replaced by Egyptian ones, and heard of streets being renamed, until—as is the case now—I didn't know a single one" (F, 6). Aciman's generation growing up in Egypt in the mid-1950s and mid-1960s watched Egypt assert its Arab identity. It witnessed Jews singled out as foreigners, traitors, imperialists, and agents of Israel. Pan-Arabism was a popular movement, inspired by the eloquence of Nasser and the promises of Arab unity, economic growth, and independence from the West. It linked Egypt's liberalism and cosmopolitanism with colonialism and marked them as anti-Egyptian.

"I am elsewhere.... Some people have an identity, I have an alibi...."[2]

In this redefined Egypt, those who did not fit into the category of Arab and Muslim were compelled to rethink their relationship to the country. Aciman's writings on Egypt are vivid accounts of the psychological suffering endured by the child and young adolescent living during this period. This psychological stress would affect his sense of self and the way he experienced the world around him. He explains in the essay "A Literary Pilgrim Progresses to the Past" that he writes about Alexandria, "the mythical home of paradox," to help him "give a geographical frame to a psychological mess," such that "Alexandria is the nickname I give this mess" (A, 89). As the narrator of *Eight White Nights* (2010) puts it, expressing your thoughts and feelings is a tricky business when you do not know who you are: "Being myself was like asking a mask to mimic a face that's never been without masks. How do you play the part of someone trying not to play parts?" And driving the point further: "[D]id one score more points by feigning indifference or by feigning to feign indifference ... ?" (E, 142). Aciman's attachment to Egypt is both feigned and, in a structural sense, fundamental. In a psychology of relentless displacement, Egypt is the only element that can be counted on always to be present. It is constitutive of who Aciman is and *how* he is. This is a complicated affair, as he confesses in the essay titled "Temporizing" in *Alibis*:

> My impulse when I see something beautiful or moving or even something I desire in the here and now is to throw it back to Egypt, to see if it fits there, if it isn't yet another one of those missing pieces that belongs there or that should be brought back there, or that should be made to seem to have originated there, as though for something to make sense to me it has to have roots that go all the way back to Egypt, as though the act of piecing Egypt back together, of reconstructing and restoring even an imaginary Egypt out of this scatter of impressions in New York were an interminable restoration project whose purpose is to prevent all contact with the present, so that anything I encounter that strikes me must, in one way or another, correspond to something Egyptian, have an Egyptian coefficient, or else mean absolutely nothing. (A, 72)

The passage develops at some length his idea of Egypt as the grid on which he plots his life. Aciman's entire work is a meticulous, at times parodistic, elaboration of the self-scattering caused by exile. Egypt is always there as a place he remembers, as a loss he cannot get over. Egypt is an anchor that is curiously not one. It is in his work the site of manic repetition, systematic ambivalence, and diffuse unalleviated anger.

In this chapter, I sometimes conflate Aciman the man and his writerly persona and sometimes not. I do not distinguish between novels, memoirs, essays, reviews, and his responses in interviews. Separating fiction from autobiography is problematic and, in Aciman's case, it is unproductive. Aciman has gone to great lengths to fudge the lines. As he puts it, he is not "after" the facts of a historical moment. Rather, he is interested in summoning the aura, conjuring up the sense of reality that surrounded them. He is after affect. He writes: "The fiction/nonfiction distinction is immaterial, if not downright artificial," adding: "it's evoking I am after. If words must evoke, they must take all manner of oblique paths."[3] He explains: "I was always a novelist. My condition (to myself) for writing *Out of Egypt* was very simple: I would write my life and my family's as factually as I could, but it would have to read like a novel and abide by all the conventions of the novel. The partition between memoir and novel never really existed."[4] He states provocatively in the same interview: "As a memoirist, I may claim to write the easier to remember things; but I could also just be writing to sweep them away. . . . Writing always asks the past to justify itself, to give its reasons. . . . What we want is a narrative." He continues: "This is why most people write memoirs using the conventions not of history but of fiction. It's their revenge against facts that won't go away."

One of the "facts that won't go away" and to which Aciman returns obsessively is Egypt. In "Rue Delta," he evokes the last Passover Seder he and his family spent in Alexandria, all being aware it was to be their last. After the Seder, as the family gathered around listening to the nightly news on Radio Monte Carlo as they did every night, the fourteen-year-old Aciman goes out for a walk. It is April 1965. On this nighttime walk he describes the feeling of the city slipping away as of a death that takes too long to end and may never end: "It would be like taking a last, hopeless look at someone about to die or to become a stranger but whose hand still lingers—warmly—in ours" (O, 173). Aciman's writing on Egypt is predicated on rehearsing over and over this lingering movement of a hand claiming Egypt as the site of both love and inconsolable loss. Paul John Eakin puts it well when he observes that Aciman's "founding myth as a writer" is traceable to the image of "the self performing the act of recall."[5]

Out of Egypt: Portrait of a Family

In the first part of *Out of Egypt: A Memoir* (1994) the narrator evokes his lineage. It is a pointillistic portrayal. The narrator, or *I*, is not once given a name. I will call him Aciman and at times also the boy or the child. The father's last name and the last names of close family members are also not given. The origin of some of the family members is given and for others it is not. The narrative is fragmented but chronology is intelligible, relegating some of the most revealing passages about life in Egypt in the late 1950s and early '60s to the second part of the book. Aciman establishes that both his paternal and maternal families were not born in Egypt but that his mother, Régine or Gigi, was. *Out of Egypt* opens with a colorful personage, Aciman's uncle Vili, the embodiment of the Mediterranean Jew: protean, mobile, connected, and pragmatic. He is not limited by borders and nationalities. He circulates freely and is at home everywhere and nowhere: "Uncle Vili knew how to convey that intangible though unmistakable feeling that he had lineage—a provenance so ancient and so distinguished that it transcended such petty distinctions as birthplace, nationality, or religion (O, 5). Vili is forced to leave Egypt in the first wave of immigrations like a thief in the night without a chance to say his proper goodbyes to his family and aging mother. As a counterweight to this freewheeling Mediterranean Jew, Aciman juxtaposes the narrow lives of his parents and grandparents. In his discussion of the two branches of his family, the boy, Aciman, indulges in a crude social division that distinguished between so-called "European Jews" and "Arab Jews." These labels, which I explain below, were mostly imagined and created by certain individuals, and families, to gratify a view of themselves as superior—more European than Egyptian or Arab. The compulsion to label someone or some group as Other and exclude them is never more ardent than when the person or group targeted for exclusion is "almost-same" ("Presque-même"), as Jacques Hassoun explains in *The Strangers' Crossing* (*Le Passage des étrangers;* 1995). The more the excluder and the excluded resemble each other, the more anxious and more nasty the reaction of the excluder.[7] The young boy in *Out of Egypt* refers to himself and his father's family as *European Jews* and to his maternal family as *Arab Jews*. This is not because his father's side of the family traces its roots to Europe—to the Iberian diaspora of the fourteenth and fifteenth centuries or to Italy where the narrator suggests his family has citizenship (O, 16–17). Rather, Aciman writes in *Alibis* about these "paper citizenships that were to real nationalities what paper profits are to real money" (A, 82). Throughout the novel, he uses the epithets *European Jew* and *Arab Jew* to describe Jews living in Egypt, regardless of their nationality or where they were born.[7] His paternal grandparents Esther and Albert, for example, try unsuccessfully to convince their son Henri not to marry Gigi, not because she is deaf (a condition they also frowned upon), but because she is the daughter of an *Arab Jew*. Gigi's father, Jacques, is a Syrian Jew, born in Aleppo. Her mother, Adèle, is born in Turkey, like the child's father and paternal grandparents. I think the list of invitees to the celebrated three-day ball held by and for the elite of Alexandrian society helps explain the value system that informs this distinction and the fantasy that feeds it. The boy's maternal grandmother, Adèle, pined to be invited. She goes through a lot of trouble and does everything possible to curry favor with Esther. Still, she is not invited "because of her Arab Jew" husband. Aciman points out that with the exception of "the rabbi of Cairo, who was an *Egyptian Jew*, Arab Jews had not even been considered as possible guests" (O, 133).

The terms *Egyptian Jew* and *Arab Jew* are interchangeable here. Something about the rabbi's position precludes his being referred to as an *Arab Jew*. On the first night of the ball, the "wealthiest members of the Alexandrian establishment" are invited. On the third and last day, "minor business associates" and those *European Egyptians* considered "évolués," or "civilized," can attend. Examples of "évolués" are "the neighborhood Copt pharmacist and his Syrian-Lebanese wife," and a "Greek accountant" (O, 132). The improvised distinctions *European Jew, Arab Jew,* and their variants, *European Egyptian* and *Egyptian Jew,* rest on something. As it turns out, these distinctions are based on some unspecified idea of social worth. They are not based on where someone is born; the pharmacist's wife is Syrian Lebanese, like Jacques, the boy's maternal grandfather who is called an *Arab Jew*. And they are not based on wealth; Aciman's maternal grandparents, Adèle and Jacques, are wealthier than Esther and Albert. It appears at times that the distinction is established on the basis of the ability to speak a European language. Something about language seems to give moral weight to, or undermines, the user of that language. But even language does not make a difference in this case. The boy's paternal grandparents speak a classic form of Ladino, not the dialect Adèle, his maternal grandmother, uses. For Esther and Albert, Adèle's lowbrow Ladino dialect explains that she would marry an *Arab Jew* and have friendly relations with people in the lower rung of Alexandrian society. Esther and Albert both speak French, do not use Arabic, and chastise Aciman's mother—"Arab Jewish ingrate," as Esther calls her—for allowing the boy to hang around with the servants in the kitchen and speak Arabic with them (O, 177). To be fair, his father does not agree with his parents. He proclaims proudly that his son knew the name of "every cook and servant" as well as he knew "the name of every Greek god and goddess," adding that it was "as good a way as any to learn Arabic" (O, 223). By itself, the French language even when spoken with ease does not make the cut in this family. The boy's Arabic tutor, and the headmaster of a Jewish school, Monsieur al-Malek, is "An Arab Jew, [who] spoke English, French, and Arabic fluently" and is deeply disliked by the paternal side of the boy's family (O, 251). Monsieur al-Malek is an intelligent, seemingly pleasant, and kind man. But something in his comportment, his informality, his way of relating to people from different walks of life (servants, children, and snobs) offends them. Flora, the boy's aunt, remarks: "I can't stand this man" when al-Malek compliments the Johnnie Walker he is offered. She thinks he is only pretending to know what he is drinking and finds his manner irritating. On what, then, is this prejudice based? It is difficult to put a finger on what exactly it takes to be Arab or European in this family. To refer to someone as an *Arab Jew,* like the narrator's mother, his grandfather Jacques, his grandmother Adèle's acquaintances, and the teacher Monsieur al-Malek is *not* to broadcast that they were born in Egypt or in an Arab country, that they lack education, do not speak a European language, or are not wealthy. Rather, the element that fuels the prejudice seems to be their *proximity* to Arabs, be it through the Arabic language or social intercourse. In "Reflections of an Uncertain Jew," Aciman offers a barely discernible note of disapproval that Egyptians, like himself and his paternal grandparents, failed to acknowledge Egypt's Arab culture. He writes: "No one identified with Alexandria, and everyone was too busy identifying with the entire culture of Europe to understand what having a single culture really meant." He continues: "We imagined every other city in the world in order not to see the one city we were very much a part of, the way we imagined every other culture in order to avoid seeing we were basically and just Jewish" (A, 82). Considering the ugly bias, we might ask: Are we looking at the traumatized child responding defensively to what Arab Egypt had created? Are these the defensive elders rallying around the only part of cosmopolitan Egypt left for them to hold on to? To put it kindly, I would answer in the affirmative. But it is a complicated affair that gets perhaps a little clearer in the discussion on *Harvard Square* I take up later on.

At the end of *Out of Egypt*, both families leave. The boy's maternal grandparents, more affluent than his father's parents, are forced out in 1958 after the seizure of their assets. They settle in France, where Adèle succumbs to emotional shock. She had forgotten who she was, says one of the boy's aunts: "[S]he arrived in France the most pitiful sight in the world: there she was, the *grande bourgeoise* of Rue Memphis—with her grandchildren, her pianos, her tea parties—standing at Orly airport as frightened and confused as a five-year-old child" (italics in text; O, 86–87). Esther, the narrator's paternal grandmother, and his parents leave nearly a decade later in the spring of 1965. Albert, the paternal grandfather, dies in Egypt. When Aciman returns to Egypt in 1995 after having written *Out of Egypt*, he visits the cemetery in Alexandria where Albert is buried and writes touchingly about it in the essay "Alexandria: The Capital of Memory":

> "Are you happy now?" I want to ask my grandfather, rubbing the stone some more, remembering a tradition practiced among Muslims of tapping one's finger ever so gently on a tombstone to tell the dead that their loved ones are present, that they miss them and think about them. I want to speak to him, to say something, if only in a whisper. But I am too embarrassed. Perhaps this is why people say prayers instead. But I don't know any prayers. All I know is that I cannot take him with me—but I don't want to leave him here. What is he doing here anyway? In a hundred years, no one will even know my grandfather had lived or died, here or elsewhere. It's the difference between death and extinction. (F, 19)

As far as Aciman is concerned, the Mediterranean, Europe, Egypt, or Alexandria are, on the face of it, all interchangeable. These places are part of the imaginary of a man who was lacking whatever it took to figure out who and what he was. He writes in the essay "Parallax," in *Alibis*:

> I was born in Alexandria, Egypt. But I am not Egyptian. I was born into a Turkish family but I am not Turkish. I was sent to British schools in Egypt but I am not British. My family became Italian citizens and I learned to speak Italian but my mother tongue is French. For years as a child I was under the misguided notion that I was a French boy who, like everyone else I knew in Egypt, would soon be moving back to France. "Back" to France was already a paradox, since virtually no one in my immediate family was French or had ever even set foot in France. But France—and Paris—was my soul home, my imaginary home, and will remain so all my life, even if, after three days in France, I cannot wait to get out. Not a single ounce of me is French. I am African by birth, everyone in my family is from Asia Minor, and I live in America. And yet, though I lived in Europe for no more than three years, I consider myself profoundly, ineradicably European—the way I remain profoundly, ineradicably Jewish, though I have no faith in God, know not one Jewish ritual, and have gone to more churches in a year than I've gone to synagogues in a decade. Unlike my ancestors the Marranos who were Jews claiming to be Christians, I enjoy being a Jew among Christians so long as I can pass for a Christian among Jews. (A, 185)

He continues in the next paragraph: "I am an unreal Jew, the way I am an imaginary European. An imaginary European many times over" (A, 185). And in the essay "Rue Delta" he explains: "The Egypt I craved to return to was not the one I knew, or couldn't wait to flee, but the one where I learned to invent being *somewhere else, someone else*" (italics in text; A, 175).

Stalling, or How to Ruin your Life . . .

The second half of *Out of Egypt*, beginning with chapters 4 and especially 5, offers a richly detailed and compelling account of the everyday life of Egyptian Jews living in post-1956 Egypt. In chapter 4, the boy's family moves from the Smouha district of Alexandria to the elegant Cleopatra district. His parents felt Smouha was "unsafe" because it was frequented by "too many vagrants, too much dust, so few Europeans."[8] They move to a "fabulous home" in an apartment that belonged to a family who had "finally decided" to leave Egypt and "were desperate to sell" (O, 217). This opportunism should not be viewed as a moral reflection on Aciman's family. It describes the state of affairs, the devastation of fortunes, and rampant opportunism that reigned in Egypt as a result of the mass exodus.

From 1956 to 1965, the question that hovered mercilessly over the Aciman family and the remaining members of the Jewish community in Egypt was this: Do Jews still have a future in Egypt? The decision to leave or stay was particularly pressing for families with children. Many heads of families, like Aciman's father, were reluctant and stalled. This stalling cast a heavy shadow on households and created pressures that would not dissipate until the decision was made. From this one decision not made, many other seemingly less important decisions stayed up in the air or, worse still, resulted in messy, poorly thought-out resolutions. The father's resolve to teach the boy Arabic and move him to a different school is, perhaps, a case in point. Jews reluctant to leave, Aciman explains, reasoned that it is best to keep a low profile and wait out the most recent manifestations of antisemitism. There had been others as recent as 1952 and before that in 1948. As a young man in Paris, the ethnopsychiatrist Tobie Nathan reproached his father for not leaving Egypt when the writing was on the wall. Nathan explains that at that time he, Nathan, did not appreciate the fact that his father was from a world where men did not decide their destiny; it was determined for them. He observes that the curious thing was that even though men in the same position as his father believed that their decisions were predetermined, they nonetheless tried to figure things out before they acted on them. "They lived in a different world. They lived in a world where men do not decide their fate, where things that happen to them are enigmas they must decode," writes Nathan.[9] This is not classic fatalism. Because even though they believed that the decision had been taken out of their hands—the play of fate—still actions must be considered, advantages and disadvantages rehearsed by a studied reasoning, *as if* these actions had not been determined in advance. It is as if the subject called upon to act were performing a ritual drawn from its past when decisions were made and not merely accepted. Families like Aciman's found many practical reasons to stall: there were elder parents, businesses, careers, not to mention their age. Aciman's father was in his mid-forties when it became evident that Jews had no place in Egypt. And he was fifty when the family left. Aciman evokes with finesse and poignancy the anxiety that textured their lives. The simplest of activities, going to the movies or answering the phone, became sources of tension. Pressures mounted and yet Aciman's father could not come to a decision. Waiting for the decision became a test of nerves. Aciman describes the political state of affairs. Jews who stayed behind after most of their compatriots had left witnessed the further withering of civil rights, the arbitrary application of laws restricting Jews' access to work and education; they saw the arbitrary application of nationalization laws, sequestration, confiscation of assets, censorship, and a spate of garden-variety harassments. As I suggested, Egypt's politics toward Egyptian Jews had profound and damaging psychological effects. Indecision, feelings of ambivalence, anger, and depression were not uncommon. And although the very old and adults had cause to suffer, the young had it hard too. Aciman was kept in the dark about his parents' thoughts and plans. A decision deferred, if only for a short time, seems interminable for a child or adolescent. Indecision, deferring, secrecy, and ambivalence affect one's philosophical, ethical, and aesthetic disposition. Aciman's nuanced and wily aesthetics is informed by his experience of waiting it out. In the essay

"Temporizing," he explains the verb *to temporize* and suggests why it appeals so much to him:

> I immediately latched onto the word because, as one says of the children of Holocaust survivors, I am a child of temporizers. I was born in Egypt in a Jewish family whose members saw the writing on the wall but decided to wait out their foes. Don't do anything rash, put off risking what you have for what you may never get, above all lie low. . . . [W]hat it really says is this: if I kill myself a tiny bit each day before you do, won't this obviate your need for killing me? (A, 62)

Aciman is fourteen years old when his family leaves Egypt in 1965. At the height of the waves of departures, in 1956 and 1961, he is five and ten years old respectively. When his mother's family leaves, in 1958, he is six. Because waiting, delaying, lying low, and not knowing what comes next, Aciman equates his existence in those days to a slow death. Dying, disappearing, hiding, and dodging describe his consciousness both in Egypt and in exile. The exile, he explains, suffers from a "Marranism of time." "A Marrano, after all, is someone who practices two faiths simultaneously: one in secret, another in the open. Similarly, an exile is a person who is always in one place but *elsewhere* as well" (my italics added; A, 64). He continues: "A temporizer is someone who exists in two time zones but who, for this very reason, does not exist in either" (A, 64). Temporizing is both a strategy for survival in a world perceived as hostile and a form of consciousness.

Aciman's father, Henri, like his father Albert before him, was not born in Egypt. As such, he descends from a family that has been twice displaced in a relatively short time. As I suggested in the introduction, it was not uncommon to find families who counted among their own a grandparent or a parent who was not born in Egypt, who came from elsewhere. For economic advancement, to reunite with family members, willingly or compelled, Egyptian Jews knew about displacement in their lifetimes. It is not surprising that Aciman's father deferred the decision to move with his whole family, aging parents, and dependent uncles and aunts in tow. In his mid- to late forties, Henri was understandably reluctant to start a new life. But interestingly, Aciman attributes his father's reluctance to something else. Henri could not picture himself losing, conceding, and capitulating. He was so determined to not leave that "to prove" his determination and despite what looked to his wife and son like "the writing on the wall," he added another floor to his factory, invested in several apartments, commissioned new furniture, and, "to cap his list of fantasies," enrolled Aciman "in what throughout his early years in Egypt had always seemed to Henri an exclusive institution that incarnated the very peak of British splendor: Victoria College." A one-time prestigious school that prepared young men of the elite for a career in administration and the professions, Victoria College was renamed Victory College soon after

1956. Aciman refers to it throughout as VC (O, 219). The father failed to notice, Aciman explains, that the Victoria College of 1960 "had essentially become an Arab school wearing the tattered relics of British garb" (O, 220).[10]

At Victoria College, the boy resists learning Arabic. He does not understand why he should. The more pressure the father exerts on him to learn it, the more Aciman resists. When his Arabic tutor Monsieur al-Malek is asked to give his opinion on forcing the boy to learn Arabic, al-Malek answers the father with a question: "How long do you plan to stay in Egypt?" The father responds: "For as long as they'll let me. What a question!" (O, 257). Aciman explains that in times of stress his father "stalled" and when his father stressed over an idea "the idea itself was never abolished; it was simply remanded, suspended" (O, 251). Aciman's family ultimately leaves Egypt when his father's textile factory falls under government control. The fourteen-year-old Aciman is entrusted with official errands and with the purchase of their plane tickets. The father throws his responsibility on his son, suggesting his total capitulation and breakdown.

Victoria College: Dog of the Arabs . . .

Victoria College had become in the two years the boy attended the source of his deepest unhappiness. He performs poorly, failing his courses in Arabic. In school he tries to hide the fact that he is Jewish. He is one of only a few "Europeans" and "Christians," and believes himself to be the only Jew. In this post-1956 Egypt, the boy comes face to face with abject Arab antisemitism, expressed in the sordid psychological machinations devised by his teachers and the students. He writes that Arabic had become compulsory and propaganda against Jews brazen. Like the other "European boys" at Victory College, he finds it difficult to understand the language of instruction. He explains: "All we knew was street Egyptian, a sort of diluted, makeshift lingua franca that Egyptians spoke with Europeans" (O, 220). Henri wanted his son to learn Arabic, believing that in the new political climate Arabic was necessary for work and in general day-to-day life. But he was also worried that the family would be perceived as traitors by government informers who suspected Jews of rejecting the new Egypt. What will "*they* think," he reasoned, "when they see that in this house we totally disparage everything to do with Arabic culture. *They* already know everything that goes on in this house" (italics in text; O, 255). He wants his son to be "like everyone else" (O, 255) and pass unnoticed. Henri tries to put the boy in Islamic religion class instead of Christian, a decision Aciman objects to: "I did not want to study the Koran, nor did I want to be the only European in a class of Moslems; certainly I didn't want to have to take off my shoes during religion class, which is what devout Arabs did" (O, 256). His father also explores the idea of converting to the Greek Orthodox Church. He takes his son along to interview the Church Father in Alexandria. As he does with so many ideas, Henri defers the decision to convert. Thinking he is reassuring his son, he tells the boy: "Don't worry, I don't think we'll be doing anything with our Greek priest. . . . Still, I want to think about all this some more. . . . At any rate, there's no rush" (O, 269). It is against this background of uncertainty, veiled feelings, and physical and psychological coercion that Aciman, a child of ten or eleven, must ask what Egypt means to him.

The boy's resistance to learning Arabic becomes a battle waged at home and at school. Anxiously and helplessly the boy asks why he should be forced to learn Arabic when "none of the other European boys studies Arabic." The father answers through his anger that those who are leaving "may not have to worry about Arabic" but that since the family is not planning to leave, "let us at least pretend that Arabic is important to us" (O, 233). The boy fails Arabic and, since nobody at home can help him, a string of tutors are hired, one more incompetent than the next. They have no pedagogical skills and the boy's skills do not improve. Aciman points out that his father was unable, reluctant, and helpless to address what was obvious to everyone, including himself, that antisemitism permeated the school and that his son was suffering from it. Aciman writes:

> Something ugly and dangerous prevailed in class whenever the *Yahud* were mentioned. All I could do was stiffen helplessly and wish that some unknown force might come and take me away, that the ceiling might fall on Miss Sharif, that a terrible beast might squirm its way out of the sea and yawn at our classroom door. Without budging from my seat, I would try to make myself scarce, stare into the void, and drift away. (Italics in text; O, 241)

Institutional antisemitism is dramatized in the episode of a twenty-line poem the boy's class is required to memorize and that he is required to recite in front of them: "The poem was accompanied by an illustration of a young Egyptian soldier waving a scimitar at three old men clothed in three tattered flags. The first was wearing the Union Jack, the second the *bleu-blanc-rouge*, and the third, a bald, short man with wiry sideburns, a large crooked nose, and a pointed beard, was shabbily draped in the Star of David" (italics in text; O, 233). The boy brings the poem home. He understands the nature of its subject because Miss Sharif explained it in class. The illustration also makes the general idea abundantly clear. As the boy looks at the poem, he feels the eyes of his father on him and breaks into a sweat. Aciman's eyes are burning and he is on the verge of crying. His father fully understands the antisemitic picture, yet he says to him: "I don't care how you do it . . . but by tomorrow morning you'll have to know this poem by heart" (O, 234). His governess, a Greek Egyptian woman who cannot read Arabic, says to the father, in the boy's presence, "children should not be taught such ugly things." "Ugly or not ugly," the father snaps, "he'll do what everyone else does" (O, 235). Aciman writes that the poems students were taught at the school were "always about poison, Jews, vengeance, and motherland" (O, 237). The poem in question was no different:

> The poem itself was a long, high-minded, patriotic ode dedicated to the unity of the Arab world. It calumnized almost all the nations of Europe and, in its *envoi*, stirred all Arab boys and girls to free the last two Arab countries from the yoke of foreign dominion: Algeria and Palestine. France was suitably anathematized, as was England. Finally, by way of perorating her little speech, Miss Sharif inveighed against the *Yahud*, the Jews, throwing her fist in the air in an imitation of a salute, and sending the adrenaline rushing through my body each time she mentioned the word. (Italics in text; O, 241)

In class, students are expected to respond with battle cries, to ask questions, and to voice their agreement. In this atmosphere, complete with colorful posters hung along the walls "decrying imperialism, Zionism, and the perfidy of Jews," the nine-year-old narrator is picked to recite the poem (O, 241). Without so much as his father's sympathy, the boy has no choice, no way out. With the help of the servant's son, Aciman is able to memorize its words. Terrified by the prospect of forgetting it, he repeats it to himself several times before sleeping and immediately after he awakes. In the morning and throughout the day, he rehearses the poem in his mind. He is certain he has mastered the task and prepares himself to deliver it in class.

During recess in school that day, Aciman, unprovoked, starts to make fun of a boy named Amr who, "like many Arabic-speakers, had never learned to distinguish between *b* and *p* in English pronunciation" (O, 239). Aciman's behavior is understandable, psychologically speaking. Afraid of what is in store for him, he tries to alleviate his anxiety by compensating for the humiliation he feels. Later that day, during another short recess, Aciman once again ribs Amr, who, angry, conjures up the letter *b* to call him "Kalb al Arab, dog of the Arabs." Aciman, unable to contain himself, seeing himself reduced in the eyes of Amr and of his teacher, lunges at Amr. Amr fights back and the tussle is stopped by the supervising teacher. Aciman's knee is bleeding. He is sent to the headmistress who inquires what the fight was about and, upon learning from Aciman's own mouth that Amr called him "Kalb al Arab," and without giving him time to finish his complaint, she says to him in Arabic: "But you are the dog of the Arabs." She said this "smiling, as if it were the most obvious thing in the world." Aciman writes: "Stunned, I was almost sure I had misconstrued her words. I was even about to protest again. But I said nothing and went to the bathroom. . ." (O, 240). After cleaning his wound, he returns to the classroom and realizes, at that very moment, that he has forgotten the poem. The words have disappeared from his mind, only moments before he was due to recite the poem. He was seated at his desk waiting for Miss Sharif to finish her prefatory remarks about "Nasser's vision of a united, Pan-Arab nation," and knowing he would be the first to recite the work in front of the class, he recounts: "Quietly I tore out a very tiny corner of my notebook and drew a Star of David on it. It might bring me good luck. Not knowing what to do with the star, and not wishing to leave it lying about in my desk or in my pockets . . . I put it in my mouth, moved it a bit, and then let it stick to my palate, where it rested, untouched by my tongue or by my teeth, as Michel Cordahi [a Catholic boy] had told me he did with the Host" (O, 243). At this moment, Miss Sharif calls his name. "A shot of adrenaline coursed through" him "along with a cold, numbing spasm" (O, 242). All he is able to recite when he is called upon is the poem's title and its first line, which repeated the title. The poem slips out of his head under the pressure of the moment and, perhaps also, as a form of passive resistance.

After this incident, the narrator's father hires another tutor who uses the Koran to teach him Arabic, proper Arabic. Under his new tutor's methodology, he is instructed to copy and recopy the same suras from the Koran (O, 245–46). The tutor does not volunteer to explain the contents or expect him to learn what the words mean. Without a meaning to connect the words, he gets into the habit, he learns, to expect nothing from words. He is not only unaware of the text's meaning, but the text itself is made absent, passively destroyed. Numbed by Arabic letters, the boy's mind and his senses concentrate on the ambient world. At times, as he is copying, he listens attentively to the sounds his friends make as they rush to the beach, their kites flying in the air. He anticipates all their moves. At other times, he allows his eyes to glide from the page he is writing to the Matisse reproduction hanging in his room. It "beamed and beckoned in the morning light" where "between the balusters lining the artist's balcony in Nice were patches of blue—as always the sea" (O, 246). In short, the boy is learning to shut out what pains him and to sharpen his senses to what pleases him. He learns to imagine the world outside and distances himself from his unpleasant existence. He writes: "I worked quietly, studiously, filled by the vacuous bliss of medieval scribes who put in a long day's work at their desk without ever reading or understanding a word of what they've copied all day" (O, 246).

The Mediterranean as Elsewhere as Home

I suggest that in Aciman's imaginary, the Mediterranean is constructed around images and sounds that defer meaning and shut out suffering, and humiliation. Meaning dissipates, evaporates, is pushed to the side. The Mediterranean is that blue void. Aciman writes in the essay titled "In Search of Blue," that the blue of the sea meant so many things, none of which could be expressed. Only later, he explains, did the Mediterranean become the place to which he could return, in his mind's eye, to see, understand, frame his past and the experience of Egypt. He writes: "My love of the sea is in part a result of having lost Alexandria, *not* necessarily something I experienced in Alexandria. I love it precisely because it was lost. The smell of the salt, the touch of sunlight on bare skin, and above all the magic of beach life, with its strange, elaborate rituals" (my italics; F, 28–29). It is worth asking, what is it about Egypt that was lost? The Mediterranean encloses an ache within its azure blue. This pain, Aciman suggests, comes from losing a life before it was even a life worth holding on to. The Mediterranean serves as a metaphor for Aciman to evoke a history and a childhood so traumatized that it can barely sustain its own existence. It is a metaphor for a journey of self-discovery that folds back unto itself, unto sensations and perceptions. It does not open to the world. He writes:

> *What do you do with so much blue once you've seen it*? What is it if not the desire to prod some kind of admission from those we cannot have and wish we hadn't met or gotten to love and are condemned to crave.
> *What do you do with so much blue once you've seen it*? It's what you ask instead of doing, as if words could provide anything over and above raw experience. (Italics in text; F, 28)

What Aciman reveals, as I suggest in the title of this chapter, is that something about the Mediterranean as elsewhere is the best he can come up with to describe how it feels for an Egyptian Jew to have an identity and a place. A place is not the same thing as a home, for establishing roots. This is a far cry from Jacqueline Kahanoff's sense of rootedness in the Nile Valley and Edmond Jabès's sense of the Mediterranean and the desert as home of his ancestors. The Mediterranean is not home for Aciman. Rather, it is more like discovering a spot to throw a line that, unlike an anchor, is subject to the movement and scattering of waves. The Mediterranean, metaphorically speaking, is this place that collects Aciman's scattered selves, like the dabs of paint in the Impressionist paintings he admires. His picture of Egypt as loss can be made out best from a distance.

Lost Egypt was the work of nationalist hardliners who associated the Mediterranean with Europe. They turned their back on it because, in the Arab imaginary, the sea was European. For David Ohana, and for Egyptians who identified with Egyptian territorial nationalism, this was not the case; the shores of the Mediterranean were connected to each other by multidirectional exchanges that took place throughout the ages. The Mediterranean, writes Ohana: "represents a dialogue between East and West, between the classical world and the worlds of Judaism, Christianity, and Islam."[11] As I explain in the introduction and as Ohana has put it: "The Mediterranean did not create an all-inclusive culture with a singular homogeneous character. It created a variety of historical models of cultural meetings and exchanges of intellectual goods, such as the Italian Renaissance or Christian–Muslim–Jewish Andalusia" (Ohana, 4). In pre pan-Arab Egypt, to be Egyptian one could be both Muslim and Mediterranean. To be Mediterranean did not mean (and never meant) a person had no roots in one of the countries that lined its shoreline. A person could be Mediterranean and rooted in a land, be part of a distinctive community, and possess a distinct history.[12] It *did* mean, as it did for Aciman, Albert Camus, and Leïla Sebbar, for example, that when people were compelled by force or by other reasons to leave their countries they were still connected to the Mediterranean by a culture that fostered open exchange, hospitality, and freedom. The countries along its shoreline have shared histories that go back millennia. In a poignant moment I describe elsewhere, Yukel, one of Edmond Jabès's incarnations in *The Book of Questions*, feels he can no longer endure people's indifference toward him and abruptly leaves Paris for the Mediterranean.[13] He takes the train to any city at which he can see the sea, as the Mediterranean restores his sense of belonging. It is least of all a site of indifference, as he evokes here: "In its shells, I have heard the echo of my name moaning."[14] It is not only *not* the site of indifference; it is the homeland of his ancestors. Jabès writes: "The Mediterranean restored the eyes of those who came before me. This is why I want the sea to be the bond, a moving, millenary, binding in the book. And this is why my dreams, in a world torn apart by departures, feel like deliverance. Run for your life! Out there, there's perhaps something for us, life."[15] The Mediterranean is the space of reunions. People who live along its shores cannot not fall utterly in love with it. And this has as much to do with the rich civilizations it spawned as it does with its physical beauty. The Mediterranean is more than the sum of the countries that surround it. Pan-Arab nationalism devastated the psychic resources, including measured responses, of many Egyptian Jews, like the young Aciman. It put into question their sense of identity. In the face of considerable hostility and systematic humiliation, it became difficult to imagine themselves—as older generations of Egyptian Jews were able to do—as both Egyptian and Jewish.

At the end of *Out of Egypt*, in a passage to which I referred earlier, Aciman is out for a walk. It is nighttime, his family's last night in Alexandria. They have just celebrated their last Passover Seder in Egypt. With his back to the city, the fourteen-year-old considers what he is leaving behind:

> Facing the night, I looked out at the stars and thought to myself, over there is Spain, then France, to the right Italy, and straight ahead, the land of Solon and Pericles. The world is *timeless and boundless*, and I thought of all the *shipwrecked*, homeless mariners who had strayed to this very land and for years had tinkered away at their damaged boats, praying for a wind, only to grow soft and reluctant when their time came. (My italics; O, 338–339)

Aciman imagines himself as the descendent of a family stranded on Egyptian soil. He comes from elsewhere, somewhere over the Mediterranean Sea. When he looks straight ahead over the horizon and thinks of Spain, France, Italy, and Greece, he does not imagine modern Greece, but "the land of Solon and Pericles."

This picture of Aciman with his back to Alexandria suggests that he has turned his back on Egypt, an Arab Egypt. What he takes away with him on this night of Passover is Egypt's Mediterranean face, its ancient Hellenic culture. When Aciman speaks of Europe, he is thinking about what has endured of Ancient Greece in European culture. He is thinking of Europe's high culture. He is not thinking of modern Paris or Rome, cities that Aciman, like many Egyptian Jews, did not find easy to love once they lived there. Rather, he imagines being an inhabitant of "the timeless and boundless" pre-Islamist Ancient Mediterranean world. He explains in "Reflections of an Uncertain Jew" that to be an European Jew born in Egypt is to participate in the "vertiginously rich European culture" that "lasted seventy-five years" in Egypt. He evokes Walter Benjamin and Sigmund Freud to clarify what he means by European culture. To be part of European culture was to believe that one lived in a more special, more urbane, and more ancient place than any one single European capital. His father and great-uncles knew as they posed in photographs with cigarettes between their fingers that Alexandria was not Berlin, Vienna, Paris, Rome, Milan, and London. They wished and perhaps partly believed that Alexandria could be all these capital cities "all in one" (A, 80–81). Egypt was Mediterranean, open, cosmopolitan, and Hellenistic, or it was not Egypt. Aciman writes in the essay titled "Parallax": "I belonged to Europe; Egypt as far as I was concerned was simply an error that needed to be redressed. I had no love for Egypt and couldn't wait to leave; it had no love for me and did, in the end, ask me to leave" (A, 186). He continues:

> The beauty of Alexandria, of the Mediterranean, of being in a place that history had labored centuries to set in place meant nothing to me. Even the beach couldn't seduce me. If on a November day the totally deserted beaches of Alexandria seemed to belong to me and to no one else on this planet, and if the sea on those magnificently limpid mornings wasn't capable of raising a single ripple, then all I needed to seize the magic of the moment was one illusion: that this beach was not in Egypt but in Europe, and preferably in Greece. Indeed, whenever I saw a beautiful Greek or Roman statue in Egypt, I would automatically think of Greece, not of a Greek statue in Egypt. A Greek statue in Egypt was simply waiting to be taken to its rightful place in Athens even if the rightful place for a Hellenistic statue, was in fact, not Athens but Alexandria. (A, 186)

Egypt "had no love" for me. This is a shattering thought: "Exile disappears the very notion of a home, of a name, of a tongue" (A, 190). Aciman loved Egypt as much as he could love a place that from his earliest childhood made it clear that he was unwanted, made him suffer, humiliated him, dispersed his family across the globe, and made an exile of him even in Egypt. The effect of this total rejection meant, paradoxically, that Aciman could not be indifferent to Egypt. It became an obsession and "an enduring habit of mind" (P, 187).

In "From Alexandria" (1997), his article on Albert Camus, Aciman compares himself to the North African writer. Camus, like Aciman, is a man who "understood what it meant to be in two homes at the same time without being at home in either,"[16] in the latter case someone of both Algeria and France. More significantly, Aciman suggests that Camus's home was *neither* Algeria nor France. Home was the Mediterranean, the sea itself and its Hellenistic culture and not any particular country attached to its shores. After returning to Algeria from his travels in France, Camus did not return to the same place he had left, Aciman asserts: "Camus had gone back to his birthplace, a city where natives like himself would shortly become unwelcome foreigners" (MLN, 696). When Aciman returned to Egypt, it was, as he describes Camus's return to Algeria, to go "back to a place that was and yet had never been his true home, since his true home was—but then wasn't really either—set *somewhere across the Mediterranean*" (my italics; MLN, 697). By saying "somewhere across the Mediterranean," Aciman is not referring to North African shores—or European ones, for that matter. "Somewhere across the Mediterranean" is, in both the geographical and figurative sense, to be *of* the Mediterranean, to be of another place, belonging always *elsewhere.* There is, as I said earlier, something about this sea that is more than the sum of the countries on its shoreline. The Mediterranean is a cultural construct and the condition of being a part of it, *for Aciman,* is accepting that one will never wholly inhabit one shore or the other, that one is perpetually already divided, exiled, transient, *elsewhere.* Cultural remnants of Hellenism are dispersed along its route in hidden pockets or in the cultural archaeology of memory—for Aciman, though this is not the case for Edmond Jabès, for example. The older Jabès had known a different and kinder Egypt; for him the Mediterranean could still be home because he knew what home meant. Not so for Aciman and his generation, weaned too early to remember.

Aciman is not indifferent to Egypt. He cannot be, as I suggested. In "Parallax," Aciman makes the telling admission that when he is in a different place, say in Paris looking at the Seine, he finds himself "a bit more forgiving," allowing himself "to nurse some love for Alexandria" (P, 187). Egypt is the wound as well as the source of healing. This is why Egypt will always be, as for the masochist, the source of both suffering and pleasure to which he returns time and time again.

Mediterranean Seaming

The fourteen-year-old boy of "Rue Delta" in *Out of Egypt: A Memoir* is walking along scantily lighted streets at Ramadan:

> [I] was, as all European-Egyptians of my generation will always remember, accosted by *wonderful odors* of sweetened foods that were not only begging me to grasp how much I was losing in losing Alexandria, but in their overpowering, *primitive fragrance*, also trailed with them a strange sense of exhilaration

born from the presage that, finally, on leaving Egypt, I *would never have to smell these earthy smells again*, or be reminded that I had once been stranded in what seemed a blighted backdrop of Europe. I was, as always during those final days in 1965, at once apprehensive, eager, and reluctant to leave; I would much rather have been granted an eternal reprieve—staying indefinitely provided I knew I'd be leaving soon. (Italics added; 174–175)

Egypt, like a lover or a mother, engulfs the boy physically and psychically. It overwhelms his senses. He cannot help his desire to leave and to stay at the same time. Aciman seems to suggest that to stay in Egypt is to risk sinking into a pre-civilized state of culture where odors are, paradoxically, wonderful and fragrances earthy and primitive. He thus experiences Egypt at a visceral level: its culture attracts him and repulses him. In his novel *Harvard Square* (2013), Aciman depicts a short-lived friendship between the narrator, a twenty-six-year-old graduate student in comparative literature preparing to retake his Ph.D. comprehensives at Harvard and a taxi driver, no older than thirty-four, named Kalaj—short for "kalashnikof" because when he spoke it was like the rapid fire of that weapon: *rat-tat-tat, rat-tat-tat*. Kalaj was born in Tunis and has lived many years in France. He speaks French fluently, like the narrator who is an Egyptian Jew born in Alexandria. Both men have strong and ambivalent feelings toward France and the French language. It is the language they use together because it evokes Paris and their memories there, even though Paris was not "home" but their "half-way home." For both, Paris was not what they imagined it to be when they lived in Tunis and Alexandria (H, 43). In fact, both dislike France. The narrator, who remains nameless throughout the novel, points out that he and Kalaj were regulars at the Café Algiers in Cambridge that summer when he was studying because it reminded them of France, an imaginary France. France was the incurable disease they contracted as children in their respective countries and to which there seemed to be no remedy:

> [W]hat cemented our friendship from the very start was our love of France and of the French language, or better yet, of the idea of France—because real France we no longer had much use for, nor it for us. We nursed this love like a dirty secret, because we couldn't undo it, didn't trust it, didn't even want to dignify it with the name of love. But it hovered over our lives like a fraught and tired heirloom that dated back to our respective childhoods in colonial North Africa. Perhaps it wasn't even France, or the romance of France we loved; perhaps France was the nickname we gave our desperate reach for something firm in our lives—and for both of us the past was the firmest thing we had to hold on to, and the past in both cases was written in French. (H, 56)

When they met, Kalaj was not an American citizen; nor was the narrator. Café Algiers felt at times like France and France might at times have felt to them like home. But they were not fooled by this distortion. The narrator shares the following: "we were wrong everywhere, here, as in France, as in our respective birthplace that no longer was our homeland" (H, 57). Kalaj was a Berber Muslim but could not go back to Tunis because of a minor legal infraction. And the narrator could not go back to Egypt because he was Jewish. The French language they spoke together, which brought them together in the first place, conferred only provisional comfort, only serving to remind them they were not home. It was, the narrator admits: "a language we spoke with joy and bitterness in our hearts, because we spoke it with the wrong accent, because it was our mother tongue, but not our native tongue. Our native tongue—we didn't even know what that was" (H, 57).

More than because of the French language, Kalaj and the narrator are drawn to each other in their deep longing for the only place they could call home—the Mediterranean. It is the summer of 1977 in Cambridge, Massachusetts. At Café Algiers, the narrator surprises himself by missing Egypt. The poster of the town of Tipaza on the café's wall drew him into the café the first time. The poster with "its turquoise sea forever limpid and beckoning, everything in this small coffee shop reminded me of a Middle East I thought I had lost and put behind me and suddenly realized I wasn't ready to let go of. At least not yet" (H, 11). He adds:

> One look at the poster of Tipaza and your body ached for sea water and beach rituals you didn't even know you'd stopped remembering. All of Café Algiers took me back to Alexandria, the way it took Kalaj back to Tunis, and the Algerian [an employee] to Oran. Perhaps each one of us would stop by Café Algiers every day to pick up the person we'd left behind in North Africa, each working things back to that point where life must have taken a wrong turn.... Sheltered from the morning sun and wrapped in the strong scent of coffee and of cleaning fluids, each found his way back to his *mother*. (My italics added; H, 42–43)

There is something primal and visceral that connects Aciman to Egypt. The mother is not the motherland grounded in a nationalist idea but is the vast and overwhelming presence in Aciman's imaginary of the Mediterranean Sea. He looks around him at Cambridge and remarks: "This wasn't my life, wasn't my birthplace, wasn't even me, couldn't be me" (H, 11). From a distance of many years, accompanying his son for a college visit to Harvard, now his alma matter, the narrator thinks: "I wasn't even a citizen in those days and *a side of me, just a side of me*, craved to move back somewhere on the Mediterranean. This fellow was from the Mediterranean as well and he too longed to go back. We were friends" (my italics; H, 10). Typically, "just a side" of him craved to go back. As everywhere in Aciman's work, he is never *entirely* in one place. Both he and his friend suffer from an incurable homesickness that can never be satisfied because the *terra firma* it longs for is as vast and vague as the sea.

Arab Egypt

Aciman is not troubled by political correctness. His handling of Kalaj's marginalized existence in Cambridge unapologetically dramatizes a bias he has against Arabs. Aciman's views on the difference between Arab and European (and his privileging of the latter) are consistent with Tarek El-Ariss's argument that an unfavorable and unhelpful contrast between modernity as embraced by Europeans and modernity expressed as embraced by Arabs has been responsible for the over-valuation of European culture.[17] The friendship depicted between a European Egyptian and an Arab in Aciman's novel is complicated; the narrator and Kalaj are like opposite sides of the same coin. To take the comparison further, they are two sides of the same coin but one has a rough finish, the Arab side, while the other has the veneer of European culture. The narrator explains that a Berber by birth, Kalaj had grown up to love France in Tunis, while he, Aciman, since childhood had worshiped Paris in Alexandria: "Tunis had no more use for him when he jumped a navy ship in Marseilles at the age of seventeen than Egypt had for me when it expelled me for being Jewish when I was fourteen." The narrator suggests that the two of them are fundamentally the same and, paradoxically, the opposite of each other: "We were, as he liked to boast when we'd run into women at a bar, *each other in reverse*" (my italics; H, 57–58). The narrator adds:

> If I liked listening to him, it was not because I believed or even respected the stuff he mouthed off every day at Café Algiers, but because there was something in the timbre and inflection of his words that seemed to rummage through a clutter of *ancestral fragments* to remind me of the person I may have been born to be but had not become.... What I heard... was the raspy, wheezing, threatened voice of *an older order of mankind, older ways of being human*, raging, raging against the tide of the new that had the semblance and behavior of humanity but really wasn't. *It was not the clash of civilizations or of values or of cultures*; it was a question of organ, which chamber of the heart, which one of its dear five senses would humanity cut off to join *modernity*. (My italics; 52)

I do not believe that the narrator, Aciman, has sufficiently disguised his view that Kalaj is primitive when he asserts that "It was not the clash of civilizations or of values or of cultures." I suggest that it is sufficiently clear that as the narrator sees it, Kalaj has not joined "modernity," has not evolved from "an older order of mankind." If it is not clear enough that the narrator considers Kalaj savage, primitive, unpolished, and a rough version of Aciman's imagined future-self, the Harvard-educated man, he adds further about Kalaj: "He was a man. I wasn't sure what I was. He was the voice, the missing link to my past, the person I might have grown up to be had my life taken a different turn. He was savage; I'd been tamed, curbed" (H, 52). It barely changes the picture when the narrator deprecates himself in the process of comparing himself to Kalaj: "Perhaps he was a stand-in for who I was, a primitive version of the me I'd lost track of and sloughed off living in America" (H, 53). The narrator sees himself as the image of Kalaj but "without hope, without recourse, without future" (H, 281). He is terrified at the idea of turning into Kalaj, of returning to a state he left behind in Egypt. His future depends on establishing himself in America, fitting in, and making a mark: "By looking at him I was almost looking at myself. . . . He was my destiny three steps ahead of me. I could fail my exams, be sent packing to New York, and in a year from now, no one would . . . remember to think of me" (H, 203). Near the end of the novel Aciman writes: "It took someone like him to remind me that, for all my impatience with life in New England and all my yearning for the Mediterranean, I had already moved to the other side" (H, 271). The Egypt that remained when Aciman and his family left was indeed Arab Egypt; Alexandria was no longer even a shadow of its former Hellenistic European self. As Aciman writes in "Alexandria: The Capital of Memory": "There are no Europeans left, and the Jews are all gone. Alexandria is Egypt now" (F, 3). At the end, it is abundantly clear to the narrator that Kalaj is a Tunisian Arab while he, the narrator, is an *European Egyptian* without an Egypt to return to. Egypt is Arab now, in the same way that Tunisia is Arab. But Kalaj can go home. His Mediterranean, it turns out, was not the site of loss but of nostalgia, and this luxury of nostalgia is not given to the narrator. Without Cambridge, he would be utterly hopeless.

Open letter to President Obama

Aciman never skirts around, covers up, or gives short shrift to the fact that he is Jewish and born in Egypt. This is perhaps because for too long when he lived in Egypt he had to, out of fear, hide his Jewishness. And even if, hidden inside, it served him as a badge of identity, a faithful companion, reminding him not only who he was and what he was but, also, *that he was*, it had been kept too long. It was his Jewish identity, and not Judaism per se, that had grounded him all these years. Aciman's open letter to U.S. president Barak Obama brings up a very painful subject. His letter was published four days after the president gave the speech "To the Islamic World" at Cairo University on June 4, 2009. Obama was at the height of his celebrity, idolized by liberals in his own country, viewed the same way by people around the world who believed he was ushering a new era, and was soon to receive the Nobel Peace Prize. Aciman's letter to the president is titled "The Exodus Obama Forgot to Mention" and was published as a *New York Times* op-ed on June 8th.[18] In it, Aciman reproaches Obama for sweeping under the rug Egypt's record of intolerance toward its minority populations. He explains that he is an Egyptian Jew, a person with a history, a family, and a people whose presence in Egypt was expunged, first by the Egyptians themselves and now by him, the American president. Aciman's letter is powerful and unequivocal. It deserves to be cited in its entirety, but I quote at length only part of it. Aciman first reviews the groundbreaking aspects of the president's speech to the Islamic world. He acknowledges that Obama spoke of Islam's flaws "loudly and clearly," brought up "the plight of Egypt's harassed Coptic community," criticized "Holocaust deniers," "put the Israelis on notice" regarding settlements in occupied territories, and reminded the assembled that he had not forgotten "the suffering of Palestinians." Having stated this, Aciman adds a *but*: "neither he nor anyone around him, and certainly no one in the audience, bothered to notice one small detail missing from the speech: he forgot me." Aciman continues:

> The president never said a word about me. Or, for that matter, about any of the other 800,000 or so Jews born in the Middle East who fled the Arab and Muslim world or who were summarily expelled for being Jewish in the 20th century. With all his references to the history of Islam and to its (questionable) "proud tradition of tolerance" of other faiths, Mr. Obama never said anything about those Jews whose ancestors had been living in Arab lands long before the advent of Islam but were its first victims once rampant nationalism swept over the Arab world.
>
> Nor did he bother to mention that with this flight and expulsion, Jewish assets were—let's call it by its proper name—looted. Mr. Obama never mentioned the belongings I still own in Egypt and will never recover. My mother's house, my father's factory, our life in Egypt, our friends, our books, our cars, my bicycle. We are, each one of us, not just defined by the arrangement of protein molecules in our cells, but also by the things we call our own. Take away our things and something in us dies. Losing his wealth, his home, the life he had built, killed my father. He didn't die right away; it took four decades of exile to finish him off.
>
> Mr. Obama had harsh things to say to the Arab world about its treatment of women. And he said much about America's debt to Islam. But he failed to remind the Egyptians in his audience that until 50 years ago a strong and vibrant Jewish community thrived in their midst. Or that many of Egypt's finest hospitals and other institutions were founded and financed by Jews. It is a shame that he did not remind the Egyptians in the audience of this, because, in most cases—and especially among those younger than 50—their memory banks have been conveniently expunged of deadweight and guilt. They have no recollections of Jews.
>
> In Alexandria, my birthplace and my home, all streets bearing Jewish names have been renamed. A few years ago, the Library of Alexandria put on display an Arabic translation of "The Protocols of the Elders of Zion," perhaps the most anti-Semitic piece of prose ever written. Today, for the record, there are perhaps four Jews left in Alexandria.
>
> When the last Jew dies, the temples and religious artifacts and books that were the property of what was once probably the wealthiest Jewish community on the Mediterranean will go to the Egyptian government—not to me, or to my children, or to any of the numberless descendants of Egyptian Jews.

> It is strange that our president, a man so versed in history and so committed to the truth, should have omitted mentioning the Jews of Egypt. He either forgot, or just didn't know, or just thought it wasn't expedient or appropriate for this venue. But for him to speak in Cairo of a shared effort "to find common ground . . . and to respect the dignity of all human beings" without mentioning people in my position would be like his speaking to the residents of Berlin about the future of Germany and forgetting to mention a small detail called World War II.

An eloquent and moving text, the open letter to Obama is Aciman's hue and cry about the indignities served Egyptian Jews and other Jews in the rest of the Arab world. It reveals the animus he harbors and his grief. We hear the child inside the adult angry about the injustice his father suffered. We hear about "things" being taken away and stolen. "Things," as in material objects, are not trivial, he says. The "things we call our own" are home; "take away our things and something in us dies." Something "dies," cries the child—his father dies, that's who. He also and most touchingly embraces his coreligionists, speaks on their behalf. But it is the child in him that speaks in the open letter to Obama. A letter in which he calls Alexandria "home." He describes how terrible it feels at the moment when after being bullied, fleeced, and kicked out of Egypt he is now shoved aside by the "leader of the Free World." He is a man in pain who cannot believe he is being humiliated, ignored, and erased yet again by another man he possibly admires. Aciman's commitment to his identity as an Egyptian Jew is as solid as things get in Aciman, as solid as they get for a subject who finds it already hard to be present to himself.

I have argued that Aciman's Egypt is constructed on the shoulders of both an imaginary and an actual Mediterranean. In his work, something about Egypt is taken on, accepted, loved, and regretted while something else is rejected, erased, elided. Like the moon, Aciman's Egypt presents one of its faces to the Earth while the other stays behind. In his imaginary, Egypt's hidden face is Arab. It is Egypt's dark side, its cruel side. The face of Egypt he sees in his past, wants to see, and misses is an Egypt whose culture is Mediterranean, Hellenistic, open, diverse, outward looking, and hospitable.

Notes

I use the following abbreviations and editions of André Aciman's works:
(A) *Alibis: Essays on Elsewhere*. New York: Picador, Farrar, Straus and Giroux, 2011.
(E) *Eight White Nights*. New York: Picador, Farrar, Straus, and Giroux, 2010.
(F) *False Papers: Essays on Exile and Memory*. New York: Picador, Farrar, Straus & Giroux, 2001.
(H) *Harvard Square*. New York: W.W. Norton, 2013.

(L) *Letters of Transit: Reflections on Exile, Identity, and Loss.* New York: The New Press, 1997.
(O) *Out of Egypt: A Memoir.* New York: Farrar, Straus and Giroux, 1994.

   1. Julia Clancy-Smith, *Mediterraneans. North Africa and Europe in an Age of Migration, c. 1800–1900* (Berkeley: University of California Press, 2011), 9.
   2. André Aciman, "Parallax," in *Alibis: Essays on Elsewhere* (New York: Picador, Farrar, Straus and Giroux, 2011). Further references to *Alibis* will be included in the text as (A).
   3. Noah Charney, Interview in *Daily Beast*, November 28, 2012, http://www.thedailybeast.com/articles/2012/11/28/andr-aciman-how-i-write.html.
   4. André Aciman, "How Memoirists Mold the Truth" (*New York Times*, April 6, 2013), 2.
   5. Paul John Eakin, *Living Autobiographically* (Ithaca, N.Y.: Cornell University Press, 2008), 163–169.
   6. Jacques Hassoun, *Le Passage des étrangers* (Paris: Austral, 1995), 13. See also the discussion in chapter 1.
   7. See Lital Levy's concise assessment of the interest in discussions of the "Arab" in Jewish identity in "Historicizing the Concept of Arab Jews in the 'Mashriq,'" *Jewish Quarterly Review* 98, no. 4 (Fall 2008): 452–469. For an application of that distinction on the ground, as it were, see Joyce Zonana, "'And she loved brown people': Jacqueline Shohett Kahanoff's Affirmation of Arab Jewish Identity in *Jacob's Ladder*," in *Sephardi and Mizrahi Jews in America. The Jewish Role in American Life: An Annual Review of the Casden Institute for the Study of the Jewish Role in American Life*, edited by Steven J. Ross, vol. 13, 53–73, 4 (West Lafayette, Ind.: Purdue University Press, 2016). See also Ella Shohat, *Taboo Memories, Diasporic Voices* (Durham. N.C.: Duke University Press, 2006).
   8. Richard Smouha, ed. *The Smouha City Venture: Alexandria 1923–1958*. Printed by Create Space, An Amazon.com Company, 2014. Smouha City was, and still is considered a western suburb of Alexandria. It was conceived and developed by Joseph Smouha and his sons. The Smouha site dates from the late Roman period and before: stone objects have been found that indicate the existence of a Ptolemaic monument (Smouha, 173). The suburb of Smouha City was built by draining Lake Hadra. It took approximately five years to design, plan, and build. It was conceived as an urban community with various types of residential housing, schools, places of worship, a hospital, a celebrated racing club, a golf course, tennis courses, and its own post office. In 1925, after a competition that attracted architects and city planners from Italy, France, Britain, and Egypt, Joseph Smouha unveiled his plan for the homogeneous modernist townscape. In this way, the design broke with Alexandria's eclectic architecture. The first villas were purchased in 1933–1935; its first inhabitants represented the upper middle class of Alexandrian bourgeoisie. A Jew born in Baghdad in 1878, Joseph Smouha was sent to Manchester, England, in 1892. There he began what became a successful career as a cotton trader and broker. Because of his expertise as a trader, and his knowledge of Arabic, he was sent by the British government to Egypt in 1919 to address the economic problem of the British pound, which at that time was losing value rapidly. He remained in Egypt and became a successful urban developer. This information is taken from an excellent study put together by his grandson, Richard Smouha, with contributions from the architect and research fellow Cristina Pallini, and the archeologist and Egyptologist Marie-Cécile Bruwier. The study imparts a wealth of information on business practices, the workings of the municipal government of Alexandria in the selling

and development of land, the intersection of European, Egyptian, and Levantine business interests; it also provides a wealth of information on aspects of life in turn of the century Alexandria before and after the monarchy; the working conditions of the *fellah* (Smouha, 78), and on sequestration, confiscation of property and the laws put in place by both the Nasser and Mubarak administrations. The book features a good number of early maps of Alexandria as well as photographs. Many of the maps and photographs have been in family archives. Their rendition in the book are of excellent quality.

9. Nathan's text: "[I]l vivait ailleurs, dans ce monde où les hommes ne décident pas de leur destin; où ce qui leur arrive n'est pas de leur ressort mais constitue un message sibyllin qu'il leur faut décoder." Tobie Nathan, *Ethno-roman* (Paris: Grasset, 2012), 181–182; my translation.

10. The archival research of Sahar Hamouda and Colin Clement discredit in part Aciman's school years in Victoria College, 1959–1961. Aciman was enrolled under the name André Adjiman. Aciman was the only Jew in his grade, though there were two others in the school. Sahar Hamouda, *Victoria College: A History Revealed*, edited by Sahar Hamouda and Colin Clement, Colin (Cairo: The American University, 2002).

11. David Ohana, *Israel and Its Mediterranean Identity* (New York: Palgrave Macmillan, 2011), 4. Further references to this work will be included in the text as (Ohana).

12. Critics of the Mediterranean paradigm, such as Michael Herzfeld and Ian Morris, argue that the discourse of a unified Mediterranean culture and *zeitgeist* sacrifices local attributes to secure their model. I think that the case of Egypt resists such a critique and serves as an exemplar of what we look at when we speak about local identities and their relationship to the wider Mediterranean. On this subject of local cultures and local histories, see Nile Green in "Rethinking the 'Middle East' after the Oceanic Turn," in *Comparative Studies of South Asia, Africa and the Middle East* 34, no. 3 (2014): 556–564, where Green proposes a new and dynamic spatial model for mapping geographical categories along different lines than conventional nation states. Green's "arena" model would be able to account for an Islamicate Mediterranean.

13. Aimée Israel-Pelletier, "Edmond Jabès, Jacques Hassoun, and Melancholy: The Second Exodus in the Shadow of the Holocaust," *MLN* French 123, no. 4 (September 2008): 797–818.

14. Jabès's text: "dans ses coquillages, j'ai écouté gémir l'écho de mon nom." In Edmond Jabès, *Le Livre des Questions,* vol. 1 (Paris: Editions Gallimard, 2002), 362; *The Book of Questions*, vol. I, translated by Rosemarie Waldrop (Middletown, Conn.: Wesleyan University Press, 1991), 327. Further reference to the French original is included in the text as (LQ) and (BQ) for the English translation.

15. Jabès's text: "La Méditerranée a régénéré les regards qui ont précédé le mien; c'est pourquoi j'ai voulu que la mer soit, dans le livre, le lien mouvant, millénaire, et c'est aussi pourquoi mes songes, dans un monde déchiré de départs, ont le sens d'un sauvetage. Sauve qui peut! Là-bas, il y a peut-être pour nous, la vie" (LQ, 362–363). Rosemarie Waldrop's translation: "The Mediterranean has revived eyes before mine. This is why I want the sea to be the moving, millenary bond in the book. It is also why my dreams have the sense of a lifeline in a world torn by departures. Gangway! Down under there is perhaps a life for us" (BQ, 327).

16. André Aciman, "From Alexandria," *MLN* 112, no. 4 French Issue (September 1997): 683–697, 697. Further references to this article will be included in the text as (MLN).

17. Tarek El-Ariss, *Trials of Arab Modernity: Literary Affects and the New Political* (New York: Fordham University Press, 2013). El-Ariss takes issue with both those who consider that Arab culture is derived from Western Enlightenment concepts and those who, like Ahmad Lutfi al-Sayed and Taha Hussein, considered modernity a universal narrative of systematic innovation and progress. El-Ariss argues that Arab literary modernity is often portrayed as a violent somatic confrontation with and within modernity (3). In his own words, his work "challenges the Eurocentric framework that treats Arabic modernity as borrowing from the West, or as a process that started in the Arab-Muslim world independently of Europe" (13).

18. André Aciman, "The Exodus Obama Forgot to Mention," *New York Times,* June 8, 2009; http://www.nytimes.com/2009/06/09/opinion/09aciman.html.

Epilogue

> My father was a wandering Aramean. He went down to Egypt, and sojourned there, few in number; and he became there a nation, great, mighty and populous. And the Egyptians dealt ill with us, and afflicted us, and laid upon us hard bondage.
> Deut. 26:5, 6

> ... everything always continues. The pharaohs barely belong to the past.[1]
> Edmond Jabès

WHEN JEWISH MEN and women living in Egypt for centuries or decades thought about Egypt, they did not necessarily think they lived in the ancient land of their ancestors. Not necessarily. Nor were they necessarily thinking about God's injunction to never again live in the land of Egypt (Deut. 28:68). But they would have harbored images and scenes of an ancestral past that was continually reinforced in prayers and rituals: Egyptian Jews, even those with the scantiest knowledge of Judaism, would have found it difficult to miss the connection. The Egyptian landscape, its flora and fauna, the Nile, the Pyramids, and the Sinai were there to remind them that they shared the same land as their biblical ancestors.[2] In the imaginary, all thoughts and images find a place, and contradictions meet no resistance. Egyptian Jews internalized this remarkable conjoining of the present and the biblical past.

Tobie Nathan, a writer and ethnopsychiatrist whose work focuses on immigrant and minority populations, argues that myths, habits of thought, and other cultural baggage shape cognition, perceptions, and psychology.[3] They constitute the "toolbox," or symbolic structure internalized by patients. This structure informs mental disorders and allows for healing to take place. He observes that symbolic structures acquired from ancestors are more powerful than those acquired later. The way to reach patients who are suffering is to begin by learning directly from patients themselves where to find the toolbox they brought with them when they left their native country. It is with these tools that healing will take place. In the toolbox of Egyptian Jews are ancestral myths that have enormous weight. Nathan, Kahanoff, Hassoun, and Jabès are not alone in recognizing that Egyptian Jews like themselves have a privileged relationship with the founding myth of Judaism. In their imaginary there exists virtually no distinction between ancient people and their modern counterparts. Whether the biblical ancestors were historically real or constitute an enduring myth, Nathan contends that Second Exodus Jews are the *actual* Jews referred to in the Bible as having left Egypt: "The Jewish community of Egypt is unique. It is the only generation that came out of Egypt. It is not Moses but Nasser who took us out of Egypt" (my italics).[4]

It is commonplace among Egyptian Jews to note that the passage in the Haggadah relating that the Jews left *Misrayim* with Moses always struck them as peculiar, considering they were living there in flesh and blood. This feeling, they explain, was less a source of confusion than of amusement. There was something transgressive about it. It suggested they had played a trick on God. After all, they had stayed behind when God thought they had all left with Moses. In fact, God insisted that Moses go after the last Jews and bring them out of Egypt. The first transgression of the Egyptian Jews, then, is to have disobeyed God's commandment, using subterfuge by hiding from Moses. But there is something more egregious than even disobedience and trickery. Was not God's first commandment, proffered in Sinai to the Jews, all about his success in getting the most recalcitrant among them to leave? Were not his words an injunction to *not forget* that he, the Eternal, brought them forth from Egypt to be a free people, his chosen? (Exodus: 20:2). By staying behind, were Second Exodus Jews not in effect calling into question the meaning of the Exodus? The modern iteration of the story is therefore one of resistance, a tale of both pride and self-reproach. It is the story of the capitulation of the last remaining Jews of Egypt. In the end, God prevails and the last Egyptian Jew is forced out by Nasser.

What is remarkable about this narrative of the Second Exodus is that it adds an affective dimension to the archetypal First Exodus narrative. Second Exodus Jews resisted *not* because they could not help being tricksters; nor because they were not interested in God's promise to lead them to freedom. Nor did they resist because they were cowardly, or lazy, or materialistic and did not want to spend forty hard years in the desert. Rather, they stayed behind, hid from view, and resisted Moses's call because they loved Egypt too much to leave. They were attached physically and emotionally to Egypt, to their native land. On an emotional level, then, and in their collective imaginary, Egyptian Jews who disobeyed God had chosen Egypt over and above anything else. What is the price to be paid for such disobedience?

In Deuteronomy 28, God reframes the interdiction to never set foot in Egypt by proclaiming in no uncertain terms that a return to Egypt is the ultimate punishment of the Jew. Egypt is the site and emblem of unimaginable humiliation. In Deuteronomy 28:1, God tells the Jews that if they observe faithfully his commandments, he will set them "high above all the nations of the earth." But if they disobey, terrible misfortunes will befall them. The most frightful of these is a return to Egypt where they will meet with conditions worse than slavery: "The Lord will send you back to Egypt in galleys, by a route which I told you you should not see again. There you shall offer yourselves for sale to your enemies as male and female slaves, but *none will buy*" (my italics; Deut. 28:68). Worthlessness, "none will buy," is a more cruel punishment than enslavement. Worthlessness means the other's most complete indifference. The punishment that falls upon Second Exodus Jews is to find themselves on the scene of precisely where love itself is, namely Egypt, and to experience the feeling of *worthlessness*. Worthlessness is the source of Jewish Egyptian melancholy. And melancholy, as opposed to mourning, is never ending.[5] God's most cruel punishment is psychological. Victor Teboul, a Jewish Egyptian novelist, expresses this with sublimity: "It was our fault, we should not have gone back." If the love for Egypt were not powerful, Teboul asks, would Jews have returned time and again despite God's powerful interdiction? I cite more fully from the quotation above: "Hadn't we already left Egypt under the pharaohs? It was a hospitable country but always tyrannical; and just as before we were robbed, imprisoned, and enslaved. It was our fault, we should not have gone back."[6]

The psychological nature of God's punishment is clear in the experience of Second Exodus Jews. During Passover and throughout the year in prayers devoted to celebration and remembrance, they are reminded of Egypt, the Egypt they loved, and are reminded of God's displeasure with them. When Egyptian Jews hear the word for Egypt, *Misrayim*, in prayers, they do not hear it the same way other Jews do. In their collective imaginary, every utterance of the word singles them out. Multiplied in prayers countless times, it resonates with affect. It reminds them of Egypt, certainly. It also reminds them that God has not forgotten their transgression; they are not among his chosen people; they are, indeed, *worthless*. The lesson learned in France, Israel, the United States, and everywhere they settled was that Egypt had been, all along, nothing more than a living proof of the Jewish condition of eternal exile. The Egyptian landscape, Egypt's geography and climate, the Mediterranean and the Nile are sites of tremendous feelings for these contemporary Jews who disobeyed God.

I have been insisting that for Egyptian Jews, and for the writers I discuss in this book, Egypt is a real place, one that figures a home that is lost. Egypt is where the roots of the Jewish people will always be even though the Jews themselves are gone. Tobie Nathan, whose family left Egypt in 1957, recalls that on the last Passover he spent with his father who was ninety-one or ninety-two-years-old, there were about twenty people gathered around the table to celebrate once again "the exodus from Egypt" ("la sortie d'Egypte") when his father uttered these words: "the main thing is that we're together. . ." Nathan gives these words their full expression as follows: "You can go out and see the world, see things, see people but you cannot leave your people. The main thing is that we're together."[7] Nathan then tells the story of a bird who could fly anywhere he wanted. But if you watched closely you would notice that the bird always came back to the same branch. The bird comes back to his people and to his ancestral place. The flight from Egypt is a lived experience for the Jewish Egyptian community. Regardless of where their grandparents trace their origins, Egyptian Jews are aware that they have reenacted the biblical narrative *in their own time*. Nathan muses that in a peculiar way: "We are *of* Egypt. And we are of *the departure* from Egypt."[8] And to return is like to never have left. Egyptian Jews are the *alpha and omega* of this foundational narrative. During the Passover Seder, *all* Jews around the world are instructed to act *as if* they personally went out from Egypt. In a fundamental sense, all Jews did. But not all can say, as Egyptian Jews can, they actually and personally lived that experience.

Notes

1. Jabès describing life in Egypt, the concept of time, the Egyptian people, and the landscape: "Nulle part il n'y a interruption—tout continue toujours. C'est à peine si les pharaons appartiennent au passé," Marcel Cohen, *Edmond Jabès: du désert au livre* (Paris: Pierre Belfond, 1980), 35. My translation.

2. Maurice Fargeon, editor of the *Annuaire des juifs d'Egypte et du proche Orient* (1942), argued that "some Jews did not leave Egypt at the time of Moses but remained and moved to Assyut, where they formed a tribe of warriors." Quote is from Joel Beinin, *The Dispersion of Egyptian Jewry: Culture, Politics, and the Formation of a Modern Diaspora* (Berkeley: University of California Press, 1998), 33.

3. Ethnopsychiatry is not the same as cross-cultural psychiatry where therapists bring to the task their own theories and assumptions from, say, Freud, Winnicott, or other Western healers.

4. Nathan's words: "La communauté juive d'Egypte est spéciale. Elle est *la seule génération* qui soit sortie d'Egypte. Ce n'est pas Moïse mais Nasser qui nous a fait sortir d'Egypte" (my translation, my italics). "Tobie Nathan avec Dayan-Roseman, Maison du Barreau, février 2015." Internet site: www.akadem.org/sommaire/colloques/livres-des-mondes-juifs-et-diasporas-en-dialogue-2015. My translation.

5. Aimée Israel-Pelletier, "Edmond Jabès, Jacques Hassoun, and Melancholy: The Second Exodus in the Shadow of the Holocaust," *MLN* French 123, no. 4 (September 2008): 797–818.

6. Victor Teboul's text: "C'était notre faute, il n'aurait pas fallu y retourner. N'avait-on pas déjà quitté l'Egypte sous les pharaons? C'était un pays accueillant mais toujours asservissant; on avait encore une fois été spoliés, emprisonnés. C'était notre faute, il n'aurait pas fallu y retourner," Victor Teboul, *La Lente découverte de l'étrangeté* (Montréal: Les Editions des Intouchables: 2002), 94. My translation. Teboul has written several semiautobiographical novels about Egypt, exile, relational ethics, and identity.

7. Nathan's text: "L'essentiel, c'est d'être ensemble . . . Tu peux partir à la découverte du monde, des choses, des êtres et des hommes, mais tu ne peux quitter ton peuple. L'essentiel, c'est d'être ensemble," *Ethno-Roman* (Paris: Grasset, 2012), 177–178. My translation.

8. Nathan's words: "Nous sommes *de* l'Egypte et *du départ* de l'Egypte" (my italics; op. cit., Akadem).

Bibliography

Abécassis, Frédéric. "Approche d'un champ: l'enseignement étranger en Egypte, 1921–1952." *Egypte-Monde Arabe* 18–19, no. 2 (1994): 169–194.
———. "Entre droit et pratiques: Comment les juifs d'Egypte sont devenus étrangers." In *The History and Culture of the Jews of Egypt in Modern Times,* edited by Ada Aharoni, Aimée Israel-Pelletier, and Zamir Levana, 260–277. Tel Aviv: Keness Hafakot, 2008.
Abulafia, David. *The Great Sea.* New York: Oxford University Press, 2013.
———. "Mediterraneans." In *Rethinking the Mediterranean*, edited by W. V. Harris, 64–93. Oxford: Oxford University Press, 2006.
———. "Thalassocracies." In *A Companion to Mediterranean History*, edited by Peregrine Horden and Sharon Kinoshita, 139–153. Oxford: Wiley Blackwell, 2014.
Aciman, André. *Alibis: Essays on Elsewhere.* New York: Picador, Farrar, Straus and Giroux, 2011.
———. *Eight White Nights.* New York: Picador, Farrar, Straus, and Giroux, 2010.
———. *False Papers: Essays on Exile and Memory.* New York: Picador, Farrar, Straus and Giroux, 2001.
———. *Harvard Square.* New York: W.W. Norton, 2013.
———. *Letters of Transit: Reflections on Exile, Identity, and Loss.* New York: The New Press, 1997.
———. *Out of Egypt: A Memoir.* New York: Farrar, Straus and Giroux, 1994.
Aharoni, Ada. "The Image of Jewish Life in Egypt in the Writings of Egyptian Jewish Authors in Israel and Abroad." In *The Jews of Egypt: A Mediterranean Society in Modern Times,* edited by Shimon Shamir, 192–198. Boulder, Colo. and London: Westview, 1987.
Al-Sayyid Marsot, Afaf. *A Short History of Modern Egypt.* Cambridge: Cambridge University Press, 1985.
Alcalay, Ammiel. *After Jews and Arabs: Remaking Levantine Culture.* Minneapolis: University of Minnesota University Press, 1993.
———. "Desert Solitaire: Edmond Jabès, Resident Poet." *Voice Literary Supplement* (February 1994): 13.
Anderson, Benedict. *Imagined Communities.* London: Verso, 1983, 2006.
Ariss-el, Tarek. *Trials of Arab Modernity: Literary Affects and the New Political.* New York: Fordham University Press, 2013.
Asad, Talal. *Formations of the Secular. Christianity, Islam, Modernity.* Stanford, Calif.: Stanford University Press, 2003.

Astro, Alan, ed. *Discourses of Jewish Identity in Twentieth-Century France*. New Haven, Conn.: Yale University Press, 1994.
Auster, Paul. "Book of the Dead." In *The Sin of the Books: Edmond Jabès*, edited by Eric Gould, 3–25. Lincoln: University of Nebraska Press, 1985.
Ayalon, David. "The Spread of Islam and the Nubian Dam." In *The Nile: Histories, Cultures, Myths*, edited by Haggai Erlich and Israel Gershoni, 17–23. London: Lynne Rienner, 2000.
Bagnall, Roger. "Egypt and the Concept of the Mediterranean." In *Rethinking the Mediterranean*, edited by William V. Harris, 339–347. Oxford: Oxford University Press, 2005.
Bar-Av, Avraham. *17 Sheikh Hamza Street, Cairo*. Israel: Rimonim, 2011.
Barda, Racheline. In *Encyclopedia of Jews in the Islamic World*, vol, 2, pp. 132–142, edited by Norman Stillman. Leiden. Boston: Brill, 2010.
Beinin, Joel. *The Dispersion of Egyptian Jewry: Culture, Politics, and the Formation of a Modern Diaspora*. Berkeley: University of California Press, 1998.
Benbassa, Esther. *The Jews of France: A History from Antiquity to the Present*, translated by M. B. DeBevoise. Princeton, N.J.: Princeton University Press, 1999.
Biale, David. *Cultures of the Jews: Volume I. Mediterranean Origins*. New York: Schocken, 2002.
Blum, Robert, ed. *Anthologie des écrivains d'Égypte d'expression française*. Cairo, 1937.
Booth, Marilyn, and Anthony Gorman, eds. *The Long 1890s in Egypt: Colonial Quiescence, Subterranean Resistance*. Edinburgh: Edinburgh University Press, 2014.
Botman, Selma. *Egypt from Independence to Revolution, 1919–1952*. Syracuse, N.Y.: Syracuse University Press, 1991.
Cabasso, Gilbert, ed. *Juifs d'Egypte: Images et textes*. Paris: Editions du Scribe, 1984.
Cahen, Didier. *Edmond Jabès*. Paris: Pierre Belfond, 1991.
Carlino, Tiziana. "The Levant: A Trans-Mediterranean Literary Category?" in *Trans-* 2 (2006), Littérature et Image, https://trans.revues.org/129.
Chakrabarty, Dipesh. "The Climate of History: Four Theses." *Critical Inquiry* 35 (2009): 197–222.
Charney, Noah. Interview with André Aciman, *Daily Beast*, November 28, 2012. http://www.thedailybeast.com/articles/2012/11/28/andr-aciman-how-i-write.html.
Clancy-Smith, Julia. *Mediterraneans. North Africa and Europe in an Age of Migration, c. 1800–1900*. Berkeley: University of California Press, 2011.
Cohen, Erik, H. *The Jews of France Today: Identity and Values*. Leiden: Brill, 2011.
Cohen, Marcel. *Edmond Jabès: du désert au livre*. Paris: Pierre Belfond, 1980.
Cohen, Rachel. "Bamia. Mémoire d'enfance, le retour en Égypte avec le cousin." In *Lettres de l'enfance et de l'adolescencence*, edited by Françoise Petitot. 111–118. Paris: Eres, 2002/4, http://www.cairn.info/revue-lettre-de-l-enfance-et-de-l-adolescence-2002-4.htm.
Cohen, Susan, D. "Cultural Mixing, Exile, and Femininity in Paula Jacques's Lumière de l'œil." *French Review* 67, no. 5 (April 1994): 840–853.
Cole, James R. *Colonialism and Revolution in the Middle East: Social and Cultural Origins of Egypt's 'Urabi Movement*. Princeton, N.J.: Princeton University Press, 1993.
Cooke, Miriam, Erdag Goknar, and Grant Parker, eds. *Mediterranean Passages: Readings from Dido to Derrida*. Chapel Hill: University of North Carolina Press, 2008.

Dammond, Liliane S., and Yvette M. Raby. *The Lost World of the Egyptian Jews: First-Person Accounts from Egypt's Jewish Community in the Twentieth Century.* New York: iUniverse, 2007.
Dayan-Rosenman, A. "The Israeli-Palestinian Conflict in France: A Conflict in Search of Novelistic Representations." In *Israeli-Palestinian Conflict in the Francophone World*, edited by Nathalie Debrauwere-Miller, 81–92. New York, London: Routledge, 2010.
Debrauwere-Miller, Nathalie. "La 'Conscience d'un Cri' dans la poétique d'Edmond Jabès." *French Forum* 30, no. 2 (Spring 2005): 97–119.
Derrida, Jacques. *Demeure: Fiction and Testimony*, translated by Elizabeth Rottenberg. Stanford, Calif.: Stanford University Press, 2000.
——. "Edmond Jabès and the Question of the Book." In *Writing and Difference*, 77–96. New York: Routledge, 1967.
——. *Monolingualism of the Other or the Prosthesis of Origin.* Stanford, Calif.: Stanford University Press, 1998.
Di-Capua, Yoav. *Gatekeepers of the Arab Past: Historians and History Writing in Twentieth-Century Egypt.* Berkeley: University of California Press, 2009.
Dobie, Madeleine. "For and Against the Mediterranean: Francophone Perspectives." *Comparative Studies of South Asia, Africa and the Middle East* 34, no. 2 (2014): 389–404.
Douer, Alisa. *Egypt. The Lost Homeland: Exodus from Egypt, 1947–1967. The History of the Jews in Egypt, 1540 BCE to 1967.* Berlin: Logos, 2015.
Eakin, Paul John. *Living Autobiographically: How We Create Identity in Narrative.* Ithaca, N.Y.: Cornell University Press, 2008.
El-Ariss, Tarek. *Trials of Arab Modernity: Literary Affects and the New Political.* New York: Fordham University Press, 2013.
Erlich, Haggai, and Israel Gershoni, eds. *The Nile: Histories, Cultures, Myths.* London: Lynne Rienner, 2000.
Esposito, John. L. *Islam and Politics.* Syracuse, N.Y.: Syracuse University Press, 1991.
Fahmy, Ziad. *Ordinary Egyptians: Creating the Modern Nation through Popular Culture.* Stanford, Calif.: Stanford University Press, 2011.
Fenoglio, Irène. "Le Destin poétique d'Edmond Jabès dans les désécritures de la décennie blanche." In *Edmond Jabès: L'Eclosion des énigmes* edited by Daniel Lançon and Catherine Mayaux, 28–42. Paris: Presses Universitaires de Vincennes, 2007.
——. "Egyptianité et langue française." In *Entre Nil et Sable: ecrivains d'Egypte d'expression française (1920–1960)*, edited by Marc Kober, Irène Fenoglio, and Daniel Lançon, 15–25. Paris, France: Centre National de Documentation Pédagogique, 1999.
Garner, Georg. "Fin-de-Siècle, Paris: Actualités d'un malaise." In *Che vuoi? Revue de Psychanalyse* 12 (1999): 49–62.
Gerard, Daniel. "Le choix culturel de la langue en Egypte." *Egypte-Monde Arabe* 27–28 (1996): 253–284.
Gershoni, Israel, and James Jankowski. *Egypt, Islam, and the Arabs: The Search for Egyptian Nationhood, 1900–1930.* New York: Oxford University Press, 1986.
——. *Confronting Fascism in Egypt: Dictatorship versus Democracy in the 1930s.* Stanford, Calif.: Stanford University Press, 2010.
——. *Redefining the Egyptian Nation: 1930–1945.* Cambridge: Cambridge Middle University Press, 1995.

Goitein, S. D. *Jews and Arabs: Their Contacts through the Ages.* New York: Schocken, 1955.
——. *A Mediterranean Society: An Abridgment in One Volume*, revised and edited by Jacob Lassner. Berkeley: University of California Press, 1999.
Goldberg, Harvey E., ed. *Sephardi and Middle Eastern Jewries: History and Culture in the Modern Era.* Bloomington: Indiana University Press, 1996.
Gorman, Anthony. *Historians, State and Politics in Twentieth-Century Egypt: Contesting the Nation.* London: Routledge, 2003.
Green, Nile. "Rethinking the 'Middle East' after the Oceanic Turn." *Comparative Studies of South Asia, Africa and the Middle East* 34, no. 3 (2014): 556–564.
Halawani, Mary. *I Miss the Sun.* Sphinx Productions, 26-minute film, 1983.
Halim, Hala. *Alexandrian Cosmopolitanism: An Archive.* New York: Fordham University Press, 2013.
Hammerschlag, Sarah. *Broken Tablets: Levinas, Derrida, and the Literary Afterlife of Religion.* New York: Columbia University Press, 2016.
Hamouda, Sahar. *Victoria College: A History Revealed*, edited by Sahar Hamouda and Colin Clement. Cairo: The American University Press, 2002.
Hand, Seán, and Steven T. Katz, eds. *Post-Holocaust France and the Jews, 1945–1955.* New York: New York University Press, 2015.
Handelman, Susan. "'Torments of an Ancient Word': Jabès and the Rabbinic Tradition." In *The Sin of the Book: Edmond Jabès*, edited by Eric Gould, 55–91. Lincoln: University of Nebraska Press, 1985.
Hanley, Will. *Identifying with Nationality: Europeans, Ottomans, and Egyptians in Alexandria.* New York: Columbia University Press, 2017.
Harris, W. V., ed. *Rethinking the Mediterranean.* Oxford: Oxford University Press, 2006.
Hassoun, Jacques. *Alexandries. Roman.* Paris: Editions de la Découverte, 1985.
——. *Alexandrie et autres récits de Jacques Hassoun.* Paris: l'Harmattan, 2001.
——. *La cruauté mélancolique.* Paris: Flammarion, 1995.
——. *Les contrebandiers de la mémoire.* Paris: Syros, 1994.
——. *L'exil de la langue. Fragments de langue maternelle.* Paris: Payot, 1979.
——. "Glossaire," in *Juifs du Nil*, 2nd ed. Paris: Editions du Scribe, 1984.
——. *Histoire des Juifs du Nil.* Paris: Minerve, 1990.
——. *Jacques Hassoun extraits d'une oeuvre.* Paris: l'Harmattan, 2009.
——. *Le passage des étrangers.* Paris: Austral, 1995.
Hassoun, Jacques and Abdelkibir Khatibir. *Le Même livre.* Paris: Editions de l'éclat, 1985.
Hawkins, Beth. *Reluctant Theologians: Franz Kafka, Paul Celan, Edmond Jabès.* New York: Fordham University Press, 2003.
Hochberg, Gil, Z. *In Spite of Partition: Jews, Arabs, and the Limits of Separatist Imagination.* Princeton, N.J.: Princeton University Press, 2007.
——. "'The Mediterranean Option': On the Politics of Regional Affiliation in Current Israeli Cultural Imagination." *Journal of Levantine Studies* 1 (Summer 2011): 41–65.
——. "'Permanent Immigration': Jacqueline Kahanoff, Ronit Matalon, and the Impetus of Levantinism." *Boundary 2* 31, no. 2 (Summer 2004): 219–243.
Horden, P., and N. Purcell. *The Corrupting Sea: A Study of Mediterranean History.* Oxford: Wiley Blackwell, 2000.
Hourani, Albert. *Arabic Thought in the Liberal Age, 1798–1939.* Cambridge: Cambridge University Press, 1983.

Ilbert, Robert. *Alexandrie 1830–1930: Histoire d'une communauté citadine*. Cairo: Institut Français d'Archéologie Orientale, Bibliothèque d'Etude, 1996.
Israel-Pelletier, Aimée. "Edmond Jabès, Jacques Hassoun, and Melancholy: The Second Exodus in the Shadow of the Holocaust," *MLN* French Issue 123, no. 4 (September 2008): 797–818.
———, Aharoni, Ada, and Levana Zamir, eds. *The History and Culture of the Jews of Egypt in Modern Times*. Tel Aviv: Keness Hafakot, 2008.
Jabès, Edmond. *The Book of Margins*, translated by Rosemarie Waldrop. Chicago: University of Chicago Press, 1993.
———. *Le livre de l'hospitalité*. Paris: Gallimard, 2012.
———. *Le livre des questions I*. Paris: Gallimard, 2002.
———. *Le livre des questions II*. Paris: Gallimard, 1997.
———. *Le livre des ressemblances*. Paris: Gallimard, 1991.
———. *Un Etranger avec sous le bras, un livre de petit format*. Paris: Gallimard, 1989.
Jacob, Wilson Chacko, *Working out Egypt: Effendi Masculinity and Subject Formation in Colonial Modernity, 1870–1940*. Durham, N.C.: Duke University Press, 2011.
Jacques, Paula. *Au moins il ne pleut pas*. Paris: Stock, 2015.
———. *Deborah et les anges dissipés*. Paris: Mercure de France, 1991.
———. *Gilda Stambouli souffre et se plaint*. Paris: Mercure de France, 2002.
———. *Kayro Jacobi, juste avant l'oubli*. Paris: Mercure de France, 2010.
———. *La descente au paradis*. Paris: Mercure de France, 1995.
———. *Les femmes avec leur amour*. Paris: Mercure de France, 1997.
———. *L'héritage de tante Carlotta*. Paris: Mercure de France, 1987.
———. *Light of My Eye*, translated by Susan Cohen-Nicole. Teaneck, N.J.: Holmes & Meier, 2009.
———. *Lumière de l'oeil*. Paris: Mercure de France, 1980.
———. *Rachel-Rose et l'officier arabe*. Paris: Mercure de France, 2006.
———. *Nuits magnétiques*. "Sept jours et six nuits ou le temps d'un retour au pays natal." Radio Broadcast on *France Culture* (June 1993; rebroadcast June 1999).
———. *Un baiser froid comme la lune*. Paris: Mercure de France, 1983.
Jaron, Steven. *Emond Jabès: The Hazard of Exile*. Oxford: Legenda, 2003.
Kahanoff, Jacqueline Shohet. "Afterwords: From East the Sun." In *Mongrels and Marvels: The Levantine Writings of Jacqueline Shohet Kahanoff*, edited by Deborah A. Starr and Sasson Somekh. Stanford, Calif.: Stanford University Press, 2011.
———. "Childhood in Egypt." In *Mongrels and Marvels: The Levantine Writings of Jacqueline Shohet Kahanoff*, edited by Deborah A. Starr and Sasson Somekh, 1–13. Stanford, Calif.: Stanford University Press, 2011.
———. "A Culture Stillborn." In *Mongrels and Marvels: The Levantine Writings of Jacqueline Shohet Kahanoff*, edited by Deborah A. Starr and Sasson Somekh, 114–127. Stanford, Calif.: Stanford University Press, 2011.
———. "Israel: Ambivalent Levantine." In *Mongrels and Marvels: The Levantine Writings of Jacqueline Shohet Kahanoff*, edited by Deborah A. Starr and Sasson Somekh, 193–212. Stanford, Calif.: Stanford University Press, 2011.
———. *Jacob's Ladder*. London: Harvill Press, 1951.
———. "A Letter from Mama Camouna." In *Mongrels and Marvels: The Levantine Writings of Jacqueline Shohet Kahanoff*, edited by Deborah A. Starr and Sasson Somekh, 164–176. Stanford, Calif.: Stanford University Press, 2011.

———. "To Live and Die a Copt." In *Mongrels and Marvels: The Levantine Writings of Jacqueline Shohet Kahanoff*, edited by Deborah A. Starr and Sasson Somekh, 128–135. Stanford, Calif.: Stanford University Press, 2011.
———. "To Remember Alexandria." In *Mongrels and Marvels: The Levantine Writings of Jacqueline Shohet Kahanoff*, edited by Deborah A. Starr and Sasson Somekh, 213–231. Stanford, Calif.: Stanford University Press, 2011.
———. "Wake of the Waves." In *Mongrels and Marvels: The Levantine Writings of Jacqueline Shohet Kahanoff*, edited by Deborah A. Starr and Sasson Somekh, 136–152. Stanford, Calif.: Stanford University Press, 2011.
———. "What about Levantinization." *Journal of Levantine Studies* 1 (Summer 2011): 13–22.
Kaplan, Edward. "The Problematic Humanisn of Edmond Jabès." In *The Sin of the Book: Edmond Jabès*, edited by Eric Gould, 115–130. Lincoln: University of Nebraska Press, 1985.
Kedourie, Elie. *Islam in the Modern World, and Other Studies*. New York: Holt, Rinehart, Winston, 1980.
Khuri-Makdisi, Ilham. *The Eastern Mediterranean and the Making of Global Radicalism, 1860–1914*. Berkeley: University of California Press, 2013.
Kinoshita, Sharon. "The Mediterranean and 'the New Thalassology.'" *PMLA* 124, no. 2 (2009): 600–608.
Kober, Marc, Irène Fenoglio, Daniel Lançon, eds. *Entre Nil et sable. Ecrivains d'Egypte d'expression française (1920–1960)*. Paris: Centre National de Documentation Pédagogique, 1999.
Krämer, Gudrun. "'Radical' Nationalists, Fundamentalists, and the Jews in Egypt or, Who Is a Real Egyptian?" In Gabriel R. Warburg and Uri M. Kupferschmidt, *Islam, Nationalism, and Radicalism in Egypt and the Sudan*, 354–371. New York: Praeger Special Studies. Praeger Scientific, 1983.
———. *The Jews in Modern Egypt 1914–1952*. Washington: University of Washington Press, 1989.
La Capra, Dominick. *Writing History, Writing Trauma*. Baltimore: Johns Hopkins University Press, 2001.
Lagnado, Lucette. *The Man in the White Sharkskin Suit*. New York: HarperCollins, 2007.
Lançon, Daniel. *Jabès L'Egyptien*. Paris: Jean-Michel Place, 1998.
Landau, Jacob M. "The Decline of the Jewish Community in Eighteenth-Century Cairo: A New Interpretation in the Light of Two Iberian Chronicles." In *The Jews of Egypt: A Mediterranean Society in Modern Times*, edited by Shimon Shamir, 15–29. Boulder, Colo. and London: Westview, 1987.
Lang, Berel. "Writing-the-Holocaust: Jabès and the Measure of History." In *The Sin of the Book: Edmond Jabès*, edited by Eric Gould, 191–206. Lincoln: University of Nebraska Press, 1985.
Laskier, Michael. *The Jews of Egypt: 1920–1970*. New York: New York University Press, 1991.
Levy, Lital. "Historicizing the Concept of Arab Jew in the 'Mashriq.'" *Jewish Quarterly Review* 98, no. 4 (Fall 2008): 452–469.
———. "The Nahda and the Haskala: A Comparative Reading of 'Revival' and 'Reform.'" *Middle Eastern Literatures* 16, no. 3 (2013): 300–316.
Luthi, Jean-Jacques. *Introduction à la littérature d'expression française en Egypte (1798–1945)*. Paris: Editions de l'école, 1974.

Malino, Frances. "Prophets in Their Own Land? Mothers and Daughters of the Alliance Israélite Universelle." *Journal of Jewish Women's Studies & Gender Issues* 3, Motherhood (Spring–Summer 5760-2000): 56–73.

Malki, Elliot. *Starting over Again: A Jewish Egyptian Story*. Film directed by Ruggero Gabbai. Milano: Forma International Production, 2015.

Mandel, Maud. "The Encounter between 'Native' and 'Immigrant' Jews in Post-Holocaust France: Negotiating Difference." In *Post-Holocaust France and the Jews, 1945–1955*, edited by Seán Hand and Steven T. Katz, 38–57. New York: New York University Press, 2015.

Marglin, Jessica M. "Mediterranean Modernity through Jewish Eyes: The Transimperial Life of Abraham Ankawa." *Jewish Social Studies* 20, no. 2 (2014): 34–68.

Maslowski, David. "Les Modèles culturels des juifs d'Egypte de la fin de la domination ottomane (1882) jusquà la révolution des officiers libres (1952)" M.A. Thesis, Université de Paris 1. Panthéon-Sorbonne, 2012–2013.

Mayer, Thomas. "The Image of Egyptian Jewry in Recent Egyptian Studies." In *The Jews of Egypt: A Mediterranean Society in Modern Times*, edited by Shimon Shamir, 199–212. Boulder, Colo. and London: Westview, 1987.

Meddeb, Abdelwahab, and Benjamin Stora, eds. *A History of Jewish–Muslim Relations: From the Origins to the Present Day*. Princeton, N.J.: Princeton University Press, 2013.

Mendelson-Maoz, Adia. *Multiculturalism in Israel: Literary Perspectives*. West Lafayette, Indiana: Purdue University Press, 2014.

Miccoli, Dario. *Histories of the Jews of Egypt. An Imagined Bourgeoisie, 1880s–1950s*. New York: Routledge Studies in Middle Eastern History, 2015.

———. "Moses and Faruq. The Jews and the Study of History in Interwar Egypt 1920s–1940s." *Quest—Issues in Contemporary Jewish History* 4 (November 2012). http://www.quest-cdecjournal.it/focus.php?id=319.

———. "Moving Histories. The Jews and Modernity in Alexandria 1881–1919."*Quest—Issues in Contemporary Jewish History* 2 (October 2011): 149–171.

Mitchell, Timothy. Colonising Egypt. Berkeley: University of California Press, 1988.

Mizrahi, Maurice. *L'Egypte et ses juifs: Le Temps révolu, XIXe et XXe siècles*. Geneva: Imprimerie Avenir, 1977.

Mole, Gary. "Edmond Jabès and the Wound of Writing: The Traces of Auschwitz." *Orbis Litterarum* 49 (1994): 203–306.

Morris, Ian. "Mediterraneanization." *Mediterranean Historical Review* 18, no. 2 (2003): 30–55.

Naggar, Carole, and Jacques Hassoun. "Le Caire. Mille et une villes." *Autrement* 12 (February 1985): 43–47.

———. *Egypte, Retour. Récit*. Paris: Nahar Misraïm, 2007.

Naguib, Nefissa. "The Fragile Tale of Egyptian Jewish Cuisine: Food Memoirs of Claudia Roden and Colette Rossant." *Food and Foodways* 14, no. 1 (2006): 35–53.

Nathan, Tobie. *Café Littéraire du mercredi—Tobie Nathan—Ce Pays qui te ressemble* (November 2015). https://www.youtube.com/watch?v=dt9zhRN2FeQ.

———. *Ce pays qui te ressemble*. Paris: Stock, 2015.

———. *Ethno-roman*. Paris: Grasset, 2012.

———. *France-Inter* radio interview with Patrick Cohen, September 11, 2015. https://www.franceinter.fr/emissions/le-7-9/le-7-9-11-septembre-2015.

———. Interview with Jean-Pierre Elkabbach on Bibliothèque Médicis, Public Sénat, October 30, 2015. https://www.youtube.com/watch?v=Iv6enTbzSkU.
———. "Jour de fête." In *Une enfance juive en méditerranée musulmane*, edited by Leïla Sebbar, 261–269. Saint-Pourçain-sur-Sioule: Bleu Autour, 2012.
———. "Tobie Nathan, "Rentrée Littéraire 2015." https://www.youtube.com/watch?v=FY-DYARHi9U.
Nolden, Thomas. *In Lieu of Memory: Contemporary Jewish Writing in France*. Syracuse, N.Y.: Syracuse University Press, 2006.
Ohana, David. *Israel and Its Mediterranean Identity*. New York: Palgrave Macmillan, 2011.
———. "The Mediterranean Option in Israel: An Introduction to the Thought of Jacqueline Kahanoff." *Mediterranean Historical Review* 21, no. 2 (December 2006): 239–263.
Parris, David L. *Albert Adès et Albert Josipovici: ecrivains d'Egypte d'expression française au début du XXe siècle*. Paris: L'Harmattan, 2010.
Perry, Glenn E. *The History of Egypt*. Westport, Conn.: Greenwood, 2004.
Phillips, Adam. *Becoming Freud: The Making of a Psychoanalyst*. New Haven, Conn.: Yale University Press, 2014.
Porte, Michelle. *Jabès and Egypt*. Film produced in 1989. In *Mediterranean Memory* http://www.medmem.eu/en/notice/INA00055. Collection title: Océaniques, ID: INA00055 Source: INA (FR), 1989.
Reynolds, Nancy Y. *A City Consumed: Urban Commerce, the Cairo Fire, and the Politics of Decolonization in Egypt*. Stanford, Calif. Stanford University Press, 2012.
Rodrigue, Aron. "Alliance Israélite Network." In *Encyclopedia of Jews in the Islamic World*, edited by Norman A. Stillman, vol. 1, 171–180. Leiden: Brill, 2010.
Rothberg, Michael. *Multidirectional Memory: Remembering the Holocaust in the Age of Decolonization*. Stanford, Calif.: Stanford University Press, 2009.
Samuels, Maurice. *The Right to Difference: French Universalism and the Jews*. Chicago: University of Chicago Press, 2016.
Sanua, Victor D. *Egyptian Jewry: Guide to Egyptian Jewry in the Mid-Fifties of the 20th Century. The Beginning of the Demise of a Vibrant Egyptian Jewish Community*. 2nd ed. New York: Franklin Printing, n.d.
———. "Emigration of the Sephardic Jews from Egypt after the Arab-Israeli Wars." *Proceedings of the Eleventh World Congress of Jewish Studies*, vol. 3, 215–222. Jerusalem: World Union of Jewish Studies, 1994.
———. "A Jewish Childhood in Cairo." In *Fields of Offerings: Studies in Honor of Raphael Patai*, edited by Victor D. Sanua, 283–298. Rutherford, N.J.: Fairleigh Dickinson University Press, 1983.
Sardas, Jacques. *Without Return: Memoirs of an Egyptian Jew 1930-1957*. Dallas: Thebes Press, 2017.
Scharfman, Ronnie. "Par quelle porte entrer dans ce livre où il n'y a que des portes ou que leur seuil?" In *Ecrire le livre autour d'Edmond Jabès, Colloque de Cerisy-la-Salle*, edited by Richard Stamelman and Mary Ann Caws, 285–290. Paris: Editions Champ Vallon, 1989.
Schreier, Joshua. *Arabs of the Jewish Faith: The Civilizing Mission in Colonial Africa*. New Brunswick, N.J.: Rutgers University Press, 2010.
Sebbar, Leïla. *Une Enfance juive en Méditerranée musulmane*. Auvergne: Bleu Autour, 2012.
Segré, Victor. *Un Aller sans retour: L'histoire d'un communiste juif Egyptien*. Paris: L'Harmattan, 2009.

Sezgin, Paméla Dorn. "Jewish Women in the Ottomon Empire." In Zion Zohar, *Sephardic and Mizrahi Jewry*, 216–235. New York: New York University Press, 2005.

Shamir, Shimon, ed. *The Jews of Egypt: A Mediterranean Society in Modern Times*. Boulder, Colo. and London: Westview, 1987.

Smouha, Richard. ed. *The Smouha City Venture: Alexandria 1923–1958*, edited by Richard Smouha, Cristina Pallini, and Marie-Cécile Bruwier. CreateSpace, An Amazon.com Company, 2014.

Starr, Deborah. *Remembering Cosmopolitan Egypt: Literature, Culture, and Empire*. New York: Routledge, 2009.

Starr, Deborah A., and Sasson Somekh. *Mongrels or Marvels: The Levantine Writings of Jacqueline Shohet Kahanoff*. Stanford, Calif.: Stanford University Press, 2011.

Stillman, Norman, ed. *Encyclopedia of Jews in the Islamic World*. Leiden. Boston: Brill, 2010.

———. *Jews of Arab Lands in Modern Times*. Philadelphia: The Jewish Publication Society, 1991.

Stoddard, Roger E. "Comment je lis Edmond Jabès: La Réponse du bibliographe." In *L'Eclosions des énigmes*, edited by Daniel Lançon and Catherine Mayaux, 297–309. Paris: Presses Universitaires de Vincennes, 2007.

Szwarc, Sandrine. *Les Intellectuels juifs de 1945 à nos jours*. Paris: Le Bord de L'eau, 2013.

Tageldin, Shaden M. *Disarming Words: Empire and the Seduction of Translation in Egypt*. Berkeley: University of California Press, 2011.

Teboul, Victor. *La Lente découverte de l'étrangeté*. Montréal: Les Editions des Intouchables, 2002.

Toledano, Ehud R. *State and Society in Mid-Nineteenth Century Egypt*. Cambridge: Cambridge Middle East, 2003.

Toledano-Attias, Ruth. "La dénationalisation des juifs d'Egypte." In *La fin du judaïsme en terre d'islam*, edited by Shmuel Trigano, 51–85. Paris: Denoël, 2009.

Trigano, Shmuel. *La fin du judaïsme en terres d'islam*. Paris: Denoël, 2009.

Vatikiotis, Panayotis, J. *The History of Modern Egypt from Muhammad Ali to Mubarak* Baltimore: Johns Hopkins University Press, 1991.

Vergès, Françoise. "Wandering Souls and Returning Ghosts: Writing the History of the Dispossessed." *Yale French Studies* 118/119 (November 2010): 136–154.

Weiss, Jason. *Writing at Risk: Interviews in Paris with Uncommon Writers*. Iowa City: University of Iowa Press, 1991.

Wilson, Colette. "Multidirectional Memory and Exile in Jacques Hassoun's Polyphonic Novel *Alexandrias. A Novel*." *Journal of Romance Studies* 13, no. 2 (Summer 2013): 94–115.

Wilson, Jacob C. *Working out Egypt: Effendi Masculinity and Subject Formation in Colonial Modernity, 1870–1940*. Durham, N.C. and London: Duke University Press, 2011.

Winter, Michael. "Egyptian Jewry during the Ottoman Period as a Background to Modern Times." In *The Jews of Egypt: A Mediterranean Society in Modern Times*, edited by Shimon Shamir, 9–14. Boulder, Colo. and London: Westview, 1987.

Yerushalmi, Yosef Hayim. *Zakhor: Jewish History and Jewish Memory*. Seattle: University of Washington Press, 1989.

Zohar, Zion, ed. *Sephardic and Mizrahi Jewry: From the Golden Age of Spain to Modern Times*. New York: New York University Press, 2005.

Zonana, Joyce. "'And She Loved Brown People': Jacqueline Shohett Kahanoff's Affirmation of Arab Jewish Identity in *Jacob's Ladder*." In *Sephardi and Mizrahi Jews in America. The Jewish Role in American Life: An Annual Review of the Casden Institute for the Study of the Jewish Role in American Life*, ed. Steven J. Ross, vol. 13, 53–73. West Lafayette, Ind.: Purdue University Press 2016.

Index

Aciman, André, 4, 13, 22, 46, 176–178; on Arab antisemitism, 185, 186, 187; on Arab Egypt, 195–196; on Camus, 192; on the distinction Arab Jew/European Jew, 179–181; on Egyptian Jews' decision to stay or leave, 182–185; experience of exile and, 177, 184, 191, 197; on identity, 181; Mediterranean paradigm and, 188–194; open letter to Obama, 22, 196–198; on pre-Islamic Egypt, 191; at Victoria College, 184–188, 200n10

Aciman, André, works of: "Alexandria: The Capital of Memory," 176, 181, 196; *Alibis: Essays on Elsewhere*, 177, 179, 182; *Eight White Nights*, 177; *False Papers: Essays on Exile and Memory*, 176, 189; "From Alexandria," 192; *Harvard Square*, 193–196; *Out of Egypt: A Memoir*, 178–182, 185–188, 192–193; "In Search of Blue," 188

Adorno, Theodor, 110

"Afterword: From East the Sun" (Kahanoff, 1968), 86, 87, 88–89, 90, 96

Aharoni, Ada, 4, 20

Alawiyya Dynasty, 9

Alcalay, Ammiel, 81, 119, 127

Alexandria, 11, 19, 69, 177; Chatby cemetery, 39; Cleopatra district, 182; Jewish presence in, 8; Lycée de l'Union Juive pour l'Enseignement, 34; population growth, 5, 6; Smouha district, 182, 199n8; Victoria (Victory) College, 184–188

Alexandria Quartet (Durrell), 93

Alexandrias. A Novel [*Alexandries. Roman*] (Hassoun, 1985), 22, 53–60; "Alexandria," 59–60; "Giulia," 57–58; "Léa," 58–59; "The Travel Journal of Sedaka Raoul Viterbo," 55–57

"Alexandria: The Capital of Memory" (Aciman), 176, 181, 196

Algeria, 29, 109, 187, 192

Alibis: Essays on Elsewhere (Aciman, 2011), 177, 179, 182

Alliance Israélite Universelle (AIU), 22, 79–80, 81, 98n13

Anatomy of French Judaism (Rabonovitch, 1962), 109

Anderson, Benedict, 4

antisemitism, 108, 144, 166, 167. *See also* Egypt, antisemitism in

apatrides (stateless) status, 40, 45, 162, 163

Aqqad, Abbas Mahmud al-, 15

Arabia, 16

Arabic language, 9, 12, 16, 48, 51, 97n4, 116; Aciman and, 180, 181, 183, 185, 186, 188; Hassoun and, 33–34, 53, 59; Jabès and, 104, 127; *Jacob's Ladder* on value/status of, 71, 76, 84, 88; name of Egypt in, 119; in Paula Jacques novels, 158

Ashkenazi Jews, 11, 22; in *At Least It's Not Raining*, 169–171; in *The Book of Questions*, 112, 114, 115, 131; in *Deborah and Those Reckless Angels*, 157; in *Jacob's Ladder*, 88

Askénazi, Léon, 109

ASPCJE (Association pour la Sauvegarde du Patrimoine Culturel des Juifs d'Egypte), 38, 64n29

assimilation, 86

At Least It's Not Raining [*Au moins il ne pleut pas*] (Jacques, 2015), 166, 169–171

217

Aunt Carlotta's Legacy [*L'Héritage de tante Carlotta*] (Jacques, 1987), 144–145, 150, 152–156, 165
Auster, Paul, 107, 113, 116, 124

Balzac, Honoré de, 70
Bastille group, 38
Beauvoir, Simone de, 34
Begin, Menachem, 36
Behna Films, 13
Beinin, Joel, 8, 13
Beirut, 19
Benjamin, Walter, 191
Ben Jelloun, Tahar, 53
Benzakein, Félix, 17, 35
Biale, David, 18–19, 20
Bible, 8, 166; Deuteronomy, 27–28, 128, 202, 204; Exodus, 4, 203
Blanchot, Maurice, 100, 117
Bonan, Zaki, 13
Book of Hospitality, The (Jabès, 2012), 118, 125
Book of Questions, The (Jabès, 1997–2002), 22, 120, 123, 131–132; *The Book of Yukel*, 121, 126, 190; Egypt as screen memory of Judaism, 115–120; exile theme, 101, 112–115; on memory, 101; readers and questioning process, 115–119; as reflection on the Holocaust, 110–112, 113, 114, 131; *Return to the Book*, 121–123, 128, 131; Talmudic inspiration for, 115
Book of Resemblances, The (Jabès, 1991), 113, 123–124, 131
Brazil, 20
Britain, 14, 35; domination of Egypt, 69; Egyptian revolt against, 17, 70–75; influence over parliamentary monarchy, 26n32; occupation of Egypt (1882), 6, 7, 72
Byzantine empire, 8

Caillois, Roger, 103
Cairo, 11, 19, 87; Abassieh district, 83; Bassatine cemetery, 39, 64n29, 154, 155; Darb el Labbanah neighborhood, 129; Garden City district, 69, 77, 84; Jewish presence in, 8; as "Paris on the Nile," 5; population growth, 5, 6

Caliphate, end of (1924), 14
Camp David Accords (1978), 36
Camus, Albert, 103, 190, 192
capitalism, 20
Castro, Léon, 17, 102
Cattaoui, Joseph Aslan, 17
Ce pays qui te ressemble (Nathan), 88
Chansons pour le repas de l'ogre (Jabès, 1947), 106
Chedid, Andrée, 81
Christians, 9, 14; Catholics, 87, 106; excluded from Egyptian citizenship, 104; French influence in Egypt and, 125; Greek Orthodox, 87, 106, 185–186; in *Jacob's Ladder*, 69, 82, 87, 88; Syrian and Lebanese, 15, 82
cinema, 79
citizenship, 9, 36, 40, 103–104, 144, 164
City Consumed, A (Reynolds), 105
civil rights, 41, 183
Clancy-Smith, Julia A., 176
class divisions, 84
Cocteau, Jean, 102–103
Cohen, Albert, 146
Cohen, André, 34, 35, 38
Cohen, Jacques, 13
Cohen, Marcel, 105, 108, 113, 118, 128, 137n60
Cohen, Rachel, 39
Cohen, René, 103
Cohen-Levinas, Danielle, 135n26
Colloquium of French-Speaking Jewish Intellectuals (Colloque des Intellectuels Juifs de Langue Française; CIJLF), 108, 110, 135n26
colonialism, 95, 98n13, 177
communism, 34, 63n19, 63n21, 102, 144; French Communist Party, 36, 38; Israeli Communist Party, 37; nationalism combined with, 35
Confronting Fascism in Egypt (Gershoni and Jankowski), 20
Constitution, Egyptian, 14, 17, 79
conversos, in Spain, 41
Copts, 3, 8–9, 15, 38, 47, 106; French influence in Egypt and, 125; in *Jacob's Ladder*, 88; mentioned in Obama speech, 197

cosmopolitanism, 11, 25n25, 38, 43
Country that Looks Like You, The [*Ce Pays qui te ressemble*] (Nathan, 2015), 163
Cultures of the Jews: Mediterranean Origins (Biale), 18–19
"Culture Stillborn, A" (Kahanoff), 127
Curiel, Henri, 36, 38, 102
Curiel, Raoul, 102

Damanhur, city of, 6
Débat-Unir, 36
Deborah and Those Reckless Angels [*Deborah et les anges dissipés*] (Jacques, 1991), 150, 156–158, 169
Debrauwere-Miller, Nathalie, 110
depersonalization, 129–130
Derrida, Jacques, 100, 101, 102, 115, 133n4
Descent to Paradise [*La Descente au paradis*] (Jacques, 1995), 146, 148–150, 158–159, 162
Deschamps, Pierre, 80
desert, 88, 101, 127, 129–131
Di-Capua, Yoav, 7, 12, 103
Dickens, Charles, 70
DMNL (Democratic Movement for National Liberation), 35
Dostoyevsky, Fyodor, 55
Dreyfus Affair, 29, 108
Dror movement, 35, 37
Durrell, Lawrence, 93

Eakin, Paul John, 178
Écorce du monde, L' (Jabès, 1955), 106
effendiyya class, 13, 25n23
Egypt, 5, 167; Arab identity of, 195–196; cultures in history of, 3; debt burden in 19th century, 6; immigrants attracted to, 7; "Liberal Age," 14, 17; modernization of, 13, 79; Peace Treaty (1977–1979) with Israel, 21, 128; population growth, 6, 8. See also nationalism
Egypt, ancient/biblical, 5, 101, 202; Exodus of Jews from, 21, 119; in Jabès, 101, 123–124; in *Jacob's Ladder*, 91, 92; in Nathan, 204–205; Pharaonic era, 14, 15, 16, 17; Ptolemaic, 8; in Teboul, 204

Egypt, antisemitism in, 17, 24n13, 45, 197; Nasser's politics and, 158; at Victoria College, 185, 186
Egypt, Return [*Egypte, Retour: Récit*] (Naggar, 2007), 31–32
Egyptian Jews, 46, 57; confidence during "Liberal Age," 14; contributions to modernization efforts, 13; in Egyptian politics, 17; "European Jews" and "Arab Jews," 179–180; excluded from Egyptian citizenship, 104; founding myth of Judaism and, 203; in France, 36, 38; French favored over British by, 75, 97n4; history of interaction with other Jews, 11; Holocaust survivors and, 146; hostility toward, 7–8; identity of, 3–4; imaginary of, 3, 4, 40, 81, 101; indigenous, 8, 9, 10, 80; Israel and identity of, 160–162; newcomer, 9, 11; population of, 7, 23n12; restrictions against, 20–21, 40; Western culture and, 18
Egyptian Jews, attachment to Egypt, 3, 5; in Aciman, 22, 177; in Jabès, 101, 126; in Jacques, 22, 141, 145, 156, 158, 161, 162, 171; in Naggar, 31
Egyptian Jews, expulsion of (1957), 10, 18, 26n34; Aciman's open letter to Obama and, 197; decision to leave or stay in decade preceding, 182–183; Jabès and, 120, 129; as reenactment of biblical narrative, 205; referenced in *Descent to Paradise*, 148; as Second Exodus, 21, 22, 56, 203
Egyptology, 16
Eight White Nights (Aciman, 2010), 177
El-Ariss, Tarek, 195, 201n17
Eliot, T. S., 150
Éluard, Paul, 103, 106
English language, 88, 105
Enlightenment, 12, 80, 107, 124, 165
ethnopsychiatry, 4, 34, 183, 202, 205n3
European culture, 3, 20, 24n13, 76, 82, 121; Alliance Israélite Universelle (AIU) and, 80; ancient Greece and, 191; belief in superiority of, 81; modernity and, 79, 195; Zionism and, 93
Europeanization, 22, 77

exile, 3, 46, 50; Aciman and, 177, 184, 191, 197; First Exile from Babylonia, 28; forgotten language and, 52; healing wounds of, 48; Jabès and, 101, 107, 111–112, 116; Jacques and, 146–147, 151, 152–156; nostalgia and, 12; transmission through generations and, 29–30; as universal experience, 51
"Exodus Obama Forgot to Mention, The" (Aciman, 2009), 196–198

Fahmy, Ziad, 13–14, 18, 25n25
False Papers: Essays on Exile and Memory (Aciman, 2000), 176, 189
Farid, Muhammad, 16
fascism, 29, 102
father: identification with, 38; imaginary or symbolic, 47; mediated place of, 37–38; name of, 45, 47–48; wounding of, 49–50, 162
Fatimid period, 9
Fédida, Yves, 5, 64n29
fellah (fellahin), 13, 59, 89, 91, 127, 159
feminism, 34, 84, 89
Fenoglio, Irène, 62n15, 104, 105
Filbert, Elian J., 102
film industry, Egyptian, 13, 25n22
First Temple, destruction of (586 BCE), 8
France, 6, 29, 50, 120, 193–194, 204; collaboration with Nazis, 170; cultural exchange with Egypt, 102; Egyptian Jews as immigrants in, 140, 153; as inhospitable country for immigrants, 124–129, 162–166; Judaism after Auschwitz, 107–109; May 1968 rebellion, 32, 33, 38
French language, 9, 24n13, 33; Aciman and, 180, 193, 194; Hassoun and, 51, 53; Jabès and, 104–106; *Jacob's Ladder* on value/status of, 69, 70–71, 73, 76, 84–85, 88; Jacques and, 147; Kahanoff and, 97n4
Frenkel Brothers, 13
Freud, Sigmund, 46, 49, 191, 205n3
"From Alexandria" (Aciman, 1997), 192

Gabbai, Ibram, 38
Gabbay, Emile, 38

Garner, Georg, 52
Geniza period, 8, 10
Gershoni, Israel, 14, 15, 26n32
Getting to Know the Jews of France [*À la rencontre des Juifs d'Egypte*] (1984), 38
Ghallab, Muhammad, 16
Gide, André, 103
Gilda Stambouli Suffers and Complains. [*Gilda Stambouli souffre et se plaint.*] (Jacques, 2002), 164–169
globalization, era of, 6
Goitein, S. D., 8, 10
Greco-Roman culture, 3
Greeks, 12, 38, 95, 106
Green, André, 33
Groupement des amitiés françaises, 102–103
Guattari, Félix, 33

HADETO (al-Haraka al Dimuqratiya li al-Taharrur), 35, 38
Hakim, Raymond, 13
Hakim, Robert, 13
Hakim, Tawfiq al-, 15, 16
Hammerschlag, Sarah, 100–101, 133n4
Handelman, Susan, 116
Hanley, William, 11
Hara, Jews of, 79, 82
Haret el-Barabra, 146, 153
Haret el-Yahoud, 146, 149, 156, 163
Haroun, Magda, 21, 26n37
Harvard Square (Aciman, 2013), 193–196
Hassoun, Jacques, 4, 21, 27–28, 78, 129, 203; anti-British nationalist movements supported by, 102; concept of the One (*le Un*), 22, 41–43; concept of the stranger, 40–41; Dror movement and, 35, 37; on ethnicity, 43, 44; expelled from Egypt, 35–36; on the father and the cure, 47–51, 63n27; on immigrants and adaptation, 29–31, 32, 36–38; Levantinism and, 87, 89, 98n18; "moral tales" or vignettes of, 45, 49; mother tongue concept of language, 46, 52–54; as psychoanalyst, 37, 50; reclaiming of Egyptian identity of Jews and, 31–36; return to Egypt, 39–44, 128; on smuggling as call to action, 31;

transmission concept of, 21, 27, 28–29, 30, 156; on the "wounded father," 50, 162; Zionism and, 56–57
Hassoun, Jacques, works of: *Alexandrias. A Novel* (*Alexandries. Roman*), 22, 53–60; *A History of the Jews of the Nile* (*Histoire des Juifs du Nil*), 47; *Language in Exile* (*L'Exil de la* langue), 52; *The Same Book* (*Le Même livre*), 51; *Smugglers of Memory* (*Les Contrebandiers de la mémoire*), 27, 29, 30–31, 51, 58; *The Strangers' Crossing* (*Le Passage des étrangers*), 40–44, 45–46, 50, 179
hate crimes, 41
Hawkins, Beth, 118
Haykal, Muhammad Husayn, 15
Hebrew language, 33, 48, 51; chanting in, 116; Kahanoff and, 97n4; name of Egypt in, 119–120
Herodotus, 15
History of the Jews of the Nile, A [*Histoire des Juifs du Nil*] (Hassoun, 1984), 47
Hitler, Adolf, 109
Hochberg, Gil, 95, 96, 97n4, 98n18, 99n26
Holocaust, 100, 101, 109–112, 114, 131, 184; deniers of, 197; Judaism in France after, 107–109; memory of, 101; survivors of, 146, 168, 170
Hussayn, Taha, 15, 201n17

Ibn Khaldun, 17
I Build my Dwelling [*Je bâtis ma demeure*] (Jabès, 1959), 107
identity, Egyptian, 4, 14, 15, 55, 88–89; Arab identity of Egypt, 176, 195–196; Israel and identity of Egyptian Jews, 160–162; Jewish Egyptian, 17, 21, 46–47, 60, 68, 77, 158–160; Nile River and framing of, 16; racial and ethnic, 42–44
Illusions sentimentales, Les (Jabès), 106
imagined communities, 4
immigrants, 6, 7, 46, 51, 140; children of, 29, 85, 145, 162; France as inhospitable country for, 124–129; progressive politics and, 36–38; smuggler/contraband metaphor and, 31; waves of Jewish immigration, 10

imperialism, 34, 51, 70, 187
indigeneity, 8, 46
"In Search of Blue" (Aciman), 188
International Films, 13
Iran, 15
Irish Catholics, 69
Islam, 12, 15, 18, 197
Ismaïl Pasha, 6
Israel, Elie, 13
Israel, Saul, 119
Israel, state of, 32, 56, 204; Egyptian Jews as immigrants in, 140, 166–169; Egypt's failed wars against, 21; identity of Egyptian Jews problematized by, 160–162; Jews from Arab lands in, 171; kibbutz culture, 166, 167; Levantinism and, 92–96; Peace Treaty (1977–1979) with Egypt, 21, 128; proclamation of, 156, 169; treatment of Palestinians, 57, 170
Italians, 106
Ittihad Party, 17

Jabès, Arlette, 102, 103, 127
Jabès, Edmond, 4, 13, 22, 46, 100–102, 169, 203; approach to the Holocaust, 109–112; on belonging, 100, 128; on depth, 116–117, 129; early writing career of, 106–107; Egyptian desert and, 129–131, 189; experience of exile and, 39, 101, 107, 111–12, 119, 126; family background, 102–104; on France as inhospitable country, 124–129; French language and, 104–106, 137n60; on Judaism after Auschwitz, 107–109; Kahanoff and, 112, 127; Mediterranean concept and, 120, 121–122, 137n52, 189, 190, 192; melancholy of, 119, 122, 127, 129; on readers and the questioning process, 115–119; return to biblical/mythic past and, 48; rootedness and, 88, 89, 119, 123, 137n60; on time and continuation, 202
Jabès, Edmond, works of: *The Book of Hospitality*, 118, 125; *The Book of Resemblances*, 113, 123–124, 131; *Chansons pour le repas de l'ogre*, 106; *I Build my Dwelling* (*Je bâtis ma demeure*), 107; *L'écorce du monde*, 106; *Les Illusions sentimentales*,

106; *L'Obscurité potable*, 106. See also *Book of Questions, The*
Jabès, Henri, 102
Jacob (biblical), 5, 48, 77
Jacob, Max, 113
Jacob's Ladder (Kahanoff, 1951), 22, 28, 68–70, 129; allegory of revolt against British domination in, 70–75; as *bildungsroman*, 68–69; on Egyptian Jewish identity, 75–76; Levantinism in, 86–92; matrineal society in, 84–86; rewriting of biblical canon and, 76–79; women and modernity in, 79–84. See also Israel, state of: Levantinism and
Jacques, Paula, 4, 13, 22, 35, 46, 57; on Ashkenazi Jews, 157, 169, 170; experience of exile and, 146–147, 151, 152–156; on France as inhospitable country, 162–166; immigrants to France in novels of, 124, 140; on the Holocaust, 167, 168; on Israel and Egyptian Jews, 158, 161, 166–171; on Jewish/Muslim relationship, 158, 160–161, 171; resistance as theme in, 140–146
Jacques, Paula, works of: *At Least It's Not Raining* (*Au moins il ne pleut pas*), 166, 169–171; *Aunt Carlotta's Legacy* (*L'Héritage de tante Carlotta*), 140, 144–145, 150, 152–156, 165; *Deborah and Those Reckless Angels* (*Deborah et les anges dissipés*), 150, 156–158, 169; *Descent to Paradise* (*La Descente au paradis*), 146, 148–150, 158–159, 162; *Gilda Stambouli Suffers and Complains.* (*Gilda Stambouli souffre et se plaint.*), 164–166, 167–169; *Kayro Jacobi Just before Oblivion* (*Kayro Jacobi juste avant l'oubli*), 161, 166; *A Kiss as Cold as the Moon* (*Un Baiser froid comme la lune*), 141–144, 163–164; *Light of My Eye* (*Lumière de l'oeil*), 140, 147–148, 150–152, 159–160, 166–167, 169, 171; *Magnetic Nights* (*Nuits Magnétiques*), 36, 39; *Rachel-Rose and the Arab Officer* (*Rachel-Rose et l'officier arabe*), 146; *Women with Their Love* (*Les Femmes avec leur amour*), 146, 160–161, 166–169
Jacques Hassoun: de mémoire (film, 2008, dir. Pérez), 48

Jankélévitch, Vladimir, 44, 108
Jankowski, James, 14, 15, 26n32
Jaron, Steven, 103, 133n6
Jewish diaspora, 31, 54
Jews. See Ashkenazi Jews; Egyptian Jews; Mizrahi Jews; Sephardic Jews
Joseph (biblical), 5
Judaism, 4, 11, 37, 116, 196; in disarray after the Holocaust, 101, 107–109; founding myth of, 203; indestructible union with Egypt, 78; in Paula Jacques novels, 158, 160

Kabbalah, 109
Kafka, Franz, 137n60
Kahanoff, Jacqueline, 4, 13, 22, 46, 78, 101, 203; on Egypt and Israel, 93–95; as feminist, 84, 89; on Jabès's *Book of Questions*, 112; Jewish Egyptian identity and, 77; language choice and, 97n4; Levantinism notion of, 34, 86–87; literary forebears of, 70; memory of "oneness," 89; return to biblical/mythic past and, 48, 76–79; rootedness and, 88–89, 94, 189
Kahanoff, Jacqueline, works of: "Afterword: From East the Sun," 86, 87, 88–89, 90, 96; "A Culture Stillborn," 127; "Israel: Ambivalent Levantine," 86–87; "A Letter from Mama Camouna," 89; "To Live and Die a Copt," 89; "To Remember Alexandria," 92–96; "Wake of the Waves," 91; "What About Levantinism?" 95, 96. See also *Jacob's Ladder* (Kahanoff, 1951)
Kaplan, Edward, 116, 117
Kayro Jacobi Just before Oblivion [*Kayro Jacobi juste avant l'oubli*] (Jacques, 2010), 161, 166
Khatibi, Abdelkebir, 51, 98n18
Khuri-Makdisi, Ilham, 6, 18, 19–20, 99n21
Kiss as Cold as the Moon, A [*Un Baiser froid comme la lune*] (Jacques, 1983), 141–144, 163–164
Krämer, Gudrun, 8, 9, 18, 24n13

Lacan, Jacques, 33, 63n27
Ladino language, 180
Lançon, Daniel, 133n6

Lang, Berel, 110, 111, 120
Language in Exile [*L'Exil de la langue*] (Hassoun, 1993), 52
Laskier, Michael, 24n13, 26n34
League of Youth against Racism and Antisemitism (La Ligue des Jeunes Contre le Racisme et l'Antisémitisme), 102
Lebanon, 16, 19, 20
"Letter from Mama Camouna, A" (Kahanoff), 89
Levantinism, 20, 34, 81, 82, 90, 91, 171; aesthetics of, 22, 86, 99n18; Israel and, 92–96; in *Jacob's Ladder*, 22, 86–92
Levinas, Emmanuel, 100, 108, 109, 133n4
Levi-Strauss, Claude, 103, 150
Lévy-Valensi, Eliane Amado, 108
Liberal Constitutional Party, 16
liberalism, 12, 25n25; cultural, 14; end of, 20–22; as false promise, 13; Turkish revolution and, 18
Light of My Eye [*Lumière de l'oeil*] (Jacques, 1980), 140, 147–148, 150–152, 159–160, 166–167, 169, 171
Lutfi al-Sayed, Ahmad, 15, 17, 119, 201n17
Lycée de l'Union Juive pour l'Enseignement (Alexandria), 34
Lycée Français network, 79, 106, 153

Magnetic Nights [*Nuits Magnétiques*] (Jacques, 1993), 36, 39, 48
Mahmud, Hafiz, 16
Maimonides, 128
Malino, Frances, 81
Malki, Elliot, 28, 61n1
Mamluks, 9
Mano, Guy Lévis, 106
Mansura, city of, 6
Marglin, Jessica M., 16
Marxism: Hassoun and, 29, 34, 35, 37, 38, 43; Jews as adherents of, 63n22
Maslowski, David, 13, 25n22, 25n25
Mathatheia Films, 13
Mayer, Thomas, 7
Mediterranean Sea, 3, 6, 200n12; Aciman and, 188–194; East-West dialogue and, 189; Jabès and, 120, 121–122, 128, 137n52, 189

melancholy: feeling of worthlessness and, 204; Hassoun and, 30, 37, 41–42, 54, 60, 128; Jabès and, 119, 122, 127, 129; Kahanoff and, 93
Memmi, Albert, 108, 109
memory, 3, 30, 31, 54; cultural archaeology of, 192; of the dead, 130; screen memory, 46, 120; writing and, 117
Miccoli, Dario, 13, 80
Michaux, Henri, 103
Middle East, 17, 100
minorities, Egyptian, 5, 9, 11; Armenians, 12, 38; Constitution (1923) and, 14; discourse of modernity, 13; Egypt's record of intolerance for, 196; French influence in Egypt and, 125; Greeks, 12, 38, 95, 106; language and, 51–60; smuggler/contraband metaphor and, 31. *See also* Copts; Egyptian Jews
Mission Laïque Française, 80
Mizrahi, Togo, 13
Mizrahi Jews, 80, 169; Algerian, 109; in *Jacob's Ladder*, 69, 76, 84, 88
modernity, 12, 13–14, 84, 135n26; European versus Arab conceptions of, 195, 201n17; Pharaonic heritage and, 16; urban middle class and, 69–70
Mole, Gary, 110, 131–132
Mongrels and Marvels (Starr and Somekh, 2011), 95
Monolingualism of the Other (Derrida), 115
Morad, Leila, 20
Moses (biblical), 4, 5, 101, 126, 129, 132, 203
"mother tongue," 22, 46, 52, 53–54, 182, 194
Mourad, Leila, 13
Muhammad Ali, 5, 9, 12
Musa, Salama, 15, 16
Muslim Brotherhood, 35, 63n21
Muslims, 13, 14, 38, 47; in *Jacob's Ladder*, 69, 72–74, 78, 79, 82, 87, 88; in Paula Jacques novels, 146, 158; Persian, 15; relations with Jews, 22

Naddara, Abou (Yaqub Sanua), 102
Naggar, Carole, 4, 31, 32, 39, 129
Naguib, Nefissa, 12
Nahar Misraïm (ASPCJE journal), 64n29

Nahum, André, 81
Napoleon I, 108
Nasser, Gamal Abdel, 102, 119, 148, 153; mass departure of Jews and, 176, 203; pan-Arabism and, 45, 177, 187
Nathan, Tobie, 4, 11, 21, 22, 33, 39, 203; on *apatrides*, 162–163; on Arabic and Hebrew words for Egypt, 119–120; *Ce pays qui te ressemble*, 88; ethnopsychology of, 34, 202; family history and departure of Jews from Egypt, 183; Levantinism and, 87, 99n18; Passover experience of, 204–205; as psychoanalyst, 32; on rootedness, 88; on statelessness, 163
nationalism, 7, 140; Egyptian territorial, 3, 5, 12–20, 77, 93; Islamic/Muslim, 9, 14, 15, 17–18; Turkish, 15. See also *apatrides* (stateless) status
nationalism, Arab, 7, 12, 14, 15; Egyptian Jews' view of, 17–18; Jewish solidarity strained by, 101; liberal rejection of, 17; success in 1950s and 1960s, 158
nationalism, pan-Arab, 5, 20, 21; Egyptian Jewish identity and, 190; of Nasser, 45, 177, 187
nationality, 140, 160, 179; anxiety of being without, 22, 163; documents of, 7; Egyptian, 7, 9, 11, 40, 158, 159; French, 125; Italian, 103–104; as modern phenomenon, 11; as new phenomenon, 40
Nazism, 11, 29, 41, 101, 102, 168
Nébi Daniel, 64n29
Neher, André, 108–109
Nile River, 3, 77, 120, 131, 202; Egyptian identity and, 16; in Naggar, 31–32; in Paula Jacques novels, 149–150
Nile Valley, 14–15, 16, 189
North Africa, 5, 16, 100, 109; Egypt's separation from, 15; French-speaking immigrants to France from, 124; in World War II, 17
nostalgia, 45, 50, 54, 58, 87, 153, 155; exile and, 12; Mediterranean as site of, 196; pathetic geography and, 44; symptoms of, 47
Nouveaux Colloques des Intellectuels Juifs, 135n26

Obama, Barak, 196–198
Obscurité potable, L' (Jabès, 1936), 106
Ohana, David, 189
"Open Letter to President Barak Obama" (Aciman), 22
origins, fetishization of, 43
Other, the, 34, 179
Ottoman empire, 3, 9, 11; dissolution of, 14, 40; Jews under rule of, 80
Out of Egypt: A Memoir (Aciman, 1994), 178–182, 185–188, 190, 192–193

Palestine, 8, 11, 102, 167, 187
Palestinians, 57, 127, 170, 197
Passover, 22, 76, 101; in Aciman's "Rue Delta," 178, 191; in *Jacob's Ladder*, 68, 76; in *A Kiss as Cold as the Moon*, 141, 142; in *Out of Egypt*, 190; in Tobie Nathan, 204–205
Pérez, Paul, 48
Phillips, Adam, 33
Picciotto, Maurice de, 27
Poland, pogroms in, 11
Promised Land, myth of, 30, 50, 168
psychoanalysis, 32–33, 34, 45, 47, 50, 54; Lacanian, 34, 48, 63n27; upheavals of 1960s in France and, 33, 38

Rabonovitch, Wladimir, 109
Rachel-Rose and the Arab Officer [*Rachel-Rose et l'officier arabe*] (Jacques, 2006), 146
"'Radical' Nationalists, Fundamentalists, and the Jews in Egypt, or Who is a Real Egyptian?" (Krämer), 18
Renan, Ernest, 15
Revolution, Egyptian (1919), 15, 16
Reynolds, Nancy Y., 6, 105
Roden, Claudia, 12
Rodrigue, Aron, 79–80
Roman empire, 8
Rome group, 36
Rommel, Erwin, 109
Rossant, Colette, 12
Rothberg, Michael, 54
Russia, pogroms in, 11, 168

Sadat, Anwar, 36
Saïd, Mahmoud, 77
Salem, Nagua, 13
Same Book, The [*Le Même livre*] (Hassoun, 1985), 51
Sanua, Yaqub (Abou Naddara), 102
Sartre, Jean-Paul, 34, 103
Scharfman, Ronnie, 118
Schreier, Joshua, 98n13
Sebbar, Leïla, 3, 190
Seghers, Pierre, 106
Sephardic Jews, 10–11, 80, 102, 103; Algerian, 109; in *At Least It's Not Raining*, 169–171; in *The Book of Questions*, 112–113, 114, 115, 131; experience of exile, 133n4; in *Jacob's Ladder*, 69, 76, 84, 88
Sezgin, Paméla Dorn, 80
Shamir, Shimon, 9, 18, 103–104
Sharaf, Muhammad, 16
shu'ubiyya movement, 15, 18
Simon-Nahum, Perrine, 135n26
Six-Day War (1967), 93, 96
Smouha, Joseph, 199n8
Smugglers of Memory [*Les Contrebandiers de la mémoire*] (Hassoun, 1994), 27, 30–31, 58, 59; transmission case studies in, 29; on universality of exile, 51
socialism, 20
Société d'Etudes historiques juives d'Egypte, 13
Somekh, Sasson, 95
Soupault, Philippe, 103, 106
Spain, expulsion of Jews from, 80, 141–143
Stambouli, Raymond, 34, 38
Starr, Deborah, 95
Starting Over (documentary film, dir. Gabbai, 2015), 12, 28, 61n1

Stillman, Norman, 17, 64n33
Strangers' Crossing, The [*Le Passage des étrangers*] (Hassoun, 1995), 40–46, 50, 58, 179
Suez Canal, 5, 6, 20, 140
Suez War (1956), 34, 36, 164
synagogues, 10, 26n37, 57, 116–117; Eliahou Hanabi (Alexandria), 64n29; Reb David Ibn Abi Zimra (Cairo), 104

syncretism, cultural, 19, 20
Syria, 16, 19, 20

Taine, Hippolyte, 15
Talmud, 10, 109, 115
Tanta, city of, 6, 8
Teboul, Victor, 4, 204
theater, 79
This Country That Is Like You [*Ce pays qui te ressemble*] (Cohen, 2015), 35
Toledano-Attias, Ruth, 24n13
"To Live and Die a Copt" (Kahanoff, 1973), 89
"To Remember Alexandria" (Kahanoff, 1976), 92–96
"To the Islamic World" (Obama speech, 2009), 196
Tovar, Jeshurum, 18–19
transmission, cultural, 20, 22, 28–29; in *Aunt Carlotta's Legacy*, 156; in *Jacob's Ladder*, 75–76
Tut-Ankh-Amon, discovery of tomb of, 14

Um Kulthum, 20
United Nations convention on stateless persons, 163, 164
United States, 22, 143, 204
Urabi rebellion, 6, 103

Voies Communistes, 36
Voies Nouvelles, 36

Wafd party, 14, 15, 17
"Wake of the Waves" (Kahanoff, 1962), 91
Wakim, Beshar, 13
wandering Jew, 56
Weiss, Jason, 116, 127, 130
West, the, 18, 71
Westernization, 9, 24n13
"What About Levantinism?" (Kahanoff, 1968), 95, 96
Wiesel, Elie, 111
Wilson, Colette, 54, 55
Women with Their Love [*Les Femmes avec leur amour*] (Jacques, 1997), 146, 160–161, 166–169
World War I, 17
World War II, 17, 100

Yerushalmi, Yosef Hayim, 21
Yishuv, 11
Yom Kippur war (1973), 93

Zaghlul Sa'd, 17
Zamir, Levana, 12

Zionism, 7, 24n13, 56, 93, 95, 167, 170; Arab denunciation of, 187; hegemonic culture of, 86–87; seen as betrayal of Egypt, 35
Ziwar Pasha, 17
Zola, Émile, 70

AIMÉE ISRAEL-PELLETIER is Professor of French at the University of Texas at Arlington. She is the author of books and articles on French literature and film. She was born in Cairo in 1949 to a Jewish family compelled to leave Egypt under the regime of Gamal Abdel Nasser. Her family was admitted to France in March 1961 as refugees in transit. In December 1961, HIAS helped her family settle in New Jersey. She went on to obtain a Ph.D. and began her career as a scholar of French literature. With this book, she returns to her roots to pay homage to her Jewish Egyptian heritage.

www.ingramcontent.com/pod-product-compliance
Lightning Source LLC
Chambersburg PA
CBHW020650230426
43665CB00008B/380